STENDHAL'S VIOLIN

STENDHAL'S VIOLIN

A Novelist and his Reader

ROGER PEARSON

CLARENDON PRESS · OXFORD
1988

Oxford University Press, Walton Street, Oxford OX2 6DP

Oxford New York Toronto
Delhi Bombay Calcutta Madras Karachi
Petaling Jaya Singapore Hong Kong Tokyo
Nairobi Dar es Salaam Cape Town
Melbourne Auckland

and associated companies in
Beirut Berlin Ibadan Nicosia

Oxford is a trade mark of Oxford University Press

Published in the United States
by Oxford University Press, New York

British Library Cataloguing in Publication Data

Pearson, Roger
Stendhal's violin: a novelist and
his reader.
1. Stendhal—Criticism and
interpretation
I. Title
843'.7 PQ2441
ISBN 0-19-815851-3

Library of Congress Cataloging in Publication Data
Data available

Typeset by Dobbie Typesetting Service, Plymouth, Devon
Printed in Great Britain
at the University Printing House, Oxford
by David Stanford
Printer to the University

'Un roman est comme un archet, la caisse du violon *qui rend les sons* c'est l'âme du lecteur.'

(*OI*, ii. 699)

'L'épigraphe doit augmenter la sensation, l'émotion du lecteur, si émotion il peut y avoir, et non pas présenter un jugement plus ou moins philosophique sur la situation.'

(*OI*, ii. 129)

'Mon but est de faire en sorte que chaque spectateur interroge son âme, se détaille sa propre manière de sentir, et parvienne ainsi à se faire un jugement à lui, une manière de voir modelée d'après son propre caractère, ses goûts, ses passions dominantes, si tant est qu'il ait des passions, car, malheureusement, il en faut pour juger des arts.'

(*OC*, xlvii. 14)

for
Vivienne
s.q.n.

Preface

'Pour bien parler de Stendhal, il faudrait un peu sa manière.'
(André Gide)[1]

Lecteur bénévole,
Ecoutez le titre que je vous donne. En vérité, si vous n'étiez pas bénévole et disposé à prendre en bonne part les paroles ainsi que les actions des graves personnages que je vais vous présenter, si vous ne vouliez pas pardonner à l'auteur le manque d'emphase, le manque de but moral, etc., etc., je ne vous conseillerais pas d'aller plus avant. (*LL*, i. 93)

This *captatio benevolentiae*, with which Stendhal once thought to begin *Lucien Leuwen*, will not, it is hoped, be thought too direct or too ingenuous an opening to a work of literary criticism. It has seemed appropriate in view of the purpose and critical method of the present study. The purpose is to go beyond the traditional interpretation of Stendhal's novels as egotistical exercises in wish-fulfilment and to propose that Stendhal's aim was to play upon his readers' reactions—partly by manipulating their expectations as novel-readers, partly by provoking responses which mirror the responses of the central characters to their own experience, and partly, in more general terms, by seeking to 'blesser le moins possible la vanité du lecteur'.[2]

As to critical method, this has been much influenced by its subject. Tzvetan Todorov has written of his desire to see the literary critic 'begin at last to play the role he has always been intended to play, that of a participant in a double dialogue: as reader, with his author; as author, with his own readers'.[3] Some such ambition underlies what follows, though with the important addition of a third element—the dialogue of a reader with other readers of his author. Hence the extensive reference to other critical works on Stendhal.

My account of Stendhal is divided into six parts. The first presents a broad survey of his aesthetics and draws particular attention to the relationship between literary and musical imitation. The next four offer interpretations of his four main novels, and each is intended

[1] *OC*, v. p. i.   [2] *JL*, i. 331, 400.
[3] 'All against humanity' (a review of Robert Scholes's *Textual Power*), *Times Literary Supplement*, 4 Oct. 1985, pp. 1093–4.

both to be informative about the reception of the novel in question and to propose new ways of reading it. The final part deals briefly with *Lamiel*, Stendhal's last and unfinished novel, and then closes with a number of provisional conclusions. What follows, therefore, is what Jonathan Culler calls a 'story of reading', and Culler himself has given a lucid account[4] of just how fraught such an enterprise may be. In the relationship between text and reader, where does 'truth' lie? With the reader who brings meaning to what are otherwise only black marks on paper, or with the text which compels the reader to respond in a particular way? As Sartre puts it in '*Qu'est-ce que la littérature*: 'pour le lecteur, tout est à faire et tout est déjà fait'.[5] Equally, when I impute responses to Stendhal's reader, as I repeatedly shall, what reader have I in mind? The 'actual' reader, the 'contemporary' reader, the 'implied' or 'intended' reader, the 'narratee', the 'ideal' reader, etc., etc.? I have dispensed with these terms in the interests of simplicity and because I believe it will be possible to infer from the context which of these I have in mind. Nevertheless the question remains: am I talking about an 'innocent' reader who reads 'for fun' (Stendhal's 'femme de chambre') or a 'knowing' reader who is aware of the various tricks which novelists get up to? For, as Culler argues, 'to read is to operate with the hypothesis of a reader, and there is always a gap or division within reading. Our most familiar versions of this division are the notion of "suspension of disbelief", or our simultaneous interest in characters as people and in characters as devices of the novelist's art, or our appreciation of the suspense of a story whose ending, in fact, we already know.'[6]

In fact I shall be talking about both kinds of reader and indeed about this very division, because it is itself central to Stendhal's own concerns as a writer and, in particular, as a novelist. Stendhal recognized that there was more to novel-writing than a good yarn and a tug at the heart-strings:

la sensibilité n'exige pas heureusement de grands efforts d'esprit; le plus plat romancier parvient à vous arracher une larme, et à faire souffler votre bougie

---

[4] See *On Deconstruction. Theory and Criticism after Structuralism* (London, 1983), 31–83, especially 64–83. This may be complemented by Susan R. Suleiman and Inge Crosman (eds), *The Reader in the Text. Essays on Audience and Interpretation* (Princeton, 1980) and Jane P. Tompkins (ed.), *Reader-response Criticism. From Formalism to Post-Structuralism* (Baltimore and London, 1980). See also Culler's own extensive bibliography.
[5] Quoted by Culler, p. 76.   [6] Ibid. 67–8.

à trois heures après minuit: il faut un Cervantès, un Lesage, ou un Mérimée pour faire naître ce sourire délicieux qui indique le plaisir de l'esprit.[7] Yet he was also adamant that such intellectual pleasure should not be at the expense of emotional and imaginative participation. Apart from the fact that 'l'art du poète est de présenter le plus de plaisir possible au spectateur',[8] the requirement that the reader be involved in this way provides important protection for the novelist against the dangers of abstraction and empty virtuosity. 'Or, qu'est-ce qu'un roman sans émotion?',[9] asks Stendhal. His answer: an unduly philosophical work which pronounces upon the human condition without providing reliable evidence, or a self-consciously artificial work demanding approval as 'literature'.

For Stendhal the reader's illusions are as important as his judgements. But this raises a problem for the critic of Stendhal. How can he know what illusions are engendered by the Stendhalian text in readers other than himself? This is a problem which Stendhal himself addressed in the imaginary dialogue between a Romantic and an academician in the first chapter of *Racine et Shakespeare*, a dialogue which presents an interesting example of reader-response, or rather spectator-response, criticism. Given that the purpose of tragedy is to move the spectator and hence to achieve 'ce degré d'illusion nécessaire à une émotion profonde'[10], should one follow the example of Racine or Shakespeare? Racine, says the academician, because the unities of time and place are conducive to the suspension of disbelief. No, says the Romantic, the suspension of disbelief comes not from trying to convince an audience that it is not in a theatre but from making it forget periodically that it is. Like Culler's divided reader 'les spectateurs savent bien qu'ils sont au théâtre, et qu'ils assistent à la représentation d'un ouvrage d'art, et non pas à un fait vrai';[11] and when an audience applauds during a performance, it is applauding the actor not the character. But it can also experience moments of 'illusion parfaite'. Now there is, of course, illusion of an absurd kind, which the Romantic illustrates by telling the story of the soldier on duty in a Baltimore theatre during a performance of *Othello*. As Othello is on the point of killing Desdemona in Act V, the soldier shoots the actor playing Othello because 'il ne sera jamais dit qu'en ma présence un maudit nègre aura tué une

---

[7] OC, xlix. 59–60.   [8] JL, ii. 75.   [9] OI, ii. 231.
[10] RS, 53.   [11] RS, 58.

femme blanche.'[12] This is the illusion of those who mourn the deaths of characters in contemporary soap opera. But there is illusion of another kind: brief, fleeting moments when the spectator forgets both himself and the dramatist's expertise in the use of his medium (e.g. Racine's fine verse) and is completely absorbed in the spectacle before him. Like happiness the suspension of disbelief consists for Stendhal not in a permanent state but in 'ces instants délicieux et si rares d'*illusion parfaite*'.[13] The task of the tragedian (for the Romantic of this dialogue) and the novelist (for Stendhal) is to provide catchable quarry in this aesthetic 'chasse au bonheur' despite the spectator/reader's self-consciousness about his own activity. For the Romantic more such moments are provided by Shakespeare than by Racine:[14] for Stendhal the Happy Few are those who weep at Rossini's *Otello*.[15]

But do such moments of illusion occur? 'Il me semble', says the Romantic, 'que ces moments d'*illusion parfaite* sont plus fréquents qu'on ne le croit en général, et surtout qu'on ne l'admet pour vrai dans les discussions littéraires'. And if you, academician, will not accept this, then 'j'avoue que je ne puis rien vous répondre':

vos sentiments ne sont pas quelque chose de matériel que je puisse extraire de votre propre cœur, et mettre sous vos yeux pour vous confondre. Je vous dis: Vous devez avoir tel sentiment en ce moment; tous les hommes généralement bien organisés éprouvent tel sentiment en ce moment. Vous me répondrez: Pardonnez-moi le mot, *cela n'est pas vrai*. Moi, je n'ai rien à ajouter. Je suis arrivé aux derniers confins de ce que la logique peut saisir dans la poésie.

Which is not to say that the nature of literary response thereby ceases to be problematic:

il n'y a que des charlatans qui prétendent enseigner l'algèbre sans peine, ou arracher une dent sans douleur. La question que nous agitons est une des plus difficiles dont puisse s'occuper l'esprit humain.[16]

---

[12] Ibid.   [13] *RS*, 59.
[14] *RS*, 60. Cf. *VIT*, 93: Shakespeare saw in tragedy 'une représentation du caractère et des passions des hommes, qui doit toucher les spectateurs, en vertu de la sympathie et non par une vaine admiration pour les talents du poète'.
[15] *VR*, i. 181.   [16] *RS*, 59–60.

I should like to thank the editors of *Forum for Modern Language Studies* for permission to use material from my article 'Stendhal's *Armance*: The Comedy of "Une Chasse au malheur" ', and M. Victor Del Litto, editor of *Stendhal Club*, for permission to use material from my article 'A la recherche du temps présent. Quelques réflexions sur l'art de la chronique dans *Le Rouge et le Noir*'. I should like also to acknowledge the numerous debts which I have incurred in the writing of this book: to the many people who have written about Stendhal and to whom I have referred so extensively; to the librarians of the Taylor Institution Library and the Bibliothèque nationale for their generous help; to the Provost and Fellows of The Queen's College, Oxford, and the Board of the Faculty of Medieval and Modern Languages at Oxford for granting periods of leave and financial assistance towards travel abroad and attendance at conferences on Stendhal; to Alban Krailsheimer for his interest and stimulating suggestions; to Patricia Lloyd for the skill and patience with which she has typed the manuscript; to Virginia Llewellyn Smith for her generous encouragement and assistance; and lastly to my friend and colleague Ian Maclean for his unstinting altruism and unfailingly acute yet tactful advice. Without the benevolence of his reading, this book would never have been completed.

Roger Pearson

The Queen's College, Oxford
23 January 1987

Contents

Note on References

The following abbreviations have been used in the footnotes. For full bibliographical information see the Bibliography.

Arm: *Armance* (Classiques Garnier)

CHA: *Chroniques pour l'Angleterre* (ed. McWatters and Dénier)

COA: *Courrier anglais* (ed. Martineau)

CP: *La Chartreuse de Parme* (Classiques Garnier)

Corr: *Correspondance* (Bibliothèque de la Pléiade)

DLA: *De l'amour* (Classiques Garnier)

HPI: *Histoire de la peinture en Italie* (Divan)

JL: *Journal littéraire* (= OC, vols 33–5)

LL: *Lucien Leuwen* (Garnier-Flammarion)

MT: *Mémoires d'un touriste* (Maspero)

O: *Œuvres* (Editions Rencontre)

OC: *Œuvres complètes* (Cercle du Bibliophile)

OI: *Œuvres intimes* (Bibliothèque de la Pléiade)

RN: *Le Rouge et le Noir* (Classiques Garnier, ed. P.-G. Castex)

RS: *Racine et Shakespeare* (Garnier-Flammarion)

VHMM: *Vies de Haydn, Mozart et Métastase* (= OC, vol. 41)

VIT: *Voyages en Italie* (Bibliothèque de la Pléiade)

VR: *Vie de Rossini* (Divan)

These choices of edition reflect a compromise between availability, on the one hand, and reliability and scholarship on the other. The decision not to refer to the novels in the Bibliothèque de la Pléiade edition derives from the fact that this is about to be superseded.

I

THE MIRROR AND THE VIOLIN

'J'abhorre d'être cru sur parole; croire ainsi est une habitude
surannée que je ne voudrais pas contribuer à donner au lecteur.'

(*MT*, i. 261)

Joining the Happy Few

'Tout l'effet du poète est dans le cœur de ses auditeurs. Ce n'est que là que sont ses véritables victoires.'

(*JL*, i. 427)

'READING the novels of Stendhal', it has been said, 'is like riding a surfboard—one is not exactly oblivious of the past or the future, but they do not help much to balance the perilous present. The longer one stays on top of the wave, the more exhilarating the triumph; and there is a special climactic thrill about getting all the way in a single unbroken sweep.'[1] The tenor of these remarks, if not the West Coast analogy, is typical of most critical reaction to Stendhal. He is enjoyably tricky. Perhaps the finest essay yet written on him, that by Jean-Pierre Richard, ends on a similar note: 'parler de Stendhal, c'est chaque fois se condamner à l'impression que l'on n'a rien dit, qu'il vous a échappé et que tout reste à dire. Il faut alors se résigner et le rendre à son imprévisible et merveilleux jaillissement.'[2]

A critic embarking on a study of Stendhal is faced with many such warnings about the difficulty of his journey, and indeed meets with it at once in the entertaining debates about his subject's pseudonym. How should we pronounce it? Why did Henri Beyle choose it? On the first question Gérard Genette argues for St*a*ndhal on the basis of the pun 'vous allez encore vous stendhaliser' addressed by Beyle to Adolphe de Mareste in a letter of 1818,[3] but the more common

---

[1] Robert M. Adams, *Stendhal: Notes on a Novelist* (London, 1959), 206.

[2] 'Connaissance et tendresse chez Stendhal', in *Littérature et sensation* (Paris, 1954), 15–116. Cf. F. W. J. Hemmings, *Stendhal. A Study of his Novels* (Oxford, 1964), 95: 'no one who ventures to speak or write about Stendhal can fail to be painfully aware at almost every turn of how much he is forced to disregard, of the many reservations and attenuations that have to be suppressed.' Cf. also Victor Brombert, *Stendhal et la voie oblique. L'auteur devant son monde romanesque* (New Haven and Paris, 1954), 150–1.

[3] *Corr.*, i. 886 (3 Jan. 1818). See Genette, ' "Stendhal" ', in *Figures II* (Paris, 1969), 155–93 (192).

St*ai*ndhal may be justified if one thinks that 'scandaliser' was pronounced in the Paris of 1818 as it would be today in the Midi. As for the second question, it is a pity to have to reject the thesis that a love of Scotland led to the choice of an anagram of Shetland,[4] but it does seem clear that the pseudonym derives from the town of Stendal in present-day East Germany. First used to designate the author of Beyle's third published work *Rome, Naples et Florence en 1817*, it serves the fiction of a German cavalry officer, M. de Stendhal, visiting Italy and composing a guide-book on the basis of his travels, a fiction intended to put the French and Austrian authorities off the track of some fairly forthright remarks about Napoleon and the post-Napoleonic situation in Italy and Europe. Why he chose Stendal is not so clear, nor why he added an *h* in the wrong place. Stendal is the birthplace of Winckelmann, the centenary of whose birth was being celebrated that year, or perhaps Beyle had fond memories of a place he had visited during his time with the Grande Armée in Germany.[5] As for the *h*, Victor Del Litto is probably right in saying that he added it 'pour faire plus allemand, lui qui n'avait jamais réussi à se familiariser avec la langue d'Outre-Rhin';[6] others may wish to accept a more recent view that its position is full of the deepest masonic and numerological significance.[7]

In commenting on the many problems of interpretation which his works have posed, Stendhal's exegetes are in fact responding to the very notion of difficulty proclaimed by the texts themselves. In other words, Stendhal says his works are for the Happy Few, and his critics believe him. Now, as Paul Valéry once pointed out, this has done wonders for Stendhal's posthumous

[4] See *VIT*, 1313, n. 1.

[5] See Carsten Thiede, 'Stendhal à Stendal. Le pseudonyme sur les lieux', *Stendhal Club*, 16 (1973/74), 335–40, and Guy Weill Goudchaux, 'Steindal, Winckelmann et Stendhal', in V. Del Litto and H. Harder (eds), *Stendhal et l'Allemagne* (Paris, 1983), 177–89.

[6] *VIT*, 1313. Jean-Jacques Hamm suggests that the H is for Henri and thus signals the presence of the living author behind the pseudonym. See 'L'achèvement et son envers: de l'œuvre au lecteur', in Philippe Berthier (ed.), *Stendhal. Colloque de Cerisy-la-Salle (30 juin–10 juillet 1982)* (Paris, 1984), 13–31 (24).

[7] Dieter Diefenbach, 'Stendhal et la franc-maçonnerie', *Stendhal Club*, 27 (1984/5), 329–38 and 'Stendhal: un pseudonyme et ses variantes', *Stendhal Club*, 29 (1986/7), 43–8. Diefenbach's thesis stresses the connection with Winckelmann. For a different account of this see Francis Claudon, 'Stendhal et Winckelmann', *Stendhal Club*, 25 (1982/3), 297–309, and Guy Weill Goudchaux, art. cit.

reputation because 'il rend son lecteur fier de l'être'.[8] But sometimes, unfortunately, this pride has seemed more like the smug enjoyment of a cosy exclusivity, and even quite recently it has been possible to read the following remark from the pen of an otherwise excellent 'stendhalien':

> Stendhal désirait surtout s'adresser au lecteur raffiné qui partageait cette même supériorité intellectuelle, créant ainsi le sentiment d'appartenir à une petite élite qui est un des plaisirs les plus durables qu'offre la lecture du roman stendhalien.[9]

Did Stendhal really envisage the Happy Few as a band of intellectual snobs?

His first use of the phrase comes in a letter to Edouard Mounier in February 1804, and it clearly means those of like mind and taste.[10] Subsequently it appears, by way of dedication, at the beginning of the second volume of the *Histoire de la peinture en Italie* (1817), at the end of *Promenades dans Rome* (1829) and of *Le Rouge et le Noir* (1830), at the beginning of *Lucien Leuwen* (1834/5) and, most famously perhaps, at the end of *La Chartreuse de Parme* (1838-9).[11] The phrase probably has its source, not in *Henry V* (IV. iii: 'we few, we happy few, we band of brothers') but in Goldsmith's *The Vicar of Wakefield*, which Stendhal much admired and had certainly read before 1804 (whereas he may not have read *Henry V* till 1820).[12] The Vicar relates that he has given some thought to the question of whether a widowed clergyman should remarry: 'I published some tracts upon the subject myself, which, as they never sold, I have the consolation of thinking were read only by the happy *few*.'[13] Now of course the Vicar himself may be thinking of *Henry V* but the emphasis on 'few' suggests reference rather to the Bible and the 'few' who are chosen. In Stendhal's use of the phrase, however, the opposite of the 'happy few' would be not the 'many who are called', but the 'greatest number', as in Bentham's

---

[8] 'Stendhal', in Paul Valéry, *Œuvres* (2 vols, Paris, 1957–60), i. 553–82 (558).

[9] Grahame C. Jones, 'L' intrusion de l'auteur en particulier dans *Lucien Leuwen*', *Stendhal Club*, 25 (1982/3), 50–66 (54).

[10] *Corr.*, i. 87.

[11] Cf. the use of the phrase 'intelligenti pauca' or 'pauca intelligenti' as epigraphs in *HPI*, ii and *RS*.

[12] See V. Del Litto, *La Vie intellectuelle de Stendhal. Genèse et évolution de ses idées (1802–1821)* (Paris, 1959), 94.

[13] Chapter ii, para. 3. In *Vie de Henry Brulard* Stendhal claims to have learnt the first four pages of this novel by heart in order to improve his English (*OI*, ii. 814).

famous dictum about happiness. This opposition reflects the idea often expressed in Stendhal's work, and particularly in the prefaces to *Lucien Leuwen*, that democracy and republican government bring vulgarity and mediocrity, a general levelling that is inimical to good taste and good art. As he puts it in the epigraph dubiously attributed to Hobbes in the first chapter of *Le Rouge et le Noir*: 'Put thousands together / Less bad / But the cage less gay'. Not for the masses, then, the delights of Leonardo's *The Last Supper*:

quelques personnes penseront comme moi sur cet ouvrage sublime de Léonard de Vinci, et ces idées paraîtront recherchées *au plus grand nombre*; je le sens bien. Je supplie *ce plus grand nombre* de fermer le livre. A mesure que nous nous connaîtrions mieux, nous ne ferions que nous déplaire davantage.[14]

Thus the Happy Few constitute a kind of aristocracy of taste, and occasionally Stendhal defined them further. To be a member of this body in 1817 (as a reader of the *Histoire de la peinture*) you had to be under thirty-five and have an annual income of more than 2,000 but less than 20,000 francs;[15] in 1822 (*De l'amour*) you had to be one of 'ces êtres malheureux, aimables, charmants, point hypocrites, point *moraux*';[16] and in 1836 (*Vie de Henry Brulard*) someone under thirty and who did not belong to the 'parti prosaïque'.[17] Youth, imagination, charm, a comfortable income: perhaps most of us are excluded! Except of course that Stendhal often predicted that he would find his true readers only at a later time. The years 1880, 1900, 1935, 2000, these are all proposed for the moment of recognition,[18] for the moment—as he also put it—when his number would come up in the lottery of fame.[19] So at least by reading him now we are perhaps eligible for the Happy Few? May it be that our distance from the political events of the time, our possibly quite different moral viewpoint, and our exposure to writers more recent than Stendhal allow us a less prejudiced, more faithful reading of his works? Or do we simply read him with different prejudices, as Stendhal himself implies in *Vie de Henry Brulard* (which he did not intend to publish during his lifetime):

[14] *HPI*, i. 240–1 (my italics).
[15] i. 203, n. 2.
[16] p. 328.
[17] *OI*, ii. 957.
[18] Respectively *OI*, ii. 536–7 and 685; *OI*, ii, 474; *OI*, ii. 745; *OI*, i. 167.
[19] *Corr.*, ii. 153 (26 Dec. 1828), *OI*, ii. 474, 745.

j'écris ceci, sans mentir j'espère, sans me faire illusion, avec plaisir comme une lettre à un ami. Quelles seront les idées de cet ami en 1880? Combien différentes des nôtres! [...] ceci est nouveau pour moi: parler à des gens dont on ignore absolument la tournure d'esprit, le genre d'éducation, les préjugés, la religion! Quel encouragement à être *vrai*, et simplement *vrai*, il n'y a que cela qui tienne.[20]

Whichever the case, such are the criteria for membership of the Happy Few that at times this aristocracy of taste can indeed seem extremely exclusive. 'Je n'écris que pour cent lecteurs', he writes in *De l'amour*.[21] 'Si j'espère être lu', he says in the *Histoire de la peinture*, 'c'est par quelque âme tendre', someone who shows true appreciation of Raphael and Correggio for example, 'ce lecteur unique, et que je voudrais unique dans tous les sens'.[22] On occasions it can even sound as though the fewer the Happy Few, the happier Stendhal would be. The most extreme statement of this position comes in a diary entry of 1804: 'voilà vu', he says of the audience at a performance of Fabre d'Eglantine's *Philinte de Molière*, 'ce public choisi et peu nombreux à qui il faut plaire. Le cercle part de là, se resserre peu à peu et finit par moi. Je pourrais faire un ouvrage qui ne plairait qu'à moi et qui serait reconnu beau en 2000'.[23] Comments such as these may leave one with the impression that Stendhal is writing for no one but himself, that he is indeed just an egotist, a man so obsessed with himself that he needs to write it all down, in diaries, as autobiography, in the margins of books, on playing-cards, anywhere. Never was there a more compulsive *writer* and never, it seems, one so completely taken up with the intricacies of his own activities. What sort of a man is it after all who, some three months before his fiftieth birthday, notes the fact in code on the inside of his waistband: 'J. vaisa voirla5'? Or who records on his braces the year, month, day, hour and minute of a long-awaited and much desired sexual conquest? And who then records these two acts of inscription?[24] The answer is—a novel-reader:

[20] *OI*, ii. 536-7.
[21] p. 328. Cf. p. 14: 'il me serait doux de plaire beaucoup à trente ou quarante personnes de Paris que je ne verrai jamais, mais que j'aime à la folie, sans les connaître.' Cf. also *LL*, i. 93: 'ce conte fut écrit en songeant à un petit nombre de lecteurs que je n'ai jamais vus et que je ne verrai point, ce dont bien me fâche: j'eusse trouvé tant de plaisir à passer les soirées avec eux!'
[22] i. 206.
[23] *OI*, i. 167.
[24] *OI*, ii. 533 and *OI*, i. 887. For comment see Valéry's preface to Debraye's edition of *Lucien Leuwen* in *Œuvres*, i. 567, and Genette, ' "Stendhal" ', 167.

exprimer ce qu'on sent si vivement et si en détail, à tous les instants de la vie, est une corvée qu'on s'impose, parce qu'on a lu des romans, car si l'on était naturel on n'entreprendrait jamais une chose si pénible.[25]

The idea that Stendhal wrote above all for himself has had great currency in the reception of his works, and it informs the traditional approach to his own novels. The doyen of Stendhal studies, Victor Del Litto, summarizes this view as follows:

dans toute l'œuvre romanesque stendhalienne, la majeure et la mineure, il y a un élément dominant: l'*égotisme*, ou, en d'autres mots, le besoin de tout ramener à son moi intérieur, l'habitude de ne voir les hommes et les choses que par le truchement de ce moi, l'exigence de l'introspection, la chasse au bonheur.[26]

According to this view Stendhal's novels are examples of wish-fulfilment. 'Sublimation', 'compensation', 'revanche imaginaire', 'victoire imaginaire', even 'auto-punition', these are the notions that pervade the major critical works of Martineau,[27] Prévost,[28] Starobinski,[29] Brombert,[30] Richard[31] and others.[32] Georges Blin's magisterial thesis[33] offers but one version of this in arguing that Stendhal not only found solutions to the problems of his personality by imaginatively recreating himself in his characters but also demonstrated, by his authorial intrusions, his superiority over these very characters.

But this view of Stendhal as an essentially solipsistic writer is quite wrong, for, even in his most intimate works, he is obsessed by the idea of being read and more especially, as we have seen, of being misread.

---

[25] *DLA*, 60.

[26] *Romans et nouvelles* (Paris, 1968), 9. Cf. *OI*, i. pp. ix–x. Much more recently Anne-Marie Meininger has written that 'l'œuvre romanesque de Stendhal est une des formes de son égotisme' (in her edition of *Lucien Leuwen* for the Collection de l'Imprimerie Nationale (2 vols, Paris, 1982), i. 66).

[27] *Le Cœur de Stendhal* (2 vols, Paris, 1952–3), i. 416.

[28] *La Création chez Stendhal* (Paris, 1951), 306.

[29] 'Stendhal pseudonyme', in *L'Œil vivant* (Paris, 1961), 189–240 (201, 212).

[30] *Stendhal et la voie oblique*, 118 ff.

[31] 'Connaissance et tendresse', 105.

[32] e.g. Paul Hazard, *La Vie de Stendhal*, 18th edn (Paris, 1927), 175, and F. M. Albérès, *Le Naturel chez Stendhal* (Paris, 1956), 320. In 1927 Valéry's preface to Debraye's edition of *Lucien Leuwen* includes the following comment on Stendhal's creation of powerful politicians and bankers: 'il se venge en les créant de n'être pas ce qu'ils sont. Tout écrivain se récompense comme il peut de quelque injure du sort' (Valéry, *Œuvres*, i. 558).

[33] *Stendhal et les problèmes du roman* (Paris, 1954) and *Stendhal et les problèmes de la personnalité* (Paris, 1958).

Stendhal is a writer acutely conscious of a public, and this is most
obvious in the fact that so much of his published work was to be
used: by the art-lover, the opera-goer, the tourist[34] and—one might
say—the novel-reader. For Stendhal envisages the novel first and
foremost as a source of entertainment: certainly not as a form of
confession, nor as a monumental, Balzacian record of a whole
society, nor yet as a 'pure', Flaubertian work of art 'sans attache
extérieure',[35] but rather as some instrument of pleasure which must
meet certain consumer standards: 'le roman est un livre qui amuse
en racontant',[36] 'le roman doit raconter; c'est là le genre de plaisir
qu'on lui demande,'[37] 'le propre d'un roman doit être que le lecteur
qui le commence le soir veille toute la nuit pour le finir',[38] etc. But
even in the works not intended for publication there is the same
awareness that he is not writing in a void. In the diaries, for example,
two of the notebooks contain remarks addressed to the person who
may find them, asking him not to read them, both as a matter of
honour and because he will find them boring.[39] And it is no
coincidence that Stendhal was such a prolific and cogent correspondent.
Whether writing a diary or a letter, he was always engaged in an
act of communication rather than mere self-expression.[40]

One such letter, to his sister Pauline in May 1804, asks her to
keep all his letters because they will come in useful later on—for her
because she will be able to go back over some of the things she has
not understood (in what is essentially a correspondence course in
philosophy and drama!),[41] for him because 'elles me donneront
l'histoire de mon esprit.'[42] Again this looks like egotism, but one

---

[34] Stendhal was the first to give this word wide currency in French. See Del Litto's
comments in *MT*, i, 14.

[35] Flaubert's letter to Louise Colet of 16 Jan. 1852.

[36] *LL*, ii. 591.

[37] *OI*, ii. 243.

[38] *CA*, iii. 218. Cf. *Corr.*, ii. 97 (23 Dec. 1826): 'si le roman n'est pas de nature
à faire passer la nuit à quoi bon le faire?' Cf. also his definition of 'littérateurs' as
'gens donnant du plaisir avec des paroles imprimées' (*OC*, xli. 240).

[39] *OI*, i. 336 (footnote headed 'LISEZ'), *OI*, i. 655 (footnoted 'Avis'). See also *OI*,
i. 834 (epigraph).

[40] Note also that *Souvenirs d'égotisme* and *Vie de Henry Brulard* are written as
if they were letters to a friend: *OI*, ii. 451-2, 466, 536-7. For discussion of the diary
and its reader see Béatrice Didier, 'Le secret du journal', *L'Arc*, 88 (1983), 5-9. Note
further that the four biographies of composers are presented as letters.

[41] Cf. Victor Brombert, *Stendhal. Fiction and the Themes of Freedom* (Chicago
and London, 1968), 33.

[42] *Corr.*, i. 93 (11 May 1804).

must remember his remark that he kept a record of things because he had read novels. Essentially he sees himself as a story that is unfolding, and letter, diary-entry and marginal jotting are addressed to a future self who will be able to compare notes with his precursor. Literally so: 'quant aux nouvelles vues qu'un roman suggère pour la connaissance du cœur humain, je me rappelle fort bien les anciennes; j'aime même à les trouver notées en marge.'[43] Now of course this is all part of the would-be Idéologue's quest for happiness through a knowledge of self based on rigorous analysis of the available evidence,[44] and as such is still self-centred. But there is an ulterior aim not only to share such knowledge, as it were altruistically, with the world, but also to study the logic of his response to experience and how and why it may or may not have changed. It is a form of consumer research. Stendhal likes to note his own reactions to particular sentences or paragraphs in a book in order to go back to these notes later as if they were those of someone else, thus obtaining a measure of objective distance with which to authenticate his findings, and then to consider how a given piece of text caused a particular response.[45] This research is precisely akin to that which he used to carry out in the Théâtre des Français when, as a young, aspiring dramatist he would note on a copy of the play the places where the audience laughed, cried, yawned or slept:

[le poète] doit voir l'effet que les passions qu'il peint chez ses protagonistes produisent dans le cœur des spectateurs. Etudier ce qui s'y passe, cela vaut mieux qu'étudier Aristote. Le parterre des Français m'est doublement utile: j'étudie la pièce et les spectateurs, je vois d'abord ce qu'ils sont, ensuite leurs rapports.[46]

---

[43] *DLA*, 36.

[44] '*Nosce te ipsum* Je crois avec Tracy et la Grèce que c'est le chemin du bonheur. Mon moyen, c'est ce journal': *OI*, i. 710.

[45] Similar 'dédoublement' is at work when he reviews his own novels—*Armance* for the English press, *Le Rouge* for an Italian periodical. In the latter case the 'reviewer' claims to have forgotten the plot and to have had to borrow Janin's version as a result! This lapse of memory, if such it was, may even have given Stendhal an idea for overcoming his mental block about constructing plots. Much better at elaborating on a given story than inventing one from scratch, Stendhal resorted, in the creation of later parts of *Lucien Leuwen*, to writing down the story, leaving it for five or six months and then coming back to it as if it were the work of someone else. The plagiarist (for sections of *VHMM* and *HPI*) became a self-plagiarist. See *OI*, ii. 184; and cf. *OI*, ii. 206, 255–6, 258, and *LL*, ii. 582. See also F. W. J. Hemmings, 'Les deux *Lamiel*. Nouveaux aperçus sur les procédés de composition de Stendhal romancier', *Stendhal Club*, 15 (1972/3), 287–316 (288–9).

[46] *JL*, i. 427. Cf. *RS*, 68. See François Landry, *L'Imaginaire chez Stendhal. Formation et expression* (Lausanne, 1982), 56.

The trouble with the novel is that you cannot really observe with accuracy how it is being read, so the alternative is to watch yourself read. This Stendhal did with great assiduity, such was his fascination with the process of reading.

But how did he use the results of his research? The better to 'sell' us a view of life which we might not normally accept? While it is evident from the various descriptions of the Happy Few already quoted that Stendhal expected much consumer resistance from the general reader and regarded him or her[47] as a kind of enemy whose lurking presence put constant pressure on him to go back over his work and tone things down,[48] does it necessarily follow that what Stendhal sought to protect from such antipathy was a coherent message or set of values susceptible of unambiguous exposition? Victor Brombert implies as much in *Stendhal et la voie oblique*. According to this widely accepted thesis[49] Stendhalian irony disarms the feared, unsympathetic reader by anticipating his objections and by playing with his moral reactions to the point where these are 'anaesthetized'.[50] While it has the great merit of stressing the participating, creative role demanded of Stendhal's reader, this argument suggests nevertheless that such reader-participation is a mere diversion while we are sold the pass: 'Stendhal réussit non seulement à faire passer pour vraisemblables et vraies les plus grosses absurdités romanesques, mais encore à paralyser notre jugement moral. Nos propres croyances, en effet, ne nous gênent pas'[51]—the pass being an idealized, 'beyliste' conception of the world which prizes love, imagination, energy and freedom above all else. Adherents of this view refer also to a form of 'mise-en-abyme' in the Stendhalian novel whereby such a model of communication is exemplified by Lucien courting Mme d'Hocquincourt while wanting to be heard and understood by Mme de Chasteller, or by Fabrice speaking obliquely to Clélia in salon and pulpit:

---

[47] Cf. Geneviève Mouillaud, *'Le Rouge et le Noir' de Stendhal. Le roman possible* (Paris, 1973), 32–3, 161. Cf. also Béatrice Didier, 'Le secret du journal', 8, and Ellen Constans, 'Stendhal et le public impossible', in Philippe Berthier (ed.), *Stendhal: l'écrivain, la société, le pouvoir* (Grenoble, 1984), 33–55.

[48] *OI*, ii. 118.

[49] Which has subsequently been developed with much expertise by Shoshana Felman in *La 'Folie' dans l'œuvre romanesque de Stendhal* (Paris, 1971).

[50] Brombert takes his cue from Alain's notion of paralysis. See *La Voie oblique*, 162, Alain, *Stendhal* (Paris, 1935), 18, and cf. Prévost, *Création*, 111.

[51] p. 163.

ne doit-on pas voir aussi dans le sermon l'emblème du roman lui-même: un message où l'auteur prend le masque d'un narrateur pour transmettre un message symbolique à quelques destinataires particuliers, qui se cachent dans un public vaste et anonyme. Mais qui sont ces *happy few*, sinon des cryptographes?[52]

But this is the problem with the notion of the Happy Few: it implies that there is a right reading of Stendhal, that there is a message to be decoded if we can but establish the appropriate key.[53] But what if there are several keys? What if membership of the Happy Few depends on achieving not the right reading but the right response, one that can live with mixtures of comedy and tragedy, that can tolerate ambiguity and paradox without trying to resolve them, that can feel the thrill of romance while yet acknowledging the call of reason, that can imagine and also judge? Joining the Happy Few entails no submission to moral anaesthetic: it requires an open mind.

And this is the point of Stendhal's consumer research. He is not interested in devising novels which will seduce the reader into easy complicity, but in novels which will engage his every faculty: 'tout ouvrage dont le grand mérite est d'être bien calculé sur le degré de bêtise du spectateur ou du lecteur m'ennuie. Ceux qui me plaisent furent calculés pour plaire aux plus spirituels des contemporains, par ex[emple] le Dante.'[54] But such calculation is aimed not merely at pleasing the reader, for there is also an important moral consideration. Reading is dangerous. Perhaps a book cannot actually change the reader's nature[55] but it can, particularly if it is a novel, have a powerful and damaging effect:

[52] William J. Berg, 'Cryptographie et communication dans *La Chartreuse de Parme*', *Stendhal Club*, 20 (1977/8), 170–82 (180). Cf. Landry, *Imaginaire*, 333–4; Peter Brooks, 'L'invention de l'écriture (et du langage) dans *La Chartreuse de Parme*', *Stendhal Club*, 20 (1977/8), 183–90 (189); and Jean Rousset, 'Les échanges à distance', *Etudes de lettres*, IV. vii. 3 (July–Sept. 1984), 3–12. Cf. also *Armance* where Octave speaks to ladies of society in order to be heard by Armance (*Arm.*, 44).

[53] Cf. Bardèche, *Stendhal romancier* (Paris, 1947), 415: 'nous qui possédons depuis près d'un demi-siècle la grille qui permet de lire les romans de Stendhal'. Even a much more modern critic like Jean-Jacques Hamm argues something similar: 'le signe stendhalien est ambivalent. Ouvert à une multiplicité de significations, il exige une connaissance absolue des valeurs qu'il cache. Les "happy few", les privilégiés comprendront ce que le signe signale' ('L'achèvement et son envers', 28–9).

[54] *JL*, iii. 232.

[55] 'Un livre ne peut changer l'âme du lecteur. L'aigle ne paîtra jamais dans les vertes prairies, et jamais la chèvre folâtre ne se nourrira de sang. Je puis tout au plus dire à l'aigle: Viens de ce côté, c'est vers cette région de la montagne que tu trouveras les agneaux les plus gras; et à la chèvre: C'est dans les fentes de ce roc que croît le meilleur serpolet': *HPI*, i. 58.

dans les romans on ne nous offre qu'une nature choisie. Nous nous formons nos types de bonheur d'après les romans; parvenus à l'âge où nous devons être heureux d'après les romans, nous nous étonnons de deux choses: la première, de ne pas éprouver du tout les sentiments auxquels nous nous attendions; la deuxième, si nous les éprouvons, de ne pas les sentir comme ils sont peints dans les romans. Quoi de plus naturel cependant, si les romans sont une nature choisie?[56]

The novelist has chosen but one way of presenting the world, and the less shaded this presentation, the greater will be the disparity between the preconceptions it has fostered and the reader's own experience of reality, and the greater too will be the pain of disillusion. As an enthusiastic reader of *Don Quixote*, Stendhal came to an early understanding of this problem, and during his early twenties his diary and his letters to Pauline are full of warnings about 'these damned books'[57] and the need to look on any written text as but one prediction of how things may turn out in reality. He was particularly struck by a sentence from Hobbes's *Discourse on Human Nature* which he noted in translation: 'au lieu de lire les livres, il faut lire ses propres conceptions, et c'est dans ce sens que je crois que le mot fameux *connais-toi toi-même* peut être digne de la réputation qu'il a acquise.'[58] And this is what he had in mind as a novelist. While his heroes exemplify the dangers—and delights—of preconceiving life according to imagined models, his own narratives eschew moral conclusion in order to force the reader to 'lire ses propres conceptions'. Moreover such a strategy not only secures the reader from the kind of disillusion which was to kill Emma Bovary, it prevents a uniformity of response which is inimical to the individualism and singularity which Stendhal valued in human beings. For him Molière was an immoral writer because in inducing the audience at Louis XIV's court all to laugh at the same things

[56] *JL*, i. 140. Stendhal adds a footnote: 'voilà l'histoire de ma vie, mon roman était les ouvrages de Rousseau.'
[57] *Corr.*, i. 371 (25–7 Nov. 1807). Cf. ibid. 371–2, 161–2 (29 Oct.–16 Nov. 1804), 121 (6 July 1804), 54–5 (8 Feb. 1803). Cf. also *OI*, i. 79, and ii. 761, 876.
[58] *JL*, i. 366. This translates the end of chap. v, para. 14 (entitled 'Translation of the discourse of the mind into the discourse of the tongue, and of the errors thence proceeding'): 'I may in a manner conclude, that it is impossible to *rectify* so many errors of any one man, as must needs proceed from these causes, without beginning *anew* from the very first grounds of all our knowledge and sense; and instead of books, reading over orderly one's own conceptions: in which meaning, I take *nosce teipsum* for a precept worthy the reputation it hath gotten.' See Del Litto, *La Vie intellectuelle*, 149, and *OI*, i, pp. x–xvi.

he thereby instilled a dreadful conformity, 'l'horreur de n'être pas comme tout le monde'.[59] To join the Happy Few, not only must one have an open mind, one must also be oneself—'unique dans tous les sens'.

For this to happen the reader needs to be cured of dependence on an omniscient author, which of course is just what seems not to happen in Stendhal's case. Georges Blin recognizes that the technique of limited point of view does much to enhance the realism, or 'vérisme', of Stendhal's novels by suggesting the relativism proclaimed in the preface to *Armance* ('la même chose, chacun la juge d'après sa position') but sees this as being destroyed by the intrusions of an author who wants his own point of view to predominate.[60] More subtly Brombert speaks of 'le miracle d'une pseudo-objectivité'[61] whereby a very personal writer, the opposite of 'impersonal' Flaubert or Joyce, persuades to his own opinions from behind a mask of irony and apparently judicious dispassion. Jean Starobinski envisages a more Protean figure caught up in the dialectic of Beyle and Stendhal, a dialectic of authorial self-affirmation and pseudonymic self-effacement, of the 'désir d'être soi' and the 'plaisir d'agencer d'impossibles magies pour cesser d'être soi',[62] such—one may infer—that in the novels authorial assertion alternates with vicarious adventure. But what if the very partiality of the intrusions makes these equally 'relative', if the purpose of the mask is to conceal the author behind a narrator whose attitudes may be different from his, if both mask and pseudonym make the novel more independent of its author (Beyle) and present it to the reader as a phenomenon with which he must come to terms unaided? Is it not the case in each of the four major novels that the narrator's extensive commentary offers no help in the elucidation of a central mystery: what is Octave's secret, why does Julien shoot Mme de Rênal, what is Lucien really like, where does Fabrice go wrong? In the search for coherence, the Happy Few must go it alone and, as Roland Barthes has put it: 'la naissance du lecteur doit se payer de la mort de l'Auteur.'[63]

---

[59]   *RS*, 216, 219. Subsequently Stendhal tended to blame Louis XIV for this more than Molière himself. See *VIT*, 408, 913, and *MT*, i. 342.

[60]   This is the thesis of *Stendhal et les problèmes du roman*.

[61]   *La Voie oblique*, 163.

[62]   'Stendhal pseudonyme', 201. Cf. the beginning of Baudelaire's *Mon Cœur mis à nu*: 'De la vaporisation et de la centralisation du *Moi*. Tout est là.'

[63]   *Le Bruissement de la langue* (Paris, 1984), 67.

To suggest that Stendhal's principal aim is to remove himself from his novels and emancipate the reader from authorial oppression is to reject the usual implications of his famous analogy between novel and mirror and to prefer the less well known comparison with a violin from which this study takes its title. As an image for the mimetic function of art the mirror is not only highly traditional (Plato's *Republic*, Book X, Hamlet's 'mirror up to nature', etc.)[64] but also rather simplistic, since clearly all depends on the quality of the mirror and its angle of reflection. Needless to say, Stendhal was aware of this problem. Comparing the long descriptive passages to be found in Walter Scott with the psychological insights afforded by *La Princesse de Clèves* he rounds on such naïvety; 'rien de ridicule comme ce conseil donné par les gens du monde: *imitez la nature*. Eh! je le sais bien, morbleu! qu'il faut imiter la nature; mais jusqu'à quel point? Voilà toute la question.'[65] Nevertheless the analogy has stuck. Georges Blin writes of 'l'esthétique du miroir',[66] while Castex agrees in seeing the mirror as an emblem of Stendhal's art and talks of 'un miroir où se reflètent dans une vérité irrécusable les personnages et la société où ils évoluent'. Castex rightly stresses that Stendhal has added the notion of movement to the well-known image and draws a parallel with cinematography[67] which is echoed by John Mitchell's juxtaposition of Stendhal's 'mirror that moves' with the fixed and static 'fresque de la société' to which Balzac refers in the 'Avant-Propos' to the *Comédie Humaine*.[68]

But Stendhal's own use of the analogy is often playful, if not downright ironic. As Victor Brombert was the first to point out,[69] Stendhal's most celebrated reference to the novel as mirror, that in *Le Rouge et le Noir* (ii. 19), under the nicely pompous page-heading 'La Morale et la Poésie', is a nonsense. Here the narrator intervenes in the text to express his anxiety at depicting Mathilde's 'mad' love for Julien and to apologize to the putative reader on the grounds

---

[64] See M. H. Abrams, *The Mirror and the Lamp. Romantic Theory and the Critical Tradition* (New York, 1953), and Udo Schöning, *Literatur als Spiegel. Zur Geschichte eines kunsttheoretischen Topos in Frankreich von 1800 bis 1860* (Heidelberg, 1984).

[65] 'Walter Scott et la Princesse de Clèves', in OC, xlvi. 223.

[66] *Stendhal et les problèmes du roman*, part I.

[67] P.-G. Castex, *'Le Rouge et le Noir' de Stendhal* (Paris, 1967), 177–8. Castex acknowledges a debt to Jean-Louis Bory, 'Le cinéma: périlleux salut du roman', *Revue des Lettres Modernes*, 5 (1958), 249–55 (250–1).

[68] *Stendhal: 'Le Rouge et le Noir'* (London, 1973), 16.

[69] *La Voie oblique*, 15–17.

that he can but describe what he sees in nature: 'eh, monsieur, un roman est un miroir qui se promène sur une grande route.'[70] Yet just before this he has called Mathilde 'ce personnage [qui] est tout à fait d'imagination', and just afterwards he asserts that 'le caractère de Mathilde est impossible dans notre siècle'. So the novel is a fiction, not a representation of reality at all. The other use of the image in *Le Rouge* (in the epigraph to i. 13 falsely attributed to Saint-Réal[71]) is no less ironic if one is prepared to agree with Grahame C. Jones's suggestion of a pun on the name of the seventeenth–century historian[72]—which suggestion may be reinforced by the presence in the same novel of a rather redundant Mlle de Sainte-Hérédité.[73] Of course in the first of these two references to the mirror-novel there is a note of seriousness in the narrator's advice that we blame not the novelist nor even the muddy reality he depicts but rather the government officer responsible for the mud, and a similar note is struck in the preface to *Armance* and (implicitly) in the third preface to *Lucien Leuwen*. But in these two cases Stendhal is stressing that his novels are not making party-political propaganda even if they do, inevitably, touch on political issues by depicting contemporary reality. There is no suggestion of a full-blown pronouncement on the aesthetics of novel-writing, and again the point is made with humour—by the immodest and unlikely parallel between *Armance* and a hugely popular comedy, and by the fanciful comparison of a hostile reader of *Lucien Leuwen* to a sick man smashing a mirror because it reflects his green face. Indeed the second preface to *Lucien Leuwen* adds an interesting rider: 'excepté pour la passion du héros, un roman doit être un miroir'. Whatever interpretation one places upon this cryptic comment—that the hero should be larger than life, should display the energy that is no longer to be seen in contemporary society, should offer us through his inner musings an imaginative and heroic conception of life that is at variance with the harsh reality which it is the job of the rest of the novel to depict[74]—the fact remains that for Stendhal there is more to the novel than mirror

[70] *RN*, 342.

[71] See Louis Bassette, 'Sur une épigraphe de *Rouge et Noir*. Stendhal et Saint-Réal', *Stendhal Club*, 9 (1966/7), 241–53.

[72] 'Réel, Saint-Réal: une épigraphe du *Rouge* et le réalisme stendhalien', *Stendhal Club*, 25 (1982/3), 235–43.

[73] *RN*, 294.

[74] See also Michel Crouzet, *Stendhal. Quatre études sur Lucien Leuwen* (Paris, 1985), 107.

images. And indeed his only serious uses of the analogy indicate that
he saw a mirror-novel as a novel that was boringly unimaginative
and limited in its appeal:

[M. Picard] n'a pas beaucoup d'esprit, de profondeur et d'imagination; mais
c'est peut-être pourquoi il a de la vérité. Dans ses romans, comme dans ses
comédies, M. Picard rend ce qu'il voit comme un *miroir*. Ce genre de mérite
donne peu de plaisir aux personnes qui habitent le pays, mais doit être fort
précieux aux étrangers.[75]

As foreigners interested less in the details of life in France in 1825
than in the art of Stendhal's novels, it may be better to turn our
attention from the mirror to the violin. The image of the soul as the
body of a violin from which sounds are called forth by the bow of
experience is a favourite one of Stendhal's and dates back to his first
contacts with the Idéologues and their projected scientific analysis of
emotional and intellectual experiences. Thus in 1802 Stendhal notes
in his diary: 'les passions sont les effets des objets extérieurs sur nous.
Il ne faut donc pas s'étonner que le même archet produise des sons
différents sur des violons dont les caisses ne se ressemblent pas',[76]
and four years later he tries to inculcate a similar lesson into Pauline:

tu me sembles cependant assez avancée pour commencer la véritable étude, la
plus utile du moins, celle de toi-même, la véritable sagesse. Lorsque tu connaîtras
ton instrument, tu pourras dire: Tel archet, jouant dessus, produit malheur,
tel autre, bonheur; mais voilà les archets que je suis destinée à rencontrer
dans le monde [...] Ces archets donnés, il faut donc modifier la caisse de mon
violon de manière à ce qu'ils produisent ce son si rare nommé bonheur.[77]

External phenomena—the opposite sex, political changes, landscape,
Saint-Simon's memoirs,[78] the novel—these are but the causes: what is
important, and most interesting, are the effects, the notes they produce.

Now of course the notion of the soul as a sounding-box has as
long a history as the mirror of mimesis, perhaps longer.[79] Equally,
musical instruments have since Orpheus's lyre been a recurrent source
of imagery to describe the poet or writer's task, and Madeleine Simons
makes the interesting point that in French literature of the nineteenth

---

[75] *CHA*, iii. 152. Cf. Brombert, *La Voie oblique*, 16. In a rough draft for the
preface to *Armance* Stendhal uses the mirror analogy to indicate a fidelity to reality
which is unacceptable in art (*Arm.*, 259).

[76] *JL*, i. 29.   [77] *Corr.*, i. 283–4 (7 Feb. 1806).

[78] *OI*, ii. 371; *OI*, i. 729; *OI*, ii. 542, *MT*, i. 100; cf. *OI*, ii. 419; *OI*, ii. 274.

[79] Madeleine Simons traces it back to the Pythagoreans in her *Sémiotisme de
Stendhal* (Geneva, 1980), 158–60.

century there is a move away from images of harmony between poet and universe to images of discordance, as the lyre of Lamartine[80] gives way to the 'cloche fêlée' of Baudelaire and the 'chaudron fêlé' of Flaubert. But what is original about Stendhal's violin is not only the choice of instrument, but also the fact that it is the reader, not the writer, who is the sounding-box. The novelist simply wields the bow that produces the sound: the nature and quality of the sound depend on the reader. To join the Happy Few we must accept to be played upon, to enjoy 'la rêverie qui est le vrai plaisir du roman'.[81]

F. W. J. Hemmings ends the introductory chapters of his study of Stendhal's novels by quoting this phrase from De l'amour and referring to the sentence from Vie de Henry Brulard which compares a novel to a violinist's bow. Hemmings comments that this analogy 'is meaningful only in the context of an unusual reliance on the reader's response. And Stendhal was, as we have seen, prepared to accord unlimited confidence to the reader, provided he was a reader after Stendhal's own heart, one of the "happy few" '.[82] Not only might one take issue with the idea of 'unlimited confidence', but also, and more importantly, with the implication that there is a right reading of Stendhal which only those endowed with a particular kind of sensibility can achieve. Hemmings states:

[Stendhal's] novel, then, was to be evocative rather than instructive, passionate rather than reflective, emotional rather than intellectual. One might add that in that case its appeal was bound to be personal rather than universal, directed as it was to the sensibility which is variable in kind rather than to the intelligence which is variable only in degree.[83]

My own view is that the Stendhalian novel is designed to be both passionate and reflective, both emotional and intellectual, and that its appeal is potentially universal if its readers will acknowledge and defer the choices of reading which each individual novel presents.

---

[80] And of Hugo, with or without the 'corde d'airain' mentioned at the end of Les Feuilles d'automne. Cf. also Hugo's 'boîte sonore' in the preface to Les Voix intérieures, and Nerval's 'luth constellé' in 'El Desdichado'.

[81] DLA, 36. Cf. OI, ii. 542: 'je vois que la rêverie a été ce que j'ai préferé à tout.'

[82] Stendhal, 59.

[83] Ibid. Cf. also Stephen Gilman, The Tower as Emblem. Chapters VIII, IX, XIX and XX of the Chartreuse de Parme (Frankfurt am Main, 1967), 23–4, 60. Gilman use the violin analogy to argue that Stendhal conquers and inhabits his reader in order to impart the message of 'beylisme': 'only by accepting our role as musical instrument may we come to know what it means to be Stendhal' (60). Once again there are the implications of a univocal text and a passive reader.

2

Comedy and the novel

'Je regarde le roman comme la comédie au XIXe siècle.'

(*JL*, iii. 187)

IF we are to believe Stendhal's version of events in *Vie de Henry Brulard*, it was at the age of eleven that he first decided to become a writer. Having just thrilled to the abbé Terrasson's *Séthos*, the rather weighty novel which later prompted him to compare a novel with a violinist's bow,[1] he chanced on some 'mauvais romans' belonging to his uncle, Romain Gagnon. After a month or so of avid and illicit reading he discovered Andréa de Nerciat's *Félicia, ou mes fredaines*, a much reprinted libertine novel which, in the polite words of Philippe Berthier, 'l'échauffe de demi-visions tantalisantes et le conduit à d'improbables orgies.'[2] For the pubescent Beyle the die was cast: 'dès ce moment ma vocation fut décidée: vivre à Paris en faisant des comédies comme Molière.'[3] Like most young aspirant writers of the time he saw the theatre as offering the surest and speediest road to success and accordingly devoted himself with single-minded determination to one aim: '*to make* chef-d'œuvre'.[4] From his late teens to his early thirties the diary-entries, marginal jottings and drafts of projected plays (*Les Deux Hommes, Letellier*, etc.) all testify to the vigorous research of an apprentice-dramatist who is examining theatrical masterpieces, in both text and performance, to discover the secrets of his chosen craft. Other ambitious projects are postponed: histories of Napoleon or the Revolution must wait fifteen years, an *Art poétique* till he is fifty, a history of Rome till his old age.[5] The immediate task in hand is to become a 'comic bard'.[6]

---

[1] It also gave Mozart the plot for the *Magic Flute*. See *VHMM*, 307, n. 1.
[2] *Stendhal et la Sainte Famille* (Geneva, 1983), 186–7.
[3] *OI*, ii. 699.   [4] *OI*, ii. 270.   [5] *JL*, i. 16, ii. 26.
[6] *OI*, i. 571, 578. Madeleine Simons gives a very thorough account of this apprenticeship in *Sémiotisme de Stendhal*. See also Paulette Trout, *La Vocation romanesque de Stendhal* (Paris, 1970).

Realizing from the start that genius does not mean the chance receipt of inspiration from on high but rather 'une plus grande dose de bon sens'[7] acquired through concentrated observation and reflexion, he draws up reading lists[8] and inventories of possible subject matter,[9] considers how to improve his command of French[10] and his written style,[11] examines the problem of rhyme,[12] defines and analyses human nature and behaviour in the most abstract, and sometimes aphoristic, of terms,[13] and resolves above all to live and experience:

j'ai vingt ans passés, si je ne me lance pas dans le monde et si je ne cherche pas à connaître les hommes par expérience *je suis perdu.* Je ne connais les hommes que par les livres, il y a des passions que je n'ai jamais vues ailleurs. Comment puis-je les peindre? Mes tableaux ne seraient que des copies de copies.[14]

Central to his plan is the desire to know human beings well enough to know how to make them laugh, and many pages are devoted to the nature of laughter, comedy, and the joke,[15] and to the principal differences between comedy and tragedy.[16] What emerges from these pages is a fairly straightforward theory: tragedy makes us see ourselves in others, comedy makes us compare ourselves with others. Tragedy depicts a passion with which we identify strongly, comedy a character at whose mistakes we laugh or smile.[17] In particular comedy appeals to our vanity by offering a pleasurable sense of superiority over others. While the passions of tragedy are to a large extent timeless, what is ridiculous varies from age to age,[18] and person to person, and from this the future novelist-violinist derives an important rule: '*my comedy* doit changer suivant les spectateurs.'[19] If comedy is to please, the character's mistake(s) must be neither too obvious[20] nor too odious.[21] By 'l'odieux' Stendhal means something, perhaps of a political or financial nature,[22] which may be so controversial or so reprehensible to the spectator/reader as

---

[7] *JL*, i. 19.   [8] e.g. *JL*, i. 18, 43–7 103–9; ii. 1.
[9] *JL*, i. 66, 96–100, 175–6, 242–4.   [10] *JL*, i. 20.
[11] *JL*, i. 316; ii. 134, 361–79.   [12] *JL*, i. 262–8.
[13] *JL*, i. 310–11, 421 ff.   [14] *JL*, i. 130.
[15] *JL*, i. 146, 167, 216, 340, 347, 389, 409–28; ii. 4–5, 29, 110–13, 131–3, 135–8, 154, 297–9, 301–4.
[16] *JL*, ii. 70–1, 120, 135, 139–41.   [17] *RS*, 137, *OI*, i. 81.
[18] *JL*, ii. 113.   [19] *JL*, ii. 56.   [20] *JL*, ii. 110.
[21] *OI*, i. 118, 638.   [22] *RS*, 70.

to make him angry and thus banish the mood of pleasant gaiety which should be the product of comedy.[23] Comedy is not satire.[24] There should not be too great a distance between spectator and character,[25] but rather a proximity of interests which permits of sympathy[26] and even affection. Comedy should engender not impotent hatred but a warm vision of happiness.

Stendhal's early ambition to become the Molière of his century is of great importance to an assessment of his art as a novelist,[27] because the conception of comedy to which it led him turned out to be more easily realized in the novel than the play. His switch of genre had a number of causes, of course, not the least of which was his inability to master the alexandrine and work within the constraints of traditional drama. Stendhal was no versifier. Equally there was an important sociological reason. In his view the Revolution had transformed theatre audiences by filling auditoria with vulgar *nouveaux riches* whose idea of a good night out was 'le genre grossier et exagéré de M. V[ict] or Hugo, Alex[andre] Dumas, etc.'[28] The Happy Few—'êtres qui ont l'intelligence des *scènes fines*'[29]—still attended, but they were so outnumbered by the bourgeois 'plus grand nombre' that a play's success depended on pleasing the latter. Certainly one couldn't hope to please both: 'une jeune femme ne peut être blonde et brune'.[30] But the main reasons for Stendhal's rejection of comic drama in favour of the novel derive from the generic characteristics of each, and it was indicative of the way things would turn out that Stendhal's earliest definitions of comedy were exemplified by a novel, Fielding's *Tom Jones*:

le poète comique me présente un jeune hom[me] semblable à moi qui, par l'excès de ses bonnes qualités, devient malheureux et qui, par ces mêmes qualités, devient heureux; cela, me procurant la vue du bonheur, m'intéresse et me fait sourire. Tom Jones est un exemple. Plus le malheur du personnage

---

[23] *RS*, 116.

[24] *LL*, i. 341, note c, and ii. 573, and see Michel Crouzet, *La Poétique de Stendhal* (Paris, 1983), 285. See also *Arm.*, 1 (and Martineau's note 4), 3.

[25] See Richard, 'Connaissance et tendresse', 38–41.

[26] On this key term see Crouzet, *Poétique*, 195–205.

[27] See Gisela M. Moinet, 'La quête de la comédie chez Stendhal', in *Stendhal et l'Allemagne*, 135–51.

[28] *OI*, ii. 235.   [29] *OI*, ii. 236.

[30] *OI*, ii. 235. Cf. *OI*, ii. 219–20, *VIT*, 705 and *RN*, 709–10. See also Ellen Constans, 'Stendhal et le public impossible'.

avec qui je me suis identifié est grand, plus je réfléchis profondément pour trouver les moyens de m'en sortir, plus il m'intéresse.[31]

One characteristic of comic drama which was to make it unsuitable as a medium for Stendhal was already evident to him in 1804: 'le théâtre n'est point propre du tout à faire voir les motifs secrets qui font faire les actions que nous voyons tous les jours dans la nature.'[32] Yet the hidden springs of human motivation were coming increasingly to fascinate this apprentice of life, and he could see too that if 'le caractère d'un homme' meant his 'façon habituelle d'aller à la chasse au bonheur',[33] then comedy of character could derive from a whole range of entertainingly mistaken pursuits of happiness[34] which would go beyond boringly predictable[35] comedies of type (such as the miser, hypochondriac or misanthrope).[36] Thus it was not just the intellectual poverty of contemporary theatre audiences which might cause him to 'peindre [...] des choses un peu grosses'[37] but the medium itself. Given his interest in the subtle and nuanced minutiae of human behaviour and given the new conception of comedy which would require more intricate story-lines than a play may furnish,[38] the novel seemed a much more appropriate choice: 'tout peut se dire au contraire dans un roman'.[39] It was the only place for 'un vrai un peu détaillé'.[40]

A further obvious characteristic of comic drama is the absence of the tragic, yet in the definition of comedy quoted above where Stendhal sees Tom Jones as a model, there is at least one element of tragedy as he defined it, namely emotional identification with the

---

[31] JL, ii. 141. Cf. RS, 203–4. On the subject of Stendhal's admiration for Tom Jones, see Blin, Problèmes du roman, 210–14, H.-F. Imbert, 'Stendhal et Tom Jones', Revue de Littérature Comparée, 30 (1956), 351–70, and K. G. McWatters, Stendhal lecteur des romanciers anglais (Lausanne, 1968), 99–129. See also MT, i. 62.

[32] JL, ii. 43.

[33] OI, ii. 247. Cf. OI, i. 842; JL, iii. 14; HPI, ii. 111; LL, i. 337; OI, ii. 392; and Corr., iii. 396 (16 Oct. 1840).

[34] Corr., i. 125 (7 July 1804), RS, 70.

[35] OI, i. 960–1. Cf. VIT, 37, 518.

[36] Note his anxiety about Le Rouge et le Noir: 'je déplore le manque d'intrigue de Julien qui est peut-être trop un développement de caractère as mutanda mutandis, [sic] le célèbre Miseoantropos (je n'ose pas écrire le nom)' (OI, ii. 130).

[37] Corr., ii. 485 (2 Nov. 1832).

[38] Though Stendhal resolved to avoid over-complication and to maintain a happy balance between length and intricacy, a lesson he learned from Tartuffe. See OI, ii. 174, 244.

[39] Corr., ii. 485 (2 Nov. 1832).

[40] OI, ii. 198.

central character(s). To the laughter bred of superior disdain is added the smile of sympathetic recognition,[41] a mixture which Stendhal first encountered in the *opera buffa* of Cimarosa: 'en écoutant *il Matrimonio segreto*: Il y a la comédie qui fait sourire, et celle qui fait rire.'[42] The model of Cimarosa remained with him in the writing of *Letellier*, and in Moscow on 30 September 1812 he wrote in the margin of his manuscript:

credo ch'el amor mio per Cimarosa vienne di ciò ch'elli fa nascere delle sensationi pareilles a quello che desidero di far nascere un giorno. Quel misto d'allegria et di tenerezza del Matrimonio è affato congeniale con me.[43]

In traditional comedy the object of ridicule may appear lacking in humanity and thus cause us sadness, whereas in the comic operas of Cimarosa and Mozart our affection for the characters is enhanced by their only too human failings and we may enjoy 'la plus étonnante réunion de plaisirs': 'l'imagination et la tendresse sont actives à côté du rire le plus fou'.[44] At the same time it may even be true—and it was for Stendhal—that tragedy and *opera seria* leave us untouched because of their very intention to touch us, whereas *opera buffa* is in the end moving because it has first engaged us in pleasant laughter.[45] The *misto Cimarosa* thus works two ways: sympathy sustains good humour, while laughter prepares for warm tears.

Stendhal's ambition, as stated in the Moscow note, to produce such effects himself was later to be realized in his novels. 'Une farce tragique',[46] 'a comic work with a tragic hero'.[47] 'the affectionate

---

[41] Cf. Michael Bishop, 'Laughter and the Smile in Stendhal', *Modern Language Review*, 70 (1975), 50–70, and especially 63: 'if laughter hinges on a psychology of dissimilarity, it is clear that the smile stems from a psychology of resemblance.' Cf. also Léon Cellier, 'Rires, sourires et larmes dans *La Chartreuse de Parme*', in *Omaggio a Stendhal, II*, Atti del 6° Congresso Internazionale Stendhaliano (Parma, 1967), 18–33, and 'Rires, sourires et larmes dans *Le Rouge et le Noir*', in *De Jean Lemaire de Belges à Jean Giraudoux. Mélanges d'histoire et de critique littéraire offerts à Pierre Jourda* (Paris, 1970), 277–97.

[42] *JL*, ii. 123.

[43] *OI*, i. 828. Cf. *Corr.*, i. 660 (2 Oct. 1812). See Richard, 'Connaissance et tendresse', 97; Geoffrey Strickland, *Stendhal. The Education of a Novelist* (Cambridge, 1974), 97–8; Jean-Luc Seylaz, 'L'effet Cimarosa dans les romans stendhaliens', *Stendhal Club*, 25 (1982/3), 40–9; Crouzet, *Poétique*, 235 ff.; and Francis Claudon, 'Stendhal et Cimarosa', in *Stendhal e Milano*, Atti del 14° Congresso Internazionale Stendhaliano (2 vols, Florence, 1982), ii. 563–89.

[44] *HPI*, ii. 172, note 1.   [45] *OI*, ii. 912–13. Cf. *VIT*, 80.

[46] Richard N. Coe, '*La Chartreuse de Parme*. Portrait d'une réaction', in *Omaggio a Stendhal, II*, 43–61 (58).

[47] Raymond Giraud, *The Unheroic Hero in the Novels of Stendhal, Balzac and Flaubert* (New Brunswick, N. J., 1957), 69–70.

ironical smile',[48] 'a smile at the edges of our sympathy',[49] such are the phrases employed by his critics to convey the subtle emotional effects of his story-telling. In abandoning comic drama for the novel, Stendhal was taking up a much surer bow with which to play upon the sensibilities of the Happy Few. No longer ambitious to be a Molière orchestrating the laughter of a conformist public audience, he chose instead to perform upon the souls of private individuals the music of Mozart and Cimarosa (the 'Molière de l'Italie!'),[50] a poignant music of gaiety and tenderness, the music of grace.[51]

[48] Bishop, 'Laughter and the Smile', 54.
[49] Michael Wood, *Stendhal* (London, 1971), 14.
[50] *VIT*, 24. Cf. ibid. 296.
[51] See Richard N. Coe, 'From Correggio to Class Warfare: notes on Stendhal's ideal of "la grâce" ', in D. G. Charlton, J. Gaudon and A. R. Pugh (eds), *Balzac and the Nineteenth Century. Studies in French Literature presented to Herbert J. Hunt* (Leicester, 1972), 239–54.

3

Story-telling

'Permettez-moi un mot sale: je ne veux pas branler l'âme
du lecteur.'

(*Corr.*, iii. 401–2)

In exchanging comedy for the novel Stendhal may seem to have
chosen to appear on stage himself, or even to have crossed the
footlights, the better to explain and comment on his own creations.[1]
The margins of *Letellier* contain a further note, portentously entitled
'Principe de Moscou', which suggests as much:

en comédie on ne peut pas dessiner avec un trait noir comme on fait dans
le roman. Dans le roman, en traitant ce sujet [of *Letellier*], je décrirais le
caractère de Saint-Bernard, par exemple, en dix lignes, mais, en comédie,
il faudrait le faire conclure de ce qu'on voit, car écouter un caractère de La
Bruyère est froid au théâtre.[2]

Stendhal's reputation as an egotist and the apparently intrusive
presence of a narrator in all his novels may suggest that he forsook
dramatic dialogue in favour of narrative in order to communicate
his thoughts more directly. But nothing could be further from the
truth. From the earliest days of his apprenticeship he recognized that
direct 'philosophical' commentary was detrimental to the depiction
of human life, be it in his own diary,[3] in a play[4] or in a novel. In
February 1805, having just read Mme de Staël's *Delphine*, Stendhal
writes:

il y a une manière d'émouvoir qui est de montrer les *faits*, les *choses* sans
en dire l'effet, qui peut être employée par une âme sensible non philosophe
(connaissance de l'homme). Cette manière manque absolument à Mme de
Staël; son livre a absolument besoin de moments de repos [...]

---

[1] Cf. Prévost, *Création*, 486.   [2] *JL*, ii. 384 (dated 1 Oct. 1812).
[3] *OI*, i. 54: 'l'art d'écrire un journal est d'y conserver le dramatique de la vie; ce
qui en éloigne, c'est qu'on veut juger en racontant'.
[4] *JL*, ii. 160: 'il y a une grande différence entre être philosophe dramatiquement
et l'être simplement dans un livre. Le poète ne doit pas dire *la vérité* aux spectateurs;
il ne doit pas leur dire: "Geoffroy est ridicule", mais leur faire dire après avoir écouté
sa pièce: "Que ce G[eoffroy] est ridicule!" '

and adds in a footnote: 'tel qu'il est, et sans repos, le livre fait trop sur l'âme (sur mon âme) l'effet d'un cours de philosophie.'[5] And in June of that year he notes that philosophical generalities are especially inimical to comedy: '*For my happyness by the fame of great bard*, m'habituer à revenir facilement d'une maxime générale [...] au fait dont elle est extraite et qui la développe. *Particularly for my comic genius.*'[6]

Having learnt this lesson early, Stendhal never forgot it, and he kept reminding himself of it in the margins of his novels,[7] particularly *Lucien Leuwen*: 'jamais de réflexion philosophique sur le fond des choses qui, réveillant l'esprit, le jugement, la méfiance froide et philosophique du lecteur, empêche *net* l'émotion. Or, qu'est-ce qu'un roman sans émotion?';[8] 'non, rien qui fasse penser, mais au contraire quelque chose qui dispose à l'émotion, qui est le moyen de force du roman';[9] 'le roman doit raconter [...] la dissertation, la recherche ingénieuse à la La Bruyère, sont des dégénérations'.[10] In this case it is the emotional impact of the story which Stendhal seeks to preserve in the face of an evidently strong temptation on the part of a rather bored consul in Civitavecchia to voice his opinions about life under Louis-Philippe. In the case of *Lamiel*, however, it is the novelty of his plot which must not be overshadowed by undue comment.[11] Here, interestingly, he implies that such comment may nevertheless have a use: 'sur chaque incident se demander: faut-il raconter ceci philosophiquement ou le raconter narrativement selon le système d'Arioste',[12] and this 'maxime', as he calls it, casts retrospective light on his narrative practice in earlier novels. The comparative fullness of narratorial comment on, say, Julien's experiences at Vergy or Fabrice's thoughts about astrology and the contrasting absence of comment on the shooting of Mme de Rênal or the withdrawal to the charterhouse are carefully judged narratorial decisions and need to be taken into account in any discussion of *Le Rouge* and *La Chartreuse*.

If Stendhal insists, then, that a novelist is first and foremost a story-teller, it is partly because he sees the emotional involvement of the

---

[5] *OI*, i. 201.   [6] *OI*, i. 333.

[7] e.g. *Armance*: '*making this novel I was very* mélan[colique]. Voici la conviction que j'avais: c'est l'action qui fait le roman, et non pas la dissertation plus ou moins spirituelle sur les objets auxquels pense le monde' (*OI*, ii. 101 [1828]).

[8] *OI*, ii. 231.   [9] *OI*, ii. 240.   [10] *OI*, ii. 243.

[11] *OC*, xliv, 16, note 1. Cf. ibid. 15, note 1.

[12] *OI*, ii. 354.

reader as a primary aim. At the same time he recognizes also that any 'philosphical' gloss is open to misunderstanding, particularly by future generations: 'remarquez que les considérations générales sont toujours comprises par le lecteur, suivant *les habitudes de son propre siècle*.'[13] But most of all there is the danger that the novelist will allow such gloss or comment to replace events and facts, and of course 'hors la géométrie, il n'y a qu'une seule manière de raisonner, celle des faits'.[14] Constantly he warns both himself and others against this danger. Already in 1804, when he briefly envisages writing a three-act opera called *Don Carlos*, he writes:

dans l'indication *of my* car [actère] s, je mets, comme les mauvais romanciers, un maximum sans le prouver; il faut guérir de ce défaut et, au lieu de dire: D [on] Carlos était le plus brave des hommes, lui faire faire l'action la plus brave possible avec les circonstances les plus propres à faire ressortir la bravoure.[15]

Detail is all important, as Domenico Cimarosa himself had recognized,[16] and Stendhal's use of Dominique as a pseudonym[17] is particularly appropriate in the passage in the margin of *Promenades dans Rome* where he compares his own story-telling, rather unfairly perhaps, with that of Mérimée ('Clara Gazul'):

Dom [ini] que est partisan des détails. Exemple: 'Il la fit descendre de cheval sous un prétexte', dirait Clara. Dom [ini] que dit: 'Il la fit descendre de cheval en faisant semblant de voir que le cheval avait perdu un de ses fers et qu'il voulait l'attacher avec un clou.' Abréger l'*explication* de ce détail, mais le mettre au lieu de *sous un prétexte*.[18]

Stendhal's aversion to a vague, discursive style seems to have been particularly strong when he was writing *Le Rouge et le Noir* and *Lucien Leuwen*. '*La haine des détails* est ce qui perd notre littérature,' he wrote to Sutton Sharpe in January 1830,[19] and this view lies behind the lean and vigorous narrative style of *Le Rouge*, which Stendhal subsequently, and wrongly, found excessive: 'l'horreur de Dom [ini] que pour les longues phrases emphatiques des gens d'esprit

---

[13] *MT*, i. 361. Here Stendhal has just narrated the true story of Gilles de Retz which, he believes, is best left to speak for itself. Cellini's autobiography is explicitly proclaimed as the model of such narrative 'pudeur'.

[14] *Corr.*, i. 45 (29 Jan. 1803).   [15] *JL*, ii. 179.   [16] *OI*, ii. 140.

[17] Amongst nearly a hundred. See Adams, *Notes on a Novelist*, 5–6, and Starobinski, 'Stendhal pseudonyme'.

[18] *OI*, ii. 140.   [19] *Corr.*, ii. 172.

de 1830 l'a jeté dans l'abrupt, dans le heurté, le saccadé, le dur.'[20] During the composition of *Lucien Leuwen*, Hugo seems to have replaced Chateaubriand as the most representative exponent of the style he wanted to avoid: 'jeune fille assassinée à côté de moi. J'y cours, elle est au milieu de la rue; à un pied de sa tête un petit lac de sang d'un pied de diamètre. C'est ce que M. V[ict]or Hugo appelle être *baigné* dans son sang'.[21] And if he was happy to steal the story-line of Mme Jules Gaulthier's *Le Lieutenant*, he was equally unhappy about her style: 'ne jamais dire: "La passion brûlante d'Olivier pour Hélène". Le pauvre romancier doit tâcher de faire croire à la *passion brûlante*, mais ne jamais la nommer: cela est contre la pudeur.'[22]

What is at issue here is what Nigel Balchin has fetchingly called a 'gentlemanly refusal to push the larger emotions down the reader's throat'.[23] The reader must perceive, and even feel, these emotions for himself, must draw his own general conclusions from the particulars with which he is presented. Story-telling must be matter-of-fact. So much so, indeed, that some readers may be left at a loss for an explanation:

je ne dis point: 'il jouissait des doux épanchements de la tendresse maternelle, des conseils si doux du cœur d'une mère', comme dans les romans vulgaires. Je donne la chose elle-même, le dialogue, et me garde de dire *ce que c'est* en phrases attendrissantes. C'est pour cela que le présent roman sera inintelligible pour les femmes de chambre.[24]

But not for the Happy Few, who are left discreetly to their own devices the better to enjoy what Stendhal saw as one of life's great pleasures, calm and inconclusive reflection upon the power and strange consequences of human passion.[25] In the first volume of his *Mémoires d'un touriste*[26] Stendhal describes an evening the tourist spent at a friend's château in Burgundy when the conversation turned to true stories of love. Having chosen, with irony, one of the less 'energetic' of these because his contemporary readership has the soul of a seventy-year-old and hates 'l'énergie sous toutes ses formes'[27] he tells a story of working-class adultery ending in attempted murder,

[20] *OI*, ii. 143. Cf. ibid., the note dated 1 July.
[21] *OI*, ii. 191.   [22] *Corr.*, ii. 643 (4 May 1834).
[23] Introduction to David Footman, *Pig and Pepper. A Comedy of Youth*, 2nd edn (London, 1954), 10.
[24] *OI*, ii. 211.   [25] *OI*, ii. 468.
[26] These memoirs are purportedly written by a thirty-four-year-old commercial traveller in iron.
[27] *MT*, i. 80.

suicide and prosecution, in short a story not far removed in content
or import from those of Berthet, Lafargue and even Alessandro
Farnese, upon which Stendhal's own novels are based. The tourist's
reasons for recounting this story tell us a lot about Stendhal's
intentions as a novelist:

elle [this story] est rigoureusement vraie dans tous ses détails; mais a-t-elle
un autre mérite? Dans ces moments de philosophie rêveuse où l'esprit, non
troublée par aucune passion, jouit avec une sorte de plaisir de sa tranquillité
et réfléchit aux bizarreries du cœur humain, il peut prendre pour base de
ses calculs des histoires telles que celle-ci.[28]

Is this not the sort of effect which the novelist-violinist sought to
have on his own readers? Stendhal adds a further comment:

telle est leur [such stories] unique supériorité sur les romans, qui, arrangés
par un artiste en émotions, sont bien autrement intéressants, mais en général
ne peuvent servir de base à aucun calcul.

While it is tempting to seize on the phrase 'un artiste en émotions'
as a singularly appropriate description of Stendhal himself, what he
has in mind here is the novel in which events seem already to have
been mulled over at length by a novelist who then presents them in
a particular light. But what Stendhal wants to do is to present events
in no particular light and thus offer the reader more scope for
'rêverie'.

In exchanging comedy for the novel Stendhal at first thought he
was actually forgoing the opportunity to do this:

dans un récit, on me dicte mes sensations; ainsi le poète ne peut toucher qu'une
classe d'auditeurs. Quand, au contraire, nous voyons un fait se passer sur
le théâtre, chacun de nous en est touché à *sa manière*, le bilieux d'une façon,
le flegmatique d'une autre. Par là, la tragédie s'empare d'une partie des
avantages de la musique.[29]

But later, as his analogy with the violin suggests, he saw that in the
novel he could in fact achieve this particular effect of drama and
music, namely, room for the reader's emotional and intellectual
manœuvre. The key lay in style and register. Where Balzac wanted
to rival the comprehensiveness of the 'état civil', Stendhal looked
instead to the dispassionate tone of the Code civil.[30] The story-

[28] *MT*, i. 75.   [29] *RS*, 161.
[30] Cf. *Corr.*, ii. 763 (21 Dec. 1834).

teller's task was to record facts—not dull, boring facts,[31] of course, no dead details of dress and furnishing, but facts of life, interesting facts that would stimulate the reader to conjecture. While Stendhal occasionally worried that he had overdone the lack of physical description in his novels,[32] it is clear that he preferred to leave the visual aspects of character and setting as much as possible to the reader's imagination.[33] Not only did he profess himself bored by the descriptive side of novel-writing,[34] but he felt that the reader's imagination would provide the various physical details which he, the reader, would find most life-like. And in the case of the heroine, the fewer details given by the novelist, the greater the (male) reader's ability to substitute his own ideal.[35] Rather the details, or 'petits faits vrais',[36] which Stendhal wanted to register were details about human behaviour, circumstantial evidence as data for surmise.[37] These facts were to be presented in as plain and straightforward a language as possible, without prejudice as it were, and most certainly without the floweriness and pomposity which Stendhal saw as the characteristic fault of much contemporary writing.[38]

From his earliest days he thought that language, or style, should be a transparent varnish: 'il ne doit pas altérer les couleurs, ou les faits et pensées sur lesquels il est placé'.[39] This particular remark was prompted by a reading of Fénelon who, along with

---

[31] Cf. *OI*, ii. 624–5: 'tous les faits qui forment la vie de Chrysale [in *Les Femmes savantes*] sont remplacés chez moi par du romanesque. Je crois que cette tache dans mon télescope a été utile pour mes personnages de roman, il y a une sorte de bassesse bourgeoise qu'ils ne peuvent avoir: et pour l'auteur ce serait parler le *chinois* qu'il ne sait pas.'

[32] *OI*, ii. 197.   [33] *HPI*, ii. 41.   [34] *OI*, ii. 434, 457.

[35] *OI*, ii. 241.   [36] *Corr.*, iii. 402 (28–9 Oct. 1840).

[37] Cf. his article 'Walter Scott et la Princesse de Clèves': this name and title 'indiquent les deux extrêmes en fait de romans. Faut-il décrire les habits des personnages, le paysage au milieu duquel ils se trouvent, les formes de leur visage? ou bien fera-t-on mieux de peindre les passions et les divers sentiments qui agitent leurs âmes?'; *OC*, xlvi. 221.

[38] Cf. *OI*, ii. 326 (16 Sept. 1838). For the best account of Stendhal's attitudes to language and contemporary usage, see Michel Crouzet, *Stendhal et le langage* (Paris, 1981).

[39] *JL*, ii. 364. See also *Vies de Haydn, de Mozart et de Métastase*: 'le style, qui, comme un vernis transparent, doit recouvrir les couleurs, les rendre plus brillantes, mais ne les altérer' (*OC*, xli. 367). Cf. *JL*, i. 459, where Stendhal (in 1804) aspires to a kind of 'degré zéro de l'écriture': 'la première qualité d'un style est donc qu'il ne cause pas la plus petite idée fausse dans la tête du lecteur qui sait sa langue. Dans cette phrase même, *la plus petite idée fausse* est mauvais. Il fallait: la plus petite différence entre ce qui existe et ce que le lecteur entendra. Il faut que si le lecteur était dieu il pût refaire d'une chose tout ce que vous lui en avez dit.'

Montesquieu[40] and the Président de Brosses,[41] was a favoured stylistic model. Fénelon also taught him that a 'natural' style was essential to his new conception of comedy:

le style de Fénelon, étant parfaitement naturel, admet le comique comme le tragique, et toutes les autres choses de la nature. Celui de Rousseau, ayant une certaine dose d'affectation tragique, emphatique, n'admet pas le comique.[42]

Elsewhere, in the *Histoire de la peinture en Italie*, he talks of style not as a transparent varnish but as a limpid mirror: 'en exagérant le moins du monde, en faisant du style autre chose qu'un miroir limpide, on produit un moment d'engouement, mais sujet à de fâcheux retours'.[43] Moreover it is a mirror which should not call attention to itself: 'une glace ne doit pas faire remarquer sa couleur, mais laisser voir parfaitement l'image qu'elle reproduit.'[44]

Naturalness, facility, lightness of touch, an effortless and uncontrived fluency that suggests the immediacy of conversation,[45] these are the oft-stated aims of a writer who achieved in the novel what he had aimed at in the theatre:

résumé *of all my dramatic* doctrine. Pour peindre un caractère d'une manière qui me plaise, il faut qu'il y ait beaucoup d'incidents qui le prouvent et beaucoup de naturel dans la manière d'exposer ces incidents.[46]

The result of this aesthetic is a kind of enigmatic transparency,[47] a matter-of-factness that is at once emotive and intellectually

---

[40] As well as the many statements to this effect in the diaries and marginalia one may note that Stendhal had five volumes of Montesquieu rebound with 'Stile' on the spine. These are the volumes now in the Bibliothèque Jacques Doucet in Paris and referred to by Del Litto in *OI*, i. 1564, note f. See A. Blanchard de Farges, 'Un peu de Stendhal inédit. Petite récolte de notes marginales', *Le Correspondant*, 81 (1909), 1077–119 (1109–14).

[41] *OI*, i. 927 (5 May 1815): 'le style qui me plaît le plus est celui de De Brosses, qui dit beaucoup et des choses très fortes, en peu de mots et très clairement, avec grâce, sans pédanterie [...] Je crois ce goût d'autant plus réel en moi qu'il se rapporte à mon goût pour la comédie et à mon éloignement pour la tragédie.' See also *Corr.*, iii. 141 (25 Nov. 1835).

[42] *JL*, ii. 362.   [43] *HPI*, i. 122.   [44] *HPI*, i. 271.

[45] *OI*, ii. 399, 400. In the case of *La Chartreuse de Parme*, of course, this was achieved by improvised dictation: *OI*, ii. 398. Cf. *OI*, ii. 234, 243.

[46] *OI*, i. 927.

[47] See Genette, ' "Stendhal" ', 192, and Mitchell, '*Le Rouge et le Noir*', 8.

suggestive and which may be reminiscent of the effects of painting
or music. The enigmatic, or suggestive quality of Stendhal's 'petits
faits vrais' is comparable with the 'magie des lointains' achieved
by Ghirlandaio and to be found later in the works of Poussin
and Correggio:

> la magie des lointains, cette partie de la peinture qui attache les imaginations
> tendres, est peut-être la principale cause de sa supériorité sur la sculpture.
> Par là elle se rapproche de la musique, elle engage l'imagination à finir ses
> tableaux; et si, dans le premier abord, nous sommes plus frappés par les
> figures du premier plan[,] c'est des objets dont les détails sont à moitié cachés
> par l'air que nous nous souvenons avec le plus de charme; ils ont pris dans
> notre pensée une teinte céleste. Le Poussin, par ses paysages, jette l'âme dans
> la rêverie; elle se croit transportée dans ces lointains si nobles, et y trouver
> ce bonheur qui nous fuit dans la réalité. Tel est le sentiment dont le Corrège
> a tiré ses beautés.[48]

While some of Stendhal's work is, for a variety of reasons, literally
unfinished,[49] all of it may be regarded as metaphorically unfinished
in the sense that each work requires our imagination to complete
the picture, not only by conjectural solution of mysteries such as
Octave's ailment, Julien's shooting, Lucien's future, or Fabrice's
withdrawal but also, more importantly, by speculative gazing into
the magic distance of the unsaid, be it the nature of Julien and Mme
de Rênal's shared idyll in prison or the bliss that follows Clélia's 'entre
ici, ami de mon cœur', both of which evince the 'charme' and 'teinte
céleste' to be found in Ghirlandaio. Stendhal's 'pudeur' needs the
complement of our 'rêverie' if we are to experience the 'beau
idéal'.

At the same time the lucid, mirror-like quality which Stendhal
aspires to in his style is comparable with the effects of those 'peintres-
miroirs' whom Stendhal professes to admire only slightly less than
Raphael or Correggio, his masters of the 'beau idéal':

> reproduire exactement la nature, sans art, comme un miroir, c'est le mérite
> de beaucoup de Hollandais, et ce n'est pas un petit mérite; je le trouve surtout

---

[48] *HPI*, i. 181-2. See Richard, 'Connaissance et tendresse', 44-5, 83-4, Genette,
' "Stendhal" ', 191-2, and Margaret Tillett, *Stendhal. The Background to the Novels*
(London, 1971), 42-3.

[49] See Michel Crouzet's introductory essay 'De l'inachèvement' in *Romans
abandonnés*, ed. Crouzet (Paris, 1968) and Jean-Jacques Hamm, 'L'achèvement et
son envers'.

délicieux dans le paysage. On se sent tout à coup plongé dans une rêverie profonde, comme à la vue des bois et de *leur vaste silence*. On songe avec profondeur à ses plus chères illusions; on les trouve moins improbables; bientôt on en jouit comme de réalités. On parle à ce qu'on aime, on ose l'interroger, on écoute ses réponses. Voilà les sentiments que me donne une promenade solitaire dans une véritable forêt.[50]

Thus, as Ann Jefferson puts it, 'performative readings become the only relevant index of life-likeness however improbable or *invraisemblable* the issues in question',[51] or as Stendhal puts it earlier in *Racine et Shakespeare*:

les imitations des arts produisent de la peine ou du plaisir, non pas parce qu'on les prend pour des *réalités*, comme disent les *auteurs surannés*, mais parce qu'elles présentent vivement à l'âme des réalités. Quand notre imagination est égayée (*rallegrata*) et rafraîchie par un beau paysage de Claude Lorrain, ce n'est pas que nous supposions les arbres que nous voyons capables de nous donner de l'ombre, ou que nous songions à puiser de l'eau à ces fontaines si limpides; mais nous nous *figurons vivement* le plaisir que nous aurions à nous promener auprès de ces fraîches fontaines et à l'ombre de ces beaux arbres, balançant leurs rameaux au-dessus de nos têtes.[52]

In arguing this theory of mimesis Stendhal is in fact taking up an idea about music which, as he told Félix Faure in October 1812, he had found in Rousseau:

rien ne me purifie de la société des sots comme la musique; elle me devient tous les jours plus chère. Mais d'où vient ce plaisir? La musique peint la nature; Rousseau dit que souvent elle abandonne la peinture directe impossible, pour jeter notre âme, par des moyens à elle, dans une position semblable à celle que nous donnerait l'objet qu'elle veut peindre. Au lieu de peindre une nuit tranquille, chose impossible, elle donne à l'âme la même

---

[50] *RS*, 178–9. Cf. *HPI*, i. 123: 'un auteur très froid peut faire frémir; un peintre qui n'est qu'un ouvrier en couleur, s'il est excellent, peut donner les sentiments les plus tendres: il n'a qu'à ne pas choisir, et reproduire comme un miroir les beaux paysages des lacs de la Lombardie.' Cf. also *HPI*, i. 189.

[51] 'Stendhal and the Uses of Reading: *Le Rouge et le Noir*', *French Studies*, 37 (1983), 168–83 (181).

[52] *RS*, 159. For a full account of the influence of painting on Stendhal's work see Philippe Berthier's excellent study *Stendhal et ses peintres italiens* (Geneva, 1977).

sensation en lui faisant faire les mêmes sentiments qu'inspire une nuit tranquille.[53]

This idea had gained considerable currency during the eighteenth century,[54] but it was Rousseau who had given it fullest expression, both in the *Dictionnaire de musique* and in the *Essai sur l'origine des langues*.[55] It would be difficult to exaggerate the importance which it assumed in Stendhal's aesthetic thinking or the effect which it had upon his subsequent career as a writer.[56] Indeed it may even have prompted his first published work. The *Lettres sur le célèbre*

[53] *Corr.*, i. 659 (2 Oct. 1812). Stendhal presumably met the idea in Rousseau's *Dictionnaire de musique* (1755–65) under the heading 'Imitation': 'tout ce que l'imagination peut se représenter est du ressort de la poésie. La peinture, qui n'offre point ses tableaux à l'imagination, mais au sens et à un seul sens, ne peint que les objets soumis à la vue. La musique semblerait avoir les mêmes bornes par rapport à l'ouïe; cependant elle peint tout, même les objets qui ne sont que visibles: par un prestige presque inconcevable elle semble mettre l'œil dans l'oreille; et la plus grande merveille d'un art qui n'agit que par le mouvement, est d'en pouvoir former jusqu'à l'image du repos. La nuit, le sommeil, la solitude, et le silence, entrent dans le nombre des grands tableaux de la musique. On sait que le bruit peut produire l'effet du silence, et le silence l'effet du bruit; comme quand on s'endort à une lecture égale et monotone, et qu'on s'éveille à l'instant qu'elle cesse. Mais la musique agit plus intimement sur nous en excitant, par un sens, des affections semblables à celles qu'on peut exciter par un autre; et, comme le rapport ne peut être sensible que l'impression ne soit forte, la peinture dénuée de cette force ne peut rendre à la musique les *imitations* que celle-ci tire d'elle. Que toute la nature soit endormie, celui qui la contemple ne dort pas, et l'art du musicien consiste à substituer à l'image insensible de l'objet celle des mouvements que sa présence excite dans le cœur du contemplateur: non seulement il agitera la mer, animera la flamme d'un incendie, fera couler les ruisseaux, tomber la pluie et grossir les torrents; mais il peindra l'horreur d'un désert affreux, rembrunira les murs d'une prison souterraine, calmera la tempête, rendra l'air tranquille et serein, et répandra de l'orchestre une fraîcheur nouvelle sur les bocages: il ne représentera pas directement ces choses, mais il excitera dans l'âme les mêmes mouvements qu'on éprouve en les voyant.' Most of this passage may also be found under the heading 'Opéra' and as the last paragraph of chapter xvi of the earlier (?) *Essai sur l'origine des langues, où il est parlé de la mélodie et de l'imitation musicale*. Stendhal's ideas about 'la magie des lointains' show that he departs from Rousseau's view that painting cannot evoke the unseen.

[54] See Béatrice Didier, *La Musique des lumières: Diderot—'L'Encyclopédie'—Rousseau* (Paris, 1985), 24. The opening chapter of Didier's study, entitled 'Le beau musical: de l'imitation à l'expression', offers a useful survey of the eighteenth-century debate about musical imitation.

[55] See *La Musique des lumières*, 37–8.

[56] Just as it would be difficult to explain why it has so far escaped critical attention. Helmut C. Jacobs's exhaustive *Stendhal und die Musik. Forschungsbericht und Kritische Bibliographie 1900–1980* (Frankfurt am Main, 1983) demonstrates how often critics have returned to the influence of music on Stendhal's work and how seldom they have considered even a connexion with Rousseau, let alone an important debt. Jacobs is right to conclude that in future 'ein Vergleich der Musikanschauung Stendhals mit derjenigen Rousseaus und Carpanis dürfte [...] im Vordergrund [...] stehen' (49).

compositeur Haydn, which form the first and most substantial part of the *Vies de Haydn, de Mozart and de Métastase* (1814), are, as every admirer of Stendhal has had to concede, a blatant plagiarism of Giuseppe Carpani's *Le Haydine ovvero Lettere sulla vita e le opere del celebre maestro Giuseppe Haydn* (1812).[57] The question has often been asked why Stendhal should have chosen this particular work to plagiarize. Richard N. Coe has answered[58] that Stendhal was drawn to the aesthetic ideas which inform Carpani's work, and to three ideas in particular: first, that the pleasure afforded by music is sensuous rather than intellectual; secondly, that the capacity to appreciate certain aspects of art varies from country to country; and, finally, that since music is vocal in origin, the notion of what constitutes ideal music will alter according to the language spoken by the listener. Although Coe recognizes Carpani's debt to Montesquieu, Helvétius, Cabanis and the abbé Dubos, he nevertheless sees Carpani as a decisive influence on Stendhal's thinking. Yet Stendhal had met these ideas many times before, and in the same writers, and there is every reason to accept Robert Alter's suggestion that this explains Stendhal's unreadiness to accept the charge of plagiarism.[59] Moreover he had, as Coe himself notes, been working on the *Histoire de la peinture en Italie* since 1811, and so had every justification in claiming originality for his own particular formulation of the theory that beauty is relative.[60]

A more likely reason for Stendhal's choice of Carpani derives from the growing interest in music to which he alludes in the letter to Félix Faure of October 1812 and which was doubtless stimulated further

---

[57] For an account of the circumstances of this plagiarism and annotations describing its extent see *OC*, xli.

[58] See *Lives of Haydn, Mozart and Metastasio by Stendhal (1814)*, trans. and ed. Richard N. Coe (London, 1972), pp. ix–xxxii. Coe suggests that Stendhal did not enjoy Haydn's music, but there is evidence that he did, especially *The Creation*. See *OI*, i. 673 and cf. *OC*, xli. 186. Also Stendhal twice compared his writing to a Haydn symphony: see *OI*, i. 624 and *LL*, ii. 440. For the suggestion that Stendhal may even have sensed an *alter ego* in Haydn, see Jean-Jacques Hamm, 'Stendhal et l'autre du plagiat', *Stendhal Club*, 23 (1980/1), 203–14 (211–12).

[59] Robert Alter, in collaboration with Carol Cosman, *Stendhal. A Biography* (London, 1980), 127 and note 3.

[60] In his open letter to Carpani Stendhal describes these as 'questions que M. Bombet [i.e. Stendhal] a approfondies le premier touchant les vraies causes des plaisirs produits par les arts, et particulièrement par la musique' (*OC*, xli. 477). Note also the projected volume mentioned in his diary on 10 June 1810 (*OI*, i. 595) which would have included short biographies of several painters, writers and composers (including Mozart and Haydn) and also contained discussion of aesthetics designed to educate contemporary opinion.

by the return to Milan and La Scala between September and November 1813. This interest drew him to works on composers and librettists in general, as the plagiarized sources of his lives of Mozart and Metastasio demonstrate, but he was drawn to Carpani's biography in particular because Carpani's main concern is to use Rousseau's account of musical imitation to explain Haydn's genius, especially in *The Creation*. This is evident in the fact that it is this explanation which prompts the most telling of Stendhal's own additions to, and commentaries on, Carpani's text.

Carpani notes as follows (and as translated by Stendhal!): 'tout le monde voit que la musique peut imiter la nature de deux manières: elle a l'imitation physique et l'imitation sentimentale.'[61] After discussion of 'physical' imitation, be it of cooing doves or snoring cuckolds, Carpani then observes that 'tous les arts sont fondés sur un certain degré de fausseté' but postpones elucidation of his observation. Whereupon Stendhal adds his own perceptive gloss:

l'artiste habile ne s'éloigne jamais du degré de fausseté qui est permis à l'art qu'il cultive; il sait bien que ce n'est pas en imitant la nature jusqu'au point de produire l'illusion que les arts plaisent: il fait une différence entre ces barbouillages parfaits, nommés des trompe-l'œil, et la *Sainte Cécile* de Raphaël. Il faut que l'imitation produise l'effet qui serait occasionné par l'objet imité, s'il nous frappait dans ces moments heureux de sensibilité et de bonheur qui donnent naissance aux passions.

Here is Rousseau's theory enunciated within the context of the Stendhalian 'chasse au bonheur'. This is immediately followed by a return to Carpani's much drier exposition of the same idea: 'voilà pour l'imitation physique de la nature par la musique. L'autre imitation, que nous appellerons *sentimentale*, si ce nom n'est pas trop ridicule à vos yeux, ne retrace pas les choses, mais les sentiments qu'elles inspirent'—which in turn is illustrated by Stendhal's commentary on an aria from Cimarosa's *Matrimonio segreto* and by the 'Fragment d'une lettre d'Ottilie'. In this fragment, written by Stendhal but spuriously attributed to Goethe's *Die Wahlverwandschaften*, an intriguing analogy is drawn between the sensibility of an opera-goer and a reel of golden thread. The job of the composer ('l'enchanteur Mozart', for example) is to hook on to the end of this thread, which consists of 'les souvenirs d'une âme passionnée', and to wind it off the reel. But: 'dès que le musicien

---

[61] *OC*, xli. 179.

peint un degré d'émotion que le spectateur n'a jamais éprouvé, crac! il n'y a plus de fil d'or sur la bobine, et ce spectateur-là s'ennuiera bientôt.' Which is to say, of course, that the artist's capacity to depict human experience, be it in painting, music or words, depends on the spectator/listener/reader's capacity to feel: 'à quoi tout le talent de Mozart lui sert-il, s'il a affaire à des bobines qui ne soient pas garnies?' The Happy Few must be well provided with golden thread.

There follows a statement of Stendhal's own musical tastes:

lorsque la musique réussit à peindre les images, le silence d'une belle nuit d'été, par exemple, on dit qu'elle est pittoresque. Le plus bel ouvrage de ce genre est la *Création* de Haydn, comme *Don Juan* ou le *Matrimonio* sont les plus beaux exemples de la musique expressive [...]

after which Stendhal returns to Carpani's text and to Carpani's account of 'sentimental' imitation in the *Creation*. In this way Stendhal upstages Carpani by presenting his own application of Rousseau's idea first. Indeed long before this, in Lettre V, he introduces into Carpani's narrative a quite fictitious account of how he himself met the nineteen-year-old Haydn and used Rousseau's idea to explain to him how he, Haydn, had succeeded in the musical depiction of a storm.[62] Carpani, on the other hand, merely has Rousseau's idea relayed to Haydn by Haydn's close friend and collaborator Baron Van Swieten and then only when the composer was sixty-three and about to write the *Creation*.[63]

Thus Rousseau's idea about musical imitation recurs on four separate occasions in Stendhal's first published work, and it is central both to Carpani's treatment of Haydn and to Stendhal's treatment of Carpani. Moreover it is the idea from which follows the well-known theory about the relativity of beauty which figures in subsequent pages of the *Vies de Haydn, de Mozart et de Métastase* and the *Histoire de la peinture en Italie*. For the principle that the artist, be he musician or writer, cannot faithfully imitate a given natural phenomenon but can only hope to provoke in the listener/reader the response which that phenomenon would itself have provoked in nature leads on to the question of the response itself. Individuals vary in their response to both natural and artistic phenomena, and there are so many factors affecting this response and relating to nationality, class, sex, and other personal, social and historical circumstances that an artist may well despair of creating

[62] 46-7.   [63] 176-7.

beauty for more than a handful of people whose responses may happen to 'fit'—in other words, the Happy Few:

il est sans doute parmi nous quelques âmes nobles et tendres comme Mme Roland, Mlle de Lespinasse, Napoléon, le condamné Lafargue, etc. Que ne puis-je écrire dans un langage sacré compris d'elles seules! Alors un écrivain serait aussi heureux qu'un peintre; on oserait exprimer les sentiments les plus délicats, et les livres, loin de se rassembler platement comme aujourd'hui, seraient aussi différents que les toilettes d'un bal.[64]

Stendhal's hypothesis of a small, understanding readership represents not a desire for an exclusive circle of admirers but a fear of failure. Just as the Vicar of Wakefield thinks that his tracts will have been read only by 'a happy *few*', so Stendhal worries that he will have achieved the 'beau idéal' for only a handful of people.

But he need not have feared, for he had in fact found the secret to this 'langue sacrée'. The answer to the writer's problem of the plural and unpredictable response of his readership is, as we have seen, to leave his work as 'open' as possible, to leave room for 'rêverie'. The telling story told without commentary and in the dispassionate style of the Code civil creates 'la magie des lointains'. Thanks to Rousseau Stendhal had discovered also how he might guide the reader's imagination and influence the images with which it peoples this distance: 'je ne désire être compris que des gens nés pour la musique; je voudrais pouvoir écrire dans une langue sacrée.'[65] What if we are all born musical? What if the writer were to represent human experience by the same means as Rousseau's composer imitates nature? It is one of the principal aims of the present study to show that this is the key to Stendhal's art as a novelist, for it is hoped to show that his novels are so written as to cause the reader to experience through the act of reading what the protagonists experience through the act of living. My argument is that such coincidence of experience between hero and reader is the product of an art which combines the non-committal clarity of a mirror and the resonance of a violin, the product of a writer bent upon a new approach to the 'beau idéal' who finds in the novel his ideal bow.[66]

[64] *VIT*, 880. Cf. 366: 'je regrette souvent qu'il n'y ait pas une langue sacrée connue des seuls initiés; un honnête homme pourrait alors parler librement, sûr de n'être entendu que par ses pairs.'

[65] *VIT*, 633.

[66] A proposition which runs directly counter to Georges Blin's view that 'chez Stendhal, sa théorie des beaux-arts et son idéal d'écrivain se combattent' (*Problèmes du roman*, 33).

II

GAIETY AND TENDERNESS IN *ARMANCE*

The Reader Empowered

'Dès que j'aurai corrigé mon caractère mélancolique par mauvaise habitude et par engouement de Rousseau, j'en aurai, j'espère, un très aimable: la gaieté du meilleur goût sur un fond très tendre.'

(*OI*, i. 315)

'La principale crainte que j'ai eue en écrivant ce roman, c'est d'être lu par les femmes de chambre et les marquises qui leur ressemblent.'

(*Arm.*, 261)

1

Tragedy and comedy

'La tragédie n'étant pas ma nature, me scie; la comédie m'intéresse
comme instruction.'

(*OI*, i. 711)

THE paradox of Stendhal's first novel *Armance* is that it was
inspired by a joke and yet has always been read as a tragedy. The
circumstances of its genesis are well known. The duchesse de Duras,
hostess of one of the leading salons of the Restoration, had recently
become known to a wider public by publishing two novels, *Ourika*
(1824) and *Edouard* (1825). The former tells of a negress who
conceives an impossible love for the son of her rich benefactress and
dies of a broken heart, the latter of an advocate's son who conceives
an equally impossible love for a duchess and meets a welcome end
at the battle of Brandywine. Wanting for her next novel a plausible
alternative to the obstacles of race and class, Mme de Duras lit upon
the idea of sexual impotence, and the result was *Olivier ou le secret*.
When it came to the question of publication, however, she soon
realized that, while blacks and lawyers were one thing, sexual
impotents were quite another, and she contented herself instead with
readings from her new novel to her salon faithful.[1] Word soon
spread, and one of Stendhal's friends, Hyacinthe Thabaud, more
commonly known by his pseudonym Henri de Latouche, saw an
excellent opportunity to indulge in the then popular pastime of the
literary hoax. Accordingly he wrote a novel on the same theme and
with the same title and arranged for it to be published anonymously
by the same publisher and in the same format as the duchess's
previous novels. Fanning the flames of the consequent *succès de
scandale*, Stendhal's own review of the novel for the *New Monthly
Magazine* early in 1826 attributes it to the duchess and then, after
a tongue-in-cheek eulogy of its style, proceeds to deplore its
publication on the most absurd of grounds:

[1] It was eventually published in 1971 by Corti, in an edition by Denise Virieux.

en vertu de la doctrine métaphysique de l'association des idées, le nom de la duchesse rappelle un mot désagréable. Les critiques grossiers ne manqueront naturellement pas de faire valoir cette circonstance, et toute personne sage regrettera qu'elle ait dû être présente à l'esprit du noble auteur pendant tout le temps qu'elle mit à écrire et à corriger son joli petit volume.[2]

The subsequent history of the genesis of *Armance* is less clear, though no less proof against the charge of obscenity. Stendhal began composition of the novel between 31 January and 8 February, when his own '*impuiss*[ance] *of making*' (260)[3] obliged him to set it aside. After receipt of Clémentine Curial's letter of 15 September breaking off their relationship,[4] he returned to it 'comme remède' and finished a draft version by 10 October.[5] This he submitted, after some revision, to Mérimée. Mérimée's reply has been lost, but it prompted the famous letter of 23 December which is often appended to editions of the novel and in which Stendhal is quite luridly explicit about his hero's impotence (here called 'babilanisme') and about how Armance manages to enjoy her wedding-night despite it. After further revision, including the renaming of the hero (at Mérimée's instigation) and of the novel itself (together with a subtitle, added at the instigation this time of his publisher), a final version was published in August 1827, almost two years after Parisian society had first heard of Olivier and his secret. The joke was stale, and anyway the change in the hero's name left Stendhal having to explain, even to close friends like Sutton Sharpe and Mme Gaulthier,[6] what the original point had been. Small wonder, then, that such little impact as *Armance* made was unfavourable, and that Stendhal himself may have regarded the work as a failure.[7] Even when he

---

[2] *CA*, ii. 423. Is the 'mot désagréable' in question merely 'rat', or does Stendhal have in mind a double pun upon the second of the duchess's names: Claire Lechat de Kersaint Duras?

[3] Throughout Part II simple page-reference of this kind is to the Classiques Garnier edition by Henri Martineau.

[4] *OI*, ii. 93. The impotence of Clémentine Curial's own husband is mentioned by Stendhal in a letter to Mme Jules Gauthier on 6 August 1828 (*Corr.*, ii. 148).

[5] Hemmings argues that this version was the reworking of a first draft completed between 31 January and 8 February. See 'Les Deux *Lamiel*', 288–9. It is of interest that, during the second period of composition, he read, or re-read, Mme de Duras's *Edouard*. See *Arm.*, 264.

[6] See *Corr.*, ii. 139 (23 Mar. 1828) and 148 (6 Aug. 1828) respectively.

[7] *OI*, ii. 412. Romain Colomb, Stendhal's cousin and literary executor, reports that *Armance* was for Stendhal 'l'objet de sa prédilection', but in the manner of a child with rickets. See *OC*, xlix. 313.

reviewed it himself for the *New Monthly Magazine* in April/May of 1828, the lame attempt to attribute its hostile reception to the fact that it depicts 'les salons et les mœurs de 1827, sujet fort délicat à traiter' is followed by a more genuine-sounding concession: 'c'est à coup sûr un écrit bien fautif.'[8] As to the claim that a second edition was 'actuellement sous presse', that was pure hype or, as he called it, 'puff'. And indeed when a subsequent edition did finally appear, its editor felt obliged to describe the novel as 'un coco d'Amérique creusé avec un mauvais couteau' (p. xxix), a view echoed more recently by Margaret Tillett, who sees *Armance* quite simply as 'that novel to which it is useless to apply the criteria of common sense'.[9]

Is it useless? The main source of apparent nonsense is the theme of impotence. Originally Stendhal had wanted to retain the name Olivier because 'ce nom seul fait *exposition* et exposition non indécente' (249). But then why, when he substituted the name Octave and anyway diverted attention on to the eponymous Armance, did he not include clear indications of Octave's problem to supplement the cryptic 'D'ailleurs un tel sujet!...' with which the preface ineffectually ends? The classic response to this question has been not only that Stendhal faced a problem of delicacy but also, and more especially, that he sought to avoid unwanted comedy. Thus F. C. Green argues that any explicit reference to Octave's sexual impotence would have compromised the tragic tone of *Armance* and concludes with the observation that 'one might as well try to be tragic about housemaid's knee in English fiction as to wring the hearts of French novel readers on the subject of *impuissance*.'[10] Yet while Green's assessment of the limitations of English fiction may be accurate enough, his knowledge of what will or will not wring the hearts of French readers seems to be less sure. Despite, and indeed sometimes because of, an awareness of the nature of Octave's problem as it is 'revealed' by Stendhal in his marginalia and letters,

---

[8] *CA*, iii. 365.

[9] *Background*, 74. Cf. Auguste Bussière's famous comment: 'on croit se promener dans une maison de fous', in Emile Talbot (ed.), *La Critique stendhalienne de Balzac à Zola* (York, S. Carolina, 1979), 97.

[10] *Stendhal* (Cambridge, 1939), 193. This argument is accepted by Georges Blin, in his 'Etude sur *Armance*' in *Armance*, ed. Georges Blin (Paris, 1946), p. xx, and by Grahame C. Jones, *L'Ironie dans les romans de Stendhal* (Lausanne, 1966), 33–4; and by Geneviève Mouillaud, 'Stendhal et le mode irréel. A propos de l'impuissance dans *Armance*', *Modern Language Notes*, 83 (1968), 524–42 (541).

Armance has more often been read with reverence than with levity, and there is an almost unanimous consensus among both French and English-speaking critics that the novel is tragic. For Blin '*Armance* est une tragédie, et c'est déjà la tragèdie du héros stendhalien spécifique';[11] for Bardèche there is 'quelque chose de racinien' in the ending and an 'absence de l'humour' in the text as a whole.[12] Del Litto asserts that '*Armance* s'apparente à la tragédie classique, et non pas à la comédie',[13] while Richard N. Coe believes 'the narrative of *Armance* [...] is anything but comic in essence.'[14]

But what more implausible thesis could there be? That a man who had wanted to be the Molière of his time and who was renowned among the salons of Paris for his wit and all too ready sense of fun should sit down at the age of forty-three to write a solemn tragic novel about a pathological condition so foreign to his own experience?[15] It is, nevertheless, something of a hazardous exercise to question the critical consensus by suggesting ways in which *Armance* may be read as a comedy. In the first place there are few things more tedious than having a joke explained, particularly if one has understood it already, and there is the risk of being accused of what Stendhal in *Vie de Henry Brulard* refers to in a similar context as 'de l'esprit à la *Charles Nodier*, de l'esprit ennuyeux'.[16] And indeed commentary is redundant when it comes to Mme de Malivert's extravagant horror of impious literature, her husband's terror of becoming a widower, the commandeur de Soubirane's bluff meridional approach to life and his obsession with speculation on the Bourse, or Mme de Bonnivet's mysticism and her fond belief that the gilt moulding of her drawing-room ceiling harbours an attentive genie ready to 'magnetize' her soul. At the same time one may even appear callous. Impotence and suicide are after all more serious matters than housemaid's knee.

---

[11] 'Etude sur Armance', p. xx.   [12] *Stendhal romancier*, 146–7.
[13] *O*, v. 16.
[14] 'The Anecdote and the Novel: a Brief Enquiry into the Origins of Stendhal's Narrative Technique', *Australian Journal of French Studies*, 22 (1985), 3–25 (10). Cf. also Hemmings, *Stendhal*, 70; *Armance*, ed. H.-F. Imbert, 16; Jones, *Ironie*, 25, 33 (but cf. the same author's 'L'emploi du point de vue dans *Armance*', *Stendhal Club*, 18 (1975/6), 109–36, and his reference (135) to 'une comédie qui tourne mal'); C. O'Keefe, 'A Function of Narrative Uncertainty in Stendhal's *Armance*', *French Review*, 50 (1976/7), 579–85 ('a veritable comedy—or, more properly, tragedy—of errors': 584); D. Place, 'The Problems of Stendhal's *Armance*', *French Studies*, 33 (1979), 27–38 (37); and Tillett, *Background*, 89.
[15] Despite the evidence of chapter iii of *Souvenirs d'égotisme* and the chapter entitled 'Des Fiasco' in *De l'amour*. See George M. Rosa, 'Byronism and "Babilanisme" in *Armance*', *Modern Language Review*, 77 (1982), 797–814 (799).   [16] *OI*, ii. 924.

But here one must put the question that has bedevilled critics of *Armance* almost since the beginning: is Octave impotent? Or rather, given that the novel contains no explicit evidence that he is[17] and that one is nevertheless conscious that Stendhal had such a disability in mind when he wrote *Armance*, how should one read the novel? There would appear to be four ways of doing so: (i) one accepts that Octave is impotent and interprets the novel predominantly in that light;[18] (ii) again one accepts that Octave is impotent but this time seeing his disability as either subordinate to or symbolic of more important social and political aspects;[19] (iii) one rejects the external 'key' as constituting a *hors-texte* (although this does not necessarily preclude an examination of the theme of impotence, be it physical, psychological, political or linguistic);[20] or (iv) one attempts a preliminary reading of the novel in simulated ignorance of the external 'key' and subsequently re-assesses this reading in the light of Stendhal's declarations. This fourth method, that of Georges Blin in his well-known study of *Armance*, will be adopted here, and adopted not only because it seems reasonable to investigate whether the novel has any coherence without reference to external evidence,[21] but more especially because the customary 'explanations' of certain

---

[17] It is difficult to agree with those who believe the novel to contain sufficient 'hints' to make the external evidence redundant. Cf. Blin, 'Etude sur *Armance*', p. lix, Del Litto's introduction in *O*, iv. 14, and Strickland, *Stendhal*, 131. As will be seen presently, many of these hints are susceptible of alternative interpretations.

[18] Cf. Del Litto's introduction; Gide's preface (repr. in *OC*, v); Green, *Stendhal*; Hemmings, *Stendhal*; Jones, *Ironie*; H. Levin, *The Gates of Horn* (New York, 1963); and Thibaudet, *Stendhal* (Paris, 1931). Among the several disadvantages of such an approach are the reduction of the text to a pathological case-report and the invitation to a literal-mindedness bordering on the comic. Both disadvantages are exemplified by Martineau's assessment of the novel: 'il paraît vraisemblable qu'Octave n'est pas *impotens* par malformation organique ou physique. Cette tare n'aurait point échappé à l'œil inquiet et vigilant de sa mère' (*Arm.*, pp. xiv-xv).

[19] Cf. Bardèche, *Stendhal romancier*; Brombert, *Fiction*; Michel Crouzet, 'Le réel dans *Armance*. Passions et société ou le cas d'Octave: étude et essai d'interprétation', in *Le Réel et le texte* (Paris, 1974), 31–110; E. Gans, 'Le secret d'Octave: secret de Stendhal, secret du roman', *Revue des Sciences Humaines*, 40 (1975), 85–9; and H.-F. Imbert, *Les Métamorphoses de la liberté, ou Stendhal devant la Restauration et le Risorgimento* (Paris, 1967), 365–445.

[20] Felman, '*Folie*'; Françoise Gaillard, 'De la répétition d'une figure: *Armance* ou le récit de l'impuissance', *Littérature*, 18 (May 1975), 111–26; Jean-Marie Gleize, '*Armance* oblique', in *Le Réel et le texte*, 111–21; Simons, *Sémiotisme*; and Emile Talbot, 'The Impossible Ethic: A Reading of Stendhal's *Armance*', *French Forum*, 3 (1978), 147–58. Cf. also Crouzet, *Langage*, 185–94.

[21] See Jean Bellemin-Noël, *L'Auteur encombrant: Stendhal/'Armance'* (Lille, 1985), especially 29, 35.

passages in the novel as allusions to impotence are by no means conclusive. Thus Octave's exclamation in chapter ii: '*Je l'aimerais*! moi, malheureux!' could well suggest that Octave, like Fabrice before his imprisonment, believes himself to be psychologically incapable of love. Similarly in chapter iv his 'horror' of love and his solemn oath not to fall in love may be comparable with Lucien Leuwen's rejection of sentiment as the waste of a young man's time. Admittedly his later references to 'les choses les plus étranges sur mon compte' (188) and the 'secret affreux' which will explain his 'fatales bizarreries', as well as his Zadigian 'mais' (222–3), suggest something less nebulous, but he could well have in mind that mental instability which, were he not an aristocrat, would have led to his being certified insane (28) and which his mother hopes to alleviate by marrying him to Armance (103). And his supposedly most telling statement: 'mais quel est l'homme qui t'adore? c'est un *monstre*' (224) is less conclusive when one thinks that Octave, never one for understatement,[22] would have applied the term 'monstre' to himself if he had not tended his injured footman (31). Equally, his rapid departure midway through the second act of Scribe's *Le Mariage de raison* (where a door-key is proffered as an invitation to conjugal sex) may indicate not the tragic embarrassment of an impotent theatre-goer but a somewhat Puritan aesthetic sensibility ('les mots les plus agréables et les plus fins lui semblaient entachés de grossièreté': 38). Above all, perhaps, one should remember that Octave commits suicide not necessarily because he is impotent but more probably because he is led to believe the women he loves no longer loves him.[23]

If then, in the first instance, Octave's secret malady is not to be sexual impotence,[24] what might it be? Clearly nothing other than

---

[22] Notwithstanding Armance's comment that 'son cousin parlait trop bien pour exagérer ses idées' (227).

[23] A fact stressed again recently by Bellemin-Noël (*L'Auteur encombrant*, 24) who notes that Stendhal, in the letter to Mérimée, misinterprets his own novel on this very point.

[24] Interpretations based on the idea of such impotence are further undermined if one accepts H.-F. Imbert's contention that the letter to Mérimée 'fut écrite après coup, un jour que Stendhal entend jouer au roué et au carabin devant son ami' (*Métamorphoses*, 372). Certainly the content and tone of the letter are atypical of Stendhal's correspondence as a whole, although that may be because recipients of such letters prefer to destroy them. Note also Pierre Barbéris's suggestion that Mérimée's own tendency to 'fiasco' (as publicized by George Sand) may account for Stendhal writing in the way he does in this letter. See '*Armance*, Armance: quelle impuissance?', in Berthier (ed.), *Stendhal. Colloque de Cerisy-la-Salle*, 67–86 (85–6). Barbéris argues here that Octave is not impotent but has resolved to remain chaste with the woman he loves, and that he commits suicide as a consequence of his act of defilement (on his wedding-night).

the *mal du siècle*, and here the text is quite explicit. The doctors
called in by Mme de Malivert are sure that Octave 'n'avait d'autre
maladie que cette sorte de tristesse mécontente et jugeante qui
caractérise les jeunes gens de son époque et de son rang' (8), a diagnosis
which is later repeated (30) and also arrived at by Armance (33).
The narrator shares this view, even if he expresses it more
laconically: 'on échappe difficilement à la maladie de son siècle:
Octave se croyait philosophe et profond' (85). This aspect of the
novel has not escaped critical attention,[25] but once again one must
question the degree of reverence with which it has been treated. Of
the few critics who allow a measure of comedy in *Armance*, Blin
concedes merely some 'persiflage furtif',[26] Hemmings that 'the over-
scrupulous young man is slightly comic',[27] Brombert that Stendhal
does ironize Octave's behaviour but only to forestall an irreverent
reader,[28] and Jones, while illustrating the ironic distance between
narrator and hero, nevertheless believes that 'l'auteur semble hésiter
à déprécier son héros'.[29] Only one critic has declared unequivocally
that *Armance* is 'une parodie de *René*'[30]—which indeed, on one
level, it most certainly is. And of course there is plenty of external
evidence that Stendhal had little time for the agonized posturings
of René and his would-be heirs. He himself had been a victim of
the fashion, indeed at the same age as Octave. He explains in a long
letter to his sister in 1804 how the disparity between the exalted
notions about human nature with which the protagonists of
La Nouvelle Héloïse had imbued him and the less than sublime

---

[25] Cf. especially Albérès, *Le Naturel chez Stendhal*, 338–9; Crouzet, 'Le réel
dans *Armance*', 38, 59–60, 64, 74; Levin, *Gates of Horn*, 114; U. Mölk,
'Stendhal's *Armance* und die Motivgeschichte des impotenten Helden', *Romantische
Zeitschrift für Literaturgeschichte*, 1 (1977), 413–32; and Custine, *Aloys ou le religieux
du Mont Saint-Bernard*, ed. P. Sénart (Paris, n.d. (1971)), pp. vii-xxii. Imbert takes
the opposite view in *Métamorphoses*, 423. Cf. also Martineau who refuses to allow
it *because* Octave is impotent (*Arm.*, p. xi). Bellemin-Noël's thesis in *L'Auteur
encombrant* is that the novel is 'une étonnante illustration de la *métapsychologie
de la mélancolie*' (23) and that Octave suffers from a 'psychose maniaco-
dépressive' (29).
[26] 'Etude sur *Armance*', p. lvii.
[27] *Stendhal*, 87.
[28] *La Voie oblique*, 6–10.
[29] *Ironie*, 13.
[30] J. M. Sykes, '*Armance*, roman romantique?', *Stendhal Club*, 16 (1973/4),
127–35 (135). Del Litto in his introduction sees non-parodistic parallels with *Adolphe*,
particularly in the use of seasons and climate to mirror the psychology of the
protagonists (*O*, iv. 17).

behaviour of real people made him 'sans cesse plus misanthrope, nourri dans ma folie par la mélancolie, qui est un sentiment profond et doux à la vanité'. He warns her against this 'folie dont j'ai eu tant de peine à me guérir, si tant est que je le sois', both here[31] and in a subsequent letter of 1805 which leaves one in no doubt about his attitude to the *mal du siècle*:

tous les philosophes chagrins, J.-J. Rousseau, Mme de Staël, le sont pour n'avoir pas pris le monde du bon côté. C'est un homme qui fendant une racine de noyer au milieu de la cour, s'efforcerait tout le matin de faire entrer son coin par le gros bout [,] ne parviendrait qu'à casser sa masse, et, sur les midi, dégoûté de ses efforts, irait pleurer dans un coin de la cour; bientôt il s'exalterait la tête, se mettrait à croire qu'il y a de l'honneur à être malheureux, et, de suite, qu'il est excessivement malheureux [...] En général les malheureux de ce genre, dans le monde, ne sont que *sots*. Les trois quarts de ces mélancolies ne sont que des sottises. C'est malheureusement la maladie des jeunes gens du siècle [...] on dirait à les entendre le monde composé d'une infinité de petites solitudes qui se touchent où chaque malheureux attend la mort avec impatience. Ils partent de là pour se faire croire de bonnes gens et ils sont tout simplement des ennuyés *ennuyeux*, avec le caractère que l'éducation leur a donné. Tu vois à Grenoble [...] la comédie du sentiment, à Paris, *où la tête est meilleure*, ce comique est aussi plus relevé, plus profond, on donne la comédie de la mélancolie. Tâchons, ma chère Pauline, de n'être pas dupes de cette farce.[32]

Stendhal's attitude here is reflected in his growing aversion to Alfieri, an aversion which in 1811 gave rise to the conviction that:

un *com[ic] ba[rd]* doit arranger sa vie d'une manière toute différente de celle d'Alfieri. Il eût eu plus d'esprit, plus de talent et plus de bonheur en ne voulant pas lutter de caractère et d'orgueil avec des institutions inébranlables; il fallait regarder la vie comme un bal masqué où le prince ne s'offense pas d'être croisé par le perruquier en domino. Il y aurait dans le caractère d'Alfieri pris de ce côté-là le sujet d'une comédie destinée à

---

[31] *Corr.*, i. 162.
[32] *Corr.*, i. 219. This rejection of fashionable melancholy and the wish to 'se dérousseauiser' is a recurrent theme in Stendhal's writing between 1804 and 1811. See *JL*, i. 140 (and footnote), 403 (June 1804), *Corr.*, i. 261 (23 Dec. 1805), 287–8 (15 Feb. 1806), *OI*, i. 315 (10 April 1805), 321 (25 April 1805), 427 (30 Sept. 1806), 446 (28 May 1806), 469 (30 Sept. 1806). See also Strickland, *Stendhal*, 27–33.

ramener ces bilieux pleins de vertus au beylisme.[33] Elle ridiculiserait *Le Misanthrope* de Molière (qu'on n'aille pas croire que je ne respecte pas cet homme étonnant).[34]

'Comédie de la mélancolie', 'comédie destinée à ramener ces bilieux pleins de vertu au beylisme', might these phrases be apt descriptions of *Armance*? Certainly one of the more important aspects of the novel is its debt to *Le Misanthrope*. If there is something of Tartuffe in Julien Sorel, then there is much of Alceste in Octave. The parallel is made explicit in chapter vii ('il était devenu misanthrope et chagrin; chagrin comme Alceste sur l'article des filles à marier'), and it is implicit throughout. Alceste's famous declaration in the first scene of *Le Misanthrope*: 'Je veux qu'on soit sincère, et qu'en homme d'honneur, / On ne lâche aucun mot qui ne parte du cœur' is echoed

---

[33] This is the first recorded use of the term 'beylisme'. In the same diary entry Stendhal complains that his friend Louis Crozet is the opposite of 'beyliste' because his current love-affair is making him 'triste et attristant' (*OI*, i. 662). Four days later he implicitly defines 'beylisme' further by describing the two faults in his own character which prevent him being happy: (i) 'ma maudite horreur pour ce qui est *bas*'; (ii) 'la *folie* de m'amuser à m'imaginer qu'on m'insulte pour composer ensuite des réponses bien hautes et bien insolentes, et me voir donnant des soufflets [...] comme Alfieri tuant Elie pour lui avoir tiré un cheveu' (*OI*, i. 665). Six days later he refers to 'mes deux défauts provenant de *misanthropie*' (*OI*, i. 668). See also *Corr.*, i. 657 (24 Aug. 1812) and especially 659 (2 Oct. 1812): 'je lisais les *Confessions* de Rousseau il y a huit jours. C'est uniquement faute de deux ou trois principes de *beylisme* qu'il a eu tant de malheurs. Cette manie de voir des devoirs et des vertus partout a mis de la pédanterie dans son style et du malheur dans sa vie. Il se lie avec un homme pendant trois semaines: crac, les *devoirs* de l'amitié, etc. Cet homme ne songe plus à lui après deux ans; il cherche à cela une explication noire. Le *beylisme* lui eût dit: "Deux corps se rapprochent; il naît de la chaleur et une fermentation, mais tout état de cette nature est passager. C'est une fleur dont il faut jouir avec volupté, etc." Saisis-tu [Félix Faure] mon idée? Les plus belles choses de Rousseau sentent l'empyreume pour moi, et n'ont point cette grâce *corrégienne* que la moindre ombre de pédanterie détruit.' For commentary on this passage see Crouzet, *Poétique*, 152–3. On 'la grâce', the stylistic equivalent of 'beylisme', see Coe's 'From Correggio to Class Warfare: notes on Stendhal's ideal of "la grâce" '.

[34] *OI*, i. 663 (17 Mar. 1811). Cf. also Stendhal's reference in his marginalia to 'le Ridicule des jeunes gens dont ce roman veut les avertir', (259; cf. also 258, and 258–9). Stendhal's idea of presenting a comic version of *Le Misanthrope* reflects, of course, the Romantic misconception of the play as a tragedy of sincerity, a misconception which has its roots in Rousseau's *Lettre à D'Alembert sur les spectacles*. See E. D. Sullivan, 'The Actor's Alceste: Evolution of the Misanthrope', *Modern Language Quarterly*, 9 (1948), 74–89, and 'Molé's Interpretation of Molière's Misanthrope', ibid. 492–6. Also O. E. Fellows, *French Opinion of Molière (1800–1850)* (Providence, 1937), 72–3. For Stendhal's comments on Molière's Alceste as an admirable, non-comic character, see *JL*, i. 345, 347, 409. Cf. *JL*, iii. 8 (1813), where he has come to the view that Rousseau was wrong not to see *Le Misanthrope* as a comedy.

by Octave's first statement in the first chapter of the novel: 'pourquoi me montrerais-je autre que je ne suis?' which, curiously, is an alexandrine.[35] Equally, the denouement of *Le Misanthrope* is echoed in Octave's reaction on realizing that he loves Armance: 'il ne lui restait que la solitude et l'habitation au fond de quelque désert' (129). If one combines these allusions with those to *René* ('je suis ici dans un désert d'hommes': 87) and the *Rêveries du promeneur solitaire* ('moi seul, je me trouve isolé sur la terre. Je n'ai et je n'aurai personne à qui je puisse librement confier ce que je pense': 31–2), it is clear that as misanthrope and outsider, Octave has an impeccable literary pedigree.

But is he a comic figure? At the beginning of the novel Octave's sense of alienation is presented in a tentative and vaguely critical tone:

peut-être quelque principe singulier, profondément empreint dans ce jeune cœur, et qui se trouvait en contradiction avec les événements de la vie réelle, tels qu'il les voyait se développer autour de lui, le portait-il à se peindre sous des images trop sombres, et sa vie à venir et ses rapports avec les hommes. (6)

The excess of gloom on these two counts, however, soon leads in the course of the novel to a number of blatant absurdities. Thanks to his forebodings about his future (namely, that he is condemned to the unfulfilling life of a rich young nobleman and membership of a hidebound and obsolescent class) Octave thinks of adopting a number of alternative life-styles, the heterogeneity of which implies a certain lack of conviction: in turn, that of a monk, a research chemist, the son of a textile manufacturer, an industrial chemist, a person in charge of a cannon or steam-engine, a travelling mathematics tutor called M. Lenoir, a valet like his own Pierre Gerlat but in service with a rich young Englishman (for which role he is sufficiently motivated to acquire the skill of boot-polishing), and finally a conductor of agricultural experiments amongst the peasants of Brazil. His eventual choice of the role of latter-day crusader in the cause of Greek independence from the Turks seems by comparison to be rather unoriginal.

Under the second heading, that of his dealings with other people, the consequences of Octave's gloom are no less colourful. Convinced that he is an 'être à part' and that communication with others is

---

[35] In *Vies de Haydn, de Mozart et de Métastase* Stendhal describes the alexandrine as 'un cache-sottise' (OC, xli. 311), and he later repeats the joke in the preface to *Racine et Shakespeare*.

impossible, he believes the only resource would be to 'trouver une belle âme [...] de s'y attacher pour jamais, de ne voir qu'elle, de vivre avec elle et uniquement pour elle et pour son bonheur. Je l'aimerais avec passion...' (24). But at once he exclaims in disbelief (while nearly getting run over by a carriage): '*je l'aimerais!* moi, malheureux!...'. As suggested before, one can here regard Octave as believing himself to be psychologically incapable of love. In fact what Octave is saying is that because he is unhappy, *therefore* he will never fall in love. The despair wrought in him by this a priori reasoning is expressed in the most extravagant terms (24–5) and leads him to contemplate taking his own life. But the role of suicidal *homme fatal* is short-lived, and his thoughts turn to a more mundane matter, the refurbishment of his bedroom. He thinks of raising the ceiling and installing three seven-foot mirrors; he alone would have a key to this room and a servant would come and dust it on the first of every month. And, as the narrator wryly reports: 'l'homme qui pendant trois quarts d'heure venait de songer à terminer sa vie, à l'instant même montait sur une chaise pour chercher dans sa bibliothèque le tarif des glaces de Saint-Gobain' (26). The expenses involved in altering his room would, it appears, amount to 57,350 francs. Moreover it would seem that the schemes of the misanthropic interior designer are no more original than those of the would-be aristocratic drop-out. The family drawing-room, located directly beneath his bedroom, also has a raised ceiling and its windows have been replaced by mirrors.[36]

Taken together with the instances of somewhat ludicrous paranoia (the fragmentary diary written in the Greek alphabet and then concealed in the secret drawer of his desk, the radical newspapers read behind locked doors in a nondescript restaurant and then burned), these details from the portrait of Octave suggest a rather sub-standard version of Alceste or Jean-Jacques. Equally, the relation

---

[36] Robert Chessex suggests that 'glaces' here (9) means not mirrors but panes of glass cooled in water with which the inferior 'vitres' of blown glass were replaced by householders bent on house improvement. See 'Ambiguïté fâcheuse', *Stendhal Club*, 22 (1979/80), 374–5. But the context leaves the ambiguity intact. Stendhal is stressing the sterility of the hôtel de Malivert and deliberately evoking 'une image vivante de la vie morale de cette famille' by describing the lifeless, immobile lime-trees which are pruned three times a year and the division of the lonely garden into bizarre compartments by stiff borders of box. Accordingly he stresses an absence of light in 'le salon [...] si sombre'; and hence: 'une tenture de velours vert, surchargée d'ornements dorés, semblait faite exprès pour absorber toute la lumière que pouvaient fournir deux immenses croisées garnies de glaces au lieu de vitres.' Why have immense casements with better glass if you want to convey gloom?

between Octave's actions and his elaborate moral code suggests something less than that Cornelian moral grandeur with which he has sometimes been credited.[37] A sense of duty is apparently Octave's strong point and indeed the only thing that motivates him: 'on eût dit que si le devoir n'avait pas élevé sa voix, il n'y eût pas eu chez lui de motif pour agir.' His uncle, in tones of exasperation with which one may come to sympathize, tells him he is 'le devoir *incarné*', to which Octave makes the awesome reply: 'que je serais heureux de n'y jamais manquer! [...] que je voudrais pouvoir rendre mon âme pure au Créateur comme je l'ai reçue!' (6). It appears that the eighteen months he devoted to the study of chemistry at the Ecole Polytechnique was a 'devoir que je m'étais imposé' (14). In chapter ii, when he is contemplating suicide, he at first thinks little of the duty he owes his family to carry on the family name: 'c'est un bien petit devoir qui m'attache à eux.' But: 'ce mot *devoir* fut comme un coup de foudre pour Octave. Un *petit devoir*! s'écria-t-il en s'arrêtant, un devoir de peu d'importance!... Est-il de peu d'importance, si c'est le seul qui me reste?' (25), and at once his resolve to live assumes the dimensions of extreme moral heroism. As one who is frequently swearing solemn oaths to himself, he now swears to 'surmonter la douleur de vivre': 'eh bien! je suis malheureux! reprit-il en se promenant à grands pas; oui, je suis malheureux, mais je serai plus fort que mon malheur.—Je me mesurerai avec lui, et je serai plus grand. Brutus sacrifia ses enfants, c'était la difficulté [!] qui se présentait à lui, moi, je vivrai' (27). These grandiose pronouncements occur just after he has worked out how much his new room will cost.

This exaggerated sense of personal duty is one aspect of Octave's main concern, which is to earn his self-respect, something he also hopes to achieve by eschewing all affectation and pretension. But does Octave live up to the principle expressed in his initial question: 'pourquoi me montrerais-je autre que je ne suis?'? The defiance of social convention implied here is seldom evident in his subsequent behaviour, and indeed his quest for Armance's approval leads him to play the social game with much success. At the same time the very existence of his 'secret affreux', whatever it may be, suggests that in fact he spends his whole time appearing other than he is. Certainly his mother sees in him not honesty but 'une profondeur de dissimulation incroyable à cet âge' (16). At the beginning of the novel

[37] Blin, 'Etude sur *Armance*', p. xlv, Imbert, *Métamorphoses*, 374, and Talbot, 'The Impossible Ethic', 150.

he may talk openly with Armance, but the narrator points out that this is only because 'ces deux êtres n'avaient que de l'indifférence l'un pour l'autre' (20). When there is something at stake he dissembles, particularly with his family. For their benefit he pretends to like his room the way it is, he pretends to enjoy the company of his uncle, and he pretends to be in a good mood when he isn't. (Admittedly he is honest with his mother on the subject of the horse she has bought him, but he is careful not to let his honesty go unnoticed: 'faut-il qu'une fois en sa vie ton fils n'ait pas été sincère avec la personne qu'il aime le mieux au monde?': 11.) Doubtless most of these are understandable and venial deceptions in the cause of familial harmony, but in chapter v the narrator is obliged to warn the reader that Octave is only 'cet être, qui se croyait si exempt de fausseté' (52). And his later deceits are less anodyne, even if those on whom they are practised may well deserve them. In order to see more of Armance he cultivates her aunt, the marquise de Bonnivet, and convinces her that he is a soul in peril of eternal damnation whom she can save if only she will see him more often and guide him with her piety. Later, when he thinks that the frequency of their meetings may be endangering her reputation and may therefore cause her to reduce the number of occasions on which he can see Armance, he decides to reassure public opinion by pretending to be an ardent admirer of the comtesse d'Aumale. The degree to which he is play-acting at this point is reflected in his decision to entertain the comtesse by dressing up as a magician, and subsequently in his plans, mentioned earlier, to adopt a pseudonym and to pretend to be someone else. This contradiction between role-playing and the desire to be honest puts Octave under a lot of pressure and, as with Julien in *Le Rouge et le Noir*, the pressure is periodically released in extraordinary fits of rage. During these 'accès de fureur' he appears momentarily to lose his reason, and his actions are marked by 'une violence extrême, une méchanceté extraordinaire' (28). The most notorious of these fits causes him to throw his footman out of the window and down on to a laurel bush. The footman survives but, as the narrator remarks: 'on peut comprendre maintenant les chagrins de Mme de Malivert' (29). This evidently comic incident has a certain significance in that the fit of rage has been brought on by an hour spent playing charades. It is as if Octave can only pretend for so long before the pressure this creates has to find an outlet in violence.

The notion of 'devoir' and the ambition of sincerity, then, are two aspects of Octave's pursuit of self-esteem, and both are ironized. So too is the third: his belief that he knows himself. In an early conversation with his mother he remarks with great equanimity: 'j'ai par malheur un caractère singulier, je ne me suis par créé ainsi; tout ce que j'ai pu faire, c'est de me connaître' (12). But of course the first half of the novel gives the lie to this as, unbeknownst to himself, he falls in love with Armance. He believes that his assiduity in visiting the pious marquise de Bonnivet derives from a desire for the opportunity to prove to Armance that he is unaffected by the restoration of his family's fortune. But as the narrator observes: 'ce sage de vingt ans était loin de pénétrer la véritable cause du plaisir qu'il trouvait à se laisser convertir' (53), and the point is repeated at the end of chapter vii: 'ce qui est admirable, c'est que notre philosophe n'eut pas la moindre idée qu'il aimait Armance d'amour. Il s'était fait les serments les plus forts contre cette passion, et comme il manquait de pénétration et non pas de caractère, il eût probablement tenu ses serments' (73). These observations nicely undermine Octave's somewhat pompous complacency: '"c'est par lâcheté et non par manque de lumières que nous ne lisons pas dans notre cœur", disait-il quelquefois, et à l'aide de ce beau principe, il comptait un peu trop sur sa clairvoyance' (54).

When a chance remark by the comtesse d'Aumale half-way through the novel reveals to him that he is in love with Armance, he is filled with extravagant self-disgust: 'je me jugeais sans cesse moi-même et je n'ai pas vu ces choses! Ah! que je suis méprisable!' (133). The extent of his blindness and the suddenness of his realization make him the most despicable of men: 'mais j'étais donc sur le chemin qu'ont suivi les plus vils scélérats? Quoi! hier soir, à dix heures, je n'ai pas aperçu une chose qui, quelques heures plus tard, me semble de la dernière évidence? Ah! que je suis faible et méprisable!' (134). After this shock he becomes much more circumspect in judging his own motives. Having decided to leave France to go and prove his courage by fighting for the Greeks against the Turks, he wonders whether he ought to return to Andilly before his departure. But he quickly suspects that his apparent desire to say goodbye to his mother is in fact a desire to see Armance again, and this leaves him bewildered: 'mais toute ma conduite n'est-elle pas une duperie?' (155). This circumspection soon gives way to more subtle self-deception. He fights a duel, apparently to satisfy his honour, and is happy to be wounded. The narrator remarks: 'je ne sais quel espoir vague et criminel il fondait sur la blessure qui allait le retenir quelques jours chez sa mère, et par conséquent pas fort loin d'Armance' (160). The 'quelques jours' transpire to be several months. After that his one remaining problem in the pursuit of Armance is the oath he swore to himself never to love. Getting over this takes him a week. At first he decides that it doesn't matter if he breaks the oath since he is going to die anyway. But what happens if he survives? He decides that to stick to his oath would constitute weakness of character: 'car enfin, ce serment ne fut fait que dans l'intérêt de mon bonheur et de mon honneur' (175).

These are just some of the ironies which surround Octave's anguished aspiration to the lofty ideals of dutifulness, sincerity and self-knowledge, and several of them are just as clearly to be found in the character and behaviour of Armance. As the marquis de Malivert notes, there is between them 'une funeste analogie de caractères' (213).[38] In her case, one presumes, there is no question of any 'natural disqualification for efficient marriage',[39] and yet she is just like Octave in her aversion to love and marriage. While Octave is anxious to appear unconcerned about his new-found fortune, Armance doesn't want to seem to be after his money by paying him any attention. When, in order to reassure him, she tells him: 'vous avez toute mon estime', she at once thinks she has somehow compromised herself, and her reaction is like that of Octave when he realizes his own love for her: 'quoi! se dit-elle, après quelques moments, si tranquille, si heureuse même [...] il y a une demi-heure, et perdue maintenant! perdue à jamais, sans ressource!' She too talks of her 'fatal secret' and her 'fatal amour', thinks like Octave that she is 'faible' and 'méprisable', decides that religious retreat is the only solution (though here, like Octave redesigning his room as a refuge from the world, she is careful to envisage 'un couvent [...] avec une vue pittoresque'), and all this, of course, in the name of 'devoir':

là jamais je n'entendrai parler de lui. Cette idée est le *devoir*, se dit la malheureuse Armance. Dès ce moment le sacrifice fut fait. Elle ne disait pas,

---

[38] Cf. Blin, 'Etude sur *Armance*', p. xxxv; Del Litto's introduction, *O*, iv. 16; Jones, *Ironie*, 40–3, 47, and 'L'emploi du point de vue', 116, 119, 135; O'Keefe, 'A Function of Narrative Uncertainty', 581–2; and Talbot, 'The Impossible Ethic', 151–7.

[39] Quoted from H. B. Samuel in Hemmings, *Stendhal*, 70. Cf. Martineau's equally splendid description of Octave as 'un amoureux platonique par décret de la nature' (*Cœur*, ii. 14) and H.-F. Imbert's 'un disgracié de Vénus' (*Armance*, ed. Imbert, 12).

elle sentait (le dire en détail eût été comme en douter), elle sentait cette vérité: du moment que j'ai aperçu le *devoir*, ne pas le suivre à l'instant en aveugle, sans débats, c'est agir comme une âme vulgaire, c'est être indigne d'Octave. (67)

In an orgy of self-denial she strips the walls of her room bare of every conceivable ornament, including an engraving of the San Sisto Madonna. The only serious hitch in Armance's venture into the world of interior decoration concerns not the price of Saint-Gobain mirrors but the propriety of wallpaper. This she decides reluctantly to forgo on the grounds that it had not been invented when the religious orders were founded. And all this because she said to Octave: 'vous avez toute mon estime.'

Throughout the novel Armance persists in this exaggerated view of what her honour demands. She pretends to Octave that she is likely to marry someone else and pretends to herself that anyway 'le mariage est le tombeau de l'amour'. 'Il peut y avoir des mariages agréables', she concedes in a misquotation of La Rochefoucauld, but 'il n'y en est aucun de délicieux' (104). She would tremble to marry Octave, much preferring their 'pure et sainte amitié'. Should this be threatened, then death would be the only answer. Even when she herself inherits a fortune towards the end of the novel and thereby becomes an eligible match for Octave, she still believes she is somehow a 'fille perdue': 'le mariage n'est pas fait pour ma position, je ne l'épouserai pas, pensait-elle, et il faut vivre beaucoup plus séparée de lui' (197). Again she thinks of becoming a nun, and in the end she is pretty well forced into marriage with the man she loves, and only because she has been accidentally (and slightly) compromised.

If then Octave and Armance are to be seen as participants in a comic 'chasse au malheur', what is the norm of behaviour from which they depart? In *Armance* it is the norm of 'beylisme', of 'beylisme' not in the sense of mere hedonism[40] but in the sense of what Gide was to call 'disponibilité'.[41] Octave and Armance have preconceived their lives: they believe they will never be happy; when they are, they believe this happiness will not last; and at the end it is as if, in order to prove themselves right, they make sure that it does not. Octave ensures the

---

[40] The term used by Hemmings, *Stendhal*, 88. See above, note 33.
[41] As well as the evident similarities with *La Porte étroite* (cf. Blin, 'Etude sur *Armance*', p. xlvii, and *OC*, v. 352) one may note a certain resemblance between Octave and Lafcadio in *Les Caves du Vatican*, particularly the Octave who 'essaya de se causer une douleur physique assez violente toutes les fois que son esprit lui rappelait Armance' (152).

'tragic' end that he had always predicted for himself, and Armance enters the conventual life that she had always believed she should adopt. Yet they had an alternative. In chapter xxiii, recovering from the duel, Octave realizes the mistake he has been making, a mistake which Julien and Lucien will also make: 'au lieu de conformer ma conduite aux événements que je rencontrais dans la vie, je m'étais fait une règle antérieure à toute expérience' (176). Here Octave learns one of the Stendhalian secrets to happiness, and the way in which he learns it constitutes one of the more interesting aspects of the novel.[42]

In chapter v Octave is unhappy because Armance will not speak to him: 'par ce malheur réel Octave fut distrait de sa noire tristesse, il oublia l'habitude de chercher toujours à juger de la quantité de bonheur dont il jouissait dans le moment présent' (44). The stress here is on 'juger'. Octave is right to look for happiness in the present (and in this respect he is several steps ahead of Julien) but he is wrong to evaluate it, particularly as his criteria of dutifulness, sincerity and self-knowledge mislead him. His happiness increases as his love for Armance leads him to take a more balanced and less excessively misanthropic view of society: 'il se disait qu'excepté dans la classe des femmes dévotes ou laides, chacun songeait beaucoup plus à soi, et beaucoup moins à nuire au voisin qu'il n'avait cru l'apercevoir autrefois' (83). Love has momentarily cured him of his absurd paranoia: 'il s'aperçut enfin que ce monde qu'il avait eu le fol orgueil de croire arrangé d'une manière hostile *pour lui*, n'était tout simplement que mal arrangé.' So debonair is he at this point that he becomes a spokesman for 'beylisme'; 'tel qu'il [le monde] est, il est à prendre ou à laisser. Il faut ou tout finir rapidement et sans délai par quelques gouttes d'acide prussique ou prendre la vie gaiement' (84). Thus one-third of the way through the novel Octave has already discovered part of the Stendhalian recipe for happiness, and his erstwhile 'chasse au malheur' looks like becoming a true 'chasse au bonheur'. But the trouble is that he has no confidence in this change of direction: 'en parlant ainsi, Octave cherchait à se convaincre bien plus qu'il n'exprimait une conviction.' He cannot profit from his discovery because he is still preoccupied with notions of moral worth, with a personal code of self-esteem which is his 'règle antérieure à toute expérience'. Eventually, though, he does accept

---

[42] Cf. Crouzet, 'Le réel dans *Armance*', 87, 104–5; Felman, 'Folie', 163 ff.; and Imbert, *Métamorphoses*, 403 ff.

his discovery and is prepared to love Armance or, as he puts it, to adapt his behaviour to events as they occur. His readiness to confess his 'secret affreux' to Armance is evidence of this. But this new approach founders, of course, on the forged letter which leads him to believe that Armance is not marrying him for love. At once his newly won 'disponibilité' vanishes and his predisposition to 'malheur', his 'vocation de défaite',[43] makes him believe the evidence of the letter rather than the evidence of Armance's behaviour and conversation.

Read in this way *Armance* offers an entertaining critique of the attitude of mind known as the *mal du siècle* and presents its sufferers as engaged upon a wilful 'chasse au malheur' in defiance of the real happiness which life, and particularly love, may have to offer. The extravagance of language and gesture (the repeated use of 'fatal', 'malheureux', the letter written in blood, the night of anguish spent swooning in a wood, etc.), the disparity between noble moral aims and the practical accommodations of everyday living, between the 'théorie de la vie' (50) and the 'événements de la vie réelle' (6), these are the ingredients of Stendhal's 'comédie de la mélancolie'. The real 'malheur' in *Armance* is that Octave's lesson in 'disponibilité' is so quickly forgotten, and it is ironic that the forged letter should accuse Octave of not being 'aimable et gai', for that is precisely what the experience of love had allowed him to become. Ironic, too, rather than tragic, is the account of his suicide. He whose love for Armance began beneath a portrait of Byron[44] sets off for Greece, ostensibly to fight with courage and perhaps to die like Byron at Missolonghi, but instead to take his own life without ever setting foot on Greek soil: 'et à minuit, le 3 de [*sic*] mars, comme la lune se levait derrière le mont Kalos, un mélange d'opium et de digitale préparé par lui délivra doucement Octave de cette vie qui avait été pour lui si agitée' (245). The understatement of the relative clause and the contrast between the romantic setting and the chronological and pharmacological precision encourage not catharsis but a wry, if sympathetic smile. If only... Indeed *Armance* lacks that sense of inevitability which is characteristic of tragedy. Rather it is a novel

[43] Felman, '*Folie*', 87.
[44] Cf. Brombert, *Fiction*, 55; Peter Brooks, *The Novel of Worldliness. Crébillon, Marivaux, Laclos, Stendhal* (Princeton, 1969), 228; Crouzet, 'Le réel dans *Armance*', 66–8, Hemmings, *Stendhal*, 79; Imbert, *Métamorphoses*, 444; and George M. Rosa, 'Un présage de la mort d'Octave dans *Armance*', *Stendhal Club*, 23 (1980/1), 15–21.

of the might-have-been, which is doubtless why it contains so many subjunctives and conditional clauses,[45] and in particular ten within the first two paragraphs. In fact it appears from the first paragraph that what Octave really wanted to do all along was to join the army, but his father prevented it. *Armance* might have been *Lucien Leuwen*.

---

[45] Cf. Mouillaud, 'Stendhal et le mode irréel', 530.

2

By steam and sail

'La même chose, chacun la juge d'après sa position.' (2)

IT is suggested, then, that Octave's ills are imaginary,[1] as imaginary as those of the eponymous heroine. Just as Octave talks of his 'fatal secret' and regards himself as an 'être à part', so Armance has her own 'fatal secret'[2] and wallows in the problems afforded by her 'position'[3] and her 'situation': 'il manquait à l'horreur de ma situation d'avoir mérité ses mépris' (66); 'le mariage n'est pas fait pour ma position' (197); 'je porte une juste peine [...] de la fausse position dans laquelle je me suis placée' (203). Her terms are as nebulous as Octave's, and the reality of her inheritance makes as little difference to her 'position' as the experience of love to Octave's conviction that he can never be happy. Dispensing with the 'key' of impotence in this way, far from leaving one with an obscure text, actually permits a coherent, if not more coherent reading of the novel. As Shoshana Felman neatly puts it: 'ce n'est pas, en effet, la clé qui manque, mais un manque qui en est la clé.'[4]

Of course it may be objected, as C. W. Thompson has,[5] that to dispense with the key is simply to pander to a prevailing taste for the lacunary in order to avoid the problems of interpretation posed by Stendhal's declarations in his marginalia and letters. With scrupulous and well-judged scholarship Thompson himself adduces much contemporary evidence to suggest that by 'impuissance' is meant homosexuality, or at least a degree of sexual ambivalence sufficient to account for Octave's behaviour in the novel. Persuasive

---

[1] Cf. the narrator's footnoted remark: 'le pauvre Octave se bat contre des chimères' (112) and the epigraph to chapter xxix: 'ses maux les plus cruels sont ceux qu'il se fait lui-même.'

[2] Cf. Bellemin-Noël, *L'Auteur encombrant*, 18–19.

[3] In the context of a different thesis Imbert notes the frequent recurrence of this word and gives references for each use of it in the novel (*Métamorphoses*, 425 and notes 212 and 213).

[4] 'Folie', 170. But Felman argues that the textual 'lack' in *Armance* reflects the physical lack in Octave.

[5] See 'Les clefs d'*Armance* et l'ambivalence du génie romantique du Nord', *Stendhal Club*, 25 (1982/3), 520–47 (520–1).

as the evidence is, Thompson rightly considers that 'l'idée d'ambivalence [...] dépasse largement le domaine sexuel' and argues that Stendhal was aiming, through multiple allusions to English and German Romanticism, 'à généraliser l'image représentée par Octave en un certain type de héros qui serait propre au romantisme, et par là au génie du Nord'.[6] This ambivalent hero is tragically torn, not only between conflicting sexual desires but between dream and action, between the mist and mysticism of the North and the sun and sensuality of the South, between concealment and revelation. Certainly Thompson provides the most plausible account to date of the creative process whereby Latouche's *Olivier* became Stendhal's *Armance*,[7] and in particular whereby the idea of sexual 'singularité' grew into a reflection on Romanticism. But his disregard of the comic treatment to which many aspects of the latter are subjected in the novel places his reading within the consensus which is here being questioned. At the same time his substitution of the term 'ambivalence' for 'impuissance' and 'manque' makes for a conclusion about the genesis of *Armance* which could have come from the pen of one of those 'critiques modernisants' whom he has cautioned at the outset: 'aucune étape sur cette trace complexe ne suscite un sens définitif, valable pour l'ensemble et pour tous les temps; le sens n'a pas arrêté de changer et ne peut jamais être fixé'. The modernists' lacuna becomes 'ce flou, propre au génie du Nord, où se fondent toutes les allusions'.[8]

Given that the picturesque French slang expression for sexual ambivalence is 'marcher à voile et à vapeur', Jean-Marie Gleize's description of *Armance* as (an) 'écrit *entre* la machine à vapeur et le bateau à voile'[9] may take on a new meaning in the light of Thompson's findings. But the ambivalence which Gleize has in mind is stylistic, an ambivalence located, not in the hero this time, but in the author. For Gleize, Stendhal is torn between the plain, dispassionate style of the Code civil with which he seeks to depict a prosaic reality (where 'la machine à vapeur est la reine du monde': 112), and a more 'poetic' style, the style used in the sentence quoted above ('et à minuit [...]', etc.) to narrate Octave's suicide on board

[6] 'Les clefs d'*Armance*', 533.

[7] See also Rosa, 'Byronism and "Babilanisme" in *Armance*', for the comparable thesis that Stendhal's original intention to write a novel about impotence was superseded by an interest in, and desire to portray, various aspects of Byronism.

[8] 'Les clefs d'*Armance*', 540.

[9] 'Bordures de buis', *L'Arc*, 88 (1983), 43–8 (48).

a sailing-ship.[10] The former style creates ironic distance between language and referent, and between the reader and the story of Octave:

au lieu [...] de pousser le lecteur à s'identifier avec le personnage, ou de communier avec lui auteur dans l'orgasme du plein sens partagé, de la pleine vérité coïncidante, [Stendhal] expulse au contraire ce lecteur de l'histoire et lui indique sa place, sa position, sa condition de lecteur.

The poetic style, on the other hand, provides moments of fusion when reader feels for hero and form mirrors content (in the case of the sentence narrating Octave's death, through the rhythm of anticipation and release). Thus the prosaic age of steam is punctuated by fleeting returns to the poetic age of sail, and the author's stylistic ambivalence is reflected in the novel by 'le maintien tressé-tendu des deux régimes d'écriture; sans solution'.[11]

Thompson's ambivalent hero and Gleize's ambivalent stylist generate new and interesting readings of *Armance*, each with different consequences for the status of the reader. Thompson's reader is witness to the tragedy of the divided self and participant in Stendhal's 'jeu savant' with a vertiginous Romantic intertext, while Gleize's reader is alternately involved in and excluded from the narrative. In this connexion Gleize makes much of the following passage from the preface to *Armance* (and indeed dedicates his article to its columbine protagonists!):

si l'on demandait des nouvelles au jardin des Tuileries aux tourterelles qui soupirent au faîte des grands arbres, elles diraient: 'C'est une immense plaine de verdure où l'on jouit de la plus vive clarté'. Nous, promeneurs, nous répondrions: 'C'est une promenade délicieuse et sombre où l'on est à l'abri de la chaleur et surtout du grand jour désolant en été'. C'est ainsi que la même chose, chacun la juge d'après sa position. (1–2).

For Gleize the reader is here being told that his subjectivity will exclude him from the 'pleine vérité' of the novel known only to its author. But what if the opposite is true? What if Stendhal has written the novel precisely so as to cater for the subjective viewpoint of the reader? What if ambivalence is to be found not in the hero or the author but in the individual members of the Happy Few?

[10] Whose 'voiles' are echoed in the 'voile' taken by Mme de Malivert and Armance in the last sentence of the novel. See Bellemin-Noël, *L'Auteur encombrant*, 43 and note 22. See ibid. 89–92, for a psychoanalytical account of the 'poetic' ending.

[11] 'Bordures de buis', 47–8. For a different reading of the conflict between the prosaic and the poetic in *Armance* see Helena Shillony, 'Le dénouement d'*Armance* ou la mort du héros', *Stendhal Club*, 21 (1978/9), 193–200.

Madeleine Simons has argued that the incident of the forged letter teaches the reader how to read *Armance*. The insistence on the literal-mindedness of Soubirane encourages the reader to put two and two together rather more rapidly than he and thereby, she implies, come up with the answer: impotence.[12] Might one not also argue that Octave's response to the letter provides an object-lesson in how not to read *Armance*? Like Julien reading the letter dictated to Mme de Rênal, Octave reads an account of himself which is inconsistent with the facts (just as Mme de Rênal's letter is a description of Tartuffe, not Julien) and discovers an attitude towards him which, again like Mme de Rênal's, is belied by the previous and subsequent attitudes of the letter-writer. Prejudiced in favour of a tragic interpretation Octave misreads the letter—a misreading which is prefigured by his mother's exasperated comment in the first chapter of the novel: 'ah! ton caractère a quelque chose de mystérieux et de sombre qui me fait frémir; Dieu sait les conséquences que tu tires de tant de lectures!' (12). Likewise the reader of *Armance* may be enticed into an interpretative 'chasse au malheur', and not only by the prejudice (derived from a letter!) that Octave is impotent. He can be misled by the characters' own assertions that misfortune is their lot, misled too by the narrator's frequent tongue-in-cheek adoption of the language and values of his protagonists,[13] and misled most of all perhaps by what one might call Stendhal's technique of the spurious allusion. It has already been seen how Octave is not the tragic Alceste of Romantic conception, how his Rousseauistic sense of alienation dispatches him not to the beauties of nature but to a price-list for Saint-Gobain mirrors, and how his Byronic mission to Greece ends in maritime suicide. Equally, and despite his surname,[14]

[12] *Sémiotisme*, 297. The narrative ploy of the forged letter, previously deemed by most critics to be ham-fisted and a major flaw in the novel, has been invested with a new significance by those mindful of Lacan's seminar on Poe's *The Purloined Letter*. See Felman, 'Folie', 185, and Gaillard, 'De la répétition d'une figure', 124. Cf. also the latter's Lacanian view of Octave's taste for mirrors, 115. One should note that in the novel itself the ploy is taken from 'un roman vulgaire' (231), so that what Stendhal himself acknowledged (in the letter to Mérimée) to be a lame device becomes a form of self-irony.

[13] For an analysis of this aspect of the novel see Jones, *Ironie*, 42 ff.

[14] Much onomastic speculation has been fostered by the connotations of Malivert, Bonnivet and Aumale, as by Octave's desire for a pseudonym and the pain caused him by the initials of Armance de Zohiloff. Cf. especially Gaillard, 'De la répétition d'une figure', 116–17; Gleize, 'Armance oblique', 114; Simons, *Sémiotisme*, 276–7, n. 210; and Bellemin-Noël, *L'Auteur encombrant*, 17–19, 77, 87–8, 102 (n. 31). In the circumstances it is surprising that the initial of the heroine's surname has not been subject to the same hermeneutical extravagance as one finds in Barthes's *S/Z*.

he is no incarnation of evil, no Lucifer (6,122), nor is he tempted to barter his soul like Faust (12). A sub-Byronic lover, he is neither the jealous Othello (155, 157) nor the forcibly 'disqualified' Abelard (just as Armance, for all her desire to take the veil, is no abbess of a convent, no 'nouvelle Héloïse': 77). Nor, finally, is he Don Juan. Octave is notable for the number of his scruples, not his conquests, and it is one of the nicer ironies in Stendhal's comedy that Octave should discover the most effective antidote to misery in the playing of an act of *Don Giovanni* on the piano (27).

For *Armance*, amongst other things, is the story of how *il Commendatore* Soubirane, with whom the novel opens, conspires to destroy not a Don Juan but Don *Ottavio* de Malivert, whose aversion to marriage (in the name of 'devoir') is no less great than that of Armance or Da Ponte's Donna Anna but whose ghosts are of his own imagining. Far from being the Chopin *nocturne* that Hemmings suggests,[15] *Armance* combines a comedy of melancholy and a serious lesson in 'beylisme' with the elegance and sureness of touch of Mozart's *dramma giocosa*. The orchestra has been replaced not only by Octave's piano but also by Stendhal's violin, but whereas the pianist may privilege 'les accords si sombres de Mozart' (27), the violinist is evoking a mixture of emotions, indeed a mixture reminiscent not only of Mozart[16] but of Cimarosa. Is not *Armance* a first and highly successful attempt at inspiring the 'misto d'allegria et di tenerezza'[17] which Stendhal had found in the *Matrimonio segreto* and which, in 1812, he had hoped one day to be able to elicit by his writing? Thus the gaiety created by the comic treatment of the 'mal du siècle' is tempered by the tenderness which we may feel for Octave and Armance. Their noble ideals, their love and 'conspiracy of candour',[18] their rejection of a mercenary and hypocritical society, their suffering and the poignancy of their eventual death or retreat, all these may check our laughter and bring sympathy and reverie. 'Chacun juge d'après sa position': the position of the individual reader, necessarily as nebulous for Stendhal as the 'position' of Octave and Armance may be for us, will determine the

---

[15] *Stendhal*, 94.

[16] In the case of *Don Giovanni* the mixture could be said to derive from, on the one hand, the comedy of Leporello (the list, the disguises, the fear of the statue) and, on the other, the seriousness of Donna Elvira's outrage and the poignancy of Donna Anna's grief. *Le Nozze di Figaro* (also a *dramma giocosa*) and *Cosi Fan Tutte* offer similar mixtures.

[17] See above, i. 3.   [18] Hemmings, *Stendhal*, 93.

precise quantities of gaiety and tenderness with which he responds. Just as Stendhal himself was able to re-read *René* at the age of thirty-five *'with the* convenable tristesse' but only because he was *'thinking to M*[atilde]*'* ('sans elle je n'aurai pas pu l'achever'),[19] so we will bring to our reading and re-reading of *Armance* personal circumstances which will alter the proportions of laughter and tears, and smiles, in our response. As our position changes, so will the novel.

That a new version of *Le Misanthrope* could provide the stimulus for such an ever-changing blend of gaiety and tenderness seems to have occurred to Stendhal as early as 1804. Having been to a performance of Fabre d'Eglantine's *Le Philinte de Molière ou la suite du Misanthrope* he notes in his diary how he would have gone further than Fabre in his adaptation of the play:

il semble que Fabre ait évité exprès de lui [Alceste] donner de ces pensées misanthropiques, qui sont exagérées et, par là, comiques, mais si naturelles à une âme comme la sienne. Il n'y en a que deux ou trois légères, qui cependant font rire le public. Le défaut de la pièce est d'être trop sérieuse et pas assez tendre. J'y aurais mis du tendre par la passion mal éteinte d'Eliante pour Alceste, et du comique par ses exagérations lorsqu'il aurait vu le mal. J'aurais montré un peu davantage sa réconciliation avec l'humanité quand il a trouvé un honnête hom[me]. Un peu plus de gaieté ferait jouer cette pièce aussi souvent que le *Tartuffe*.[20]

For all that Stendhal notes faults in Fabre's treatment, it was the reception of this play six months later ('le sourire, les mots que j'entendais de tous côtés me prouvent qu'on le sent parfaitement') which gave him his first glimpse of the Happy Few, 'ce public choisi et peu nombreux à qui il faut plaire'.[21] If in the earlier diary-entry one substitutes Octave for Alceste, Armance for Eliante and 'femme honnête' for 'honnête hom[me]', one has a fairly exact description of *Armance* and its Cimarosan mixture of gaiety and tenderness. Of course more than twenty years elapsed between diary-entry and novel, but Fabre d'Eglantine's play made a profound impact on Stendhal, especially as his enthusiasm for the performance of 31 December 1804 remained linked in his memory with his first meeting, at a party later that evening, with Mélanie Guilbert.[22] Also there

[19] *OI*, ii. 27 (4 Oct. 1818).   [20] *OI*, i. 95 (7 July 1804).
[21] *OI*, i. 167 (31 Dec. 1804). Cf. *OI*, i. 145 (10 Nov. 1804) and 454 (20 Aug. 1806).
[22] See *OI*, i. 361, 369.

is the possibility that Stendhal drew material for his novels from his diaries,[23] and that a re-reading of these may have given him the idea for his own, original 'comédie de la mélancolie'.[24] At the very least there is something curiously prophetic in Stendhal's thought (in 1804) that he might one day write 'un ouvrage qui ne plairait qu'à moi et qui serait reconnu beau en 2000',[25] and one may surmise that it was the idea of an impotent, or bisexual, 'homme fatal' which acted as a catalyst upon long-standing plans to write a touching comedy about a modern Alceste. In exchanging comic drama for the novel Stendhal was able to remove the reception of this new comedy from the context of a public theatre where personal response may in part be dictated by that of the audience as a whole and relocate it in the intimacy of an armchair. The Happy Few may be heterogeneous in their moral and political outlook, may wish to follow 'des routes différentes pour nous conduire au bonheur' (2). During this particular 'voyage dans un fauteuil' Stendhal leaves it to the reader to conclude which route to take and how to travel: by steam or sail, or both.

[23] See Castex's comment, *RN*, p. xxiii.
[24] Hemmings (*Stendhal*, 63) points out the clear parallels between *Armance* and *Les Deux Hommes*, the comedy which Stendhal was working on in 1803 and 1804. Did he perhaps refer back to this also?
[25] *OI*, i. 167.

III

TIME AND IMAGINATION IN
LE ROUGE ET LE NOIR

The Reader as Tourist

'Le *temps* qui, de toutes les choses de ce monde, est celle qui se
prête le plus à l'imagination.'

(*RS*, 158)

'Un roman: c'est un miroir qu'on promène le long d'un chemin.'

(*RN*, 72)

1

The chronicle

'M. de S. [...] osa raconter une aventure qui eut lieu en 1830.'

(715)[1]

IN an article written for the *New Monthly Magazine* in 1826 Stendhal recommended the Englishman proposing to visit France for the first time to read a year's back-numbers of the *Gazette des Tribunaux*. This publication, which provided full and reliable accounts of the court cases of the time, appeared every weekday, so the English traveller would have had much to read. But his industry would have been rewarded, since the *Gazette* had three great virtues in Stendhal's eyes: it was 'fort amusante', it gave an exact picture of contemporary French society, and it contained a wealth of incidental facts to which men and women had testified on oath.[2] Indeed it was almost as good as a novel, for its contributors wrote 'avec moins de talent peut-être mais avec autant de vérité que le célèbre Le Sage'.[3] Lively narrative, topicality and accuracy, use of the telling detail, these are also the qualities to which Stendhal aspired in writing *Le Rouge et le Noir*, and his own projected review of the novel, intended for the Italian readers of the Florentine literary review *Antologia*, stresses how original and up-to-date are its insights into the society of post-revolutionary France and how much more useful these will be to the foreigner 'qui cherche encore des images de la société française dans les contes de Marmontel ou dans les romans de Mme de Genlis' (713). Anyone, for example, looking for the gaiety and relaxed atmosphere of life under Louis XVI, had better content himself with the novels of the Baron de Besenval,[4] because things have changed 'du tout au tout' since then: 'rien de semblable aujourd'hui, tout est

---

[1] Throughout Part III simple page-reference of this kind is to the Classiques Garnier edition by P.-G. Castex.

[2] *COA*, iii. 43.

[3] *COA*, iii. 43-4. But in the words of H.-F. Imbert: 'la *Gazette des Tribunaux* est le musée des horreurs du temps' (*Métamorphoses*, 575).

[4] Whom Stendhal approved of (*OI*, i. 695) but whose memoirs are read by M. de Rênal merely as a source of models to imitate (38).

triste et guindé dans les villes de six à huit mille âmes. L'étranger y est aussi embarrassé de sa soirée qu'en Angleterre' (713).

Stendhal's claims for *Le Rouge et le Noir* are on the whole well founded, as is Erich Auerbach's celebrated contention in *Mimesis* that it is the first work of European literature in which the life story of the hero is fully integrated into the social and political context of his time.[5] The novel presents a comprehensive, and damning, account of French society in 1830. It includes a wide variety of social representatives ranging from the inmates of Valenod's workhouse to the king himself, but while each level of society may differ in appearance, hypocrisy, deviousness and callous self-interest are displayed by almost everyone—from Julien's father with his peasant cunning, through Julien's companions in the seminary at Besançon who will do anything for a good meal and a quiet life, to the mostly anonymous members of the secret cabal who pursue their own ends in engineering the invasion of France by a foreign power. There are a few honourable exceptions, such as Chélan, Pirard and Chas-Bernard for the Church and, among the vapid youth of Restoration Paris, at least Croisenois is man enough to die in a duel defending Mathilde's reputation. Equally, of course, the portrayal of the marquis de la Mole demonstrates Stendhal's admiration for the skilful politician and man of the world, a type which is to be represented again by Leuwen *père* and Count Mosca. But overall the picture is bleak. The industrialization of Verrières and the environmental nonchalance of its mayor, the political expediency that allows the ultra and the liberal to swap parties from one election to the next, the propagandistic purpose and architectural inadequacy of the restoration of the abbey at Bray-le-Haut, the feud between Jansenists and Jesuits, the all-pervasive influence of the Congrégation,[6] the torpor that besets inhabitants of the Faubourg Saint-Germain and the fatuity of their salon life, all these are part of 'la vérité, l'âpre vérité' (3) which Stendhal set out to chronicle.

So too are the world of crime and the processes of law. During the period 1826–1830 an average of 111 people were condemned to death each year in France, the majority for murder (arson and

---

[5] See chap. xviii: 'insofar as the serious realism of modern times cannot represent man otherwise than as embedded in a total reality, political, social, and economic, which is concrete and constantly evolving—as is the case today [1946] in any novel or film—Stendhal is its founder' (*Mimesis*, trans. Willard R. Trask, 2nd impr. (Princeton, 1968), 463).

[6] See Castex, '*Le Rouge et le Noir*', 47–9.

forgery, as well as treason, also being capital offences under the Code pénal of 1810), and of those some seventy were executed.[7] Any English tourist who followed Stendhal's advice would have read of these cases in the *Gazette des Tribunaux*, and he might perhaps have been struck, as Stendhal was, by two particular ones, those of Antoine Berthet and Adrien Lafargue. Long recognized as prototypes of Julien Sorel, these two assassins met with remarkably different fates. Berthet, a short, thin man with a pale complexion, the son of a blacksmith in Brangues, had spent four years in a seminary in Grenoble training to be a priest. At the age of twenty-one ill health forced him to leave, and his protector, the village priest, secured him a post as tutor to one of the two children of M. and Mme Michoud, a well-to-do couple living in Brangues. Whether Mme Michoud became his mistress remains uncertain, but some aspect of their relationship led to Berthet's dismissal after a year. After two years in another seminary, Berthet returned to Brangues in 1825 and began to write to Mme Michoud accusing her of having got him the sack and of being now the mistress of his successor as tutor. There followed a series of reverses: expulsion from another seminary in Grenoble after one month, dismissal—again after one year—from a post as tutor to the de Cordon family, possibly because he seduced Mlle de Cordon and possibly after M. de Cordon had received a letter from Mme Michoud. Although M. Michoud was trying behind the scenes to help Berthet and actually got him a job working for a notary, Berthet became increasingly bitter and blamed his repeated failure to be accepted by a seminary (and the consequent frustration of his ambition to become a priest) on Mme Michoud, whom he now repeatedly threatened to murder. On Sunday 22 July 1827, during Mass in the church at Brangues, Antoine Berthet shot Mme Michoud and then himself. Both survived. Berthet was subsequently found guilty of attempted murder 'avec toutes les circonstances aggravantes'. He was condemned to death and executed on 23 February 1828.

Adrien Lafargue was treated more leniently. A cabinet-maker by trade, he was a good-looking, well-spoken young man of twenty-five whose work had brought him temporarily to the town of Bagnères-de-Bigorre in the Pyrenees. At his lodgings the daughter of the house, called Thérèse, was a married woman who claimed

---

[7] See Jean Imbert, *La Peine de mort* (Paris, 1972).

to have been left by her husband. She took to Lafargue, and they became lovers. Though he had a fiancée in Bayonne, Lafargue became sincerely attached to Thérèse and was therefore all the more shocked one morning to find her in bed with a painter. Accepting her story that this was a former lover and that his sentimental appeal to their shared past had vanquished her scruples, Lafargue forgave her. On his uncle's advice he then moved out of the lodgings, but continued to see Thérèse. She however tired of him, particularly when he could not lend her three francs, and soon she had the police forbid him to see her or to enter her house. Embittered by what he saw as an abuse of his sincerity and tolerance and minded to rid the world of a 'mauvais sujet' ('il faut qu'elle meure, c'est une justice; du moins elle ne fera pas d'autres dupes': 680), Lafargue resolved to shoot her. On 21 January 1829 he went to her in her room. He fired once and missed, fired a second time and killed her. Fearing she was not dead, he then slit her throat. After this, as he had intended, he shot himself, but there was only powder in the pistol and he survived. He was found guilty of 'homicide volontaire, *sans préméditation*, [...] provoqué par des *violences graves*' (686). The sentence? A mere five years' imprisonment.

Stendhal's interest in these two murder stories is well documented,[8] and their relevance to *Le Rouge* almost self-evident. The Berthet case clearly provided Stendhal with the main shape of his plot together with many incidental details, while the Lafargue murder prompted a number of comments from Stendhal in *Promenades dans Rome* (1829) which have had a decisive influence on critical interpretation of the novel. For Stendhal the killing of Thérèse represents energy and will-power. It is an act of authentic, full-blooded passion, a spontaneous yet voluntary expression of vengeful jealousy. While wealth dispenses from effort and hard work and leaves the individual free to cultivate the delicacy and elegance of refined living, it saps his life-force, destroys all that is natural and spontaneous and turns him into a mindless imitator of models appointed by custom and fashion. Men like Lafargue, on the other hand, are the only people left with that strength of purpose which is the source of greatness:

---

[8] See Castex's edition, 649–87, as well as Claude Liprandi, *Au cœur du 'Rouge'. L'Affaire Lafargue et 'Le Rouge et le Noir'* (Lausanne, 1961) and René Fonvieille, *Le Véritable Julien Sorel* (Paris, 1971).

soustraits, par la nécessité de travailler, aux mille petites obligations imposées par la bonne compagnie, à ses manières de voir et de sentir qui étiolent la vie, ils conservent la force de vouloir, parce qu'ils sentent avec force. Probablement tous les grands hommes sortiront désormais de la classe à laquelle appartient M. Lafargue. Napoléon réunit autrefois les mêmes circonstances: bonne éducation, imagination ardente et pauvreté extrême. (687)[9]

Plainly Julien Sorel also combines these last three characteristics, and Stendhal's unflinching portrait of 'un pays d'affectations et de prétentions' (686)[10] is illuminated by the central presence of this young and energetic hero who would conquer the society of his time by playing it at its own game of hypocrisy while yet remaining free of moral taint by virtue of his own lucidity. Just when it seems that he may have lost this lucidity, he rejects the false image of himself contained within Mme de Rênal's letter to the marquis de la Mole and in an act of murderous passion recovers his real self. The violence of the deed stands as testimony to its integrity, and the aftermath— the willing acceptance of responsibility, the discovery of happiness, the poetic remembrance of things past—points to a form of authenticity that is the true quarry of every Stendhalian 'chasse au bonheur'.

This by now fairly traditional interpretation of Le Rouge and its sources is persuasive in many respects, but the sheer availability of relevant documentation[11] has in one sense done the novel a disservice. By providing some useful answers it has obscured several questions which are just as clearly raised by the story of Julien Sorel. To relate the events of the narrative so closely to a particular historical period and to two specific court cases is to see the novel as a mirror of its time and as the reflection of a coherent authorial viewpoint. Were one to see it rather as a violinist's bow, as a narrative playing upon its readers' reactions, might one not be readier to acknowledge the many interpretative problems it poses and indeed readier to welcome such problems—not as a critic who needs problems of intepretation to keep him in business,[12] but as a reader

---

[9] See also VIT, 1079–80.   [10] See also VIT, 1079.
[11] In the works of Castex, H.-F. Imbert, Liprandi and Martineau. See Bibliography.
[12] Cf. Jonathan Culler, Flaubert. The Uses of Uncertainty (London, 1974), 24: 'the critic is therefore effectively valuing, as the source of interest in Flaubert, precisely the absence of what he himself produces. He is interested in Flaubert because of the empty spaces his own discourse can fill.'

eager to give rein to surmise and to indulge in that 'rêverie' which Stendhal saw as the one true pleasure which the novel may afford?

By way of stimuli to such surmise there are, of course, the notorious questions: what is the significance of the title? why does Julien shoot Mme de Rênal? why is there no account of the July Revolution in a 'Chronique de 1830'? But there are others too. Granted, Julien has the energy and imagination which Stendhal admired in Lafargue. But how does Julien use them? Are such attributes necessarily beneficial? Is his will-power well directed? Why does he often succeed by accident rather than design? What in fact is the object of his ambition? What even does he achieve? If he does achieve something, are his means of doing so of exemplary value? Has Julien any of the greatness which Stendhal mentions in respect of Lafargue and Napoleon? Is he not as much of an imitator as the rich young men of Paris? Is it not simply that his models are different? In short, why is Julien's story *different* from those of Berthet and Lafargue?

To answer one of these questions directly, there are possibly two reasons why the July Revolution does not figure in the plot. The more banal may be that Stendhal had written most of *Le Rouge* before it occurred and did not wish to recast the novel at such a late stage. The more telling is that it was an irrelevance. After all the only reference to it comes in the fictitious 'Avertissement de l'Editeur' where the 'publisher' regards it as inimical to art: 'cet ouvrage était prêt à paraître lorsque les grands événements de juillet sont venus donner à tous les esprits une direction peu favorable aux jeux de l'imagination.' *Le Rouge* has two sub-titles: 'Chronique du XIXe siècle' (on the title-page) and 'Chronique de 1830' (at the beginning of Part I), but they are synonymous, for the July Revolution has changed nothing. Louis-Philippe may have succeeded Charles X, but vanity and hypocrisy still rule.[13] In the first chapter of Part II, which serves as a kind of interlude between the provincial and Parisian sections of the novel, the witty conversation between Falcoz and Saint-Giraud ranges widely over the various consequences of recent revolutionary and Napoleonic measures, and the narrator comments: 'la conversation fut infinie, ce texte va occuper la France encore un demi-siècle'. Regimes may come and go, but the issues, the intractable problems remain. The political malaise which the liberal Stendhal describes is chronic.

[13] See Wood, *Stendhal*, 67.

But whether it be a 'Chronique du XIXe siècle' or a 'Chronique de 1830', *Le Rouge et le Noir* is none the less a chronicle, that is to say, 'a historical record, especially one in which the facts are narrated without philosophic treatment, or any attempt at literary style' (*OED*). One might imagine this serving Stendhal as a definition both of the novel in general and *Le Rouge* in particular, but as a definition it would be disingenuous. For it is evident that Stendhal has replaced 'philosophic treatment' with thought-provoking silent commentary, just as he has dispensed with the verbiage and pretension of so-called 'literary style' in favour of a clipped and forthright narrative voice and a series of novelistic techniques which are themselves a superior and original form of literary art. What he offers in *Le Rouge* is a new kind of chronicle. As one might expect, time is of the essence, but here the reader's time matters as much, if not more, than that of the characters, and it is through its handling of temporal perspective that the work achieves its most remarkable effects.

In the following analysis of *Le Rouge et le Noir* it will be shown, first, how Stendhal creates an overwhelming sense of presentness in the novel—by extensive use of the present tense (see III. 3 below), a marked absence of prolepsis, or anticipation (III. 4), a dislocation of chronological order to enhance suddenness and surprise (III. 4), a rapidity of narrative pace which discourages the reader from taking stock or considering a wider context (III. 5), and considerable use of point-of-view technique (III. 6). Secondly, it will be argued that the narrator's own presentness in the text makes of him a contingent and biased observer whose commentary the reader is implicitly invited to look beyond and even (III. 7) to regard as contradictory. On the one hand the reader is given the illusion that he himself is present in the text; on the other, he is required to be under no illusion in response to the evidence with which he is provided (III. 1). Thirdly, it will be proposed that our customary reactions as novel-readers— involvement in the story, eager anticipation and retrospective surmise—are manipulated by Stendhal so that they become directly comparable with Julien's own experience of life. Our temporal imagination is enrolled in the service of an unfolding history (III. 8-10). In the chronicle that is *Le Rouge et le Noir* Stendhal's violin plays the music of time, and the many references to contemporary France and contemporary politics are but 'un coup de pistolet au milieu d'un concert' (360-1).

2

Arrival in Verrières: illusion and disillusion

'La petite ville de Verrières peut passer pour l'une des plus
jolies de la Franche-Comté.' (3)

THE opening chapters of *Le Rouge et le Noir* are famous for the
original way in which Stendhal introduces his reader to the fictional
world of the novel by means of an analogy with travel.[1] Just as the
book is opened by a reader possessed of some knowledge of life and
imbued with certain moral and political opinions but as yet ignorant
of the places and people he is about to encounter, so Verrières is
entered by an unknown traveller, a Parisian perhaps, who explores
the town and notes its particularities, finding some things to his taste,
others not. The traveller's enquiries are answered by the local
inhabitants, while the reader's curiosity is met by the narrator who
acts as his guide, this narrator who has himself been to Verrières
and whose eyes have gazed down upon the valley of the Doubs (7).
Such is the similarity between the traveller and the reader that the
latter may feel as if he himself is walking up the main street of
Verrières, assailed on all sides by the crashing din of M. de Rênal's
nail-factory, and indeed it is as evidence of Stendhal's supposed
'realism' that these opening pages have most often been cited. They
create a sense of immediacy, of 'being there', which seems to destroy
all notion of fiction.

This illusion of a present reality is reinforced by repeated
geographical references beyond Verrières. A town in the Franche-
Comté, nestling in the Jura mountains, close to Switzerland and
offering a view of Burgundy, once occupied by the Spanish and now
on the road taken by Italian masons as they proceed to Paris in the
spring, its gardens may not be as picturesque as those of Germany
('Leipsick, Francfort, Nuremberg, etc.') nor its plane-trees as fine as
those in England, but its new terrace is perhaps comparable with that
of Saint-Germain-en-Laye and the tyranny of 'what people will say'

---

[1] Cf. Fielding's *Tom Jones*, i. 4 and xviii. 1, where reading the novel is presented
as a journey. But Fielding does not have his reader arrive in the place(s) where the
novel is set.

is as great as in the United States. Verrières is part of the world we know, a kind of international crossroads, a significant corner of that 'global village' which we all inhabit.

But not only does the reader live in the same world as M. de Rênal, at the beginning of the novel he also lives at the same time as him. In other words narrative time and narrated time are one. What is most remarkable about these opening chapters is the way in which Stendhal, by a subtle modulation of tense, effects the transition from the present tense of a topographical guide to the past tense of conventional story-telling without forfeiting this immediacy.

The present tense of the first sentence dominates the first chapter and a half of the novel, and references to events in the past are consequently made in the *passé composé* (or simply in past participles). But the gap between narrative time and narrated time begins to open in the course of the ninth to twelfth paragraphs:

par exemple, cette scie à bois, dont la position singulière sur la rive du Doubs vous a frappé en entrant à Verrières, et où vous avez remarqué le nom de SOREL, écrit en caractères gigantesques sur une planche qui domine le toit, elle occupait, il y a six ans, l'espace sur lequel on élève en ce moment le mur de la quatrième terrasse des jardins de M. de Rênal.

Malgré sa fierté, M. le maire a dû faire bien des démarches auprès du vieux Sorel, paysan dur et entêté; il a dû lui compter de beaux louis d'or pour obtenir qu'il transportât son usine ailleurs. Quant au ruisseau *public* qui faisait aller la scie, M. de Rênal, au moyen du crédit dont il jouit à Paris, a obtenu qu'il fût détourné. Cette grâce lui vint après les élections de 182*.

Il a donné à Sorel quatre arpents pour un, à cinq cents pas plus bas sur les bords du Doubs. Et, quoique cette position fût beaucoup plus avantageuse pour son commerce de planches de sapin, le père Sorel, comme on l'appelle depuis qu'il est riche, a eu le secret d'obtenir de l'impatience et de la *manie de propriétaire* qui animait son voisin une somme de 6.000 francs.

Il est vrai que cet arrangement a été critiqué par les bonnes têtes de l'endroit. Une fois, c'était un jour de dimanche, il y a quatre ans de cela, M. de Rênal, revenant de l'église en costume de maire, vit de loin le vieux Sorel, entouré de ses trois fils, sourire en le regardant. Ce sourire a porté un jour fatal dans l'âme de M. le maire, il pense depuis lors qu'il eût pu obtenir l'échange à meilleur marché. (5–6)

The four uses of the imperfect tense in this passage 'occupait', 'faisait', 'animait' and 'était'—are consistent with the original time-sequence since they describe past states rather than events, but they also anticipate the use of the imperfect within the subsequent time-sequence and are thus the pivot of the transition. In two cases ('occupait' and 'était') they are closely linked to the first time-sequence by the immediate references to 'il y a six ans' and 'il y a quatre ans', and in the other two cases almost as closely linked by 'jouit [...] a obtenu' and 'il est vrai que'. But right in the middle of the four comes the first past historic of the novel: 'cette grâce lui vint'. Here begins the traditional time-sequence of the rest of the novel, but the change of temporal gear, so to speak, is oiled by the stylistic register: the ironic exaggeration of the phrase seems to require a past historic. (The less solemn 'cette grâce lui a été accordée' might have sufficed but not 'cette grâce lui est venue'). After this the immediate use of a *passé composé* ('il a donné') returns us once more to the original time-sequence, but only for ten lines, whereupon 'M. de Rênal vit de loin' replaces the expected 'M. de Rênal a vu de loin'. Again the narrator returns to the first time-sequence almost immediately with a *passé composé* ('a porté'), and the chapter finishes with two paragraphs in the present.

The second chapter begins by appearing to take the change to the second time-sequence for granted, and the first paragraph contains only two present tenses (of description) against four imperfects and one past historic. But again the imperfects are consistent with the first time-sequence, the past historic is 'excused' by the ironic exaggeration of 'l'heureuse nécessité d'immortaliser son administration', and the second paragraph returns us almost at once to the first time-sequence. Now the first pluperfect is introduced, still within the first time-sequence, and, as if to obscure it further, it is followed by two bold references to the present of narration itself: 'le parapet de ce mur s'élève maintenant de quatre pieds au-dessus du sol' and 'on le garnit en ce moment avec des dalles de pierre de taille' (though of course the volunteering of these pieces of information implies that the reader-traveller is no longer 'present' in Verrières). Chapter ii continues for a further two paragraphs in the present before the narrative shifts once more into the second time-sequence with 'ce jeune ecclésiastique fut envoyé de Besançon' and 'un vieux chirurgien-major [...] osa bien un jour'. The abruptness of this shift is lessened in the first case by the 'il y a quelques années' which follows and, in the second, by the reported speech of M. de Rênal. While this piece of reported speech is introduced by a past historic, its 'presentness' tends to obscure the fact that we are now in the second time-sequence. More importantly, the three past historics just used seem to create a temporal context that is situated between the first and the second time-sequences: one would expect either three *passé composé* or three pluperfects, but instead the past historic is now used as an ambiguous, transitional tense as the imperfect had been previously. The past historic rather than the imperfect has now become the pivot of the transition, and this in itself marks a definite shift in the direction of the eventual story-in-the-past.

After three paragraphs in the present, however, we revert to the use of the imperfect as a pivot, but this time to narrate the beginning of the story that will occupy the whole of the novel: 'c'était par un beau jour d'automne que M. de Rênal se promenait sur le Cours de la Fidélité.' At this point the transition from the present of the topographical guide to the past tense of conventional story-telling is almost complete. 'C'était' and 'se promenait', together with the imperfects that follow in the remainder of the paragraph, are part of the second time-sequence (the past story of Julien Sorel), yet they may still appear to be part of the first—i.e. we are still half-way between the two. There follows the beginning of the dialogue between M. and Mme de Rênal (briefly interrupted by a return to the present of narration: 'quoique je veuille vous parler [...]'), and this dialogue effects the last stage of transition; for 'disait M. de Rênal' and 'disait timidement Mme de Rênal' are temporally ambiguous phrases. Are M. and Mme de Rênal repeating themselves (i.e. are these examples of the iterative imperfect)? If not, we are still in the 'no man's land' between the two time-sequences; if they are, then the conventional past tense of narration has begun. It is probable that M. de Rênal's brief speech is one of many similar ones, given the narrator's subsequent reference to 'la longueur et les *ménagements savants* d'un dialogue de province', and we will discover in the next chapter that Mme de Rênal's question is certainly a repetition ('cette idée, qu'elle lui répétait timidement: "Quel mal ce monsieur de Paris peut-il faire aux prisonniers?"': 12). Meanwhile, between these two iterative[2] 'disait', the flashback

---

[2] While the context allows us to see these as examples of the iterative imperfect, in the rest of the novel many passages of dialogue and interior monologue are introduced by what Gérard Genette calls a 'pseudo-iterative' imperfect, i.e. one which presents scenes as repeated or habitual 'alors que la richesse et la précision des détails font qu'aucun lecteur ne peut croire sérieusement qu'elles se sont produites et reproduites ainsi, plusieurs fois, sans aucune variation.' See 'Discours du récit: *essai de méthode*', in *Figures III* (Paris, 1972), 65–282 (152). (Genette notes the presence of this eminently Proustian device in *Eugénie Grandet, Don Quixote* and *Lucien Leuwen*.) Cf. also Danièle Chatelain, 'Récit itératif et concrétisation', *Romanic Review*, 72 (1981), 304–16.

about M. Appert's visit contains the first pluperfect of the second time-sequence, so that in the middle of this dialogue which places two of the central characters directly before us for the first time, we have now moved more firmly into the time-sequence of the rest of the novel.

At the beginning of chapter iii the two pluperfects of the first paragraph appear to continue this sequence, but the past historics of the second and third ('le curé Chélan resta pensif' and 'se dit-il') mark a return to the use of the past historic as a pivot of transition (pluperfects would be more usual in this flashback). At the same time the first use of interior monologue in the novel, together with the extended dialogue between Chélan and Noiroud the gaoler, ensures that the present tense dominates even here. There is now a return to the present of narration: 'tels sont les faits qui [...]', but a present of narration which is no longer the same as the present of the story: 'dans ce moment ils servaient de texte à la petite discussion.' (If we compare this with the earlier 'on le garnit en ce moment avec des dalles de pierre de taille', the shift into the past is clear.) This is followed by another flashback in which, thanks now to the use of the pluperfect ('faites-moi destituer, s'était écrié le vieux curé': 12), the transition we have been tracing is definitively completed, and we now come to the first action and first statement of the novel which are narrated 'correctly' in the past historic: the Rênals' second child climbed on to the parapet and M. de Rênal announced that he wanted to employ Julien Sorel. The hero of the novel and the conventional narrative in the past arrive together. In the remainder of the chapter the dialogue is recorded in the past historic, the flashbacks (to the pasts of M. and Mme de Rênal) employ the pluperfect, and the final sentence demonstrates by a verbal reminder how far we have come along the temporal road since the first sentence of the novel: 'il passait, avec raison, pour le personnage le plus aristocratique de Verrières.'

Taking, as it were, two steps forward and one step back, we have moved from a narrative in the present to a narrative in the past. Yet there is no loss of immediacy: the presentness of the guide-book is gradually replaced by the presentness of direct speech, dialogue and interior monologue, and the persistence of references to the present of narration serves to maintain the link with the first temporal sequence of the novel in which narrator, reader and character were coeval. And it is these devices, as well as that of *style indirect libre* (first evident in chapter v: 'pourquoi ne serait-il pas aimé de l'une d'elles, comme Bonaparte, pauvre encore, avait été aimé de la brillante Mme de Beauharnais?': 23), which are to be used throughout the novel and which are to lend it that 'allure d'une *chose présente*'[3] which is its hallmark.

In its first sentence *Le Rouge et le Noir* evokes not only a present reality but also a world of illusion, and the way in which it confronts the reader with a problem of interpretation is typical of the novel as a whole. The verbal phrase 'peut passer' prompts a number of readings: Verrières can rightly be considered one of the prettiest towns in the Franche-Comté; Verrières may pass for one of the prettiest towns in the Franche-Comté (whereas in actual fact …); Verrières, just as well as any other town, can pass as one of the prettiest towns in the Franche-Comté. The first of these readings is apparently confirmed by the two sentences that follow:

ses maisons blanches avec leurs toits pointus de tuiles rouges s'étendent sur la pente d'une colline, dont des touffes de vigoureux châtaigniers marquent les moindres sinuosités. Le Doubs coule à quelques centaines de pieds au-dessous de ses fortifications bâties jadis par les Espagnols, et maintenant ruinées.

Pretty touches of colour, a varied landscape, some charming ruins, a dash of history, the elegant turn of phrase, these suggest the reliable world of the guide-book or the familiar world of the novel which establishes its pleasant setting before the appearance of the protagonists. But already we may discern the prettiness of the chocolate-box, perceive a certain artificiality in the regular attachment of epithet to noun and in the rather conscious pursuit of concision,[4] and soon we discover the truth about the prettiness of Verrières. It consists in what one can see *from* Verrières, either the view beyond M. de Rênal's house to the 'ligne d'horizon formée par les collines de la Bourgogne, et qui semble faite à souhait pour le plaisir des yeux' or the view from the Cours de la Fidélité ('une des vues les plus pittoresques de France',) which has often been enjoyed by the narrator and is conducive to 'la rêverie du voyageur'. We discover too why it is good to look away from Verrières—from its textile-factories as well as from the deafening and dehumanizing

---

[3] Prévost, *Création*, 322.
[4] Whereas the falseness of the repetition of 'tirant sur le bleu' should perhaps be seen as an authorial lapse.

nail-factory that is the source of M. de Rênal's fortune. Admittedly M. de Rênal's gardens are twice said to be magnificent, but we learn that the word 'magnifique' is as ironic as the polite traveller's enquiry about 'cette belle fabrique de clous' and is rather, one supposes, the term used by the inhabitants of Verrières and by M. de Rênal himself. They are magnificent because they are 'remplis de murs': they are not 'pittoresques'. And the same goes for the plane-trees that shade the Cours de la Fidélité: these too are introduced as 'magnifiques' but in the narrator's eyes they resemble 'par leur têtes basses, rondes et aplaties, à la plus vulgaire des plantes potagères'. It would be much better if they had 'ces formes magnifiques qu'on leur voit en Angleterre'. Magnificence, as much as prettiness, is in the eye of the beholder.

Even if we allow that picturesque views can make for a pretty town, we soon learn that such prettiness is only superficial. The principal merit of the fine view to the hills of Burgundy is that it permits the traveller to forget 'l'atmosphère empestée des petits intérêts d'argent dont il commence à être asphyxié'. Throughout chapters i and ii there is a movement from what pleases the eye to what disgusts the soul, from what once was fine to what now is reprehensible. Thus, in the town's mayor:

au total sa figure ne manque pas d'une certaine régularité: on trouve même, au premier aspect, qu'elle réunit à la dignité du maire de village cette sorte d'agrément qui peut encore se rencontrer avec quarante-huit ou cinquante ans. Mais bientôt le voyageur parisien est choqué d'un certain air de contentement de soi et de suffisance mêlé à je ne sais quoi de borné et de peu inventif. On sent enfin que le talent de cet homme-là se borne à se faire payer bien exactement ce qu'on lui doit, et à payer lui-même le plus tard possible quand il doit.

Compare too the town's industry: the sawmills may constitute 'une industrie fort simple et qui procure un certain bien-être à la majeure partie des habitants plus paysans que bourgeois' but it is the textile-factories that have enriched the bourgeois. And then there is the town's scale of values: a 'bonne tête' knows a bad buy when he sees one, a 'mauvaise tête' prefers the designs of Italian masons to the monstrous walls so dear to M. de Rênal.

The reader too is included in this process of revelation, and in the middle of chapter ii the narrator confirms our second reading of the first sentence:

rapporter du revenu est la raison qui décide de tout dans cette petite ville qui vous semblait si jolie. L'étranger qui arrive, séduit par la beauté des fraîches et profondes vallées qui l'entourent, s'imagine d'abord que ses habitants sont sensibles au *beau*; ils ne parlent que trop souvent de la beauté de leurs pays: on ne peut pas nier qu'ils n'en fassent grand cas; mais c'est parce qu'elle attire quelques étrangers dont l'argent enrichit les aubergistes, ce qui, par le mécanisme de l'octroi, *rapporte du revenu à la ville*.

The reader began the novel as a traveller walking through the town and seeing only the surface of things. Now he is a stranger, an outsider, beguiled by extrinsic beauty and fondly imbuing others with his own aesthetic sensibility, while all the time he is part of a materialistic world and a source of financial gain. A gullible tourist— and a book-buyer?

Finally the third reading of the opening sentence: 'Verrières, just as well as any other town, can serve as one of the prettiest, etc.' Only in the final sentence of the novel (in the last footnote) do we learn that Verrières does not after all exist. Whether or not we suspected as much is less important than the reason for Verrières's invention: 'pour éviter de toucher à la vie privée'. In this final *envoi* of the novel the narrator's remarks about the tyranny of 'what people will say' constitute a reprise of his comments in the final paragraph of chapter i on the 'gens sages et modérés qui distribuent la considération en Franche-Comté':

dans le fait, ces gens sages y exercent le plus ennuyeux *despotisme*; c'est à cause de ce vilain mot que le séjour des petites villes est insupportable, pour qui a vécu dans cette grande république qu'on appelle Paris. La tyrannie de l'opinion, et quelle opinion! est aussi *bête* dans les petites villes de France qu'aux Etats-Unis d'Amérique.

Here are the remaining answers to the questions posed by the first sentence. Verrières is not only small but petty and, far from being pretty, the ugly word of despotism, the despotism of worrying what people will say, shows there is neither freedom nor frankness in this corner of the Franche-Comté.[5] At the same time, if this tyranny is a sign of stupidity and, as the footnote explains, an invasion of privacy, then the fictional nature of Verrières—'pour éviter de toucher à la vie privée'—is a sign of intelligence. The tourist finds that he has

[5] The fact that one cannot always equate the narrator with Henri Beyle/Stendhal is illustrated here by a comment in Stendhal's diary, dated 20 Oct. 1823: 'je suis au milieu de Francs-Comtois, que je trouve les gens les plus francs du monde' (*OI*, ii. 70).

bought, not a *Guide Bleu* to the Jura mountains, but an enlightening fiction.

In the opening chapters of the novel the reader is thus led through three stages of a hermeneutic journey corresponding to the three meanings of its opening sentence. At first he believes in appearances and is taken in by the subtle narrative techniques which create an illusion of presentness. Then he is shown the truth beneath these appearances and realizes that he must place this present moment within a broader, different context. Finally it is suggested to him that the appearances of the imaginary may serve to express a more profound view of reality. Just such a journey awaits the reader-tourist in the novel as a whole.

3

'Une chose présente': the use
of the present tense

'Tous les temps des verbes ont une influence différente
sur l'âme.'

(JL, i. 460)

SINCE Jean Prévost's analysis of 'l'allure d'une chose présente' in *Le Rouge et le Noir*, critics have justifiably, if infrequently, stressed this aspect of Stendhalian narration,[1] but one wonders nevertheless whether due credit has been given to Stendhal's narrative art in this respect. Since Proust, the use of the 'éternel imparfait' in the novels of Flaubert, and particularly in *Madame Bovary*, has received much attention, and there is now widespread admiration for the way in which Flaubert, by combining the imperfects of description, repeated action and *style indirect libre*, manages to create the sense of a static, monotonous world and to blur the outlines of fact and fantasy to the point where even the most actively participating reader finds it impossible to 'conclure'. Most especially, the Flaubertian imperfect puts the description of place and physical appearance, the relation of events, and the inner musings of the protagonists all on a par. In *Le Rouge et le Noir* the present tense operates in a similar way (if with quite different effects), for it is the tense of the narrator's intrusions, the reader's putative reactions and the characters' discourse, their interior monologue, dialogue and letters.

---

[1] See for example Josiane Attuel, *Le Style de Stendhal. Efficacité et romanesque* (Bologna and Paris, 1980), 564: '*Le Rouge et le Noir* est dominé par une présence obsédante, celle du Temps.' Cf. also Hans Boll Johansen, *Stendhal et le roman. Essai sur la structure du roman stendhalien* (Aran and Copenhagen, 1979), ch. v; Charles J. Stivale, 'Le vraisemblable temporel dans *Le Rouge et le Noir*', *Stendhal Club*, 21 (1978/9), 299–315; and Christof Weiand, '*Ernestine* prototype de la narration stendhalienne', *Stendhal Club*, 26 (1983/4), 263–79, and *Die Gerade und der Kreis: Zeit und Erzählung in den Romanen Stendhals* (Frankfurt am Main, 1984). See also below, notes 6 to III. 4 and 5–7 to III. 5.

(i) *The present of the narrator*

The present tense is used by the narrator in a number of different ways. We have already seen its use to suggest the present reality of Verrières, and this *topographical* or *geographical* present continues to be employed throughout the novel. We learn of the little wood above Verrières, 'qu'on appelle le Belvédère, et qui domine le Cours de la Fidélité' (33) and of present plans to widen the streets of the town. Bray-le-Haut and its famous relic, Vergy—M. de Rênal's 'château', local traditions and nearby mountain walks—Besançon, the Rhine, all are described in the present of the guide-book. So too the physiognomy of Verrières's peasants and their cunning, what a sawmill looks like, the nature of mattress stuffing, the meanings given to certain words (139, 174). And of course the novel is full of comments in the present tense on various aspects of provincial and Parisian mores, on democracy and its consequences, on the Church, not to mention the odd remark about the way the Russians imitate the French but at a remove of fifty years or the moral conclusions to be drawn from the way in which a seminarist may eat a boiled egg.

Such comments in the *sociological* present are what constitute the *chronique* of contemporary France mentioned in the novel's sub-titles, the *portrait de mœurs* of which Stendhal makes so much in his projected review of the novel. These comments are original not only for their scope and directness—and as such they have contributed to Stendhal's reputation as a 'realist'—but also for the subtlety with which they are blended into the text. Already discreet in their brevity—often only a sentence, rarely more than a paragraph in length—they seem to spring naturally from the story itself rather than to be the observations which it is the function of the story merely to illustrate. Indeed on occasions one has the impression that a given comment may be the result of generalizing from one example, an example afforded by the story itself. In the account of the early stages of the relationship between Julien and Mme de Rênal we read:

dans une petite ville de l'Aveyron ou des Pyrénées, le moindre incident eût été rendu décisif par le feu du climat. Sous nos cieux plus sombres, un jeune homme pauvre, et qui n'est qu'ambitieux parce que la délicatesse de son cœur lui fait un besoin de quelques-unes des jouissances que donne l'argent, voit tous les jours une femme de trente ans, sincèrement sage, occupée de ses enfants, et qui ne prend nullement dans les romans des exemples de conduite. Tout va lentement, tout se fait peu à peu dans les provinces, il y a plus de naturel. (36–7)

This supposedly general truth about provincial love-affairs fits the protagonists so exactly that the particularity of their past story is assimilated into the generality of present truth. Yet this particular passage also operates the other way round: concealed in the relative clause 'qui n'est qu'ambitieux parce que la délicatesse de son cœur lui fait un besoin de quelques-unes des jouissances que donne l'argent' is a general 'truth' which is designed to make us view Julien's desire to 'faire fortune' as an indication of sensitivity. And this manipulation of the reader's moral reactions further enhances the immediacy of the story of Julien Sorel by increasing our sympathy for him. The *sociological* present, then, bridges the gap between narrative past and reading present not only temporally but morally.

The same is true of what one might call the *sententious* present. With the narrator as travel-guide and sociologist comes the narrator as moralist. The novel is sown with generalizations and maxims that suggest a knowable and typifiable humanity of which the protagonists themselves are also part, and a realm of common experience which embraces narrator, reader and character. From the paltry 'le malheur diminue l'esprit' (348) to the original, if debatable, 'les vraies passions sont égoïstes' (128) these maxims invite the reader's judgement and accordingly prompt him to consult his own experience, thereby perhaps calling to his mind a situation in which he may have been exactly comparable with the character in the novel whose situation has given rise to the maxim. Stendhal is here using a familiar device,[2] particularly when such general observations are introduced, as they often are in *Le Rouge et le Noir*, by demonstrative adjectives: 'cet air dur que le danger donne aux hommes' (55), 'cet état d'étonnement et de trouble inquiet où tombe l'âme qui vient d'obtenir ce qu'elle a longtemps désiré' (82–3), etc. These demonstratives seem to invite the reader's complicity, even to shame him into acceptance of what is said, and thereby, of course, to acknowledge the 'reality' of the fictional event which has given rise to them. For all the familiarity of this device it nevertheless serves once more to unite past and present, and as with the sociological present there are instances where the maxim or generalization seems to be prompted

---

[2] See Prévost, *Création*, 496–7; Blin, *Problèmes du roman*, 245; Genette, ' "Stendhal" ', 190; and Attuel, *Style*, 323. See also Genette, 'Vraisemblance et motivation', in *Figures II* (Paris, 1969), 71–99, especially 78–81. For a sophisticated account of sententiousness in literature see Geoffrey Bennington, *Sententiousness and the Novel. Laying Down the Law in Eighteenth-Century French Fiction* (Cambridge, 1985), particularly 3–21.

by the story itself: 'à vingt ans, l'idée du monde et de l'effet à y produire l'emporte sur tout' (63). More especially, there are a number of decidedly partisan remarks (which will be discussed later under the heading of 'Perspective') which mean that the sententious present, like the sociological present, manipulates the reader's moral values to the point where he will either accept the narrator's moral outlook or at least understand the moral viewpoint from which the narrator regards his characters.

Finally there is the present of story-telling, or *narrative* present: 'nous passons sous silence une foule de petites aventures' (253), 'nous supprimons le reste du système comme cynique' (265), etc. Several such references exist in the novel as evidence of Stendhal's use of the time-honoured technique whereby flashbacks, omissions and other narrative requirements are attributed to authorial licence. Similar, though more original, is the abbreviation of the description of the king's visit to Bray-le-Haut because all the local newspapers carried nothing else for a fortnight and the suggestion that we consult the *Gazette des Tribunaux* to see why the narrator only gives 'un extrait bien pâle' of Julien's minutes of the meeting of the 'note secrète' conspirators. But it is not so much for narrative convenience that Stendhal employs this device, if indeed at all, but rather to suggest an absence of imagination and artistry and to imply that the story pre-exists the act of narration. This illusion (illusion because there is much more to *Le Rouge et le Noir* than the stories of Berthet and Lafargue) is enhanced by the narrator's comments on Julien himself: 'j'avoue que la faiblesse dont Julien fait preuve dans ce monologue me donne une pauvre opinion de lui' (134), 'ici éclate dans tout son jour la présomption de Julien' (185), 'c'est, selon moi, l'un des plus beaux traits de son caractère' (407), etc. Such remarks suggest that the character is quite independent of his creator, and where these comments are critical, the illusion of autonomy is strengthened by the notion that the narrator is having to record something of which he does not approve. This device, familiar enough in novels before Stendhal (cf. *Tom Jones*), can appear rather lame and artificial (as it does sometimes in Gide), but in *Le Rouge et le Noir* it is saved by the fact that the comments are often not to be taken at face value. Thus, in the second of the two examples quoted above, Julien's presumption consists in his not allowing the sound of church bells to put him in mind of the wages of the bell-ringers. Instead Julien's soul 'errait dans les espaces imaginaires', something of which the narrator quite clearly approves. What we have here therefore is an example of Stendhalian antiphrasis. This will be discussed at more length later, but it may be suggested in advance that its use adds depth to the use of the present of narration. Not only does the latter suggest a story unfolding in the present and beyond the control of the narrator but also it prompts the reader to examine the facts themselves in the light of the moral values suggested to him in the commentary. The story may appear to pre-exist the act of narration but the moral interpretation one lays upon this story does not, and in this domain the autonomy of the reader is equal to that of the narrator or the character.

The narrator's numerous interventions in *Le Rouge et le Noir* constitute one of the novel's major characteristics, and this obtrusive presence may irritate or entertain according to taste. Certainly it has helped to perpetuate the confusion of Henri Beyle and Stendhal and to encourage biographically based interpretations of the novel, interpretations which reduce the role of the reader to that of a passive accomplice in the wish-fulfilling fantasy of a supreme egotist. But nothing could be further from the truth. By creating a narrator who appears to have no control over the facts of his narration and yet is possessed of very definite views on the nature of those facts, Stendhal inscribes the act of reading in the text itself. The narrator interprets or reads the facts in such an individual way that the reader himself is prompted to use his own judgement—which may or may not coincide with the narrator's. In his book *Stendhal et les problèmes du roman* Georges Blin argues that the interventions in the text, far from destroying the 'illusion' of the novel, transform the nature of fictional illusion: from being a simple 'méprise' it becomes a game of

intentionnalité sympathique, telle que, pour être annexés à ses créatures, il nous faille avoir été annexés à leur créateur [...] Il importe, à cette fin, que la voix que nous entendons soit plus que la forme audible des faits: si elle avoue la contingence du narrateur, la voix rétablit devant nous le présent de la narration [...] Sans doute ne s'agit-il là que d'un *comme si* de l'audition—le roman ne relevant pas moins de la fiction comme fiction d'un récit que comme récit d'une fiction [...] Si, cependant, le conteur mérite d'occuper de sa personne notre attention, nous escortons d'autant mieux l'événement conté que, dans cette illusion de l'écoute, nous ne pouvons pas refuser notre escorte au conteur contant.[3]

---

[3] p. 339. For brevity's sake this quotation is taken from Blin's summary of his arguments.

Blin does not distinguish between the narrator and Stendhal and, as has already been noted, his paradoxical thesis, for all its many insights into Stendhal's narrative techniques, still reduces the Stendhalian novel to a piece of biographical evidence. Yet his account of the 'intrusions d'auteur' may serve as a conclusion to this section on the present of the narrator. It is by making of the narrator (and not of the author, as Blin says) a recognizable character[4] that Stendhal achieves the liberation of the reader. Because the narrator appears contingent and relative, the reader is free to place his own interpretation on the facts laid before him. These facts have not been pre-digested, there is no pre-established pattern into which they fit, so there is still room for the reader's own judgements to come into play.

(ii) The present of the fictional reader

The use of the present tense to refer to the reader's putative reactions to the narrator's story at once places the reader on the same temporal plane as the narrator and the characters. Introduced anonymously into the novel as a tourist, the reader is soon personally identified ('cette scie à bois, dont la position singulière sur la rive du Doubs vous a frappé en entrant à Verrières') and then personally addressed ('quoique je veuille vous parler de la province pendant deux cents pages, je n'aurai pas la barbarie de vous faire subir la longueur et les *ménagements savants* d'un dialogue de province'). Here in one sentence narrator, reader and characters (M. and Mme de Rênal) come together, and the various subsequent references to 'le lecteur' ('vous' having served as a transitional term between 'le voyageur' and 'le lecteur') serve to prolong the illusion of a narrator speaking directly to us about people whose actions are as visible to us as to him.

We have seen how the autonomy of the reader is achieved by the way in which the narrator is endowed with such a striking, individual presence that we come to see him as relative and as by no means the only one entitled to moral judgement on the actions of the characters. The reader of *Le Rouge et le Noir*, in so far as he is mentioned in the text, is a multiple personality. He may be a Parisian

---

[4] Character, or 'personnage', is the appropriate term here, for the narrator has not only been to Verrières, he also knows the people who frequent the La Mole salon. See *RN*, 247, and the implications of the use of the present tense and the *passé composé* in the accounts of the comte Chalvet and M. Balland.

traveller (4) or Parisian *lycéen* (155), he may have a sense of humour (172) and be averse to sombre portrayals of seminary life (177), or he may find the reception rooms of the Hôtel de la Mole 'aussi tristes que magnifiques' (229) and the oppressive atmosphere of Mme de Fervaques's salon simply boring (396). There again he may be so incensed at the recent erection of white walls to divide the gardens of Malmaison that he interrupts the narrator's account of Julien's tearful transports of delight (223), or he may be one of those 'âmes glacées' who will regard Mathilde's love-struck piano-playing as so unbecoming as to verge on the indecent (341). The explicit references to the reader in *Le Rouge et le Noir*, limited though they are in number, serve to remind the individual reader that he too is relative and contingent and that the moral code and knowledge of life he brings to the novel may colour his interpretation of the facts as strongly as the narrator's has been. The present tense in which they are couched may bring narrator, reader and character together but it also underlines the fact that the present of the act of reading is provisional. If the characters develop in the novel, then so too perhaps does the reader.[5]

(iii) *The present of the characters*

If *Le Rouge et le Noir* has 'l'allure d'une chose présente', it is not only because of the interventions of the narrator and the involvement of the reader himself, but also because of the immediate way in which the characters appear before us—in their dialogue, interior monologue and letters. Despite the strong presence of the narrator the reader is permitted a direct and unfiltered view of the protagonists and may enjoy the illusion of access to a world of living human beings who speak and think quite independently of their creator. Of course the novel is famous for its interior monologues and, if Stendhal did not invent the device, he is certainly the first to make such extensive use of it. So familiar is this aspect that further commentary is redundant. Suffice it to say that its use is not, as Prévost and others have said or implied, restricted to the main characters. Chélan (10), Pirard (164, 169), Mme Derville (79), Croisenois (274), Mme de Fervaques (386), Frilair (443) and even

---

[5] For a fuller account of the fictional reader in the novel see Ann Jefferson, 'The Uses of Reading'.

Tanbeau (392) all have moments of interior monologue, however brief, in which we glimpse their inner selves and see them as more than mere components of the 'décor humain'.[6] Also it is worth repeating that the extensive use of interior monologue in the cases of Julien and Mathilde is absolutely in keeping with the cautious, cerebral approach to living they adopt (and with which their outbursts in speech or action, unaccompanied by interior monologue, contrast so effectively), while a study of the much more limited use of it in the case of Mme de Rênal reveals not just that she is more natural and spontaneous, more 'unthinking', but also that when she does reflect inwardly, she does so briefly. For this suggests appropriately her rapid, instinctive apprehension of the truth in contrast to the long concerted musings of Julien and Mathilde who are beset by doubt and suspicion and mentally explore each situation from every possible angle.[7]

The use of dialogue in the novel to achieve 'presentness' seems by contrast much less original, yet nevertheless it reveals certain distinctive Stendhalian features. Lampedusa has commented on the way in which the dialogue in Le Rouge seems natural because it is unmemorable.[8] Part of the reason for this is that the dialogues do not appear as major set pieces, with the possible exception of the encounter between M. and Mme de Rênal in I. xxi ('Dialogue avec un maître'). Instead the dialogue is broken up by short passages of interior monologue, style indirect libre or narratorial intervention and is also frequently presented as merely a snippet of a much longer dialogue (as in I. ii and elsewhere). Alternatively we may be given the words of one of the speakers while those of the other(s) are reported in indirect speech.[9] Mainly this technique contributes to the rapid pace of the novel. By truncating the dialogue in this way Stendhal is able to suggest the 'presentness' of his characters while preventing the dialogue from occupying a space in the text disproportionate to its importance in the story.

---

[6] Prévost, Création, 326.

[7] See Dominique Trouiller, 'Le monologue intérieur dans Le Rouge et le Noir', Stendhal Club, 11 (1968/9), 245–77. See also John T. Booker, 'Style direct libre: the case of Stendhal', Stanford French Review, 9 (1985), 137–51. Booker distinguishes between interior monologue and what he calls 'style direct libre' where the usual tags (e.g. 'se dit-il') are omitted. He finds that Stendhal makes more extensive use of 'style direct libre' (as well as interior monologue) in Le Rouge than in any of his other novels and that this contributes substantially to its 'presentness' (147).

[8] 'Notes sur Stendhal', Stendhal Club, 2 (1959/60), 155–68 (161). These notes, written in 1955, show a great debt to Jean Prévost's La Création chez Stendhal.

[9] See Prévost, Création, 325.

It is interesting to note once again that dialogue, like interior monologue, is not the prerogative of the main characters nor indeed necessarily associated with moments of dramatic encounter between characters, be they major or secondary. Often, indeed, dialogue is employed to lend immediacy to some aspect of the narrative which might otherwise seem too discursive. This is the case in the first chapter of Part II where the survey of political life in France and the comparison of Paris and the provinces, serving as a reprise of Part I and introduction to the Paris of Part II, is brought to life by being presented as a conversation between two characters who do not appear elsewhere in the novel (though Falcoz is known to us via M. de Rênal, and Saint-Giraud indirectly through mention of his brother during the scene of the assigning of a lease in Part I). Similarly, at the beginning of the description of the ball given by the duc de Retz, Stendhal establishes the social scene which will serve as the context for the reciprocal 'cristallisation' of Julien and Mathilde by presenting snatches of conversation which are merely attributed to 'un jeune homme à moustaches', 'son voisin', 'un troisième' (270–1). Indeed much of the description of the ball is given over to the dialogues in which Altamira is a participant, and the dialogues serve to suggest the public animation of a social gathering in contrast to the silent, private dreams of Julien and Mathilde. And both here and in the case of Julien's coach journey with Falcoz and Saint-Giraud it is entirely appropriate that conversations should be the principal activity.

Yet dialogue also occurs, apparently incidentally, where indirect discourse or interior monologue would have sufficed. Mathilde's dim view of the insipid lookalikes that constitute the well-born youth of Paris is already evident from her thoughts at the ball and from her cult of Marguerite de Navarre, yet her charmingly named cousin Mlle de Sainte-Hérédité makes a brief appearance as interlocutress for Mathilde in a dialogue on this subject (294). But then the following paragraph reveals the point: we are being shown an example of Mathilde's somewhat colourful language, language which only an intimate conversation with a like-minded female cousin allows her to display. As is often the case in Stendhal's novels, the evidence precedes the commentary or explanation, and dialogue, even when seemingly gratuitous, allows the characters to appear before the reader as they are and before the narrator has a chance, as it were, to add the gloss with which the reader may or may not agree.

At the same time the reader is permitted not only to hear these dialogues but to see them, for they are often accompanied by information as to the tone and gesture with which the words are delivered. The cry and the whisper, the shriek and the strangled tone, pallor and suffusion, these are the coded signs that accompany the tags 'dit-il', 'répondit-elle', etc. and which the narrator leaves it to the reader to translate respectively into surprise and conspiracy, glee and anguish, timidity or duplicity, anger or embarrassment.

When the characters are absent from one another and yet communicate, the immediacy of the dialogue is replaced by the other immediacy of the letter. Julien's humorous prediction that 'ceci va être le roman par lettres' (315) as Mathilde bombards him with yet another letter from the door of the library proves almost true. Her first letter to Julien, of which we are given an extract (307), is the first of many, and we are shown all or part of eleven separate letters in the last fourteen chapters of the novel, while several others are mentioned. In the case of Mme de Rênal's letter to the marquis de La Mole the reader is once again placed directly in front of the evidence, and it is up to him—here in the absence of any subsequent narratorial comment—to consider what connexion exists between it and the attempt on the life of its supposed authoress. The other letters, mostly the correspondence between Mathilde and her father, are less important, but once more their language and tone allow the reader to judge for himself how this relationship stands at this point and not to have to rely on the opinions of the narrator. The written word is also 'une chose présente'.[10]

---

[10] See Margaret Mauldon, 'Generic survival: *Le Rouge et le Noir* and the Epistolary Tradition', *French Studies*, 38 (1984), 414–22.

4

Anticipation and flashback

'Chronique: recueil de faits historiques rapportés dans l'ordre de
leur succession.'

(Dictionnaire Robert)

AFTER consideration of Stendhal's use of the present tense in the
novel, it will now be useful to examine how the illusion of presentness
is further enhanced by the limited use of anticipation and
flashback.[1] Certainly there is very little anticipation in the sense of
revelation to the reader of what will happen later in the story (though
there is, as will be seen later, a quite considerable and complex play
with the reader's expectations). There would appear to be only four
instances of it and the revelations are all things which Julien will
later discover: ways of simulating religious fervour (44), Frilair's
special talent as an agent for the Congrégation (196), the secrets to
a successful salon (242), and where Mathilde was hidden in the
courtroom during his trial (464). None of these reveals any major
event in Julien's future career. The first three serve rather to underline
Julien's innocence, while the fourth is more a convenient way of
informing us of Mathilde's presence. In his analysis of the novel
Prévost argues that 'l'auteur ne feint jamais d'ignorer quoi que ce
soit'[2] but the one thing he does feign not to know is the future, and
Blin is right to speak of the narrative of *Le Rouge et le Noir* as 'cette
marche vers l'inédit'.[3] One ingredient of its presentness is that we
never know what will happen next.

As for flashback, Prévost again was the first critic to consider this
aspect of the novel. 'Nous allons toujours de l'avant', he writes, 'et
sauf la brève page sur l'enfance de Julien jamais un retour en arrière:

---

[1] For an account of these in *Armance* see Charles J. Stivale, 'Ordre et duration:
la structuration temporelle d'*Armance*', *Stendhal Club*, 24 (1981/2), 141–56.

[2] *Création*, 310.

[3] *Problèmes du roman*, 153. Cf. Peter Brooks, *Reading for the Plot. Design and
Intention in Narrative* (Oxford, 1984), 76; 'the entire narrative mode of Stendhal's
novels is in fact markedly metonymic, indeed virtually serial, giving the impression of
a perpetual flight forward, a constant self-invention at the moment and of the moment.'

c'est la *chronique*, comme dit le titre du livre.'[4] We begin at the beginning and move forward, not *in medias res* in the manner of Balzac, having then to move backwards before the story begins. As John T. Booker points out in his important article 'Retrospective Movement in the Stendhalian Narration',[5] critics since Prévost have all tended to agree with him and to perpetuate the notion that the novel's 'allure d'une chose présente' results from a simple, even naïve, narrative line.[6] Booker himself is almost the only critic to have challenged this view. He notes correctly that there are many more flashbacks and what he calls 'temporal overlaps' than Prévost and others have acknowledged and shows how Stendhal has sought to disguise these: first, by reducing the number of pluperfects and using the past historic and imperfect as if no flashback had occurred; secondly, by introducing the flashbacks surreptitiously by general moral observations for which the flashbacks then appear to provide atemporal explanation or illustration, a procedure which can operate in reverse to return the reader to the narrated present. Equally there are brief flashbacks which allow the same event to be perceived from different points of view. All of this leads Booker to conclude that far from detracting from the 'allure d'une chose présente', the retrospective movement actually enhances it by allowing us to perceive directly how several characters react to the same things.

Taking flashbacks to events which occurred wholly or partly before the novel began, what Genette calls *analepses externes* and *analepses mixtes*,[7] already the first chapters have been seen to contain several: the construction of M. de Rênal's garden, the history of the Cours de la Fidélité, M. Appert's visit, M. de Rênal's and Valenod's visit to Chélan, the past histories of M. and Mme de Rênal. But the

---

[4] *Création*, 322.   [5] *Romanic Review*, 72 (1981), 26–38.

[6] See Jean Pouillon, 'La Création chez Stendhal. A propos du livre de Jean Prévost', *Les Temps modernes*, 7 (1951–2), 173–82 (179): 'on ne trouve guère chez lui ces présentations savantes, ces retours en arrière ou ces anticipations, qui supposent chez l'auteur une maîtrise extérieure de ses personnages [...] Les héros stendhaliens sont donc avant tout: présents'; Bardèche, *Stendhal romancier*, 223: 'il raconte une vie [...] Et cette vie même, il la raconte sans malice, sans détours, il suit l'ordre du temps'; Blin, *Problèmes du roman*, 152–3: 'de ce présent, le romancier [...] ne se reconnaîtra pas le droit de sortir: se bornant à accompagner le héros et à convoyer l'action, il se trouve tenu de s'interdire les prolepses et les retours récapitulatifs'; Attuel, *Style*, 130: 'le récit stendhalien est un présent dans le passé: dans le passé où il nous replace, nous suivons une action qui se déroule au moment présent, du début à sa fin, sans retour en arrière ni projection sur l'avenir, sans jeu complexe sur le temps dans l'ensemble de la composition de l'œuvre'.

[7] 'Discours du récit', 89–91.

forward movement of the narrative is maintained, not only by the modulation of tense already discussed, but also because each flashback is brief and serves as an explanation of the present—respectively, of the peculiar position of Sorel's sawmill, of the present construction of the Cours de la Fidélité, of M. de Rênal's 'air offensé', of why the Parisian's view of Mme de Rênal would be wrong, and of why Mme de Rênal is content with her husband. These flashbacks serve as a kind of running commentary and this is true of the great majority of such flashbacks in the rest of the novel.[8]

As for the *analepses internes*, or flashbacks to events which have occurred since the novel began, these too can serve as commentary on the main action,[9] but more often they allow us either to see the same event from different points of view[10] (as Booker argues) or to compare the intimate thoughts of the protagonists. Thus at the end of I. v we learn that Julien 'fut saisi d'une invincible timidité' in front of the wrought-iron gate at the entrance to the Rênal grounds, while 'l'extrême timidité de Mme de Rênal était déconcertée par l'idée de cet étranger' and 'le matin, bien des larmes avaient coulé, etc. Here the pluperfect and the adverbial phrase of time that precedes it allow us to talk unequivocally of flashback,[11] but in the case of other 'internal' flashbacks there is not at all the same sense of temporal overlap. In the following sentence, for example, the imperfect tense allows a shift in perspective that suggests continuation rather than retrospect: 'pendant que Mme de Rênal était en proie à ce qu'a de plus cruel la passion terrible dans laquelle le hasard l'avait engagée, Julien poursuivait son chemin gaiement au milieu

---

[8] See 17–18 ('dès sa première jeunesse [...] M. le maire'); 22–4 ('dès sa première enfance [...] il se pardonna'); 35–6 ('mais en sa qualité d'héritière [...] il fallait vivre': this passage is expertly analysed by Booker, art. cit.); 41–2 ('Mme de Rênal, riche héritière [...] le plus petit reproche'); 118–22 ('depuis l'instant [...] celle du galant'); 139–40 ('son existence triomphante [...] l'air audacieux envers lui'); 191–2 ('depuis dix ans [...] se disait-il'); 192–4 ('douze années auparavant [...] penser à l'abbé'); 301 ('fille d'un homme d'esprit [...] elle ne s'ennuya plus'); 424 ('les malheurs de l'émigration [...] le caractère de sa fille').

[9] e.g. 62–3: 'cependant la pauvre femme avait eu la preuve [...] elle lui ôta la main'.

[10] e.g. 98: 'une personne était plus heureuse [...] d'une noble poussière'.

[11] As we can in the following cases: 33–4 ('quelques jours avant la Saint-Louis [...] à M. Valenod'); 72–3 ('pendant son absence [...] les apparences singulières de sa maladie'); 85 ('au déjeuner [...] le danger qu'elle courait'); 122 ('elle était allée entendre la messe [...] où les prendre?'); 329–30 ('pendant que Julien [...] son existence entière); 456 ('pendant que l'âme de Julien [...] avait été prononcé'); 484 ('M. de Thaler, cet homme si riche [...] vingt-quatre ans').

des plus beaux aspects que puissent présenter les scènes de montagnes' (68).[12]

Without wishing to deny the finesse with which these flashbacks are disguised so as not to detract from the forward impetus of the narrative, one must nevertheless acknowledge that they are more or less inevitable. The majority of the 'external' flashbacks occur at the beginning of the novel as is to be expected in a traditional narrative which wants to introduce its main characters to the reader, while the 'internal' ones are generally consequent upon the periods of separation which occur between the lovers, either physical separation (Julien's absences) or psychological separation (cases of incomprehension, mistrust, quarrels). It is therefore all the more surprising to find that Stendhal seems voluntarily to create a need for flashback when a more straightforward narrative sequence would clearly be possible, and he does so at some of the climactic moments in the novel: Julien's first visit to Mme de Rênal's bedroom (81–4), Mathilde's declaration of her love (312–14), the shooting of Mme de Rênal (432–3), the day of the trial (459–60) and Julien's execution (487–8). In his essay on Stendhal Genette refers to this last event as a typical example of ' cette élision des temps forts [qui] est un des traits marquants du récit stendhalien'. For him what characterizes such a moment is the brevity of reference to the central event and a corresponding increase in attention to circumstantial detail, in this case the two paragraphs which precede the sentence: 'tout se passa simplement, convenablement, et de sa part sans aucune affectation' (487). The flashback which follows, says Genette, 'contribue encore à cet effacement de la mort en ressuscitant Julien durant l'espace d'une demi-page',[13] and he refers the reader to Jean Prévost's description of this moment as a kind of 'euthanasie littéraire'. For Genette, as indeed for Prévost, this elision of narrative is comparable with the classical rhetoric of the sublime,[14] and in the case of Julien's execution both critics are surely right. Yet this does not quite explain Stendhal's 'voluntary' use of flashback at the other climactic moments mentioned before.

It seems that in all five cases Stendhal has used flashback to preserve the suddenness of the event described: it is the elision which

---

[12] Cf. also 301–2: 'c'était pendant que ces grandes incertitudes [...] Mme de Rênal!'.

[13] ' "Stendhal" ', 181–2.

[14] Prévost, Création, 331; Genette, ' "Stendhal" ', 189.

creates the 'temps forts'. Thus the long flashback explaining how Mathilde came to write the letter to Julien in which she declares her love allows Julien's receipt of the letter to surprise us as much as it surprises him and thus to make us view his subsequent Mephistophelean glee with much greater tolerance and sympathy than prior knowledge of the letter-writer's feelings might have permitted. Similarly, the retrospective account of the exact ballistic and anatomical details[15] of the shooting preserves the brutality and shock-value of the act itself, while yet giving us the information which makes the survival of Mme de Rênal plausible. To the same end this particular flashback is followed by another which goes further back in time but is temporally symmetrical, namely the account of how Mme de Rênal came to write the letter which incited Julien to kill her. Again, this piece of information has been deferred so that we may experience Julien's shock on reading the letter.

In these two cases (Mathilde's letter and Julien's joy, Mme de Rênal's letter and Julien's fury) the function of the flashback is fairly clear: it serves to enhance the sense of immediacy by maintaining the element of surprise. But when one looks at the other instances of 'voluntary' flashback, things become more complex. In the case of Julien's trial, the first sentence of II. xli ('enfin parut ce jour tellement redouté de Mme de Rênal et de Mathilde') is followed by a retrospective account of the public interest aroused by the case and quite a long passage relating Mathilde's negotiations with Frilair and her subsequent conversation with Julien. Then we read 'le lendemain, à neuf heures', and we are back with the morning of the trial. To a certain extent one can assimilate this use of 'voluntary' flashback to the others in that the advent of the day of the trial appears sudden, but Stendhal could well have described the preparations for the trial in their 'correct' place without forfeiting the dramatic effect of his opening sentence. Or is he trying to keep us in suspense? Having announced the trial, does he then delay it to make us share the dread felt by Julien's mistresses or the impatience of the populace 'pour voir juger cette cause romanesque'? Whatever the answer, the use of flashback here seems slightly defective.[16]

---

[15] For a semiotic analysis of these, based on the work of A. J. Greimas and J. Courtés, see Jacques Geninasca, 'L'invention du détail vrai', *Stendhal Club*, 24 (1981/2), 388–402.

[16] Cf. Genette's comment on a similar hiatus in *A la recherche*, 'Discours du récit', 104–5.

The same is not true of the description of Julien's first visit to Mme de Rênal's bedroom. Here the essential information is conveyed in two sentences: 'comme elle lui parlait avec une extrême dureté, il fondit en larmes. Quelques heures après, quand Julien sortit de la chambre de Mme de Rênal, on eût pu dire en style de roman, qu'il n'avait plus rien à désirer'. The explanatory flashback that follows is as usual introduced in the pluperfect and then continued in the past historic. Then the dramatic moment is repeated, but from Mme de Rênal's point of view: 'mortellement effrayée de l'apparition de Julien, Mme de Rênal fut bientôt en proie aux plus cruelles alarmes. Les pleurs et le désespoir de Julien le troublaient vivement. Même quand elle n'eut plus rien à lui refuser, elle repoussait Julien loin d'elle, avec une indignation réelle, et ensuite se jetait dans ses bras.' But this time Julien's departure from the room is in its (chrono)logical place. Time seems momentarily to have been dislocated by their sexual encounter but is now reverting to normal. Yet not without a further loop, for the next chapter begins with half a page of renewed flashback to the moments immediately preceding Julien's departure from the room. Three returns to one event: perhaps the shock experienced by the protagonists and their consequent desire to make sense of what has happened is reflected in the manner of narration itself? Once again the narrative mode of Le Rouge et le Noir mirrors the experience of the characters.

What, finally, of Julien's execution? Here it may seem odd to speak of suddenness when Julien's death is known to be imminent. Yet the rapidity of the narrative from his last recorded speech to Mme de Rênal to the moment of execution nicely conveys the finality of death that comes as a shock however long it has been awaited. The poignancy of the moment is achieved not only by the crucial sentence itself ('tout se passa simplement, convenablement, et de sa part sans aucune affectation') in which the simplicity, rightness and lack of affectation evinced by Julien's last moments are reflected in the very style, but also by the absence of undue preparation (last words, final wishes, etc.) and of all references to the other characters. Information about these is then supplied by the retrospective passage which follows and which contains four separate flashbacks. The first, concerning Julien's previous conversation with Fouqué, explains the importance of the fine weather on the day of the execution and so offers the implicit consolation that Julien has realized his last ambition. The other three reveal Julien's arrangements in respect of

Mathilde and Mme de Rênal, of his child, and of his burial-place. Not only is there not just one flashback here (*pace* Genette), but also the information provided by the four flashbacks seems to be arranged in a temporal progression from two days before the execution to the day itself (with Fouqué's removal of Mathilde and Mme de Rênal) and then to the future (of Julien's child, of Julien's remains). Like the flashbacks involved in the description of Julien's visit to Mme de Rênal's bedroom (when, curiously, Julien is 'souffrant plus mille fois que s'il eût marché à la mort'), these ones may put us in mind of the shock-waves which follow an explosion. Only gradually, after four returns to the past, do we return to 'normal' time and the aftermath of Julien's death. The characters are still full of Julien's memory, but life must go on even after his death—if only for a page. Once he has been buried in his mountain-cave and once Mme de Rênal has joined him in whatever lies beyond the grave, the world of Julien Sorel ceases to exist. No more 'chose présente'. And the temporal sequence that began when the Rênal child clambered on to the parapet of the Cours de la Fidélité ends with the death of this tender mother who is also a faithful mistress. Time is up.

5

The passage of time

'Ce fut l'affaire d'un instant.'

(*passim*)

WE have seen how Stendhal's use of flashback contributes
paradoxically to the 'presentness' of *Le Rouge et le Noir*. Rather than
appearing to arrest the momentum of the novel it helps to preserve
the suddenness of some of the key moments in the narrative and even
to suggest a certain dislocation of time as felt by the characters
themselves. Each of these dramatic instants is like a pistol-shot, the
flashback its report. Where, however, the key moment is not attended
by circumstantial detail which it may be necessary to relate (what
Julien and Mme de Rênal said and felt before Julien left her room,
how Mathilde came to write her declaration of love, how Mme de
Rênal came to survive the shooting, the preparations for the trial,
or Julien's arrangements for the care of Mme de Rênal, Mathilde
and her unborn baby), then the suddenness is achieved by simple
brevity of narration: '[Mathilde] se trouva enceinte et l'apprit avec
joie à Julien' (413). So unexpected is this revelation, especially in
its context, that the reader's reaction is likely to be that of Julien:
'cette annonce frappa Julien d'un étonnement profond'; and the report
of this particular 'gunshot', of course, reverberates until the end of
the novel. Moments like this are highly characteristic of *Le Rouge
et le Noir*; if we do not know what the next moment will bring, that
moment seems also to arrive before we expected it. The novel takes
place in an immediate present, but the events of the present vanish
into the past with an extraordinary rapidity, leaving the reader with
a persistent sense of being overtaken. '*Le Rouge* halète', writes Jean-
Pierre Richard, 'c'est le roman d'un coureur qui oublie de reprendre
souffle',[1] while Prévost refers more poetically to 'ce galop de cheval
noir'.[2]

One of the problems facing any novelist in the recording of the
passage of time is to compress without sacrificing continuity and

[1] 'Connaissance et tendresse', 102.   [2] *Création*, 303.

coherence and yet without undue resort to the broad résumé which may destroy the immediacy of the subject.[3] Since the events of *Le Rouge et le Noir* cover a period of just under five years,[4] Stendhal's problem is considerably smaller in this respect than that faced by other 'imaginary biographers', yet for several critics he has failed to solve it. Georges Poulet, for example, takes the view that the Stendhalian accent on the 'moments heureux' in the lives of the characters, rich in perspective though they undoubtedly are (Julien on the scaffold, Fabrice discovering Clélia in prison, Lucien and Mme de Chasteller at the *Chasseur Vert*), nevertheless creates a sense of discontinuity: 'en aucun de ces épisodes, le moment ne se relie à l'ensemble des autres moments, ne forme avec eux cette totalité continue de l'existence accomplie, que nous donnent presque toujours, par exemple, les personnages de Flaubert, de Tolstoï, de Thomas Hardy, de Roger Martin du Gard.'[5] By living in the present the Stendhalian hero may lack 'une dimension essentielle, une certaine épaisseur qui est une épaisseur de durée'.[6] Agreeing with Poulet, Dominique Trouiller suggests that the use of interior monologue is a major contributing factor to this absence of 'durée': 'rigoureusement circonscrit à un moment isolé de durée, [le monologue] relève d'une perception fondamentalement discontinue du temps: des plongées verticales brisant la ligne horizontale du récit.'[7] For both these critics *Le Rouge et le Noir* is essentially a sequence of rich but unconnected moments: the *passage* of time is absent and Stendhal has sacrificed continuity to immediacy. Jean Prévost, on the other hand, takes a more positive view. The interior monologues, he argues with some justification, are themselves compressions, and 'realistic' compressions at that:

c'est que le monologue intérieur, le projet, la réflexion vraie de chacun de nous n'est qu'une longue répétition, à demi articulée, de certains mots,

[3] *Création*, 320. Cf. Percy Lubbock's distinction between 'scenic' and 'panoramic' narration in *The Craft of Fiction*, 2nd edn (London, 1965), 72.

[4] See Henri Martineau's edition for Classiques Garnier (1960), 533-7.

[5] 'Stendhal' in *Etudes sur le temps humain*, vol. iv (*Mesure de l'instant*) (Paris, 1968), 250. Cf. Paul de Man's qualified agreement with this statement at the end of 'The Rhetoric of Temporality' in *Blindness and Insight*, 2nd edn (London, 1983), 227-8.

[6] 'Stendhal', 250. Cf. 235: 'un instant rapide, où l'on sent avec énergie, voilà donc à quoi se ramène la temporalité stendhalienne'.

[7] 'Le monologue intérieur', 276. Cf. 275: 'la durée stendhalienne est une durée où quelque chose est en train de se passer *ici et maintenant*'. See also Brooks, *Reading for the Plot*, 77.

d'embryons d'idées; de loin en loin, à force de se répéter elle-même, la pensée fait un bond en avant, trouve une formule qui lui paraît neuve, et qui oriente la suite du rêve. Gardez d'un rêve ou d'une discussion avec vous-même seulement ces moments (les seuls que le souvenir garde, même si vous écrivez aussitôt après), vous obtiendrez la brièveté, l'allure des monologues du *Rouge*.[8]

Not only the interior monologues, continues Prévost, but also individual episodes leave one with the impression that Stendhal made it a rule never to allow the time of narration to exceed the time taken by the event narrated. As time presses on, so must the narrative. It is the precipitation of events in *Le Rouge et le Noir* which conveys to the reader a sense of the passage of time: Stendhal has achieved 'la concision dans le mouvement'.[9]

But is this rapidity plausible? May it not in fact be evidence of a writer desperately trying to cram the events of five years into the space of two octavo volumes? Many have thought so, particularly in respect of the denouement, and Somerset Maugham[10] is but one member of the novelist's profession to make fun of Julien's murderous flit to Verrières. No less rapid, though, is his previous journey from Strasbourg to Paris. On receipt of Mathilde's letter and after an obliging colonel has given him leave 'en quelques minutes', he gallops his way to Metz only there to abandon 'cette façon de voyager' (430), the velocity it permits being incommensurate with his 'affreuse inquiétude': 'il se jeta dans une chaise de poste; et ce fut avec une rapidité presque incroyable qu'il arriva au lieu indiqué, près de la petite porte du jardin de l'hôtel de la Mole.' Only just in time, it seems: 'cette porte s'ouvrit, et à l'instant Mathilde, oubliant tout respect humain, se précipita dans ses bras. Heureusement, il n'était que cinq heures du matin et la rue était encore déserte.' The carriage journeys in *Le Rouge et le Noir* belong more to the age of the train or the private jet (one wonders also, for example, how the narrator himself makes it down from Paris to Verrières in a day: 7), as indeed do the letters to the age of the telegraph or even the telex. If some have laughed at these improbabilities, others have striven earnestly to defend Stendhal against charges of novelistic amateurishness. Julien's journey to Verrières is the journey of a man in a trance,

---

[8] *Création*, 324. To which one might add that the recurrent use of dots in the recording of interior monologues further enhances their plausibility by suggesting the blurred interstices of reflection and fantasy.

[9] p. 335.   [10] *Ten Novels and Their Authors*, 2nd edn (London, 1963), 97.

says Martineau,[11] and one must remember, says Castex, that a *chaise de poste* went considerably faster than a diligence or a *malle-poste*.[12]

Yet it would be wrong to deny the presence in the description of the journey from Strasbourg to Paris, as indeed elsewhere in the novel,[13] of a certain resemblance to the most naïve of adventure stories, particularly as the description of the journeys to Besançon and Paris, as well as the account of Julien's first visit to Mathilde's bedroom, suggest that it would be wrong to suppose that Stendhal could not perfectly well have chosen a more conventionally plausible manner of narrating these events. 'Avec une rapidité incroyable', 'il volait en montant l'échelle' (343), are but two of the innumerable hyperboles to be found in the novel which lend it, no less than *La Chartreuse de Parme*, the gasping tone of juvenile excitement. But this is the point. The narrator ends his account of Julien's second visit to Mathilde's bedroom with the comment: 'il est plus sage de supprimer la description d'un tel degré d'égarement et de félicité'. Wiser, maybe, but less effective, for the adolescent protagonists themselves see their actions in the most 'heroic' terms, and the manner of narration helps us to experience, as it were from the inside, this living-out of a borrowed romance. And this is true of the presentation of time throughout the novel. Time appears to the reader in the same way as it does to the characters, so that the experience of time also becomes 'une chose présente'.

But how? First, by a kind of 'neutralization' of time. We have seen that Stendhal is most liable to the charge of implausibility when the reader is in a position to measure the rapidity of narration against the 'distance' covered. We know how far it is from Paris to Strasbourg or the Franche-Comté. But time in *Le Rouge et le Noir* is generally so imprecise, and the psychological distance covered within it so much less definite than the roads upon which its hero travels, that we are never led to suspect the rhythm of its advance as being in any way the result of narrative convenience. We begin 'par un beau jour d'automne' and continue from 'un jour' to 'le lendemain' to

---

[11] Ed. cit., p. xxv.   [12] 'Le Rouge et le Noir', 142–3.

[13] According to Blin 'ce passé, grimé en trompe-l'œil qu'on nomme le présent historique' is absent from the novel (*Problèmes du roman*, 153), but in fact it is used twice: by Geronimo to narrate his story (145–6), and by the narrator to describe Julien's second visit to Mathilde's bedroom (343–4). In the first instance its use seems entirely appropriate for an audience of enthralled children. Is there any reason to suppose that its use in the second instance is any different?

'quelques mois après', from autumn to winter to spring and summer. Only the combined allusions to the success of *Hernani* and the anniversary of the execution of Boniface de la Mole (286) allow Martineau to establish the date of 30 July 1830 as a reference point for all the other events in the novel and so to re-create his precise chronology which is quite foreign to the reader's own experience of the passage of time in the novel.[14] Instead time always appears to us as being subordinate to the development of the characters themselves, especially of Julien.[15] At the end of I. vi what matters is how Julien earns the respect of those around him, not only of the servants, but also of the townspeople and of M. de Rênal himself. This process covers the temporal sequence 'le soir'—'peu de jours après'—'moins d'un mois après', but we learn nothing else of what happened during those weeks. Similarly, in the following chapter, all that matters is for Julien to obtain books from the bookshop with M. de Rênal's agreement. The ruse he devises takes a month to work (39), yet once again we learn nothing of what else happened in the intervening period. In this way the chronological precision of the 'real' time of the novel is replaced by a kind of temporal penumbra which is then coloured by the characters' own experience.[16] Mme de Rênal tries to live without Julien, but the futility of her attempt is reflected in the dismissal of their two days of separation within one sentence in the midst of a dialogue between them (110); the duel with Beauvoisis 'fut fini en un instant' and occupies only a sentence, leaving the reader to echo Julien's reaction: 'mon Dieu! un duel, n'est-ce que ça!' (259); but Julien's gloating upon receipt of Mathilde's declaration of love occupies several pages (307–10). The rare examples of chronological exactitude are similar in kind: the precise date of the king's visit to Verrières (94) suggests the historic nature of this day in the minds of the participants, while the chiming of ten o'clock (51) or two o'clock (81) may be as full of significance to the timorous lover as 2.15 a.m. on a Friday morning (464) to the man who has just been condemned to death. These are moments to remember.

[14] See above, note 4.

[15] Cf. Grahame C. Jones, 'Le mouvement dramatique de la narration stendhalienne', *Stendhal Club*, 20 (1977/8), 46–56 (49): 'dans le roman stendhalien, le tempo de la narration est toujours subordonné aux besoins profonds du développement de ses caractères ou de la signification profonde de l'histoire.'

[16] A penumbra also created by the pseudo-iterative imperfect mentioned earlier. See above, note 2 to III. 2.

If the narrative of *Le Rouge et le Noir* is a reflection of the characters' own experience of time, then it is not surprising that rapidity should be its major characteristic since it is the story of a young man in a hurry. The energy of the novel is that of Julien himself and its style far removed from 'ce genre d'éloquence, qui a remplacé la rapidité d'action de l'Empire' (132).[17] But lest we confuse this Napoleonic verve with the action-packed superficiality of the adventure story mentioned earlier, a number of devices are employed to lend coherence and subtlety to this rapidity. The elision of time, for example, itself subordinate to the development of character, is further camouflaged by occurring within the individual chapters rather than between them. The beginning of II. v ('après plusieurs mois d'épreuves, voici où en était Julien') is the single exception amongst these transitions which are generally from one day to the next or even one moment to the next. Particularly at the beginning of the novel, but also elsewhere (e.g. II. xi–xii), a chapter may begin by repeating the words of the end of the last and taking up the story exactly where the last ended, if not indeed slightly before (I. xvi).[18] Secondly, while it has been seen that *Le Rouge et le Noir* is essentially unilinear in respect of the handling of time, it is not necessarily also unidimensional. Already we have noted Poulet's view that the 'moments heureux' in Stendhal's novels are rich in perspective in that they open out on to distant and beguiling temporal horizons, but these moments are rare. Yet the less epiphanous moments in Stendhal's novels are also rich in perspective, and this derives from the multiplicity of angles from which they are viewed.

---

[17] Which is why Stendhal's subsequent anxieties about the rhythm of the novel are misplaced. See *OI*, ii. 143, 149.

[18] The supposed 'mistake' involved in the transition from chapters xxi–xxii in *La Chartreuse de Parme* is also a conscious narrative device, suggesting the retelling of a story characteristic of day-dream and myth.

6

Perspective

'Je proteste de nouveau que je ne prétends pas peindre les choses en
elles-mêmes mais seulement leur effet sur moi.'

(*OI*, ii. 671)

TOGETHER with *Armance*, *Le Rouge et le Noir* marks a complete
break with the French eighteenth-century tradition of story-telling.[1]
It may contain several letters and it may be firmly focused on the
development of a single character, but it abandons the lame pretence
of the epistolary and memoir novels. Gone too are the fiction of a
discovered manuscript and the disingenuous preface that asserts the
moral utility of reading about immorality. The one residual trace
of the world of Prévost, Marivaux and Laclos is the 'Avertissement
de l'Editeur' where Stendhal, with a few deft strokes of irony,
affiliates the novel 'aux jeux de l'imagination' and implies the prosaic
sterility of the July Revolution.

In the wake of Walter Scott and, more especially, Fielding,
Stendhal 'rediscovered' third-person narration[2] but adapted it in a
way which made him an important precursor of Flaubert and the
'nouveaux romanciers' of this century. In considering the opening
chapters of the novel and the use of the present tense, we have seen
the more traditional side of the narrator of *Le Rouge et le Noir* (the
originality of the pose as travel-guide notwithstanding), and
one's first impression of the novel may suggest the presence of a
conventionally omniscient narrator. This frequenter of Parisian balls
who introduces us to the world of Verrières knows everyone's past,
can relate what is going on in the minds of the protagonists and
provides information on everything from the local dialect of the
Franche-Comté to Italian paintings in the Louvre and even the
etiquette of royal visits. But we are ready to suspend such disbelief
as this implausible omniscience may inspire because the role of the
narrator is more often that of a discreet camera, allowing us to view

---

[1] See Prévost, *Création*, 310–13.
[2] See André Le Breton, *'Le Rouge et le Noir' de Stendhal* (Paris, 1950), 216.

the events of the novel almost entirely from the point of view of the participants. The pale young peasant with clean clothes and tear-stained cheeks standing by the hall-door, the beautiful young woman so finely dressed and with such a dazzling complexion, these are the images of the first encounter between Julien and Mme de Rênal which both characters and reader will remember. And not only is it an important aspect of the 'presentness' of the novel that we should *see* events through the eyes of the characters, but even more important is the fact that we feel and understand things through them as well. Mme de Rênal's awareness of Julien's youth, cleanliness and vulnerability correspond to her expectation of 'un être grossier et mal peigné, chargé de gronder ses enfants' (25), while Julien's admiration for Mme de Rênal's beauty, grace and gentleness corresponds to his expectation of a harsh and hostile employer.

The contrasts established here between two points of view and between expectation and reality are straightforward and even a little laboured (there are constant references after the first meeting to what each had expected), but point-of-view technique is used throughout the novel with increasing verve and subtlety. First, we see things through the eyes not only of Julien, Mme de Rênal and Mathilde, but also of M. de Rênal, the marquis de La Mole and a host of secondary characters. We have already seen how interior monologue grants the reader access, however briefly, to the point of view of, amongst others, Mme Derville, Croisenois and Mme de Fervaques. The same is true of Stendhal's extensive use of *style indirect libre* in the novel, which permits only slightly less immediate contact with the thoughts of Valenod (139–40), Amanda Binet (155), Beauvoisis (259) and even Mathilde's maid (288). During the description of the king's visit to Verrières, *style indirect libre* allows us to share not only Julien and Mme de Rênal's viewpoints but also that of the people of Verrières, just as the change wrought in Mme de Fervaques by Julien's attentions is made more striking and more amusing by being shown through the eyes of her servants (398).

Secondly, the point of view may be a limited one, and this is the device which Georges Blin calls 'les restrictions de champ'.[3] We have already noted that with four minor exceptions the narrator simulates ignorance of the future which awaits his characters, and this refusal to step ahead may be seen in a number of details which show

[3] *Problèmes du roman*, part 2.

Stendhal's attempts at a coincidence between the point of view of the characters, of the narrator and thus of the reader. Physical limitation of point of view is variously conveyed in the novel. The man who awakes takes time to realize who has woken him (136, 467, 471); to hold a woman's hand in the dark is to hold not Mme de Rênal's hand but simply a hand (51, 61); to embrace a woman in a dark bedroom is a hazardous enterprise until one knows one is embracing the right one (207); and if one spends one's time desperately reciting the *Nouvelle Héloïse* to her, she may as well be anyone (326). Similarly, when one is being imprisoned as a murderer, it does not really matter who puts the handcuffs on (433). More interesting perhaps are the instances of mental limitation of viewpoint. The marquis de La Mole is twice described before Julien (or the reader) learns his name (103, 230), and Julien's initial failure to recognize Mme de Rênal in the cathedral at Besançon is conveyed in a similar manner (186). Here the point of view is only temporarily limited, and even the bizarre behaviour of the young bishop of Agde eventually becomes comprehensible (101). But in the account of the 'note secrète' (II. xxi–xxiii) the machinations of the conspirators can only dimly be grasped either by Julien or the reader, and the description of the assigning of a lease in I. xxii remains a complete mystery both to the reader and to Julien (until Mme de Rênal tells him, but not us, exactly what happened: 147).[4]

Thirdly, the way in which a given moment or event is experienced by the participants may be temporarily reflected in the manner of narration itself. There has already been occasion to mention the extensive use of dialogue in the description of the ball and of the coach journey at the beginning of Part II, the historic present in the 'adventure' of Julien's second visit to Mathilde's bedroom, and the dislocation of time for the evocation of shock at various key moments in the story. To these examples one may add the description of the king's visit to Verrières and Bray-le-Haut and the account of the 'note secrète'. In the former the public nature of the event, the pomp and circumstance and the religious solemnity are evoked not only by the choice and attribution of the epigraph but also by certain passages in the narrative which suggest the style of those contemporary newspapers which have carried the story:

---

[4] See *Problèmes du roman*, 156–9, and Mitchell, '*Le Rouge et le Noir*', 20–1.

elle parvint à rejoindre la route où le roi devait passer, et put suivre la garde d'honneur à vingt pas de distance, au milieu d'une noble poussière. Dix mille paysans crièrent: Vive le roi, quand le maire eut l'honneur d'haranguer Sa Majesté. Une heure après, lorsque, tous les discours écoutés, le roi allait entrer dans la ville, la petite pièce de canon se remit à tirer à coups précipités. Mais un accident s'ensuivit, non pour les canonniers qui avaient fait leurs preuves à Leipsick et à Montmirail, mais pour le futur premier adjoint, M. de Moirod [...] Sa Majesté descendit à la belle église neuve qui ce jour-là était parée de tous ses rideaux cramoisis. Le roi devait dîner, et aussitôt après remonter en voiture pour aller vénérer la célèbre relique de saint Clément [...] A moitié ruinée par le vandalisme révolutionnaire, elle ['cette antique abbaye'] avait été magnifiquement rétablie depuis la Restauration, et l'on commençait à parler de miracles. (98)

(The 'official' status of this last comment becomes evident when the narrator subsequently refers to 'cette magnificence mélancolique, dégradée par la vue des briques nues et du plâtre encore tout blanc'.)[5] In the case of the 'note secrète' Julien's task in taking the minutes of the meeting of the conspirators is reflected in the narrator's imitation of a newspaper account of a parliamentary debate: 'ici l'interruption partit de trois ou quatre points à la fois', 'ici il y eut interruption, mais étouffée par les *chut* de tout le monde', 'ici encore interruption'. And here again the narrator acknowledges his imitation: '*le désordre fut à son comble*, comme disent les journaux en parlant de la Chambre' (363–7).

By thus multiplying, limiting or imitating the points of view of his characters, the narrator seems to efface himself from the novel, leaving the reader in immediate contact with the worlds of Verrières, Besançon and Paris. Even where he offers us the possibility of seeing a given moment from more than one point of view—and the first meeting between Julien and Mme de Rênal belongs in this category—the effect again is one of immediacy, of 'une chose présente'. This fourth aspect of point-of-view technique, the technique of perspective, appears throughout the novel and enriches the simplicity of the unilinear passage of time. Sometimes the juxtaposition of points of view may be slow and elaborate as when we first read of Julien's reaction to Mathilde's declaration of love and then learn how she came to write it, or it may occur within a few sentences:

[5] The whole episode is in fact based on an article in *Le Moniteur Universel* (1 May 1830). See Claude Liprandi, 'Sur un épisode de *Rouge et Noir*. Un roi à Bray-le-Haut', *Revue des Sciences Humaines*, 15 (1950), 141–60.

cependant il fut sage, et se borna à répéter à son homme de minute en minute: *Monsieur, votre adresse? je vous méprise.* La constance avec laquelle il s'attachait à ces six mots finit par frapper la foule. Dame! il faut que l'autre qui parle tout seul lui donne son adresse. (255)

And the transition here from indirect discourse to direct speech is comparable with the frequent transitions from indirect discourse to interior monologue:

à peine M. de Maugiron sorti, Julien se mit à rire comme un fou. Pour profiter de sa verve jésuitique, il écrivit une lettre de neuf pages à M. de Rênal, dans laquelle il lui rendait compte de tout ce qu'on lui avait dit, et lui demandait humblement conseil. Ce coquin ne m'a pourtant pas dit le nom de la personne qui fait l'offre! Ce sera M. Valenod qui voit dans mon exil à Verrières l'effet de sa lettre anonyme. (131)

When more than two points of view are recorded, the effect is vertiginous:

Mme de La Mole, quoique d'un caractère si mesuré, se moquait quelquefois de Julien. *L'imprévu* produit par la sensibilité est l'horreur des grandes dames; c'est l'antipode des convenances. Deux ou trois fois le marquis prit son parti: s'il est ridicule dans votre salon, il triomphe dans son bureau. Julien, de son côté, crut saisir le secret de la marquise. Elle daignait s'intéresser à tout dès qu'on annonçait le baron de La Joumate. C'était un être froid, à physionomie impassible. Il était petit, mince, laid, fort bien mis, passait sa vie au Château, et, en général, ne disait rien sur rien. Telle était sa façon de penser. Mme de La Mole eût été passionnément heureuse, pour la première fois de sa vie, si elle eût pu en faire le mari de sa fille. (254)

In these examples the narrator's point of view is represented in the indirect discourse, and one can see how neutral it is. His function remains that of the travel-guide. But elsewhere it is clear that the narrator has his own very definite point of view. In considering the use of the present tense by the narrator it was suggested that his obtrusiveness and the partisan nature of his opinions makes of him another character in the story rather than the sole fount of wisdom from which the reader must inevitably draw a true understanding of the story. When, for example, the narrator says of Julien that 'il entreprenait de juger la vie avec son imagination. Cette erreur est d'un homme supérieur' (343), this comment alerts us to the fact that the narrator's worldly wisdom about love, jealousy, imagination, and other aspects of human behaviour (the sententious present) represents a quite distinct philosophy of life masquerading as general truth—a viewpoint as relative and contingent in the end as that of Julien, or Mathilde, or Mme de Rênal, something to be judged from the reader's own point of view. We have already seen how the narrator seems to encourage this independence by referring to the reader explicitly on a number of occasions. More important than these references perhaps is the way the narrator seems obliquely to anticipate the reader's moral judgements by his use of antiphrasis and, more especially, how the narrator's own judgements are fraught with such contradiction that antiphrasis may be impossible to determine. And if the narrator's viewpoint is inconsistent, what coherence can there be in that of the reader?

7

The ambivalent narrator

'La parole a été donnée à l'homme pour cacher sa pensée.'

(130)

THE use of antiphrasis in the novel has been noted by several critics and its importance to an understanding of *Le Rouge et le Noir* is demonstrated by the way in which what each critic has to say on the subject reveals his or her attitude to the fundamental question of the relations between author, text and reader. Prévost, for example, is thankful that its use is limited because 'ce serait un procédé [...] qui empêcherait toute émotion vraie dans l'âme du lecteur'.[1] So the author produces a text to move the reader? Blin warns us briefly not to be taken in by it and compares the occasional apparent severity of Stendhal's remarks on his hero or heroine with the more frequent and real severity with which he judged himself.[2] So the author produces a text to convince the reader that the author is an eminently admirable character? Others have devoted more attention to the subject, and the pertinence of their remarks is no less revealing. In *Stendhal et la voie oblique* Victor Brombert talks of 'la manie stendhalienne de présenter des qualités sous forme de défaut et de se servir de termes à valeur multiple'; 'naïf', 'ridicule', 'sot', 'sottise', and 'faiblesse' are terms of approval, while 'sang-froid' and 'prudence' are pejorative. This mania, he says, is a consequence of Stendhal's fear of his reader: 'cette timidité prend des formes variées. Apparaissant et disparaissant tour à tour, Stendhal cache son enthousiasme sous l'ironie, se désolidarise de ce qu'il admire le plus, déroute pour se faire reconnaître, et attaque afin de se défendre'.[3] But in *Stendhal. Fiction and the Themes of Freedom* Brombert's account of antiphrasis serves a different thesis, and one which quite rightly underlines the role of the reader:

[1] *Création*, 500. [2] *Problèmes du roman*, 291-8. [3] *La Voie oblique*, 51-4.

reading Stendhal is an exercise in agility. The capers and somersaults of irony, the juggling of contents, and inversions of meaning sustain a climate of ambiguity. Nothing can be more unsettling to the unprepared reader than the constant instability of the Stendhalian vocabulary, its shifts and reversals of signification.[4]

Yet the assumption is still that 'Stendhal' is the goal of interpretation and that beyond the 'climate of ambiguity' lies a stratosphere of clarity, an unambiguous author. So the author produces a text to give the reader the satisfaction of solving a difficult puzzle? Only with the short essay by Gérard Genette entitled ' "Stendhal" ' do Stendhal and the antiphrastic narrator become separate entities. Having noted previous critical interest in 'la sincérité douteuse de ces paraphrases où Stendhal semble parfois de désolidariser hypocritement de ses personnages préférés, présenter comme défaut ou maladresse ce qu'il juge en réalité comme autant de traits sympathiques ou admirables', he introduces the crucial distinction when he finds it 'presque impossible dans ces occurrences de distinguer entre l'intervention ironique de l'auteur et l'intervention supposée d'un narrateur distinct de lui dont Stendhal jouerait à contrefaire le style et l'opinion'. Consequently, he writes:

l'image du narrateur est donc, chez Stendhal, essentiellement problématique, et lorsque le récit stendhalien laisse, si peu que ce soit, la parole au discours, il est souvent bien difficile, et parfois impossible de répondre à cette question, d'apparence toute simple; *qui parle?*[5]

The fullest account of this problem is to be found in Shoshana Felman's excellent book *La 'Folie' dans l'œuvre romanesque de Stendhal*. 'Fou' and 'folie' are two of the many words which the narrator uses to applaud while appearing to condemn, and her book traces the semantic route taken by these and other terms in the course of Stendhal's novels. She argues that these terms are addressed to two sorts of reader (or 'destinataires', to use Jakobson's term), the 'lecteur moyen' and the Happy Few. They are quotations from the language of the average reader designed to enlist his sympathy and agreement (with the author) while yet being aimed at the more discerning reader who will see where Stendhal's heart really lies. To illustrate this point she quotes from *Le Rouge et le Noir*: 'maintenant qu'il est bien convenu que le caractère de Mathilde est

[4] *Fiction*, 69.   [5] ' "Stendhal" ', 188–9.

impossible dans notre siècle, non moins prudent que vertueux, je crains moins d'irriter en continuant *le récit des folies* de cette aimable fille' (342; Felman's italics), and then comments:

le 'lecteur moyen' se reconnaîtra dans le jugement sur Mathilde: '*je crains moins d'irriter* en continuant le *récit des folies* de cette aimable fille'; mais c'est aux *happy few*—véritables destinataires—qu'il appartiendra de relever, par delà l'épaule de 'l'archi-lecteur', le clin d'œil si typiquement stendhalien, d'opérer un renversement des termes, de comprendre au deuxième degré. C'est à leur intention que Stendhal prend soin de signaler, par de petits indices (l'italique, le ton ironique, les incises du genre: 'qu'on appelle', 'comme dit le vulgaire', etc.), qu'il n'est pas là où l'on pense, qu'il est toujours en deçà du mot, qu'il ne prend pas à son compte les jugements simplistes sur la 'folie'.

In this instance the antiphrasis is clear, as it can be elsewhere in *Le Rouge et le Noir*. When, for example, the narrator comments on Julien: 'j'avoue que la faiblesse dont Julien fait preuve dans ce monologue me donne une pauvre opinion de lui' (134), the 'faiblesse' in question is Julien's belief that one can be politically effective without moral compromise. But the term 'faiblesse' is a curious one to use in the context. Weakness is here synonymous with spontaneous moral judgement (springing from the emotional revulsion which Julien feels at Valenod's treatment of the inmates of the workhouse); the strength implied as its opposite is the rigorous self-control of the hypocrite and the hard-heartedness of a Valenod. Here again, then, we can see what the 'author' means and accordingly enlist in the Happy Few: we have spotted his wink.

But, as has already been argued earlier, this notion of the Happy Few has been as detrimental to criticism of Stendhal's novels as the idea of egotism, for it implies the existence within them of a secret message which waits to be decoded, implies perhaps that there is a particular set of values (usually called 'beylisme') inscribed within the comments of the narrator, be they antiphrastic or not, which alone will allow us to make sense of the events narrated. Shooting a defenceless woman in church may not immediately elicit our admiration for the assassin, but does not the secret code of values in the text make us see the energy and spontaneity of the act in opposition to the sterile caution and 'percentage mentality' of society as a whole and therefore as in some sense heroic? Maybe so, though of course in the case of the shooting the reader is left without any narratorial commentary to guide him. But there is evidence of a

[6] 'Folie', 42.

certain ambivalence in the narrator's remarks which suggests that
the reader would be wrong to trust him entirely and indeed that
certain comments which critics suppose to be antiphrastic may not
in fact be so.

We may illustrate this by examining in detail two contexts in which
the narrator refers to Julien as 'un être supérieur', first in the account
of Julien's campaign to seduce Mme de Rênal, and secondly in the
account of Julien's second visit to Mathilde's bedroom. In both these
episodes, as in the rest of *Le Rouge et le Noir* and indeed in Stendhal's
work as a whole, one of the central issues is the dichotomy between
calculation and spontaneity, between planning the future and
enjoying the present. From the beginning until the final stages of the
episode concerning Mme de Rênal (75–82), the narrator's remarks
criticize the former and extol the latter. Julien's decision to seduce
Mme de Rênal when he prefers Mme Derville elicits this comment:

tel est, hélas, le malheur d'une excessive civilisation! A vingt ans, l'âme d'un
jeune homme, s'il a quelque éducation, est à mille lieues du laisser-aller,
sans lequel l'amour n'est souvent que le plus ennuyeux des devoirs.

Julien's 'petite vanité' in thinking he will later be able to pass off his
lowly position as tutor as the result of a love-affair is followed by
the description of Mme de Rênal's happiness and unthinking
enjoyment of the present. When Mme de Rênal asks Julien if he has
another Christian name, the narrator is categoric:

à cette demande si flatteuse, notre héros ne sut que répondre. Cette
circonstance n'était pas prévue dans son plan. Sans cette sottise de faire un
plan, l'esprit vif de Julien l'eût bien servi, la surprise n'eût fait qu'ajouter
à la vivacité de ses aperçus.

If this 'sottise' does not quite blind Julien to his lack of success,
it nevertheless manifests itself again in his prickliness and his
role-playing. His only 'idée juste' is to absent himself, thereby
unintentionally making Mme de Rênal miss him. For Victor
Brombert these uses of 'sot' and 'sottise' point to Julien's 'charming
clumsiness, to his inability to live up to his own calculating schemes,
to his fundamental spontaneity [...] we must understand that he
is distressingly and delightfully timid in the author's eyes'.[7] In the
author's eyes maybe, in Mme de Rênal's eyes certainly, but why the
narrator's? Admittedly Mme Derville's dismissal of Julien's 'bien

---

[7] *Fiction*, 69.

sottes manières' as unpardonable according to the lights of 'le savoir-vivre d'une capitale de province' may cause us would-be non-provincials to wish to defend Julien against the charge of 'sottise'. But 'sot' Julien may still be if judged by the lights of the narrator's worldly experience of the art of seduction. Instead of play-acting and quoting Corneille (in fact Rotrou!) to himself, he should do something—leave for a while or simply go to her bedroom (an 'idée ridicule' which is only 'ridicule' because it is not part of his plan. Here there is indeed antiphrasis: for 'ridicule' read 'géniale'). After his 'idée ridicule', Julien is miserable: 'il était à mille lieues de l'idée de renoncer à toute feinte, à tout projet, et de vivre au jour le jour avec Mme de Rênal, en se contentant comme un enfant du bonheur qu'apporterait chaque journée.' Again, anxiety and calculation prevent happiness, as they do once more when Mme de Rênal has left Julien 'with nothing more to desire':

mais, dans les moments les plus doux, victime d'un orgueil bizarre, il prétendit encore jouer le rôle d'un homme accoutumé à subjuguer les femmes: il fit des efforts d'attention incroyables pour gâter ce qu'il avait d'aimable. Au lieu d'être attentif aux transports qu'il faisait naître, et aux remords qui en relevaient la vivacité, l'idée du *devoir* ne cessa jamais d'être présente à ses yeux. Il craignait un remords affreux et un ridicule éternel, s'il s'écartait du modèle idéal qu'il se proposait de suivre. En un mot, ce qui faisait de Julien un être supérieur fut précisément ce qui l'empêcha de goûter le bonheur qui se plaçait sous ses pas. C'est une jeune fille de seize ans, qui a des couleurs charmantes, et qui, pour aller au bal, a la folie de mettre du rouge.

But here we see that the narrator's view has changed completely. Calculation, artifice, imitation of an ideal model, preconception, these then are the hallmarks of 'un être supérieur'? But previously they were seen to constitute the 'malheur d'une excessive civilisation'! What's more, just as this scene is replayed in the minds of the characters (the triple flashback discussed earlier), so is this *volte-face*. At the beginning of the next chapter the narrator refers once more to the 'sottise' of Julien's behaviour but then to his 'folle idée de paraître un homme d'expérience'; and 'folie', as we have seen, is a term of approbation.

What should we make of the narrator's views here? Is he saying that Julien is superior because at least he tries? He has imagination and aspirations and wants more from life than the perhaps mediocre contentment which life at Vergy offers? But if happiness is not to be his lot, by what other criterion can we define his superiority?

Like the young girl's 'folie de mettre du rouge', his lack of complacency, his adventurousness, his energy, are superior to the 'noire ambition' of the Valenods and the Frilairs, the black hypocrisy of society as a whole. Then the criteria of superiority would be recklessness, gratuitousness, lack of desire for money or power. Yet are these values so great that one should sacrifice happiness to them?

The ambivalence of the narrator on these questions is reflected again in the novel in the account of another bedroom visit, the second to Mathilde's (342–4). Once again it is a question of Julien's superiority: 'il entreprenait de juger la vie avec son imagination. Cette erreur est d'un homme supérieur'. Here it might seem that a simple antiphrasis invites us to 'translate' 'erreur' into 'vérité' or 'juste entreprise'. The term 'erreur' belongs to the language of a putative reader for whom judgements on life should be made with cold rationality, whereas the reader desired by Stendhal will note that Julien's superiority derives precisely from his willingness to use his imagination. Perhaps this reader will even be flattered to note that in reading *Le Rouge et le Noir* he too has undertaken to 'juger la vie avec son imagination'. But the context belies this interpretation. At this point in the novel Julien is miserable because of Mathilde's apparent indifference towards him and which has followed so quickly upon her previous professions of love:

elle l'avait aimé, lui, mais elle avait connu son peu de mérite. Et en effet j'en ai bien peu! se disait Julien avec pleine conviction; je suis au total un être bien plat, bien vulgaire, bien ennuyeux pour les autres, bien insupportable à moi-même. Il était mortellement dégoûté de toutes ses bonnes qualités, de toutes les choses qu'il avait aimées avec enthousiasme; et dans cet état d'*imagination renversée*, il entreprenait de juger la vie avec son imagination. Cette erreur est d'un homme supérieur. Plusieurs fois l'idée du suicide s'offrit à lui; cette image était pleine de charmes, c'était comme un repos délicieux; c'était le verre d'eau glacée offert au misérable qui, dans le désert, meurt de soif et de chaleur.

These might almost be the words of Octave, that past master in the business of 'imagination renversée'. Because of his misery Julien sees everything in the blackest terms—and that is an error. Of a superior man, it would seem, because the average man has no imagination, but an *error* nevertheless. Instead of all the nonsense about glasses of iced water in the desert, he should get up and do something:

Julien n'eut pas assez de génie pour se dire: il faut oser; mais comme il regardait la fenêtre de la chambre de Mathilde, il vit à travers les persiennes qu'elle éteignait sa lumière: il se figurait cette chambre charmante qu'il avait vue, hélas! une fois en sa vie. Son imagination n'allait pas plus loin.

At last his imagination has produced the right answer: he will climb to her bedroom: 'ce fut l'éclair du génie, les bonnes raisons arrivèrent en foule. Puis-je être plus malheureux! se disait-il.' Imagination ceases and action begins. As a result: 'qui pourra décrire l'excès du bonheur de Julien? Celui de Mathilde fut presque égal.' The spontaneity and unthinking abandonment to the moment contrast markedly with the 'transports *voulus*' of their first encounter, when 'l'amour passionné était encore plutôt un modèle qu'on imitait qu'une réalité' (327), so that once more it is not at all clear wherein Julien's superiority lies. His 'erreur' of 'imagination renversée' has nearly prevented this moment of happiness with Mathilde. Only his spontaneity has saved him. Moreover the happiness enjoyed here is of the kind that both Julien and Mathilde had previously thought they ought to achieve, the delirious 'heroic' passion of romance and tragedy, rather than the quiet idyll of Vergy. So the superiority of 'imagination' can no longer be said even to reside in a rejection of the mediocre (supposing still that this is in fact how the narrator views what Vergy has to offer Julien). Furthermore Julien himself sees that 'imagination' and the self-conscious imitation of behaviour preconceived to be appropriate prevent the enjoyment of the moment, and he sees this not only after shooting Mme de Rênal (485), but also on two previous occasions: once when comparing Mathilde with Mme de Rênal (286) and once after his first visit to Mathilde's bedroom:

mon Dieu! qu'elle est belle! dit Julien en la voyant courir: voilà cet être qui se précipitait dans mes bras avec tant de fureur il n'y a pas huit jours... Et ces instants ne reviendront jamais! Et c'est par ma faute! Et, au moment d'une action si extraordinaire, si intéressante pour moi, je n'y étais pas sensible!... Il faut avouer que je suis né avec un caractère bien plat et bien malheureux. (332).

For Julien 'imagination' has led him astray: it is the error of an 'être inférieur'.

    Of the narrator all we can finally say is that he holds two separate and conflicting views: first, that the 'être supérieur' judges life with his imagination and attempts to live up to an ideal model, is one who rejects ease and mediocrity and prescribes a pattern of events to which he makes it a point of personal honour to adhere, one for whom the present must not be accepted but created; and second, that calculation and the imitation of others breeds a self-consciousness that prevents emotional fulfilment. 'L'amour de tête a plus d'esprit sans doute que l'amour vrai, mais il n'a que des instants d'enthousiasme; il se connaît trop, il se juge sans cesse; loin d'égarer la pensée, il n'est bâti qu'à force de pensées' (341): whereas such 'instants d'enthousiasme' are always 'imprévus', the reward of those who live in the present without worry for the future, a prize to be stored in the treasure-house of memory. Heroic prospects, or 'une chose présente' giving on to idyllic retrospect? The narrator offers this choice of moral vantage-points on the story of Julien Sorel, and the fascination of Le Rouge et le Noir is that these also represent the two ways in which we read this or any novel—in anticipation and with hindsight.

8

Prospects

'Mais à quoi bon ces vaines prédictions?'

(442)

WE have already seen that part of the sense of 'presentness' which *Le Rouge et le Noir* conveys derives from the narrator's refusal to reveal the story's future. On four occasions we are told of what Julien will later learn, but otherwise the narrator appears not only not to reveal the future but even to be ignorant of it, and this impression is reinforced by his occasional surmise as to what will happen to Julien: 'jamais il ne fera ni un bon prêtre, ni un grand administrateur' (185), 'suivant moi, ce fut une belle plante. Au lieu de marcher du tendre au rusé, comme la plupart des hommes, l'âge lui eût donné la bonté facile à s'attendrir, il se fût guéri d'une méfiance folle [...] Mais à quoi bon ces vaines prédictions?' In the latter case the narrator appears even to have forgotten that Julien probably no longer has a future. Even when he says, 'il ne faut pas trop mal augurer de Julien' (44), this is in no sense the comment of an omniscient narrator wishing to reassure his reader but belongs rather with the speculations of the other characters in the novel, with those of Chélan ('j'augure bien de votre esprit': 43) or the marquis de La Mole ('j'augure bien de ce petit prêtre': 238). Equally, when he comments on Julien's self-control ('un être capable d'un tel effort sur lui-même peut aller loin, *si fata sinant*': 407), the phrase 'aller loin' shows the narrator sharing the vocabulary as well as the viewpoint of Mme de Rênal, the people of Verrières (87), and Pirard (203).

'J'augure bien', 'il peut aller loin': for both narrator and character the story of Julien has yet to be written. In this apparent absence of a foregone conclusion, how does the reader react? Does he not also speculate on the future which the story holds? Not necessarily, but the novel is full of implicit invitations to do so. If the reader is like Mme de Rênal and has read either no novels or at least only a 'très petit nombre de romans' (42), then it is likely that such speculation will be minimal and the 'charme de la nouveauté' (76) all the greater. But if the reader resembles Julien or Mathilde, then his knowledge of history and literature may lead him to note parallels between *Le Rouge et le Noir* and previous fact or fiction and even to preconceive the lives of the protagonists in the very same way as they themselves do. Living in the present and taking each page as it comes, the innocent reader will experience each succeeding sentence as novel; living in anticipation of an outcome and taking each page as a preparation for the next, the knowing reader may seek to accommodate each succeeding sentence within a pattern of prediction. Each episode becomes the augury of a completed destiny which it is his to divine. A totally innocent reading may of course be impossible—even Mme de Rênal on occasions sees life in terms of a sentimental tale (26)—but the main emphasis in *Le Rouge et le Noir* is on the dangers of 'experienced' reading. If living life according to a 'modèle idéal' is the 'erreur d'un homme supérieur', so also is the tendency to see the protagonists in terms of literary or historical characters: the one prevents fulfilment and self-knowledge, the other an apprehension of their singularity. The shooting of Mme de Rênal not only reveals the 'real' Julien, it also explodes the predicted fictions with which a knowing reader may have surrounded him; and the remainder of the novel not only traces the emergence of 'l'homme qui voit clair dans son âme' (482), it also allows the reader his first accurate measurements of the distance that separates Julien from other men, be they real or imaginary.

One of the principal myths in the novel, causing the reader to predict Julien's story, is of course that of the parvenu. The word itself is used sparingly, but the whole impetus of the plot derives from Julien's ambition to 'faire fortune'. This phrase is echoed frequently—in the narrator's account (23, 34, 72), in Julien's reflections (44, 75, 133, 485) and in the advice given by Chélan (43) and Pirard (225, 226)—and, taken together with the initiation into the ways of the provincial bourgeoisie and the Parisian aristocracy, and the acquisition of manners and skills punctuated by comic moments of 'gaucherie', its use places *Le Rouge et le Noir* and its reader squarely in the tradition of the eighteenth-century parvenu novel. The reader's expectations in this direction are reinforced by the presence of the comparable myth of the foundling. The possibility that we may be reading a French *Tom Jones* is first raised by Julien's indignation at Valenod's alleged exploitation of the orphanage ('et moi aussi, je suis une sorte d'enfant trouvé, haï de mon père, de mes frères, de toute ma famille': 33) and is kept before us, never by the narrator, but by Pirard (202, 224), Beauvoisis (260), the marquis de La Mole (264, 268), Caylus (300) and Julien himself (429). The reader of Marivaux and Fielding may be led in this way to have fairly firm expectations as to the outcome of the novel.[1] Admittedly this reader may note that Julien's desire to succeed has a certain Quixotic colouring ('la résolution inébranlable de s'exposer à mille morts plutôt que de ne pas faire fortune')[2] and springs from the best of Stendhalian motives ('pour Julien, faire fortune, c'était d'abord sortir de Verrières; il abhorrait sa patrie. Tout ce qu'il y voyait glaçait son imagination': 23), but subsequent references to the moral dangers attendant upon it (43, 133, 267, 282–3) suggest the more familiar story of a man who gains success at the expense of his soul—an interpretation which is reinforced by the parallels established between Julien and both Mephistopheles (309)[3] and Tartuffe (309, 417, 418).

Already we can see how *Le Rouge et le Noir* appears to narrate a quest and an education, those two traditional features of the epic or the novel. Just as the act of reading is presented in the opening pages as a journey, so Julien's life is presented as an itinerary leading to a destination ('fortune'). Whether or not we come ultimately to see this journey as that of Everyman or as 'the rise and downfall of a romantic freak and an inexplicable genius',[4] we are always conscious of a progression. Julien's recurrent exclamation 'quelle différence' as he compares the present with the past (usually Mathilde with Mme de Rênal),[5] the narrator's periodic references to Julien becoming 'un autre homme' or his occasional reminder that Julien would not previously have acted in such and such a way, the frequent use of the adjective 'nouveau' or the adverbial phrase 'pour la première fois' to suggest an advance, be it in Julien's career or the emotional lives of the heroines, all these add to the novel's 'presentness' the sense that the passage of time means progress and change. These various words and phrases serve as markers on the temporal map, milestones by which to measure the ground covered

---

[1] For a different account of the themes of parvenu and foundling, see Brooks, *Reading for the Plot*, 62–89.

[2] This colouring remains in Julien's retrospective view of his ambition: 'j'étais aux innombrables combats que j'aurais à soutenir pour bâtir une fortune colossale' (485).

[3] Later comparisons with Mephistopheles, on the other hand, indicate a division within Julien as his authentic self re-establishes itself: 'en vérité, l'homme a deux êtres en lui, pensa-t-il. Qui diable songeait à cette réflexion maligne?' (467). The allusion here is to Goethe's *Faust* ('zwei Seelen wohnen, ach! in meiner Brust'). Cf. 469, 482.

[4] Strickland, *Stendhal*, 139. Strickland favours an exemplary reading.

[5] See Brombert, *Fiction*, 76 for a different view of this.

but, more especially, milestones which imply a road ahead. For only when these markers are replaced by those of 'fin' and 'finir' do we see journey's end: 'mon roman est fini' (427), 'tout est fini' (433), 'la fin du drame doit être bien proche' (484).

But as long as the road appears to stretch ahead, we are free to speculate about the nature of Julien's ultimate success or failure, and this speculation is fostered by the parallels with Napoleon, Richelieu and the heroes of the Revolution (Danton, Robespierre and Mirabeau). To be an obscure lieutenant from Corsica conquering not only a beautiful woman but the world itself: 'c'était la destinée de Napoléon, serait-ce un jour la sienne?' (60). But in Restoration society, of course, the Church has replaced the army as the surest ladder of success, so perhaps we may share the surmise of Mme de Rênal: 'elle croyait apercevoir plus nettement chaque jour le grand homme futur dans ce jeune abbé. Elle le voyait pape, elle le voyait premier ministre comme Richelieu'.[6] Or do we think that this man of the people's distrust of the Establishment will turn into the vengeance and hatred of a Robespierre (54, 90), or the revolutionary fervour of Danton and Mirabeau (277–9)? On the other hand, perhaps Julien's destiny lies in the more private realm of love. Starting off as a Cherubino to Mme de Rênal's 'comtesse' (cf. the epigraph to I. vi), this reader of the *Confessions* is soon playing Rousseau to Louise de Warens/Louise de Rênal (26 ff.). Though wary of meeting with the same painful fate as Abelard (320), perhaps he will find his 'nouvelle Héloïse' (157, 326). Or will he achieve success instead as a latter-day Don Juan (79)?

Just before the moment that Julien shoots Mme de Rênal, it may seem that many of these heroic prospects have been fulfilled. The parvenu in receipt of the marquis de La Mole's donations is complimented on his 'récente fortune' by the gunsmith of Verrières and the would-be foundling has been re-named Julien Sorel de la Vernaye. The imitator of Napoleon has become a lieutenant and secured the love of the most brilliant match in Paris, secured it moreover by his resemblance to a revolutionary hero and then by the cold-blooded methods of a Don Juan (or a Valmont). And is not the marquis de La Mole like Louis XIV (427) and his salon 'une véritable cour de prince souverain' (269)? Is Julien not his 'jeune ministre' (263), the one man he can dispatch to the Languedoc to settle his

---

[6] The religious connexion suggests Mme de Rênal is here (92–3) thinking of cardinal Richelieu, not the duc de Richelieu who was Prime Minister under Louis XVIII.

affairs as Richelieu once so unquestionably settled things there for Louis XIII? 'Mon roman est fini', proclaims Julien just before the arrival of Mme de Rênal's letter to the marquis de La Mole, and the reader might almost agree. This is the denouement we might have expected. But it is the romance that has finished, not the novel,[7] and the two pistol-shots in the church at Verrières shatter the illusion. *Le Rouge et le Noir* has its own story to tell: its hero is a killer. And this single fact, this 'grand fait vrai', leads us to undertake a major reassessment of this hero, a reassessment which mirrors that of the imprisoned Julien just as surely as our illusions have been reflections of those which he himself entertained. Not that the discovery of the real Julien to which this reassessment leads is achieved at a stroke.[8] Julien still occasionally looks to his models for guidance—Napoleon holds him back from suicide (439) and Danton offers him an ideal of courage and self-possession with which to face the guillotine (466, 468)—and the reader may still want to see the prison cells of Verrières and Besançon in terms of the temporary imprisonment on Elba followed by exile and death on St Helena, just as Julien's speech at his trial may call to mind once more the revolutionary hero and militant representative of an oppressed class. But despite all the residual parallels we have now to look again at Julien and, in René Girard's words, replace 'mensonge romantique' with 'vérité romanesque'.[9]

[7] Cf. Lane Gormley, ' "Mon roman est fini": fabricateurs de romans et fiction intratextuelle dans *Le Rouge et le Noir*', *Stendhal Club*, 21 (1978/9), 129–38.

[8] In view of Jean-Jacques Hamm's interesting observation that the epigraphs disappear from the text from the moment that Julien no longer has need of masks, it might be more accurate to suggest that our reassessment of Julien begins in earnest only after he has been condemned to death. Only then is his 'romance' truly finished (n.b. the page-title at the end of II. xli: 'C'en est fait'). The previous inclusion of epigraphs could then be seen as part of the strategy whereby the reader is induced to see Julien's unique experience in terms of other people's stories. See Jean-Jacques Hamm, '*Le Rouge et le Noir* d'un lecteur d'épigraphes', *Stendhal Club*, 20 (1977/8), 19–36. Cf. also Joëlle Mertès-Gleize's perceptive suggestion that the (revolutionary) discourse of others (recalled in the epigraphs) becomes superfluous when Julien's new authenticity allows him to speak for himself. See 'L'action de lire', *L'Arc*, 88 (1983), 57–63.

[9] *Mensonge romantique et vérité romanesque* (Paris, 1961). For Girard desire is triangular, the triangle consisting of the desirer, the object of desire and a mediator. The 'mensonge romantique' is the idea that we desire directly and of our own accord, the 'vérité romanesque' that we desire what others desire. In the novel (Girard deals with Cervantes, Flaubert, Stendhal, Proust and Dostoevsky) the mediator may be 'external' (Amadis de Gaule in *Don Quixote*, Walter Scott's heroines in *Madame Bovary*, Rousseau and Napoleon in *Le Rouge*) or 'internal' (e.g. it is the belief that Valenod wants a private tutor which makes M. de Rênal want to employ Julien).

Whether or not the reader accepts any or all of these invitations to see Julien as similar to such heroes of literature and history will depend on the individual reader's erudition and judgement. Critical works on the novel demonstrate that they have indeed been frequently accepted[10] and that they are sufficiently tempting for there to be the need to point out why they should not be accepted. But the individual reader may well not need such warnings, may already have seen the ways in which Julien is *different*, is 'singulier'. There is no evidence that Julien is an illegitimate foundling, and the unmercenary nature of his desire to 'faire fortune' is shown by his refusal to accept charity from Mme de Rênal, his unconcern at the increase in his pay, his offer of all his savings to Pirard, his indignation at the notion that he might be bribable and his disgust at his fellow-prisoner's passion for money. The ambiguous phrase 'faire fortune' reflects rather a nebulous dream of success, the boyish aspiration of one who is as ignorant of what this success might consist in as of how to achieve it, and it is of course one of the ironies of the novel that Julien should regard Mme de Rênal's beauty as the 'premier écueil qui avait failli arrêter sa fortune' (34) and her letter to the marquis as having 'détruit à jamais mon bonheur à venir' (438), when it is her love that brings him happiness and fulfilment.

Neither foundling nor grasping fortune-hunter, Julien is far from being the other people we might have thought him to be. The memory of Napoleon which, as he himself says, 'nous empêchera à jamais d'être heureux' (89), is not imitated[11] but travestied by Julien's story. When he punishes himself for revealing his admiration for Napoleon by binding his arm to his chest for two months (24), he unwittingly imitates a famous Napoleonic pose; and if Mathilde sees in him a resemblance to Napoleon, it is only Napoleon as mimicked by her father at balls (278). A horse and a smart blue uniform may make Julien think he is an artillery officer in the Grande Armée but he is actually escorting a king, and the rank of lieutenant and the prospect of marriage to a Parisian beauty come to him only because the lady is pregnant, as does his new title, which leads Julien to think he is descended from a nobleman exiled *by* Napoleon (429).

[10] Brooks, *Reading for the Plot*, 68, provides one of the most recent (and surprising) examples.
[11] See Moya Longstaffe's excellent article, 'L'éthique du duel et la couronne du martyre dans *Le Rouge et le Noir*', *Stendhal Club*, 18 (1975/6), 283–306 (300).

Nor is Julien like Robespierre:[12] to think so is to share the prejudice that strikes fear into the heart of the Establishment both in Verrières (90) and Paris: 'ils voient un Robespierre et sa charrette derrière chaque haie' (228). In Julien we find none of the political idealism of Danton or Mirabeau, and indeed he thinks of them mainly in order to justify his unease at selling out to the Establishment (282–4). His trial speech may sound revolutionary, but it is a piece of provocative bravado brought on by Valenod's 'regard insolent' and the thought of what Valenod will say about him to Mme de Rênal (462). Moreover it is not at all clear that the speech constitutes a form of suicide, as Frilair and several critics think,[13] for Valenod had already received his appointment as Prefect and could therefore issue different instructions to the jurors in his power, thereby indulging in 'le plaisir de le condamner à mort' (476). And even on the guillotine Julien differs from Danton in showing greater self-control (cf. 468 and 487). Nor is Julien Richelieu. He is not even in holy orders, and his role in the La Mole household is essentially that of an efficient personal secretary. The bust of Richelieu that gazes down on Julien in his bedroom prompts him to climb a ladder to Mathilde's bedroom rather than the ladder of political success, and the incident of the 'note secrète' shows how obscure are the corridors of power to Julien's eyes. Finally, as a lover, Julien shares little with his precursors in dalliance. He succeeds with Mme de Rênal because of his tearful timidity and with Mathilde because of his indifference. The reconquest of Mathilde is merely the result of following Korasoff's 'art de séduire', as it were to the letter: Julien is here no more than a second-hand Valmont.

Of all the heroic prospects which appear to open before Julien, it is ironically the story of Boniface de La Mole which offers the closest resemblance to Julien's—ironically, that is, because this prospect seems the most absurd of all and the least likely to be envisaged seriously by the reader. Mathilde's desire to relive the 'grande passion' which her sixteenth-century ancestor inspired in Marguerite de Navarre (what Jean-Pierre Richard calls her 'snobisme de l'anachronique')[14] seems so clearly the fantasy of an ardent and romantic temperament and so unlikely to be realized in the prosaic

[12] As Sainte-Beuve thought. See Talbot (ed.), *La Critique stendhalienne*, 164.
[13] e.g. Imbert, *Métamorphoses*, 570; Brombert, *Fiction*, 95; Felman, *La 'Folie'*, 206; Wood, *Stendhal*, 92–3; Brooks, *Reading for the Plot*, 82.
[14] 'Connaissance et tendresse', 69.

context of nineteenth-century France that it is all the more surprising that so many aspects of her fantasy seem to fit what eventually happens.[15] After all, her witticism in respect of Altamira ('je ne vois que la condamnation à mort qui distingue un homme': 273) and her admiration for Marguerite de Navarre's burial of the severed head of Boniface de La Mole clearly have much relevance to the denouement of the novel. The man she loves sees her constantly as a queen (270, 284, 303, 335, 444) and does indeed end up on the guillotine. Some of the parallels between fantasy and reality are of course brought about by Mathilde herself: she sends Julien to Villequier (420), the one estate which the marquis de La Mole has inherited from Boniface (268) and she buries her lover's head (488). But what is one to make of the narrator's reference to her 'amour de tête' (341) or her own assertion that 'tout est héroïque, tout sera fils du hasard' (297)? Even metaphors turn out to be literally true. It is as if providence has condemned her to live the fantasy through, that providence which she humorously believes makes her crazy (275–6) or which she seriously thinks is speaking to her in her accidental sketching of Julien's profile (340). Clearly she is obsessed by Julien's head. This capital absurdity, which is further compounded by the academician's exclamation about Mathilde herself ('c'est une tête, une tête': 287), nevertheless conceals a more serious fact: her belief in providence is similar to Croisenois's belief in occult causes (349), yet this man with whom she may therefore share an 'affinité élective' (cf. the title of I. vii), and who dies for her in a duel, is rejected by her in her determination to love Julien, the man whose passion leads him not to kill her (as she once imagines after he has raised the sword against her) but to shoot another woman. She does not see or want to see that she is on a false road. After the narrator has ironized Julien's 'triste rôle de plébéien révolté' (282 and 289) we know that her use of the term (424) is evidence of the extent of her illusion. Her desire to play Mme Roland to Julien's revolutionary Roland (339) is doubtless satisfied by her role as a nondescript Mme Michelet and her clandestine audition of Julien's pseudo-revolutionary speech at his trial, but by the end of the novel her fantasy is so far removed from the inner reality of Julien that it

---

[15] See Gilbert Durand, *Le Décor mythique de la 'Chartreuse de Parme'* (Paris, 1961), 50–2. Durand calls the story of Boniface de La Mole an 'oracle rétrospectif' and concludes that *Le Rouge* is the 'transcription moderne d'un événement de la Renaissance' and therefore directly comparable with *La Chartreuse*.

tires him (451) and strikes us as pathetic. She is left with Julien's head, but his soul has gone beyond her reach. Heroic prospects pursued to the limit prove sterile, if not grotesque, and the final implicit irony of the novel is that Mathilde's importation of Italian sculpture for Julien's grotto is likely to earn her the local reputation of 'une mauvaise tête'.

The effect of Mathilde's final fling of 'heroism' is to show the reader how wrong it is not to reassess any previous expectations in the light of the shooting of Mme de Rênal. The fond illusions of the 'prévisible' must give way to the real lessons to be learnt from the 'imprévu'. For Julien and Mme de Rênal the shooting is, to say the least, truly 'imprévu' and by its very unexpectedness surprises them into a rediscovery of their love for each other and a complete change of direction (Julien's discovery of self, Mme de Rênal's abandonment of her temporary piety). But Mathilde paradoxically is unable to accede to the true heroism of 'disponibilité'—paradoxically, that is, because she has made a cult of the 'imprévu'. Her boredom in Parisian society stems precisely from the predictable nature of its conversation:

elle avait le malheur d'avoir plus d'esprit que MM. de Croisenois, de Caylus, de Luz et ses autres amis. Elle se figurait tout ce qu'ils allaient lui dire sur le beau ciel de la Provence, la poésie, le midi, etc., etc.... (269)

and she mocks their fear of 'énergie' as being 'la peur de rencontrer l'imprévu, [...] la crainte de rester court en présence de l'imprévu' (298). Hence her admiration for the sixteenth century:

la vie d'un homme était une suite de hasards. Maintenant la civilisation a chassé le hasard, plus d'imprévu. S'il paraît dans les idées, il n'est pas assez d'épigrammes pour lui; s'il paraît dans les événements, aucune lâcheté n'est au-dessus de notre peur. Quelque folie que nous fasse faire la peur, elle est excusée. Siècle dégénéré et ennuyeux! (313)

But if 'civilisation' recuperates the unforeseen by epigram and explanation, so making every event potentially (and boringly) predictable, so also does Mathilde by seeing the unforeseen precisely as confirmation of her heroic view of life. The second night of love is superior to the first (when 'il n'y eut rien d'imprévu pour elle dans tous les événements de cette nuit, que le malheur et la honte qu'elle avait trouvés au lieu de cette entière félicité dont parlent les romans': 328), not so much because she did not expect Julien and was therefore not inhibited by anticipation as because an unexpected visit (and superhuman expertise with ladders)[16] is what ought to happen in the course of a 'grande passion' *à la seizième*. When it comes to the shooting of Mme de Rênal, Mathilde accordingly is the one person who is *not* surprised by it and who can offer a ready explanation: 'ce que tu appelles ton crime, et qui n'est qu'une noble vengeance qui montre toute la hauteur du cœur qui bat dans cette poitrine'. Not only has Julien not confounded her expectations, he has gilded them: 'elle examinait son amant, qu'elle trouva bien au-dessus de ce qu'elle s'était imaginé. Boniface de La Mole lui semblait ressuscité, mais plus héroïque' (444–5). While Julien, Mme de Rênal and the reader now embark on a revision of their ideas, Mathilde finds hers confirmed, but increasingly in contradiction of the facts. And the narrator steps in to inform us of the limits to Mathilde's notion of the 'imprévu';

cette âme altière, mais saturée de toute cette prudence sèche qui passe dans le grand monde pour peindre fidèlement le cœur humain, n'était pas faite pour comprendre vite le bonheur de se moquer de toute prudence, qui peut être si vif pour une âme ardente. Dans les hautes classes de la société de Paris, où Mathilde avait vécu, la passion ne peut que bien rarement se dépouiller de prudence, et c'est du cinquième étage qu'on se jette par la fenêtre. (449)

Despite her own previous lack of caution (346) Mathilde cannot understand Julien's act: it exceeds in its recklessness all that she has previously experienced.

The inauthenticity of Mathilde's heroism and her notion of 'l'imprévu' make her her father's daughter. The marquis de La Mole's admiration for Julien includes a taste for his unpredictability, something which his own son lacks (268). But the 'imprévu' is here the idle pastime of a bored man. Admittedly he would like to believe that Julien has felt an 'amour véritable, imprévu' (425), for then he would not have to regard him as a fortune-hunter, but when it comes to his own daughter, his taste for 'l'imprévu' is much diminished:

qui l'eût pu prévoir? se disait-il. Une fille d'un caractère si altier, d'un génie si élevé, plus fière que moi du nom qu'elle porte! dont la main m'était demandée d'avance par tout ce qu'il y a de plus illustre en France! Il faut renoncer à toute prudence. Ce siècle est fait pour tout confondre! Nous marchons vers le chaos. (421)

---

[16] For a most entertaining account of this see T. G. S. Combe, 'A Snake and Ladders in Stendhal's *Le Rouge et le Noir*', *Cambridge Review*, 104 (3 June 1983), 151–5.

The marquis's attitude to the 'imprévu' may be seen as that of one kind of reader: the unforeseen may be welcome in a novel because it is exciting, but if it calls moral values into question, then perhaps it is to be rejected as subversive. *Le Rouge* becomes a 'chronique scandaleuse'. On the other hand the reader may, as Mathilde scathingly suggests of her contemporaries, recuperate it by epigram and explanation in such a way as to deny the threat it may pose to his view of the world. And then, even if the reader's moral values are not disturbed by the event, perhaps his aesthetic values are. Do we allow that an unpredictable event may occur in a novel? Or is it to be seen as specious sensationalism? Korasoff's recipe for Parisian success is: *'faites toujours le contraire de ce qu'on attend de vous'* (265). Is this the rule that Stendhal is following?[17] Or do we say: if the short story can have a 'twist', why not the novel? Do we reject the unpredictable event as implausible? Do we perceive (and condemn) inconsistency of characterization, or do we recuperate it like Mathilde as 'heroic', an act of energy that confirms the superiority of the central character? The reception with which the shooting of Mme de Rênal has met shows that Stendhal as well as Julien is on trial and that, as with Julien, the case turns on the question of premeditation.[18] In examining this case we should remember that it is Julien's unpredictability which brings him the cross of the Légion d'Honneur (268) and that the red ribbon of this cross is indicated in the novel's title.[19]

[17] But cf. Stendhal's comment in his projected review: 'dans les folies des héros de roman vulgaire, il n'y a de bonne que la première parce qu'elle étonne. Toutes les autres sont comme les originalités des sots dans la vie réelle, on s'y attend, partant elles ne valent rien, elles sont plates' (716).

[18] Critical discussion of the shooting is pervaded with the language of the lawcourts: e.g. Emile Faguet, 'Stendhal', in *Revue des Deux Mondes*, 109 (1892), 594–633 (626): 'c'est la condamnation de l'auteur'; Henriette Bibas, 'Le double dénouement et la morale du *Rouge*', *Revue d'Histoire Littéraire de la France*, 49 (1949), 21–36 (21), refers to Faguet's 'verdict'; Castex, '*Le Rouge et le Noir*', 127: '[Rambaud] plaide coupable pour son auteur', etc., etc.

[19] Given what Claude Liprandi has described as 'la prolifération parthénogénétique des supplétives explications fantaisistes du titre du *Rouge et le Noir*, (in '*Le Rouge et le Noir*: Quiroga Rouge et Morillo Noir', *Stendhal Club*, 18 (1975/6), 219–27), a brief summary of interpretations of the title may be useful here. It was perhaps inspired by a contemporary fashion for titles which referred to colours: see Romain Colomb, 'Notice sur la vie et les ouvrages de Henri Beyle (de Stendhal)', in *Romans et nouvelles* (Paris, 1854), p. xcii; Martineau, *Le Cœur*, ii. 180; and Serge Bokobza, '*Rouge et Noir*: le blason de Julien?', *Stendhal Club*, 22 (1979/80), 37–41. (But cf. H.-F. Imbert, 'Conjectures sur l'origine scottienne du titre de *Rouge et Noir*', *Revue de Littérature Comparée*, 45 (1971), 306. Imbert's objection seems tenuous

if one remembers the contemporary use of colours to designate types of short story: e.g. *conte bleu, conte noir, conte brun, conte rose* and, inevitably, *conte de toutes les couleurs*. Cf. also Claude Duchet, '*La Fille abandonnée* et *La Bête humaine*: éléments de titrologie romanesque', *Littérature*, 12 (1973), 60–1).

Stendhal's title is most commonly seen as alluding symbolically to the army and the Church, an interpretation which originates in an article by Emile Forgues in *Le National* (1 April 1842) over the signature 'Old Nick'. Forgues claimed to have received the following explanation of the title from a friend who had consulted Stendhal directly: '*Le Rouge* signifie que, venu plus tôt, Julien (le héros du livre) eût été soldat; mais à l'époque où il vécut, il fut forcé de prendre la soutane, de là *le Noir*.' Rejecting any thought that this might be a devilish 'poisson d'avril', subsequent critics have consistently and justifiably accepted the equation of black with the Church. But the equation of red with the army has met with the objections that Napoleon's army wore blue, while their English adversaries wore red, and that the only military uniform worn by Julien in the novel is sky-blue. These objections have been countered by Liprandi in 'De "l'origine du nom Sorel" à l'origine de *Rouge et Noir*', in V. Del Litto (ed.), *Communications présentées au Congrès Stendhalien de Civitavecchia (III*ᵉ *Journée du Stendhal Club)* (Florence and Paris, 1966), 233–55, and 'Quiroga Rouge et Morillo Noir' (see beginning of this note). Liprandi equates red with the military via the red uniform and/or cloak worn by Napoleon as general and First Consul and as so depicted by Gros, David and Ingres. For Liprandi red denotes the Republic, Napoleon and the liberals, while black stands for the forces of reaction, the Church and the Congrégation. Liprandi thereby partly reinforces another interpretation of the title, advanced by Martineau (*Le Cœur*, ii. 180), according to which red denotes Julien's (supposed) republicanism and which derives from Stendhal's comment recorded on the manuscript of *Lucien Leuwen*: 'Rouge et blanc […] pour rappeler le *Rouge et le Noir* et fournir une phrase aux journalistes. *Rouge*, le républicain Lucien. *Blanc*, la jeune royaliste de Chasteller' (*LL*, i. 339). Castex (in '*Le Rouge et le Noir*', 19–20) questions Martineau's judgement on the grounds that political liberalism is not a central issue in the novel, and later (in his introduction to the Garnier edition, p. xlix, n. 1, and following Boris Reizov, 'Pourquoi Stendhal a-t-il intitulé son roman *Le Rouge et Le Noir*?', *Studi Francesi*, 11 (1967), 296–301) on the grounds that in 1830 red was not yet clearly identified as the colour of jacobin republicanism. Instead Castex prefers to take up the idea (first advanced by F. Neri in 'Note stendhalienne, *Rosso e Nero*', *Ambrogiano*, 2 May 1925) that red relates to the Legion of Honour created by Napoleon and is therefore susceptible of the military interpretation first recorded by Forgues.

At the same time Castex rejects the interpretation of the title as an allusion to games of chance, be it roulette or the card-game called 'la rouge et noire' (*OI*, i. 74 and n. 1), because Julien is not in fact faced with any gamble or risky decision in his choice of an ecclesiastical rather than military career (see '*Le Rouge et le Noir*', 19). This ludic interpretation was first advanced by Elmé Caro in 1855 (see Talbot (ed.), *Critique stendhalienne*, 182) and subsequently developed by Pierre Martino in a note published in *Le Divan*, 93 (1923), 575–7. It currently finds favour with Castex's successor at the Sorbonne, Michel Crouzet, and has been indirectly made more attractive by the content of C. W. Thompson's *Le Jeu de l'ordre et de la liberté dans 'La Chartreuse de Parme'* (Aran, Switzerland, 1982). But it has been rejected, on similar grounds to those of Castex, by Serge Bokobza in '*Le Rouge et le Noir*: jeu de hasard ou réalité politique?', *Stendhal Club*, 21 (1978/9), 163–6, who finds also that it denies the important political content of the novel. In support of his thesis that the enigmatic title is 'le signe du début de cette lutte des classes sans merci que relate le roman', Bokobza quotes from the diary of one of Charles X's officers, le colonel Edmond Marc: 'vers trois heures de l'après-midi [of 29 July 1830], comme je sortais de chez le Roi, mon service étant fini ce jour-là, je montais chez Mme Le Gros. A l'aide de son téléscope, je distinguais très bien le drapeau rouge qui flottait sur les Tuileries et celui, Noir et Rouge, qu'on avait arboré pendant le combat sur la colonne Vendôme en signe de guerre à mort' (from Edmond Marc, *Mes Journées de juillet 1830*, ed. G. de Grandmaison (Paris, 1930), 106). The reference here to the red flag flying over the Tuileries undermines Reizov's and Castex's objection to the republican interpretation on the grounds that red was not yet identified with revolutionary forces. Also the presence of a red and black flag complements Liprandi's information about the red and black ribbon suggested by the republicans and the parliamentary commission as an accompaniment to the proposed Croix de Juillet for those who fought for the Revolution (see 'De "l'origine du nom Sorel" ', 252–5, and 'Quiroga Rouge et Morillo Noir', 227, n. 14); both are evidence of the topical, revolutionary resonance of Stendhal's title. For elaboration of this see below, pp. 151, 154.

For discussion of the possible heraldic significance of the title see Imbert, 'Conjectures', and Bokobza, 'Le blason de Julien'. For further discussion of the title see Patrick Pollard, 'Colour Symbolism in *Le Rouge et le Noir*', *Modern Language Review*, 76 (1981), 323–31; Mouillaud, *Le Roman possible*, 151–236, especially 157–8; and the bibliographically rich, though otherwise inconsequential article by Maddalena Bertelà, 'Les couleurs dans quelques titres stendhaliens', *Australian Journal of French Studies*, 22 (1985), 35–42. Cf. also Gary M. Godfrey, 'Julien Sorel—Soldier in Blue', *Modern Language Quarterly*, 37 (1976), 339–48. Military and ecclesiastical, revolutionary and reactionary, energetic and repressive, passionate and apathetic, heart-on-sleeve and hypocritical, amorous and tragic, bloody and deathly, the red and the black: the endlessly debatable connotations make *Le Rouge et le Noir* a fitting title for a novel which is itself open-ended and a constant invitation to conjecture.

9

Pistol-shots

'Qui l'eût pu prévoir?'

(421)

AS Jean Prévost was the first to point out, *Le Rouge et le Noir*, along with *Armance* and *La Chartreuse de Parme*, has a double denouement.[1] The first, as we have seen, is illusory: 'mon roman est fini', says Julien, but it is only the romance that has ended. The second, consisting in the shooting of Mme de Rênal and in Julien's imprisonment and death, is precipitated by Mme de Rênal's letter to the marquis de La Mole, and thus by an act of reading. We have already seen in *Armance* how Octave's misreading of the forged letter provides an object-lesson in how not to read that novel. In *Le Rouge et le Noir* the letter serves as a paradigm of the ambiguity surrounding the protagonist. Just as the heroic prospects which open up before both character and reader almost match the reality which the novel relates, so Mme de Rênal's letter almost fits the facts. It is a masterpiece of half-truth in which accuracy and falsehood form a kind of point and counterpoint. Some truths have been transformed into a portrait of Tartuffe,[2] and the distance between Julien and this portrait is reflected in Julien's reaction: 'quel père voudrait donner sa fille chérie à un tel homme!' (432). Subsequently Julien asserts his difference and singularity by shooting the person who has misread him and thereby substitutes for all the prospects previously entertained both by himself and by the reader the single context of crime and punishment: 'j'ai donné la mort avec préméditation [...] je mérite la mort, et je l'attends' (434).

How do we react to this substitution, either morally or aesthetically? Morally we may at once condemn a man who shoots a woman in church but when we read of Julien's prediction that

---

[1] *Création*, 333

[2] See Brooks, *Reading for the Plot*, 81. Also Thibaudet, *Stendhal*, 108-28; Bibas, 'Le double dénouement', 26; Imbert, *Métamorphoses*, 547-50; Jones, *Ironie*, 56-7; Brombert, *Fiction*, 90-1; Wood, *Stendhal*, 88.

'pour le commun des hommes je serai un assassin vulgaire' (435),
are we not anxious to avoid being classed amongst the vulgar many,
and do we not seek a moral framework that will justify the act?[3]
As readers who have made many predictions as to the outcome, we
may find the event sudden and insufficiently prepared and reject it
as implausible and aesthetically invalid. Or do we prefer to think
that we saw it coming all along? The piece of paper in the pew in
Verrières church was of course prophetic,[4] we remember Julien's
previous acts of violence, in particular when he brandishes a sword
at Mathilde, we think of Mme de Rênal's faint in Besançon cathedral,
and so on. Hindsight offers many advantages.

But first the shooting, this singular event about which the narrator
offers no comment. So much has been written on the subject that
one hesitates to prolong the debate, but since the purpose of this
study is to show how Stendhal's novels play upon the reader's
reactions, it may be of interest to see how diverse, even discordant,
are the notes given back by the critical violin in this instance. Broadly
speaking there have been four principal reactions to Julien's
murderous act: it is implausible; mad; an act of vengeance;
inexplicable and therefore true to life. While each of these opinions
has had its proponents at various different times during the hundred
and fifty odd years since publication of *Le Rouge*, it is also broadly
true that they have succeeded each other historically and thus reflect
the progression in reception of Stendhal from incomprehension
through admiration for his psychological realism to recognition of
his 'modern' distrust of coherence and completion and his equally
'modern' doubts about the ability of words to describe things.

The most notorious representative of the view that the shooting
is implausible is, of course, Emile Faguet who, in 1892, in an article
for the *Revue des Deux Mondes*, considered that 'le dénouement de
Rouge et Noir est bien bizarre, et, en vérité, un peu plus faux qu'il
n'est permis' and observed with conscious or unconscious humour
that 'tous les personnages perdent la tête'. Seeing in Julien Sorel
'l'impeccable ambitieux, l'homme de sang-froid effrayant et de

---

[3] See D. J. Mossop, 'Julien Sorel, the vulgar assassin', *French Studies*, 23 (1969),
138–44.
[4] Particularly if, like Stendhal, we have just read Vigny's *Cinq-Mars* where the
hero's death is punningly foretold, at the end of chapter xx (entitled 'La Lecture'!),
by a piece of paper falling from the ceiling. See Madeleine A. Simons, 'Stendhal et
les métamorphoses du sacré. Le décor gothique: "scena tragica" et "scena comica"',
Stendhal Club, 26 (1983/4), 329–43 (336 and n. 26).

volonté imperturbable', he thought it quite implausible that such a cold-hearted schemer would sacrifice all his ambitions in this way, particularly since Mathilde's pregnancy still gives him power over the marquis de La Mole. For Faguet, Stendhal had broken off from his own story-line about Julien in order slavishly to copy the real-life shootings of Berthet and Lafargue and had thereby demonstrated his incompetence as a novelist.[5] This analysis held sway for roughly the first half of this century. Though full of admiration for the rest of the novel, Léon Blum (1916) finds the denouement impossible to accept,[6] while Pierre Sabatier (1920) agrees that Stendhal had belatedly tried to turn Julien into Lafargue,[7] and Maurice Bardèche (1947) that Julien is still master of the situation and the shooting psychologically unconvincing.[8] Blum tries to defend Stendhal by arguing that because the story was true, he did not bother to make it seem plausible, and this idea has since been taken up by Jean Prévost (1942), Michel Crouzet (1964) and Peter Brooks (1984).[9]

Another to think that Julien loses his head was Hippolyte Babou (1846), an influential journalist and one of Stendhal's first admirers: 'ce héros de dissimulation perd la tête,' he writes, 'une noire folie le saisit, et la Volonté toute puissante, qui si longtemps était restée debout malgré les plus rudes assauts de l'Instinct, tombe culbutée par une violence imprévue.'[10] The idea that Julien goes temporarily mad was to have many adherents. Albert Thibaudet (1931) alludes to 'un état de tension physique et d'aliénation',[11] and Prévost to 'ce moment d'absence morale de l'assassin, qui est une vérité clinique',[12] but it was Henri Martineau (1945) who set the seal on this thesis. In his view Julien belongs to 'une classe fort importante d'hallucinés',[13] he is 'un véritable malade' and 'en proie à une sorte d'hypnose'.[14] This idea that Julien is a kind of somnambulist or psychopath acting involuntarily has subsequently reappeared, with

---

[5] 'Stendhal', 625–7.
[6] Léon Blum, *Stendhal et le beylisme*, 3rd edn (Paris, 1947), 86.
[7] Pierre Sabatier, *Esquisse de la morale de Stendhal d'après sa vie et ses œuvres* (Paris, 1920), 55.
[8] *Stendhal romancier*, 186.
[9] See *Création*, 334; *Le Rouge et le Noir*, ed. Michel Crouzet (Paris, 1964), 20; *Reading for the Plot*, 83 and n. 23.
[10] Talbot (ed.), *Critique stendhalienne*, 139.
[11] Thibaudet, *Stendhal*, 116.   [12] *Création*, 334.
[13] *L'Œuvre de Stendhal* (Paris, 1945), 348. Martineau credits Charles du Bos with the idea (347–8).
[14] *Le Rouge et le Noir*, ed. Martineau, p. xxv.

different emphases, in the works of Henriette Bibas (1949), Jean-Pierre Richard (1954), Françoise Marill-Albérès (1956), Georges Blin (1958), Robert Vigneron (1958/9), Claude Liprandi (1961), Richard B. Grant (1962), Henri-François Imbert (1967) and Shoshana Felman (1971),[15] and may doubtless be entertained by many other readers to this day. The fact is, of course, as Grahame C. Jones has pointed out,[16] that Martineau and others are agreeing with Faguet in seeing the shooting as irrational. It is simply that Faguet blames the inadequacy of the novelist where Martineau blames the state of Julien's mind.

The most persuasive refutation of both Faguet and Martineau has been carried out by Pierre-Georges Castex, both in his study of the novel (1967) and in his edition of it for Garnier (1973) which replaced Martineau's. For Castex the shooting is a lucid act of vengeance:

cette lettre de Mme de Rênal signifie donc bien, pour Julien, un écroulement irrémédiable, et d'autant plus désespérant qu'il venait de se croire élevé au triomphe. En un instant, son ambition est ruinée, son orgueil est publiquement humilié. Tout résonne dans l'événement comme un arrêt de mort. Dans sa conscience de vaincu s'implante une idée, assez forte pour inspirer sa conduite au mépris de toute considération étrangère, et c'est celle de la vengeance.[17]

'Je me suis vengé [...] la vengeance a été atroce', 'j'ai été offensé d'une manière atroce; j'ai tué, je mérite la mort', 'j'ai donné la mort avec préméditation' (434–6), 'il y a meurtre, et meurtre avec préméditation' (455), 'mon crime est atroce, et il fut *prémédité*' (463): these and other quotations are adduced in support of Castex's thesis and to show how Julien accepts full responsibility for his crime. And when Julien reflects that 'j'ai voulu la tuer par ambition ou par amour pour Mathilde' (466), he is remembering how he felt before he read Mme de Rênal's letter: deeply in love with the woman who is expecting his child (414) and 'ivre d'ambition' (430) because of his officer's uniform.[18] Above all he has been true to himself: 'le devoir [...] a été comme le tronc d'un arbre solide auquel je m'appuyais

---

[15] Respectively, 'Le double dénouement', 25; 'Connaissance et tendresse', 35; *Le Naturel*, 95–6; *Problèmes de la personnalité*, 500; 'Beylisme, romanticisme, réalisme', *Modern Philology*, 56 (1958/9), 98–117 (111); *Au cœur du 'Rouge'*, 200–1; 'The Death of Julien Sorel', *L'Esprit Créateur*, 2 (1962), 26–30; *Métamorphoses*, 555–7; *La 'Folie'*, 86.

[16] *Ironie*, 86–7.   [17] *'Le Rouge et le Noir'*, 133–4.

[18] Bibas adds a more subtle gloss: 'ce *ou* marque admirablement le recul pris dans son esprit par une fureur passée qui ne l'intéresse plus' ('Le double dénouement', 22–3).

pendant l'orage' (481) (and 'Un Orage' is of course the title of the chapter during which he shoots Mme de Rênal[19]). Castex concludes: 'en se vengeant de celle qui l'a perdu et qui représente alors à ses yeux une caste maudite, il permet à son orgueil d'avoir le dernier mot'.[20]

Although Castex adds that Julien 'met au jour les motifs qui l'ont incité à la vengeance', many questions remain. There is still the problem of plausibility. Castex seeks to meet this in advance by arguing that Stendhal's 'intention' in writing Le Rouge was to depict the energy he found evinced by Berthet and Lafargue,[21] but is this not to argue that because similar acts were committed in reality, then Julien's own act is plausible? And what of vengeance? Castex seems to be arguing that Julien is avenging thwarted ambition, but is this not at odds with the nobility of soul which Stendhal is at pains to show in Julien? Perhaps the reference to 'devoir' may be seen to 'save' Julien morally, but how does Castex envisage this 'devoir'? Less, it seems, as a personal duty to moral values, more as a political duty to his class. Is there any evidence at all at this point in the novel that Julien has become truly a 'plébéien révolté' and that in Mme de Rênal he is shooting all who would oppress the people? No, these pistol-shots are political only in the very broad sense that one may imagine Julien finding Mme de Rênal's apparent betrayal and duplicity quite typical of her class.[22]

More convincing is the view that Julien is avenging a slur on his honour, a view which was first expounded by Henriette Bibas. For her Mme de Rênal's letter to the marquis is a description of Tartuffe, and the idea that the two people he most respects should see him as a mercenary hypocrite is beyond endurance for a man so full of 'l'horreur du mépris' (463) and who wouldn't even let his mistress buy him some underwear. He has no choice: 'le cerveau se clôt à n'importe quelle idée autre que la seule qui agisse en révulsif: tuer celle où a pris corps cette exécrable image.'[23] Whereupon, of course,

---

[19] Mossop, 'Julien Sorel, the vulgar assassin', 142.
[20] 'Le Rouge et le Noir', 149.   [21] Ibid. 134–9.
[22] For discussion of the shooting as an act of political vengeance, see Green, Stendhal, 233; Louis Aragon, La Lumière de Stendhal (Paris, 1954), 83–4; Grant, 'The Death of Julien Sorel'; Jean-Jacques Hamm, 'Le dénouement de Rouge et Noir. Un parvenu qui ne parvient à rien', Stendhal Club, 17 (1974/5), 250–66. Note Martineau's view that the shooting is symbolic of 'l'échec des aspirations forcenées de toute une génération' (ed. cit., p. xxiii).
[23] 'Le double dénouement', 27.

during his moments of quiet reflection in prison, he discovers his true self and finds happiness with Mme de Rênal. Such is the laurel wreath that crowns the hero who defends his honour.

The idea that Julien seeks to remove a false and distorting image of himself by attacking the person who presents it has since been taken up by Geneviève Mouillaud (1973),[24] while Shoshana Felman sees Julien as symbolically destroying the residual badness in himself.[25] Self-vindication is the interpretation favoured also by Gilbert Durand (1961), Harry Levin (1963), F. W. J. Hemmings (1964), Michel Crouzet (1964), and Grahame C. Jones (1966).[26] For Mossop (1969) 'it has occurred to Julien, on reading Mme de Rênal's letter, that vengeance is a matter of honour' and this marks 'the beginning of the end for the artificial personality he has created for himself'.[27] Finally, in one of the more detailed accounts of the matter, Moya Longstaffe (1976) argues that we should see this question of honour within the context of a chivalric code of values. Had the letter been written by a man, then a duel would have been the obvious course of action for Julien, whereas *Le Rouge* offers the paradox that 'Julien tire sur Mme de Rênal, non pas pour la punir, mais pour se rendre digne d'elle'.[28] The shooting is a kind of trial upon which the perfect consummation of their love depends.

Another critic who follows in the tradition of Mme Bibas is Geoffrey Strickland (1974), who accepts the broad outlines of her thesis while taking her to task for suggesting that there is no poetry in Stendhal's description of Julien's subsequent period of quiet reflection in prison. In particular he notes that Bibas's thesis still requires reference to Julien's 'état d'irritation physique et de demi-folie' to explain the enormity of the act whereby Julien seeks to retrieve his honour:

and when it has been noted, it is perfectly easy to say what is happening to him, in that one can readily think of other cases in which men have gone mad from a blow to their pride, 'over-reacted' and then repented with a correspondingly full heart. Yet this is not really an *explanation*: we know that such reactions follow one another commonly but not that they follow inevitably. Moreover, Beyle does not try to explain them. Hence perhaps the difficulties

[24] *Le Roman possible*, 145.   [25] 'Folie', 206.

[26] Respectively, *Le Décor mythique*, 100-1; *Gates of Horn*, 126; *Stendhal*, 127; ed. cit., 19-28; *Ironie*, 90.

[27] 'Julien Sorel, the vulgar assassin', 142-3.

[28] 'L'éthique du duel', 306. Longstaffe's approach is adumbrated by Crouzet, ed. cit., 27-8.

that so many readers have in following the text. The text reminds us of what is unaccountable in such an experience, commonplace though it may be.[29]

Here we have evidence of the fourth main reaction to the shooting: it is inexplicable and therefore true to life. Already in 1931 Albert Thibaudet briefly offered just such a defence of Stendhal: 'aux reproches adressées à Stendhal d'avoir créé un caractère illogique, il serait facile de répondre [...] que la vie avec ses contradictions n'est pas la logique avec son principe de non-contradiction',[30] but it was not until Gérard Genette's article 'Vraisemblance et motivation' (1969) that this approach to the question received its fullest and most theoretically based treatment. Genette distinguishes three types of narrative: (i) the *récit vraisemblable* in which motivation is implicit and corresponds to a set of norms and conventions between narrative and public (as, for example, in the case of popular sentimental fiction, detective stories and Westerns); (ii) the *récit motivé* in which motivation is explicit and may, as in *La Comédie Humaine*, take the form of psychological or sociological 'explanation' (e.g. 'comme la nature des esprits étroits les porte à deviner les minuties, [l'abbé Birotteau] se livra soudain à de très grandes réflexions sur ces quatre événements imperceptibles pour tout autre'); and (iii) the *récit arbitraire* in which motivation is implicit but enigmatic: 'ici, le récit ne se soucie plus de respecter un système de vérités générales, il ne relève que d'une vérité particulière, ou d'une imagination profonde'. By way of illustration Genette cites Julien's shooting of Mme de Rênal and, in *Vanina Vanini*, the marriage of the heroine to Prince Savelli:

ces actions brutales ne sont pas, en elles-mêmes, plus 'incompréhensibles' que bien d'autres, et le plus maladroit des romanciers réalistes n'aurait pas eu de peine à les justifier par les voies d'une psychologie, disons confortable; mais on dirait que Stendhal a choisi délibérément de leur conserver, ou peut-être de leur conférer, par son refus de toute explication, cette individualité sauvage qui fait l'imprévisible des grandes actions—et des grandes œuvres. L'accent de vérité, à mille lieues de toute espèce de réalisme, ne se sépare pas ici du sentiment violent d'un arbitraire pleinement assumé, et qui néglige de se justifier.[31]

Genette's approach to the problem of the shooting seems by far the most rewarding. Oddly it seems to have found most favour with English critics.[32] As well as Strickland, there is Michael Wood (1971) who observes with much justification that 'there is a sense in which

[29] Strickland, *Stendhal*, 153–4.   [30] Thibaudet, *Stendhal*, 115–16.
[31] 'Vraisemblance et motivation', 77.
[32] Whereas it is rejected, for example, by Brooks, *Reading for the Plot*, 82.

the whole of *Le Rouge et le Noir* depends on our feelings about Julien's crime' and argues that Julien 'wanted to kill out of feelings of vengeance and violence and malice and love and jealousy and injured memories and injured pride and no doubt much else'. But 'Julien's crime remains "inexplicable" [...] and this is the great virtue of *Le Rouge et le Noir*': 'Stendhal really means to leave us on our own here.'[33] Similarly John Mitchell (1973) comments that Stendhal 'cannot explain what is *a priori* inexplicable without robbing it of its naturalness and hence its plausibility; if it is subconscious, it is beyond words'.[34] Ann Jefferson (1983) writes: 'the shooting episode as a whole is *imprévu*, and is composed of largely inexplicable elements [...] this is an instance of what Wolfgang Iser would call a blank or a gap that needs to be filled by the reader.'[35] Indeed it is a gap which Stendhal, in his own account of the plot, is careful not to fill: 'Mathilde la [Mme de Rênal's letter] montre à Julien. Julien est furieux, il part, arrive à Verrières pendant la messe, entre, il voit Mme de Rênal et lui tire deux coups de pistolet à bout portant' (725).[36] Like Octave, it would seem, Julien is simply subject to 'accès de fureur': Octave defenestrates a footman, Julien shoots his ex-mistress.

In story-telling, then, as in Stendhal's France, the *imprévisible* is a source of greatness. In fact Genette describes such narratives as 'les œuvres les plus émancipées de toute allégeance à l'*opinion du public*',[37] and is it not 'la tyrannie de l'opinion' (6), 'l'inconvénient du règne de l'opinion' (489) which Stendhal sees as the most important symptom, and indeed cause, of France's current malaise?[38] Julien's shooting is the act of a radical not at the level of plot but at the level of narrative style:[39] a moment of energy told with energy, a premeditated act of violence. It is as if, in the course of his journey, the reader has been forced off the road at gunpoint.

[33] *Stendhal*, 86–91. [34] '*Le Rouge et le Noir*', 56.

[35] 'The Uses of Reading', 177. See Wolfgang Iser, *The Act of Reading. A Theory of Aesthetic Response* (London and Henley, 1978), ch. 8. In a recent article Michel Crouzet shows how far his own approach to the shooting has evolved since 1964 by remarking that such blanks are to be respected rather than elided or filled. The critic must recognize 'une rhétorique du non-dit'. See 'Julien Sorel et le sublime: étude de la poétique d'un personnage', *Revue d'Histoire Littéraire de la France*, 86 (1986), 86–108 (104–5).

[36] In fact, of course, Stendhal borrowed this helpfully non-committal account almost verbatim from another reader, Jules Janin. See *RN*, 700.

[37] 'Vraisemblance et motivation', 77.

[38] See also the beginning of his projected review, *RN*, 712–13.

[39] Ann Jefferson makes a similar point: 'the *imprévu* of Julien's actions at the climax of the novel is, precisely, a flouting of reading *convenances*, be they scholarly, psychological or what' ('The Uses of Reading', 178).

10

Retrospect

'Avant de passer la montagne, tant qu'il put voir le clocher de
l'église de Verrières, souvent il se retourna.'

(153)

THE aftermath of the shooting is a time of reflection, both for Julien
and the reader. Julien accepts responsibility for his act, feels
remorse—which is to say he misses Mme de Rênal,[1] tires of
Mathilde's heroism, delights in the company of Mme de Rênal and
realizes his mistake: 'autrefois', he tells her,

quand j'aurais pu être si heureux pendant nos promenades dans les bois de
Vergy, une ambition fougueuse entraînait mon âme dans les pays imaginaires.
Au lieu de serrer contre mon cœur ce bras charmant qui était si près de mes
lèvres, l'avenir m'enlevait à toi; j'étais aux innombrables combats que j'aurais
à soutenir pour bâtir une fortune colossale... Non, je serais mort sans
connaître le bonheur, si vous n'étiez venue me voir dans cette prison. (485)

Like Octave he had established a 'règle antérieure à toute expérience',
and this had put him off the scent in his 'chasse au bonheur'. But
now, unexpectedly, by accident, through having no future and being
obliged to take each day as it comes, he discovers true contentment
in the arms of the woman he loves, and in the calm that follows the
tempests of his ambition[2] his self-conscious philosophizing about
God and death gives way to poignant memories of Vergy, memories
almost more poetic and idyllic than his present, provisional bliss with
Mme de Rênal: 'les moindres incidents de ces temps trop rapidement
envolés avaient pour lui une fraîcheur et un charme irrésistibles'
(452). For Julien, as for the reader, time has rushed by, and each
moment, for all its immediacy and for all the passion with which
he has lived it, has been sacrificed to eager anticipation of the future,
but now there are moments to savour, moments of self-knowledge
and retrospective surmise, moments of re-cognition. Yes, he could
have been happy at Vergy, if only...[3]

[1] 452: just as remorse is Mme de Rênal's word for missing Julien (434).
[2] 'Chez cet être singulier, c'était presque tous les jours tempête' (61).
[3] Cf. *Armance*. See above, pp. 58–9.

During these moments of 'rêverie'[4] Julien is given to drawing parallels between Mme de Rênal and Mathilde, and it may be that there is a lesson here. Instead of making comparisons with various literary and historical figures extraneous to the novel, perhaps he— and the reader—might have looked for more useful touchstones closer at hand and seen that the two women represent the two sides of Julien's divided self, indeed that they illustrate the two conflicting views of imagination which, as we have seen, the narrator himself is unable to reconcile. On the one hand, there is Mathilde with her apparently commendable energy and imagination, her disdainful rejection of easy mediocrity in favour of a heroic pattern of life derived from novel-reading and the history of her own ancestors, and her ambitious preconceptions of which in the event she is granted only a grotesque and parodic enactment; on the other, there is Mme de Rênal who lacks 'imagination' in this sense, yet who has no need of others (35) in the way that the histrionic Mathilde, like the protagonists of *Les Liaisons dangereuses*, needs an audience (451), who is free from calculation and the desire to imitate, whose expectations have not been warped by novels (76) and for whom each day brings something unforeseen and exciting (63), who can appreciate the present moment and disregard 'le spectre de l'avenir' (76). Such a comparison would suggest that the message of *Le Rouge et le Noir* is simple enough. Julien seeks happiness along the wrong road, the road of imitation and insincerity, the unauthentic road of Mathilde, but he eventually comes to realize that happiness lies along the road of spontaneity and independent sincerity, the authentic road of Mme de Rênal. Instead of considering public opinion, '*les autres*' (456), he should have realized his own 'singularité'. One of the great ironies of the novel is that Rousseau's *Confessions*, which is initially 'le seul livre à l'aide duquel son imagination se figurait le monde', teaches him only that a private tutor does not eat with the servants (20), whereas from the very beginning he might have learnt from it the lesson he finally learns, namely the value of sincerity and honest introspection, the importance of the Delphic and Socratic device: 'know thyself'.

As the reader fingers the few remaining pages of the novel and anticipates Julien's execution, he too ceases to have a future and may pause to reconsider the textual road along which the tourist-guide

---

[4] See Landry, *L'Imaginaire*, 234–6.

has led him. Whereas Julien's uncertainty about his parentage and
ambition to 'faire fortune' may have led him to predict a happy ending
à la Tom Jones, he now finds that happiness consists not in those
traditional, bourgeois ingredients of wealth, marriage and newly
discovered noble ancestry, but in indifference to money and class,
in adultery, and in fond thoughts of a future bastard son. No wonder
Stendhal did not expect recognition for another fifty years. Moreover
the reader now discovers that this happiness, fatherhood excepted,
is a reprise of the happiness described earlier and which he, like
Julien, had failed to recognize for what it was, so anxious was he
to read on. The object of a quest is not usually to be found a quarter
of the way through the journey. Yet now, with hindsight, the reader
can see how structure and symbol combine to make Vergy the
epitome of the values which the novel proclaims.

One of the most remarkable features to be found in the structure
of *Le Rouge et le Noir* is the interplay of progression and repetition.
On the one hand, the tour which begins in Verrières continues
throughout the novel, covering terrain that is both mountainous and
flat: 'ce sont là', says the narrator during Julien's seduction of Mme
de Fervaques, 'les landes de notre voyage' (396). It brings us from
'la petite ville de Verrières', perched 'sur la pente d'une colline' and
possibly 'l'une des plus jolies de la Franche-Comté' (3), to Besançon,
'une capitale' situated on 'une montagne', a 'noble ville de guerre'
and 'une des plus jolies villes de France' (154), and then to Paris which
represents, quite simply, ' le monde' (229). On this journey from
sawmill to salon, the status of Julien changes accordingly, and 'notre
héros'[5] is transformed from 'enfant' and 'paysan' into 'fils naturel'
and 'plébéien'. As has been noted, the repeated use of such phrases
as 'quelle différence', 'il devint un autre homme', 'il voyait les choses
sous un nouvel aspect', reinforces the sense of evolution traditionally
associated with a *Bildungsroman*,[6] and there is a world of difference
between an 'amour de cœur' in the provinces for a tall, twenty-nine-
year-old mother of three children whose marital status is held in
sharp focus by the narrator's refusal to call her Louise rather than

---

[5] A label used with less and less irony as the novel unfolds: see 78, 102, 104, 152,
170, 231, 295.

[6] Bardèche's assertion that 'tout roman de Stendhal est l'histoire d'une éducation'
(*Stendhal romancier*, 199) is least questionable in respect of *Le Rouge*. Julien's
acquisition of knowledge through reading and conversation is carefully plotted: see
22-4, 39, 72, 73, 87, 90, 91, 158, 198, 235, 288. Cf. Imbert, *Métamorphoses*, 538.

Madame de Rênal, and an 'amour de tête' for an eighteen-year-old
Parisian blonde, Mathilde, also called Marguerite after Marguerite
de Navarre, who dreams of being Mme Sorel de la Vernaye but has
finally to masquerade as plain Mme Michelet. As there is a world
of difference, too, between the woman who would sincerely like to
have died at her lover's hand (434) and who follows Julien to the
grave (as a consequence of the shooting? from a broken heart?) and
the girl who was merely thrilled at the thought of being nearly killed
by her 'master' (334) and who is left clutching a severed head, in
the manner not so much of Boniface de La Mole's mistress, perhaps,
as of that other performer who claimed the head of St John the
Baptist.[7]

But such changes and contrasts begin to lose their force when one
considers the similarities and parallels which exist between the four
main sections into which the novel falls: Verrières/Vergy and the
Rênal household; Besançon and the seminary; Paris and the Hôtel
de la Mole; Besançon and prison. In Verrières and Paris Julien is
employed in an influential household, respectively of a mayor and
of a marquis about to become a government minister, and the
political life of Verrières (in particular the rivalry between ultra and
liberal) serves as a kind of microcosm of life in the capital. Verrières
has its secret societies (92) and the mysterious ways of provincial
corridors of power are no less evident in the assigning of a lease (I.
xxiii) and the widening of a street (91) than are those of metropolitan
counter-revolutionaries in the incident of the 'note secrète'. As for
the Besançon which figures in the latter pages of Parts I and II, Julien
himself notes that there is 'pas grande différence entre un séminaire
et une prison' (159). In each case the influence of Frilair and the
Congrégation is felt, first in the feud between Jansenist and Jesuit,
and then in the negotiations preceding Julien's trial. On each occasion
Julien occupies a cell offering a fine view from the top of the building
and bringing isolation from the outside world—in the first instance
because of the injury done to Mme de Rênal's reputation, and in
the second because of the injury done to her person. Both times this
isolation causes him to take stock and to change his attitudes, and
both times it ends in a reunion with Mme de Rênal: the reunion at
the end of Part I being enlivened by the comedy of ladder-assisted
arrival and trouserless departure across the walls and terraces with

[7] See Adams, *Notes on a Novelist*, 46, and F. C. St Aubyn, 'Stendhal and Salome',
Stanford French Review, 4 (1980), 395–404.

which the novel opened, and the reunion at the end of Part II rendered tragic by the imminent ascent of the scaffold and departure from life.[8]

The fulcrum of this fine equilibrium is the first chapter of Part II. Itself the description of a journey, this chapter offers not only a broad comparative survey of provincial and Parisian life but also, in the comments of Saint-Giraud, a critique of travel. Changing places offers no escape from the 'comédie perpétuelle, à laquelle oblige ce que vous appelez la civilisation du XIXe siècle', and Saint-Giraud's sophisticated decision to leave Montfleury, 'cet enfer d'hypocrisie et de tracasseries', and to 'chercher la solitude et la paix champêtre au seul lieu où elles existent en France, dans un quatrième étage, donnant sur les Champs-Elysées' not only adumbrates the paradox whereby his fellow-traveller will find happiness and moral freedom in prison but also offers a timely reminder of the paradise Julien has left behind at Vergy and the hell with which he replaced it at the seminary ('voilà donc cet enfer sur la terre, dont je ne pourrai sortir!': 160).

Most of Julien's travels seem to be an illustration of Alphonse Karr's aphorism: 'plus ça change, plus c'est la même chose'. Whether he is going to M. de Rênal's house, Besançon, Paris or even prison, the pattern is unchanging. First, the double denouement of the novel is prefigured by a series of double débuts: at Verrières church before M. de Rênal's house, at the café and hotel before the seminary, at Malmaison before the Hôtel de La Mole. Secondly, the arrivals themselves share a number of common features. At Verrières Julien is overawed by the walls and terraces of M. de Rênal's grounds and intimidated by the iron gates: 'la grille de fer était ouverte, elle lui semblait magnifique, il fallait entrer là-dedans' (25). Beyond that lies the 'porte-fenêtre' and the daunting sight of his future employer, Mme de Rênal. In Besançon he is struck by 'la hauteur des murs, la profondeur des fossés' and 'le mot café, écrit en gros caractères au-dessus des deux immenses portes' fills him with admiration: 'il fit effort sur sa timidité; il osa entrer.' 'Tout était enchantement pour lui' (154). At the seminary the sight of 'la croix de fer doré sur la porte' fills him with dread, and the awesome porter like some feline Cerberus ushers him into

---

[8] This contrast recurs between the endings of the two parts of *La Chartreuse*, but whereas the end of Part I of *Le Rouge* reminds one of Cherubino and the *Marriage of Figaro*, the end of Part I of *La Chartreuse* is more reminiscent of *Don Giovanni*. The two-volume quadripartite structure of *Le Rouge* perhaps owes something to the two- and four-act structure of these Mozart operas. Del Litto, on the other hand, sees a resemblance to a five-act tragedy (O, vii. 17–18).

this Hades ('un silence de mort régnait'; Julien is 'immobile comme frappé à mort': 161).[9] In Paris he first sees the 'vilains murs blancs' dividing the gardens of Malmaison (223), and then comes to the La Mole residence: 'le cocher souleva le marteau de bronze d'une porte immense: c'était l'HOTEL DE LA MOLE; et, pour que les passants ne pussent en douter, ces mots se lisaient sur un marbre noir au-dessus de la porte.' The 'gravité du portier' and the 'architecture magnifique' fill him with 'admiration' and 'enchantement'. He is 'ébahi' (228–9). And likewise, when he comes to enter Besançon prison, he is full of admiration for the fourteenth-century architecture (438).[10]

A most remarkable feature of the novel is the way in which so many incidents and details which are present in Part II duplicate those of Part I. If we consider Julien's mentors, we see that the marquis de La Mole obtains the cross of the Legion of Honour for Julien (266) to go with the one the chirurgien-major had left him (18). Julien is the latter's Benjamin (12) just as he becomes Pirard's (191), and Pirard in turn is a replica of Chélan in the language he uses about Julien (43, 188, 225–6). Likewise with Julien's clothes: a clerical 'habit noir' is the uniform of the private tutor (30, 95) and the secretary (224, 309) and is temporarily swapped for the blue uniform of the guard of honour (95–7) or the 'habit bleu' of the imaginary aristocrat (261). Julien's experiences follow a similar pattern in both parts of the novel. They begin with 'le premier pas' (24, 237); fear of possible danger is met with the brave exclamation 'aux armes!' (25, 310); 'castles in Spain' conflict with real experience (27, 223); there is a test to be passed, either in biblical recitation or discussion of Horace (31–2, 234–5); the respect of the servants must be gained (32, 229) even if, in the eyes of a nobleman, a private tutor is still a 'domestique' (38, 291); initial success comes through relieving the prevailing boredom (33, 242; cf. the titles of I. vi and II. xxix); there is a gift of linen (34, 37, 231); the mistress-to-be has been educated at the Convent of the Sacred Heart where her wealth has made her the object of much false flattery (35, 301); she reveals her amorous interest by leaning on Julien's arm in a singular way (37, 290);

---

[9] Julien's entry into the seminary in turn recalls details of the night he first visited Mme Rênal's bedroom: the sudden sound in an absolute silence, the reference to Saint Peter, the legs giving way, going to one's death.

[10] One wonders if this pattern of arrival at doors and passage through them lay behind Stendhal's temporary choice of Les Trois Portes as a title for the projected tripartite novel about Lucien Leuwen.

her maid is also enamoured of Julien (34 ff, 288); Julien writes down his secret thoughts but is then careful to burn them (69, 250); he must avoid the ridicule of falling from his horse (97, 238); the first night of love makes him feel like a soldier (83, 328); his mistress gives him some hair—Mme de Rênal a lock, Mathilde a whole side (149, 345); he needs to be expert with ladders (205 f., 322 ff.). At one point early in the novel it is said that 'la position morale où il avait été toute sa vie se renouvelait chez M. le maire de Verrières' (40): one wonders if it is not constantly repeated throughout the novel. At any rate there is clear evidence here that where Julien may see novelty, difference and advancement in his affair with Mathilde, the reader—in retrospect—may see mere repetition of former experience and conclude that Julien's move to Paris was a retrograde step.

This conclusion may also be suggested by other elements in Stendhal's choice and description of setting. Julien meets Mme de Rênal at her house in Verrières, but their relationship only develops in the country under the lime-tree at Vergy.[11] Here, away from the town and out of doors, their natural feelings can blossom. Julien meets Mathilde at the dinner-table, and their bookish affair begins appropriately in the library and develops in the artificial atmosphere of the salon, the opera and the ball at the Hôtel de Retz. But again the route to the bedroom leads, both literally and metaphorically, through the garden: 'ses [Mathilde's] opinions dans le jardin étaient bien différentes de celles qu'elle avouait au salon' (289), and they hold their more intimate conversations as they walk beneath its lime-trees. Whereas in Vergy the lime-tree is allowed to grow unchecked, however, the lime-trees in the La Mole garden are 'fort bien taillés' (316) (Parisian pruning being more elegant than the monstrous amputations of Verrières). Such horticultural formality exists at Vergy too, with its garden laid out like the Tuileries 'avec force bordures de buis et allées de marronniers taillés deux fois par an' (46), but Mme de Rênal and Julien shun it in favour of the orchard with its apple-trees and walnuts, there to construct their own little sandy

---

[11] Local belief that it was planted by the 15th-century Duke of Burgundy Charles le Téméraire (52) provides a nicely ironic background to Julien's endeavours to summon up enough courage to hold Mme de Rênal's hand. At the same time the connexion between Mme de Rênal and Gabrielle de Vergy (46) is of a more tragic kind (cf. 122), and the irony in this case is that the tragedy of Gabrielle becomes a story to be related by Mathilde's model, Marguerite de Navarre (in the *Heptaméron*), whereas Mme de Rênal later becomes merely a 'heroïne d'anecdotes' (473).

path for the benefit of the children, their own 'Cours de la Fidélité', offering them easy access to the breathtaking mountain vistas which are as sublime as the music of Mozart (49).

Simple, natural, out of doors, high up,[12] producing refuge 'loin des regards des hommes': these are the characteristics of the Stendhalian paradise, this Garden of Eden which Julien is soon to renounce in favour of the 'world'. But the world is a world of false enclosure. It offers not the calm and contentment of a haven or retreat, but restriction and obstacle. It is a world of walls that keep outsiders out and seem to offer tangible evidence of the solidity of class barriers (even if, as in Valenod's case, they are not quite sound-proof: 133),[13] and a world of gates, doors and even windows[14]—of gates which, as we have seen, have to be entered and of doors which may so easily be shut in one's face.[15] Only in prison does enclosure become a boon, but even then the prisoner may find too many unwelcome visitors gaining access, and it is only high up in the mountain cave near Vergy that Julien is finally at peace—as he had been in life (69).

Yet this is not quite the whole story. For all that Vergy epitomizes some cherished Stendhalian values and for all that Julien's 'chasse au bonheur' could well have ended there, imagination says no. Energy, curiosity and exploration are as important as the trusting repose of reciprocated love, it may even be better to travel than to arrive, 'la chasse' may matter more than 'le bonheur':

mais le voyageur qui vient de gravir une montagne rapide s'assied au sommet, et trouve un plaisir parfait à se reposer. Serait-il heureux si on le forçait à se reposer toujours? (147)

---

[12] See Proust, *A la recherche du temps perdu*, Bibliothèque de la Pléiade, iii. 377, and Brombert, *Fiction*, 173–4.

[13] See Martin Turnell, *The Novel in France* (London, 1950), 142–3. Cf. *OI*, ii. 68: 'la vie privée d'un citoyen [...] comme l'a si bien dit M. de Talleyrand, doit être murée'; and *RS*, 145.

[14] Cf. Le Breton, *'Le Rouge et le Noir' de Stendhal*, 222: 'on voudrait que Julien entrât moins souvent par les fenêtres'!

[15] Note also the importance of threshold: the first meeting between Mme de Rênal and Julien is an example of this with each character poised at the 'porte-fenêtre du salon qui donnait sur le jardin' and the 'porte d'entrée' respectively (26). For further discussion of the topography of the novel see Béatrice Didier, 'Lieux et signes dans *Le Rouge et le Noir*', *Studi Francesi*, 20 (1976), 40–4.

However perfect the view, there are other peaks to climb, and Julien's
wise analogy points to the tragic disjunction between happiness and
imagination which lies at the very heart of *Le Rouge et le Noir* and
is its principal concern. From the start Julien has been faced with
an ancient dilemma: 'comme Hercule, il se trouvait non entre le vice
et la vertu, mais entre la médiocrité d'un bien-être assuré et tous les
rêves héroïques de sa jeunesse' (71), and heroically he defends himself
against the lure of 'la triste prudence' (79). Heroically he abandons
the bliss of Vergy, and heroically he rejects the worldly achievements
of M. Julien Sorel de la Vernaye: 'en un mot, ce qui faisait de Julien
un être supérieur fut précisément ce qui l'empêcha de goûter le
bonheur qui se plaçait sous ses pas. C'est une jeune fille de seize ans,
qui a des couleurs charmantes, et qui, pour aller au bal, a la folie
de mettre du rouge' (82). This 'rouge' is the added lustre that
imagination lends to life, not the knowing artifice of black ambition
but the gratuitous and unthinking enhancement of blood-red vitality,
the wanton assertion that there is more to be had from life even than
all the bounty life may already have bestowed; it is make-up as make-
believe. And it is this very quality of uncalculating passion which
brings Julien the red ribbon of the cross of the Légion d'Honneur
(266) to wear against the unyielding blackness of his clerical habit,
a sign of life to cheer the uniform of his century (309) which he wears
'comme un homme qui est en deuil' (224). For the marquis de la
Mole, when Julien appears before him in red and black, he is an
equal, an aristocrat by nature, an 'homme supérieur', and for us too.
He belongs to that other Legion of Honour, the one founded by
Stendhal after the manner of Napoleon, whose members, though
not legion, make it a point of honour to 'juger la vie avec [leur]
imagination' (343), and whose names—Octave, Julien, Fabrice—
have a Roman ring to recall the energy and *virtù* upon which an
earlier empire was founded.

   Alas, Julien also resembles that other young Roman, Saint
Clement. The real Saint Clement was the third Pope and in no way
military, but the statue of Stendhal's saint is depicted as representing
a 'jeune soldat romain' who has met a violent end: 'il avait au cou
une large blessure d'où le sang semblait couler' (104). This last detail,
the thousand candles which illuminate the 'chapelle ardente'
containing the statue and the relic of the saint, the swooning girls,
all come to mind at the end of the novel when the decapitated Julien
is buried in 'cette petite grotte magnifiquement illuminée d'un nombre

infini de cierges' and Mathilde bears off her capital relic amidst the throng of mountain villagers who have come like pilgrims to witness this strange rite. Julien the latter-day apostate[16] is revealed to be more akin to an early Christian martyr.[17] Imagination not only leads Julien away from happiness, it leads him to premature death: 'le rouge' brings 'le noir'.

The wounded neck represented on the statue of Saint Clement is but one of the many details in the novel which foreshadow Julien's crime and execution and thereby create a sense of fateful inevitability in the mind of the retrospective reader. What may have appeared random at the time now takes on a providential quality such that Pirard's Jansenist words may be recalled: 'il ne faut jamais dire le hasard, mon enfant, dites toujours la Providence' (228). The parallels established by the prospective reader—parvenu, foundling, Napoleon, revolutionary hero—may now be replaced by the figure of the 'homme fatal', the man of exceptional passion and energy whose life is punctuated by intimations of premature mortality and whose superiority is the cause of his downfall. We may remember the piece of paper in the pew in Verrières church and its reference to the execution of Louis Jenrel. We may smile that Julien notes only that 'son nom finit comme le mien' (25) whereas it is an exact anagram of his own, and we may even be led by this to realize that Julien Sorel and Louise de Rênal are anagrammatically almost united.[18] We note the crimson drapery and the red light that turns

---

[16] See Castex's note 23 to i. 18. Cf. F. W. J. Hemmings, 'Julien Sorel and Julian the Apostate', *French Studies*, 16 (1962), 229–44, and Imbert, *Métamorphoses*, 595–602. Note also the parallels with Flaubert's *Saint Julien l'Hospitalier*, such as the thematic opposition of the military and the ecclesiastical, the predictions, the murder in a church (even if Mme de Rênal has little in common with a mouse!), and the revaluation of self after crime. But who was the 'Saint Julien' whom Stendhal saw canonized in 1824 for having restored life to roast larks on a Friday? See *VIT*, 655.

[17] For further discussion of the parallel with St Clement see Imbert, *Métamorphoses*, 580–2; Gilman, *The Tower as Emblem*, 26–7; Stirling Haig, 'The Identities of Fabrice Del Dongo', *French Studies*, 27 (1973), 170–6 (172); Strickland, *Stendhal*, 163; and Longstaffe, 'L'éthique du duel', 306.

[18] See Jean-Marie Gleize, 'Stendhal: le travail du texte', *Romantisme*, 1 (1971), 156–63 (158). Cf. E. B. O. Borgerhoff, 'The Anagram in *Le Rouge et le Noir*', *Modern Language Notes*, 68 (1953), 383–6, and Armand Hoog, 'Le "rôle" de Julien', *Stendhal Club*, 20 (1977/8), 131–42 (for whom Julien Sorel = je lis un rôle). For further erudite horseplay on the subject of Julien's names see Claude Liprandi, 'De "l'origine du nom Sorel" à l'origine de *Rouge* et *Noir*'; Jean-Jacques Hamm, 'Hypothèses sur quelques noms propres de *Rouge et Noir*', *Stendhal Club*, 18 (1975/6), 228–34; and Anthony Purdy, 'Un cheval nommé Sorel et une taupe régicide. Réflexions onomastiques sur *Le Rouge et le Noir*', *Stendhal Club*, 22 (1979/80), 144–52.

the holy water to blood (24–5), just as we note the crimson curtains of the equally new church at Bray-le-Haut (98), and how the red damask with which the abbé Chas-Bernard transforms Besançon cathedral, after a funeral service, to celebrate Corpus Christi (183) provides a prophetic backdrop to Mme de Rênal's collapse. And the crimson curtains are duly drawn when Julien shoots Mme de Rênal at the moment of the *élévation*, the raising of the Host, the Body of Christ.[19] Verrières even means 'church windows'.[20]

And might we not also note that, when Julien takes 'le premier pas' in Verrières church, he is said to 'faire une station à l'église' (22); that he is tried on a Friday (464); that there are three days during which he can appeal (467);[21] that he shares his champagne with two petty criminals, one of whom is irredeemable (478–9); that Fouqué must, like Joseph of Arimathaea, plead for his mortal remains (488); that this son of a sawyer is consistently referred to as the son of a carpenter. We remember the irony that Julien read Rousseau's *Confessions* without learning its lesson: is there the further irony that the man who could recite the New Testament by heart (20, 31)[22] was unwittingly foretelling his future? Has Julien been crucified for the values he proclaims by a society that fears the radical threat they pose? Has the man who won the cross of the Legion of Honour for his energy and imagination been nailed to the cross of bourgeois reaction? After all, we know who made the nails: M. de Rênal.[23]

The road which Julien and the reader-tourist travel in *Le Rouge et le Noir* is a *via dolorosa*. But wherein lies redemption? Do we look askance at Julien's imagination and exclaim, as Mirabeau does

---

[19] For further comment on these scenes and the recurrence of red, see Reizov, 'Pourquoi Stendhal'; Mouillaud, *Le Roman possible*, 151–6 and ff., and Pollard, 'Colour Symbolism'.

[20] Reviews of Langlois's *Essai historique sur la peinture sur verre* published in 1832 suggest that this usage was then on the wane. In the *Journal des Débats* (6 Mar. 1832) M. B. writes of 'ce qui reste des vitraux de couleur, des *verrières* comme on disait, de nos vieilles églises gothiques'; and in the *Revue des Deux Mondes*, (15 April 1832), 255, there is mention of 'ces verrières, commes les initiés ont continué de les appeler'.

[21] Cf. *RN*, 149, where Julien leaves Mme de Rênal only to return after three days, whereupon she resembles a 'cadavre vivant' (153); and 489 where Mme de Rênal dies three days after Julien.

[22] In his projected review Stendhal refers mistakenly to the Old Testament (*RN*, 719).

[23] For a slightly different account of the parallel between Julien and Christ, see Richard B. Grant, 'The Death of Julien Sorel'. Cf. also Imbert, *Métamorphoses*, 581–2.

in the epigraph which precedes the shooting of Mme de Rênal: 'Mon Dieu, donnez-moi la médiocrité!'? Do we content ourselves with the retrospective view that what led Julien away from the paradise of Vergy was mere foolish ambition and that the ultimate truth of the novel lies in his prison-idyll with Mme de Rênal and the discovery of his unique self? Julien, then, is a man saved at the last minute from the error of his ways? Perhaps, even, the lovers are reunited in death?[24] Redemption, according to this line of thinking, would lie in sincerity and true love.

Or do we prefer to revert to the heroic outlook of our prospective view of Julien and see him once more in terms of other people, as indeed a man of destiny, not—as it turns out—of military or political destiny so much as a quasi-religious one? Is it perhaps only through imagination that the world can be redeemed? Through the actions of great men with vision enough to transcend the predictable? Through literature too? Does the novel condemn itself to critical death to redeem the world of 1830? In the revolution of 1830 a red and black flag meant a 'fight to the death';[25] at the battle of *Hernani* a red and black ticket meant you had been chosen to fight for Hugo against the last bastion of Classical taste.[26] What better title could Stendhal have chosen for a novel which denies the happiness of rank, wealth and marriage, substitutes that of classless adultery, and turns the life of a peasant who attempts murder during Mass into another *Imitation of Christ*?

[24] The various references to the possibility of an afterlife (104, 466, 473) and the final detail that Mme de Rênal has not committed suicide (489) suggest that Stendhal is leaving this possibility of a reunion in death open for those who would believe it—and who do not see Julien as destined at once for purgatory. See Richard, 'Connaissance et tendresse', 72–3, especially 72: 'l'optimisme romanesque est si fort en Stendhal qu'il va jusqu'à balancer parfois le scepticisme incrédule'. Also Bishop, 'Laughter and the Smile', 65.

[25] See above, note 19 to III. 8.

[26] See *Victor Hugo raconté par un témoin de sa vie* (2 vols, Paris, 1863), ii. 308–9: 'M. Victor Hugo acheta plusieurs mains de papier rouge, et coupa les feuilles en petits carrés sur lesquels il imprima avec une griffe le mot espagnol qui veut dire *fer*: Hierro [Adèle Hugo here reproduces the drawing of a knotted rope spelling out the word Hierro]. Il distribua ces carrés aux chefs de tribu [previously designated as 'Gautier, Gérard [de Nerval], Pétrus Borel, etc.']'. See also Théophile Gautier, *Histoire du romantisme* (Paris, 1874), 101: 'on s'enrégimenta par petites escouades dont chaque homme avait pour passe le carré de papier rouge timbré de la griffe *Hierro*' (cf. 117: 'grâce au carré de papier rouge égratigné de la griffe *Hierro*, nous entrions au Théâtre-Français bien avant l'heure de la représentation'). The 'griffe *Hierro*' was a rebus meaning Nodo Hierro, the iron knot of Hugo's supporters and a play on the name of Charles Nodier, leader of the first Romantic Cénacle. I assume the ink was black.

It is up to the individual reader to decide whether to opt for one of these alternatives or to entertain them both. The novel itself presents the incompatibility of happiness and imagination as a problem without solution, a problem illustrated by events in 1830 but for which solution has been, and will be, sought in every age. This tourist-guide presents no design for living. Unlike Julien and Mathilde after their reading, the reader of *Le Rouge et le Noir* is left not with heroic preconceptions of life but with the resonance of an unanswered question. He is thus in a better position to obey the golden rule which Stendhal once laid down for himself:

regarder tout ce que j'ai lu jusqu'à ce jour sur l'hom[me] comme une prédiction; ne croire que ce que j'ai vu moi-même. *Joy, happiness, fame, all is upon it'.*[27]

[27] *OI*, i. 79.

IV

SINCERITY AND STYLE IN
LUCIEN LEUWEN

The Reader in Question

'Il n'y a que deux choses sur lesquelles on n'ait pas encore trouvé le moyen d'être hypocrite: amuser quelqu'un dans la conversation, et gagner une bataille.'

(*LL*, ii. 105)

'En relisant, se faire toujours la double question: de quel œil le héros voit-il ceci? De quel œil le lecteur?'

(*LL*, i. 347)

1

Text, context and choice of genre

'Si ceci ne vaut rien, j'aurai perdu un an de travail; il valait mieux
faire les *Mémoires* de Dominique.'

(ii. 579)

LE *Rouge et le Noir* appeared on 13 November 1830, somewhat
ahead of the schedule envisaged by its publisher Levavasseur who
had put 1831 on its title-page. One week earlier Stendhal had left
Paris to take up a post as consul, first in Trieste and then—when
the Austrians had refused to accept the nomination of this liberal
who had once troubled them in Milan—at Civitavecchia. After nearly
three years during which he was 'presque uniquement occupé de
[son] métier'[1] and yet found time to write *Le Juif* (January–March
1831) and *San Francesco a Ripa* (September–December 1831), the
Souvenirs d'égotisme (20 June–4 July 1832) and the unfinished *Une
position sociale* (September 1832), he returned to Paris for three
months' leave in the autumn of 1833. Amongst the many people with
whom he renewed contact was a friend of long standing, Mme Jules
Gaulthier, who asked him to look at a novel she had written called
Le Lieutenant. Having rather better things to do on leave,[2] Stendhal
took it back to Civitavecchia with him, from where, on 4 May 1834,
he wrote to its author in the following candid terms: 'il faudra le
recopier en entier et vous figurer que vous traduisez un livre en
allemand.'[3] The style was 'horriblement noble et emphatique' and
exemplified in such phrases as 'la passion qui le dévorait' or 'la passion
brûlante d'Olivier pour Hélène', certain sections were too heavily
narrative and needed the leaven of dialogue, and the denouement
fell flat: 'Olivier a l'air de chasser aux millions.' Also it would be
better entitled *Leuwen ou l'Elève chassé de l'Ecole Polytechnique* since
this would allude to Olivier's relationship with Edmond, and 'le
caractère d'*Edmond*, ou l'*académicien futur*, est ce qu'il y a de plus
neuf dans *le Lieutenant*.' In short Mme Gaulthier should cure her

---

[1] *OI*, ii. 194.   [2] *Corr.*, ii. 559–60 (11 Oct. 1833).   [3] *Corr.*, ii. 643.

style with daily doses of Marivaux's *Vie de Marianne* and Mérimée's *Chronique du règne de Charles IX* and obey one basic rule: 'en décrivant un homme, une femme, un site, songez toujours à quelqu'un, à quelque chose de réel.' As to the manuscript itself, he would return it to her when he could.

Mme Gaulthier was to take all this criticism in extremely good part: 'je vous disais bien que j'étais une grosse oie incapable de pondre un bon œuf.'[4] As for Stendhal, one sleepless night 'du 8 au 9 mai 1834' caused him to think again about the manuscript and to have the 'première idée de ne pas *send it to* Mme Jules, mais d'en *make* un *opus*. Avec cette lady, cela tomberait rapidement dans le *non lu* des cabinets littéraires pour femmes de chambre.'[5] Thus began a year of concentrated novel-writing prompted, as in the case of *Armance, Le Rouge* and *La Chartreuse*, by reading someone else's story.[6] By the end of April 1835 he felt he had completed a first draft (i. 371).[7] Meanwhile the process of revision had begun within ten days of his first putting pen to paper, and so began the curiously schizophrenic process of writing the first draft, forgetting it and then going back to improve it as if it were somebody else's.[8] Revision continued until 23 September 1835 when, midway through chapter xviii, he ceased dictation of a 'final' version bearing the title *Le Chasseur vert*. While he tinkered with the novel in October and November, and again in the autumn of the following year when he was back in Paris, the impetus had ceased, and on 23 November 1835 he began his autobiography, the *Vie de Henry Brulard*.

---

[4] *Corr.*, i. 916 (5 June 1834).

[5] *OI*, ii. 195. But cf. 194: '1er mai [18]34, *in* Rome, *lavoro after* tant de paresse. *I make Leuwen*.'

[6] Hemmings has suggested that Mme Gaulthier may in fact have derived inspiration for her novel from the following passage in *Racine et Shakespeare* (1825): 'c'est ainsi qu'un jeune homme à qui le ciel a donné quelque délicatesse d'âme, si le hasard le fait sous-lieutenant et le jette à sa garnison, dans la société de certaines femmes, croit de bonne foi, en voyant les succès de ses camarades et le genre de leurs plaisirs, croit insensible à l'amour. Un jour enfin le hasard lui présente à une femme simple, naturelle, honnête, digne d'être aimée, et il sent qu'il a un cœur' (*RS*, 110). See *Stendhal*, 134–5. Hemmings has good reason to be tentative about his suggestion, for the evidence is slim. In the passage quoted Stendhal is illustrating his point that, in feeling obliged to admire some of the more absurd conventions of neoclassical drama, theatre-goers may have been led to believe themselves incapable of authentic aesthetic pleasure. By way of illustration he has clearly chosen a well-known, typical situation. One may infer Mme Gaulthier's lack of originality not because she copies Stendhal but because she has adopted a hackneyed plot. Hence Stendhal's kindly reference to the originality of the figure of the future academician Edmond.

[7] See also *OI*, ii. 247 (30 April 1835).

[8] Cf. ii. 461, n. 173. See also above I. 1, note 45.

The result of this sixteen-month flurry of creativity was the five-volume quarto manuscript now in the Bibliothèque municipale de Grenoble containing 2,139 pages[9] and known traditionally as *Lucien Leuwen*.[10] On some sixteen hundred of these pages is the text of the novel, set out in eighteen or nineteen lines of large script on the right-hand side of each recto and accompanied on the left and verso by corrections, comments and additions which are roughly equivalent in quantity to the text of the novel itself. The remaining five hundred or so pages are blank sheets which Stendhal had bound in to accommodate the fuller treatment of certain scenes which he had deferred in the interests of narrative momentum.[11] Textually, therefore, this is by far Stendhal's most problematic work, and since Stendhal's literary executor Romain Colomb first published the chapters dictated under the title *Le Chasseur vert* in 1855, various editors have wrestled more or less successfully with its complexities.[12] Not only are there many gaps, repetitions and inconsistencies, but also, and more importantly, a large number of additions and deletions are proposed by Stendhal in the margins of his text, and each editor has to decide which of these Stendhal might

[9] MS R.301. Further pages are to be found under R.5896 (vols. v and xiii). For additional information see Crouzet's edition for Garnier-Flammarion, i. 17–20, and Anne-Marie Meininger's for the Collection de l'Imprimerie Nationale, i. 67–9. I am indebted to both editors.

[10] The numerous titles envisaged by Stendhal were, in chronological order, *Les Trois Portes*, *L'Orange de Malte*, *Le Télégraphe ou L'Orange de Malte*, *Lucien Leuwen*, *L'Amarante et le Noir*, *Les Bois de Prémol*, *Le Chasseur vert*, *Le Rouge et le Blanc*, *Le Bleu et le Blanc*.

[11] There are also some engravings. See ii. 480, and cf. ii. 585. Ostensibly Stendhal bound these in to reduce the chances of the manuscript being thrown away, but a recent article on the inclusion of engravings in *Vie de Henry Brulard* suggests there may have been a more intriguing purpose. See Carol Mossman, 'Les gravures de la *Vie de Henry Brulard*. Iconographie brulardienne: les figures d'une écriture', *Stendhal Club*, 28 (1985/6), 339–53. Mossman argues persuasively that the engravings offer an intentional, hidden commentary on the text of *Brulard*. Had Stendhal already begun to think of such a device in composing *Lucien Leuwen*?

[12] Jean de Mitty's gallant but far from ideal first edition of 1894 was followed by Henry Debraye's much more scrupulous version for Champion in 1926–7, and by Henri Martineau's various editions from 1929 to 1959 in which scholarship tends to be sacrificed to textual coherence and readability. Attempts to improve on Debraye have been made more recently by Victor Del Litto for Livre de Poche in 1973 and by Anne-Marie Meininger for the prestigious Collection de l'Imprimerie Nationale in 1982. While readers of Stendhal await the new edition currently being prepared by Del Litto for the Bibliothèque de la Pléiade, one may rely on the Debraye edition as presented by Michel Crouzet for Garnier-Flammarion in 1982. References in the text are to the two volumes of this edition. For full bibliographical details of editions of *Lucien Leuwen* see Meininger, ed. cit., i. 73–4.

have effected in a final version. This uncertainty is a direct consequence of Stendhal's decision to write as much as possible and then polish it later. In the case of *Le Rouge* he claims to have had to add material at the last minute in order to fill out the two volumes, and he does not want to be in the same position again. Better that the manuscript should be too long and that he should have to cut.[13]

As such, then, *Lucien Leuwen* is clearly unfinished, and any critic of the novel has to tread much more warily than with *Armance, Le Rouge* and *La Chartreuse* where definitive texts are available. In particular he has to decide when to attribute difficulty of interpretation to authorial subtlety and when to mere indecision or to an oversight occurring during the process of rapid, spontaneous narration which Stendhal considered conducive to an authentic style.[14] Yet compared with *Lamiel*, let alone all the 'romans abandonnées' which litter Stendhal's career as a novelist, *Lucien Leuwen* does seem complete. This impression may be due in part to the structural tidiness of the work, and in particular to the way in which major events are prepared for and the careful balance between the two parts of the novel. Thus, for example, Lucien's eventual departure to an embassy is adumbrated early on (i. 97), as is the sudden change of fortune which precipitates it (i. 99). The information which Du Poirier receives about Lucien's father and his bank in Part I points forward to M. Leuwen's dealings with the comte de Vaize in Part II: 'cette maison, lui disait-on, est du petit nombre de celles qui achètent, dans l'occasion, des nouvelles aux ministres, ou les exploitent de compte et demi avec eux' (i. 232); and this passage continues with what is almost a summary of much of Part II: 'c'était particulièrement M. Leuwen père qui se livrait à ce mauvais genre d'affaires, qui ruinent à la longue, mais qui donnent des relations agréables et de l'importance.' Lucien's work in the Ministry

[13] ii. 502, n. 466. Cf. ii. 510–11. The decision to include more physical description of the characters than he had in *Le Rouge* (i. 406, n. 434) derives, however, less from a desire for volume than from the feeling that he had been too cursory in *Le Rouge*, particularly in respect of the secondary characters, and that he had failed to help 'l'imagination du lecteur par de petits détails' (i. 397, n. 348. See also ii. 575–6).

[14] Repeatedly he asserts in the margins that he wrote first and planned afterwards. Had he been writing to a plan, he says, the effort to remember what was supposed to come next would have inhibited his imagination and prevented the fluent unfolding of dialogue and event. The novelist has to forgo preconception and remain 'disponible'. See ii. 464, n. 192; 538, note a; 582 (fol. 2 v°); 587 (fol. E v°); 592, note b. Cf. ii. 550: '*The* plan a été ma *plague* pendant tout le temps de ce roman, au contraire de *Julien*, où le plan était donné et où je ne voulais admettre aucune altération à la vérité.'

of the Interior, the use of 'agents provocateurs', and his father's
election to the Chambre des Députés, his subsequent politicking and
ultimate bankruptcy are all foreshadowed in this way. So much so
that one begins to wonder, as with Stendhal's other novels, whether
unity is the only reason for this technique. Is he trying to detract
from the suspense? Is he introducing these details early on so that
when the events actually occur they appear more plausible for having
been mentioned already?[15] Or is he even seeking to create a sense
of fateful inevitability? This problem arises most acutely in the
passage where Lucien contemplates his future as a soldier. Like Julien
he reflects on the kind of life he might have led in the Napoleonic
army, and in particular he imagines himself being wounded and then
nursed by a young country-girl in Swabia or Italy (the dream that
comes true for Fabrice in Belgium):

mais non [...] je ne ferai la guerre qu'aux cigares; je deviendrai un pilier
du café militaire dans la triste garnison d'une petite ville mal pavée; j'aurai,
pour mes plaisirs du soir, des parties de billard et des bouteilles de bière,
et quelquefois, le matin, la guerre aux tronçons de choux, contre de sales
ouvriers mourant de faim... (i. 103)

And this of course is exactly what will happen to Lucien, down to
the last detail. What should one deduce from this? That for all
Lucien's brave attempts to become his own man he has in fact no
freedom and that his career is already mapped out? That the problem
with being a soldier under Louis-Philippe is the very predictability
of military life, especially when compared with the more
adventurous, unpredictable times that were to be had under
Napoleon? Whatever reasons may have led Stendhal to this
technique, such prefiguration contributes substantially to the unity
of the novel.

So does the careful balance established between Parts I and II and
which is clearly reminiscent of the structure of *Le Rouge et le Noir*,
with Part I depicting the provinces and describing the hero's one true
love, and Part II depicting Paris (and plotting in the provinces) and
describing the hero's attempt at a calculated seduction of a Parisian
beauty. In *Lucien Leuwen* this symmetry may lead the reader to
compare the sterile virtue of Mme de Chasteller with the hidebound

---

[15] A technique which would be comparable with that whereby Stendhal introduces
the setting of a climactic scene some time before the scene occurs so that novelty of
background will not divert attention from the drama of the climactic event itself. See
Prévost, *Création*, 318–19.

inactivity of her Legitimist circle, and to contrast both with the opportunism and hypocrisy of Mme Grandet and the parliamentary representatives of the *juste milieu*. He may even speculate about the structural parallel established between Lucien's discoveries of Mme de Chasteller's (supposed) duplicity and his father's bankruptcy. Surrounding these comparisons and contrasts is the explicit framework of a 'roman d'éducation', the apprenticeship of a 'blanc-bec' (i. 110, ii, 87) who appears 'encore un peu neuf' (i. 129), 'bien jeune encore' (i. 163), who becomes 'un peu moins neuf' (i. 227) but still has many lessons (ii. 109, 142) to learn, and in whom, even within seventy pages of the end, 'le véritable caractère [...] ne paraissait point encore' (ii. 362).

Embellishing this framework and adding further to the coherence of the novel is a modicum of landscape and colour symbolism also reminiscent of *Le Rouge et le Noir*. Thus the contrast between gloomy garrison life and the delights of nascent love is reflected in the antithesis of Nancy and the woods of Burelviller. Situated on 'la plaine la plus triste du monde' boasting three trees and the prospect of some bald hillocks, approached through 'deux tristes rangées d'ormes rabougris', past an abattoir, a vegetable-oil refinery and vast gardens of cabbage (i. 123) is Nancy, 'triste bicoque hérissée de fortifications', with its main square 'traversée aux deux bouts par des fossés puants, charriant les immondices de la ville' and surrounded by 'un millier de petits tilleuls rabougris, soigneusement taillés en éventail' (i. 139). But away from Nancy, at the edge of the sad plain are the 'bois noirs magnifiques' of Burelviller, a magical place of romance and excitement where the 'café du *Chasseur vert*' offers refreshment and music and an opportunity for intimate conversation and sylvan dalliance. Here, in a Lotharingian Vergy, Lucien and Mme de Chasteller can be free of the constraints of salon life, can speak openly to each other and come close to a mutual declaration of love: 'tel est le danger de la sincérité, de la musique et des grands bois' (i. 321)!

If Stendhal considered *Le Chasseur vert* as a possible title for the novel, however, it was not only because of this café which provides a focal point for 'ces rares moments [pour lesquels] il vaut la peine de vivre' (i. 322), but also because Lucien himself is a kind of 'chasseur vert'. As a lancer, the Napoleonic equivalent of an eighteenth-century 'chasseur de cavalerie', he wears a green uniform, and his 'façon particulière d'aller à la chasse du bonheur' (i. 337) is certainly characterized by youth and immaturity. At the same time his green contrasts with the chaste white of Legitimist affiliation and of the dress which Mme de Chasteller wears to the Marcilly ball. As well as *Le Rouge et le Blanc, Le Vert et le Blanc* could also have suggested itself to Stendhal as a title, and it is fitting that Lucien's first sight of Mme de Chasteller and his subsequent chain-smoking vigils outside her house should have as their point of focus 'au milieu d'un grand mur blanc [...] une persienne peinte en vert perroquet' (i. 125)—even if he does think such a combination of colours to be in the worst possible taste. But then what lovelorn hero ever rolled his own and caused his 'princesse lointaine'[16] to suck liquorice cigarette-papers behind closed shutters? (i. 101, 246, 310).

The critic of *Lucien Leuwen* is faced, then, with an intriguing combination of, on the one hand, textual indeterminacy and, on the other, some structural and symbolic coherence. The novel is, as it were, provisionally complete or, as Anne-Marie Meininger puts it:

quand [...] Stendhal abandonne son œuvre, il la laisse achevée; le roman a un début, deux parties et un épilogue. Simplement, il n'est pas fini, c'est-à-dire pas fignolé. Épisodes esquissés, prévus, ôtés, à faire renaître peut-être, phrases et mots en l'air, tout est resté en mouvement, non fixé, et, devenu ainsi un éternel mobile de l'action et du verbe, c'est un chef-d'œuvre unique. Unique parce que les écrivains ne s'autorisent pas ce laisser-aller; ils mettent au point, civilisent, guindent. De cela, au fond, Stendhal se moquait.[17]

Here perhaps is a pointer to the most fruitful approach which one can adopt towards *Lucien Leuwen*. Reading from the perspective of 'l'ère du soupçon'[18] which finds more sincerity in the open text than in the false assurance of affirmation and closure, we may come to see virtue in such textual difficulty. This is especially true if we ask if *Lucien's story* is finished. Originally Stendhal had envisaged a three-part novel with the third part devoted to a portrayal of embassy life in Rome (or Madrid) and an account of Lucien's affair with the ambassador's wife (i.e. something approximating to *Une position sociale*). The novel would have ended with the marriage

---

[16] See Crouzet, *Quatre études*, 110. See also Jean Rousset, 'Variations sur les distances: aimer de loin', in Philippe Berthier *et al.*, *Le Plus Méconnu des romans de Stendhal* (Paris, 1983), 75–87.

[17] Ed. cit., i. 10.

[18] The phrase which Nathalie Sarraute derived from Stendhal's famous statement that 'le génie poétique est mort, mais le génie du *soupçon* est venu au monde' (*OI*, ii. 430).

of Lucien and Mme de Chasteller (i. 397–8, ii. 454, 528). Having decided not to proceed with this third part on the ground that no reader could be expected to acquaint himself, so far into the novel, with a whole new set of characters (ii. 575), Stendhal was able to proclaim that his first draft was finished ('la toile est couverte': i. 371, 372), and to devote himself entirely to revision. But this change of plan altered the significance of the main events of his plot. Mme de Chasteller's 'faux accouchement' at the end of Part I at once ceased to be the cause of the misunderstanding which traditionally interrupts the course of true love and which is just as traditionally explained when the doubting lover once more declares his faith in his beloved (cf. i. 398, n. 352).[19] Instead it became more the grotesque end of an affair, and Lucien's relationship with Mme de Chasteller merely a stage in a young man's development, albeit one which provides him with a sacred image of love by which to measure future experience. Similarly, the death of M. Leuwen and his bankruptcy at the end of Part II ceased to serve as a point of transition and became important as events in themselves, giving much greater prominence than originally envisaged to the character of Lucien's father and throwing into much greater relief the possible symbolic significance of bankruptcy and the role of money in the novel.[20] At the same time Lucien's departure for Italy contributes to a considerable impression of circularity at the end of the novel, as he goes off to earn his living for real rather than, as at the beginning, by way of an artificial attempt to prove he can do it. And his need to 'se sermonner' into seriousness as he reaches his new place of work offers a nice reminder of Ernest Dévelroy's original 'sermon' with which the novel began. Likewise the open-endedness of this conclusion may be seen to correspond to the indeterminacy of the novel's beginning, where multiple prefaces and alternative beginnings combine with chronological imprecision and the uncertainty about Lucien's reasons for being out on the streets[21] to produce the most hesitant and ambiguous of starts.

[19] For Crouzet (*Quatre études*, 106) the comedy of the novel is underpinned by 'le "mythe" de l'amour romanesque, ou le code d'une courtoisie sans âge' which, despite the lack of Part III, manifests itself in a whole series of topoi from chivalric romance. Crouzet is tacitly refuting Gilbert Durand's argument about the negation of mythic and epic patterns in the novel. See Durand, '*Lucien Leuwen*, ou l'héroïsme à l'envers', *Stendhal Club*, 1 (1958/9), 201–25.

[20] Cf. i. 373, n. 206: '10 et 11 septembre 35. Je remarque ce détail: il y a diablement d'*argent* dans ce livre.' See also Crouzet, *Quatre études*, ch. ii.

[21] See Crouzet's comments on this, i. 342–3.

Whatever the resonance of the last sentence of the novel it is clear that Stendhal's decision to suppress Part III eliminates the conventional ending of marriage and substitutes the more open one ✓ of departure and a new beginning, such that one may be put in mind of *Les Faux-Monnayeurs* and Gide's notion that a novel should be able to end with the words 'pourrait être continué'. In the case of *Lucien Leuwen* we know it could have been, and the fact that Stendhal has left it to us to imagine what happened at Capel and to wonder if Lucien and Bathilde ever met again seems all the more effective. 'On serait bien curieux de connaître Capel.' Like Edgar, 'le Parisien de vingt ans' and, by analogy, Lucien himself, the text of *Lucien Leuwen* becomes 'un brillant *peut-être*' (ii. 101).

The provisional nature of the novel needs of course to be placed in context. What were Stendhal's original ambitions in writing it? What were the constraints upon him? Why did he stop writing? Thanks to the rich documentation in the margins of the novel (what Meininger in Gidean fashion calls the *Journal de Lucien Leuwen*[22]), much evidence is available which may help to answer these questions. From the very first plan Stendhal's main aim seems to have been exhaustive topicality, since the three volumes of his projected work were to depict in turn: '1° l'*Henriquinquisme* en province; 2° le ministre comme né [*sic*][23] à Paris; 3° la cour de Rome et l'Hérodiade' (i. 398)—i.e. Legitimist circles in the provinces, the world of Louis-Philippe and *juste milieu* government, in particular the Ministry of the Interior, and the world of international politics as represented by the Court at Rome (with Mme de Saint-Aulaire, the ambassador's wife, acting as focal Herodias). Of the first he had experience through his ex-mistress Clémentine Curial (Menti),[24] of the second through various Parisian contacts, especially Joseph Lingay who worked in the Ministry of the Interior,[25] and of the third naturally through his own post as consul. Such experience was

---

[22] Ed. cit., i. 11.

[23] i.e. the comte d'Argout, one of Louis-Philippe's ministers, whose large 'nez' was a great help to cartoonists and whom Stendhal refers to elsewhere as Grandnez. See ii. 467, n. 212; 509, nn. 518 and 519.

[24] See Meininger, ed. cit., i. 26.

[25] Referred to by Stendhal as Maisonnette because he worked as secretary to the duc Decazes (whom Stendhal dubbed Maison for obvious reasons), Joseph Lingay is described in the *Souvenirs d'égotisme*. See *OI*, ii. 438 (and n. 2), 501-2, 505 (and n. 1), 506-8. Also Bardèche, *Stendhal romancier*, 255.

supplemented by extensive reading of newspapers of all political persuasions which he had sent to him from Paris.

But why be so topical? *Le Rouge et le Noir* had been a 'Chronique de 1830' and purported to depict 'la vérité, l'âpre vérité'. Did Stendhal now want to provide a similar, or indeed even more damning chronicle of the aftermath of 'les trois Glorieuses'? This may be what is implied by his cryptic comment in the margin of the novel on 5 May 1834: 'en commençant les *Bois de Prémol* en mai 1834, [...] je pense qu'il m'arrivera l'accident noté au bas de la page 250 ou 300 du second volume de *Rouge et Noir, the charge* [*sic?*] *of the present comedy*' (ii. 575). It is now thought that 'charge' here should read 'change', and that Stendhal is anticipating an imminent change of government such as occurred in 1830 when he was finishing *Le Rouge*.[26] In which case is Stendhal perhaps anxious that this novel he is now beginning will be overtaken by events and rendered out-of-date even before it is published? Such may have been his concern at the outset,[27] and he may have entertained the prospect of an early and remunerative publication,[28] but generally he seems to have been well aware that he could never publish it while still consul. Already in June 1832 he had refused an offer to publish from Henri Dupuy and declared his 'résolution de ne rien publier tant que je serai employé par le g[ouvernemen]t',[29] and on 17 February 1835, in one of his innumerable wills, he acknowledges that 'tant que pour vivre je serai obligé de servir le Budget, je ne pourrai *print it*, car ce que le Budget déteste le plus, c'est qu'on fasse semblant d'avoir des idées' (ii. 586).[30] Any fond notion of publishing it would finally have been dispelled in September by the abolition of the freedom of the press. A guarantee of this freedom had been an important part of the Charter drawn up in 1830 upon Louis-Philippe's accession, but the consequences for both monarch and government had been newspaper attacks of such virulence (and of such help to an expatriate writer in search of information) that a law to abolish it was given

[26] The note mentioned by Stendhal may be that which reads: 'cette feuille, composée le 25 juillet 1830, a été imprimée le 4 août'. See Meininger, ed. cit., i. 63.

[27] Mme Meininger thinks that Stendhal anticipated a change of government which would allow him to publish, but his use of the term 'accident' would seem to imply something negative rather than positive.

[28] See his letter to Domenico Fiore, *Corr.*, iii. 58 (15 April 1835): 'la petite chambre, avec cinq francs de revenu et cinq francs gagnés par *les Bois de Prémol* serait le bonheur suprême.'

[29] *Corr.*, ii. 456.

[30] By 'le Budget' he of course means the government, his paymaster.

royal assent on 9 September 1835. There is every reason to suppose that Stendhal ceased dictation of the *Le Chasseur vert* on 23 September because he had just received this news,[31] and in a letter of 27 September he tells the writer and critic Albert Stapfer about '*le Chasseur vert*, que je ne puis imp[rimer] tant que je mange au budget.'[32]

So, if he knew he would not be able to publish, why be so topical? The fact that he thought there might be a change of government and that he might be able to publish in 1838 or 1839 is not of much help, since by then his novel would already have begun to date: 'mais les modèles connus par mois en 1829 et 30, revus un instant en 1833, seront morts ou éloignés de la scène du monde quand l'*Orange* (ou le *Télégraphe*) paraîtra, en 1838 ou 1839' (ii. 522). It would seem rather that the motive behind this pursuit of information about contemporary France was an aesthetic one, and that Stendhal was scrupulously following the advice he had given Mme Gaulthier: 'songez toujours à quelqu'un, à quelque chose de réel.' Buried away in Civitavecchia and having spent only three months out of the last three and a half years in France he must have been concerned at being out of touch and that his depiction of Nancy and Paris might be mistaken in its detail. It was of paramount importance to be '*vrai pour tout artifice*' (ii. 468), and hence all the 'modèles' and 'pilotis' which fill the margins of his text. Every character, every event, every stylistic register, even a marble table Mme de Chasteller leans on (i. 399 n. 363), has to have a real-life counterpart so that the fiction will ring true, and Michel Crouzet's edition shows how solidly the 'pilotis' are sunk into the ground not just of Stendhal's own personal experience but also of contemporary govenment, electioneering, banking and even the royal abuse of power for financial gain.

Such documentation is not only an aid to verisimilitude ('historique', 'à vérifier' recur constantly in the margins) but also a stimulus to the creative imagination, such that Stendhal will sometimes leave the real names of his models in the text 'pour guider l'imagination' (ii. 511) before he returns to replace them with asterisks or code or imaginary alternatives. Sometimes the reality of the model threatens to interfere with his artistic aims, as when he admonishes himself for relying too heavily on his own affair with Matilde Dembowski in his description of Lucien and Mme de Chasteller:

---

[31] See Meininger, ed. cit., i. 63–4.   [32] *Corr.*, iii. 129.

'tu n'es qu'un *naturaliste*: tu ne *choisis* pas les modèles, mais prends pour *love* toujours Métilde et Dominique' (i. 391). As will be seen, part of his purpose in Part I of the novel is the comic portrayal of love *à la* Marivaux, and clearly the more desperate aspects of his own relationship with Matilde may have been adding too sombre a tone.

In the case of politics the danger was not tragedy but satire: 'j'ai suivi l'usage des peintres, que je trouve amusant, et travaillé d'après des modèles. Il faudra ôter soigneusement toute allusion trop claire qui ferait de la satire' (ii. 573). The margins are full of injunctions to obscure the topicality of the work: 'Modèle: M. Cousin. Oter la ressemblance, si on la voit. Jamais de satire' (i. 345), and the term 'personnalité' is used each time he thinks his model is too easily recognizable. Thus he changes the Minister of War's rank from marshal to general because '*Maréchal* serait personnalité' (ii. 544) and because '*Personnalité*.—C'est un vilain défaut, c'est mêler du vinaigre à de la crème' (ii. 522). The problem with satire in Stendhal's view is, as has been seen earlier,[33] that it does indeed leave a nasty taste in the mouth. It depicts 'l'odieux' (another recurrent term in the margins of *Lucien Leuwen*) and inspires in the reader a sense of frustrated anger which is quite inimical to the music of gaiety and tenderness which Stendhal seeks to call forth. He is quite explicit about this in his preface to Part II of the novel:

en arrivant à Paris, il me faut faire de grands efforts pour ne pas tomber dans quelque personnalité. Ce n'est pas que je n'aime beaucoup la satire, mais en fixant l'œil du lecteur sur la figure grotesque de quelque ministre, le cœur de ce lecteur fait banqueroute à l'intérêt que je veux lui inspirer pour les autres personnages. Cette chose si amusante, la satire personnelle, ne convient donc point, par malheur, à la narration d'une histoire. Le lecteur est tout occupé à comparer mon portrait à l'original grotesque, ou même odieux, de lui bien connu; il le voit sale ou noir, comme le peindra l'histoire. (ii. 91).

Satire is fine in the right place ('le vinaigre est en soi une chose excellente': ii. 91) but cannot be mixed with the cream of comedy, of a comedy like Fielding's *Tom Jones*, for example, where the tone is 'gai et

---

[33] See above I. 2 and n. 24.

jouant comme un enfant' (i. 341).[34] Whereas *Le Rouge* was 'vrai,
mais sec' (i. 406), what he wants now is not only to avoid the 'noble
emphase' of Mme Gaulthier by emulating the precision and clarity
of the Code civil (ii. 574), but also 'un style plus fleuri et moins sec,
spirituel et gai, non pas comme le *Tom Jones* de 1750, mais comme
serait le même Fielding en 1834' (i. 406). Just as the margins are
filled with 'modèles' and 'pilotis', so too they abound in advice about
comedy and style with repeated reminders about the comic focus of
a given scene and repeated suggestions about how to improve the
narrative pace or to lighten or invigorate the style. And when the
substance of the action has been particularly tricky, as in the
'negotiations' between M. Leuwen and Mme Grandet, he promises
himself that 'j'ajouterai le comique en polissant le style' (ii. 529).

If Stendhal's ambition in 1835 was '*to make* chef-d'œuvre', there
can be no doubt that what he aimed at was a comic masterpiece.[35]
Having gathered his material from the world of contemporary
France, he then sought to tone down its more scandalous, and
scandalizing, features ('j'ai copié les personnages et les faits d'après
nature, et j'ai constamment *affaibli*': ii. 585) and to rework it into
a timeless comedy about love and politics and the road which leads
from innocence to maturity. Yet herein lies the central problem of
Lucien Leuwen. Yes, he says in the second preface: 'cet ouvrage-ci
est fait bonnement et simplement, sans chercher aucunement les
allusions, et même en cherchant à en éviter quelques-unes.' But at
the same time: 'l'auteur pense que, excepté pour la passion du héros,
un roman doit être un miroir.' It is all very well to portray an
exceptional and apparently improbable love-affair, and indeed even
to idealize the heroine ('excuse: le lecteur n'a vu la femme qu'il a
aimée qu'un *idéalisant*': ii. 574), but the novel does reflect—
somehow, be it directly or obliquely—the world outside itself. Indeed
it *must* do so, he says, the writer does have certain moral
responsibilities. Having examined the muddy road that is Louis-
Philippe's France, can he in all sincerity proceed to direct the
mirror away from the mud and write about an endless and timeless
human comedy? Having seen the 'âpre vérité, should he not now
tell it?

---

[34] For an account of the influence of *Tom Jones* during the writing of *Lucien
Leuwen* see McWatters, *Romanciers anglais*, Part II, ch. 4.
[35] See Bardèche, *Stendhal romancier*, 296–9, and Crouzet, *Quatre études*,
8–9, 23.

Some such desire seems to underlie the description of the novel he gave to his cousin Romain Colomb and close friend Domenico Fiore in March 1835: 'c'est pour la liberté de penser, comme le *Rouge*; cela ne cherche point à choquer, mais est sévère pour la *Kanaille*.'[36] He is not concerned to shock as, say, a polemical journalist might be, but he is offering a radical critique of the Establishment, and that is dangerous. His comment that 'le roman doit être un miroir' is followed at once by thought of punishment: 'si la police rend imprudente la publication, on attendra dix ans.' ('Que de ministères de la police avant l'apparition de *this work*!', he had written earlier: ii. 466). And when we read the marginal note about the profitable windmill built by Mme de Constantin's husband: '*Prudence*: changer ce trait, on reconnaîtrait l'homme' (ii. 464, n. 193), we may well think that Stendhal's caution here is not that of a comic writer trying to avoid satire but that of a man who would dearly like to publish his exposé of the July Monarchy and wonders just how far he can go.

It may be argued therefore that the author of *Lucien Leuwen* was caught between opposing moral and aesthetic imperatives, and that for him to obey either was impossible. On the one hand he could decide to speak out, but then he ran the risk not only of being silenced by censorship and even of losing his job but also of having his novel read as a 'mere' satire. On the other he could silence himself and continue revision of the novel for its eventual publication before or after his death (the many wills he wrote bequeathing the novel show how much he felt that his recent serious illness[37] might herald imminent death). But then how would his novel be read? In both cases he comes up against a problem of readership. In the first case the reader-violin upon whom he would be playing would give back the music of *Le Charivari*, the music of satire and political cartoon.[38] In the second case the reader would be a future reader, reading from a different perspective. With *Armance* and *Le Rouge* Stendhal had known what sort of novel he could write 'against' in the reader's mind (*René* and *Le Paysan parvenu* respectively). But what would be the expectations of a posthumous reader of *Lucien Leuwen*?

[36] *Corr.*, iii. 19.   [37] See *OI*, ii. 194 (5 May 1834).
[38] Indeed he might even throw the book down in outrage and disgust, like the sick man (in the third preface to the novel) who breaks the mirror which reveals to him the greenness of his face.

We have already seen how, when Stendhal faced this problem shortly afterwards in *Vie de Henry Brulard*, he perceived an opportunity for sincerity in his ignorance of the reader: 'parler à des gens dont on ignore absolument la tournure d'esprit, le genre d'éducation, les préjugés, la religion! Quel encouragement à être *vrai*, et simplement *vrai*.'[39] But even in *Vie de Henry Brulard* the desire for sincerity eventually led to silence, as he faced the impossibility of describing his joy at visiting Italy for the first time: 'le sujet surpasse le disant.'[40] How much greater the problem was in the case of a novel. How can one be 'sincere' in a novel (as opposed to a political satire)? Sincere about what? Yes, one can try not to exaggerate or distort, one can perfect one's style, but then is one not merely engaging in idle 'exercices de style', writing in a vacuum to while away the time ('je crève d'ennui; le vrai métier de l'animal est d'écrire un roman dans un grenier')?[41] Does one not end up writing merely for oneself, performing a kind of solipsistic double-act of writer and critic, or rather of writer and reader? Is not the reason Stendhal ceased to continue polishing *Le Chasseur vert* that he felt that he had become his own violin?

For the Stendhal of *Lucien Leuwen* style had become a political issue and a test of his own sincerity, and in September 1835 he fell victim to a situation similar to that of his hero. The essential comic dilemma in which Lucien finds himself, according to his creator (ii. 495, n. 402), is that he wants to succeed and yet at the same time remain honourable. Was that not how Stendhal the novelist felt? To succeed aesthetically he must first gather facts but then transform them, and the more he transforms them, the more likely he is to have a reader; but the greater his chances of being read, the less honest he will have been about the present. The novel can only be read if it is false: its impossibility is a guarantee of its truth. Perhaps the answer was to abandon the novel and instead examine the roots of his own present self[42] in imitation of another champion of sincerity: 'j'écris maintenant un livre [*Vie de Henry Brulard*] qui peut être une grande sottise, c'est *Mes Confessions*, au style près, comme Jean-Jacques Rousseau, avec plus de franchise.'[43] Just as Lucien's journey

---

[39] *OI*, ii. 537. See above, I. i, pp. 6–7.   [40] *OI*, ii. 958.
[41] *Corr.*, ii. 487 (5 Nov. 1832).
[42] See *OI*, ii. 532: 'Je vais avoir cinquante ans, il serait bien temps de me connaître. Qu'ai-je été? que suis-je? En vérité, je serais bien embarrassé de le dire.' Stendhal's quest for identity in *Vie de Henry Brulard* is a continuation of the younger Lucien's.
[43] *Corr.*, iii. 140 (21 Nov. 1835).

south at the end of the novel is interrupted by a two-day visit to Lake Geneva and 'les lieux que la *Nouvelle Héloïse* a rendus célèbres' (ii. 435), so too, it would seem, must Stendhal pause for Rousseauistic introspection and reminiscence at Grenoble amidst the foothills of the Alps before proceeding on to the glories of *La Chartreuse de Parme*. The impasse in which both *Lucien Leuwen* and *Vie de Henry Brulard* end turns out to be a passage to Italy.

2

'Exercices de style'

'Aimerais-tu mieux un artiste parfaitement poli, gracieux, d'un ton parfait, faisant des croûtes, ou un homme au ton grossier occupé du fond des choses et non de la forme, mais produisant des chefs-d'œuvre?'

(ii. 137)

IN writing *Lucien Leuwen* Stendhal was faced, then, with a choice between cream and vinegar, between the emollient generality of comedy and the astringent topicality of satire. His stylistic dilemma was also a political dilemma. This conjunction of style and politics is the hallmark of *Lucien Leuwen*. Not only does it figure largely in the prefaces, it is also reflected in the events and characters of the novel. In many ways Stendhal's dilemma as a writer is the very subject he is writing about.

Note first, for example, how the politics of the narrator and characters seems to be wholly a matter of style. On the Left are those who lack it, republicans, Americans, 'saint-simoniens', the young; on the Right, those who have it, Legitimists and elderly admirers of 'l'inflexible génie du duc de Saint-Simon' (i. 88); in the centre, the *juste milieu*, who merely have pretensions. In particular politics seem to mean style of conversation and the ability to tell a story: 'en général, le légitimiste aura des manières plus élégantes et saura un plus grand nombre d'anecdotes amusantes; le républicain aura plus de feu dans l'âme et des façons plus simples et plus jeunes' (i. 88). It would appear that nothing is less conducive to this gift of anecdote, indeed to good literature itself, than democratic suffrage and republican good sense: 'au XIXe siècle, la démocratie amène nécessairement dans la littérature le règne des gens médiocres, raisonnables, bornés et *plats*, littérairement parlant' (i. 91); 'j'ai horreur', reflects Lucien, 'du bon sens fastidieux d'un Américain. Les récits de la vie du général Bonaparte, vainqueur au pont d'Arcole, me transportent; c'est pour moi Homère, le Tasse, et cent fois mieux encore' (i. 157).

At one end of the political and stylistic spectrum is Gauthier, the republican surveyor and newspaper-editor, who is the 'honnête homme par excellence' (i. 222) but quite lacks any style. He never lies, his manner is unaffected and he can even manage a certain eloquence 'quand il parlait du bonheur futur de la France et de l'époque heureuse où toutes les fonctions seraient exercées gratuitement et payées par l'honneur' (i. 165). But he is thoroughly boring. His simplicity of manner verges on the uncouth, his 'vérités incontestables' are always 'relatives à des objets peu amusants' (i. 222), and even when he does have some promising subject matter, he usually ruins it: 'M. Gauthier était un peu comme ces femmes honnêtes qui disent du mal des actrices; il n'amusait pas, tout en parlant d'êtres qui passent pour fort amusants' (i. 197).

In the middle of the spectrum is M. Grandet, the rising 'star' of the *juste milieu*, who lacks in honesty and intelligence what he makes up for in literary pretension: 'M. Grandet était un demi-sot, lourd et assez instruit, qui chaque soir suait sang et eau pendant une heure pour se *tenir au courant de notre littérature*, c'était son mot' (ii. 389). Gleaner of 'idées reçues' and forerunner of Flaubert's Homais,[1] he is handicapped in his literary ambition by an inability to tell the difference between literature and journalism, with the result that a remark intended to suggest the wit of Montesquieu 'ressemblait comme deux gouttes d'eau à un article de journal de MM. Salvandy ou Viennet' (ii. 391). No less handicapped is his wife, 'une bavarde effrénée', who mistakes quantity for quality and originality. She talks in a gushing, emotional way in the style of a short story by Nodier (ii. 379), while her valiant attempts to imitate Mme de Staël suggest merely 'qu'elle fait provision d'esprit dans les manuels à trois francs' (ii. 148). The conversation she expects from her salon guests is not, as Lucien at first believes, 'de l'esprit d'arrière-boutique, des anecdotes imprimées partout, des nouvelles de journaux, etc., etc.' but conversation made up of 'des anecdotes [...] moins usées, des considérations lourdes sur des sujets délicats, sur la tendresse de Racine comparée à celle de Virgile, sur les contes italiens où Shakespeare a pris le sujet de ses pièces' (ii. 200). In this salon 'un écrivain célèbre' will regale them with stories, but they are stories by or about other writers: 'une anecdote fort plaisante sur l'abbé Barthélemy, [...] une anecdote de Marmontel, ensuite une troisième sur l'abbé Delille'. Where is this famous writer's

---

[1] Comparisons between *Lucien Leuwen* and the novels of Flaubert are often more interesting than the more traditional ones with *La Comédie humaine*. See Crouzet, *Quatre études*, 12, 68, 69, 97.

own story? Lucien concludes that 'le fond de cette gaieté est sec et triste. Ces gens d'Académie [...] ne vivent que sur les ridicules de leurs prédécesseurs. Ils mourront banqueroutiers envers leurs successeurs' (ii. 203).

The style of the *juste milieu* is worthless because it is derivative and uncreative, bankrupt because it is based on a forged currency:

comme ils sont lourds et tristes, se répondant les uns aux autres par de fausses raisons, et dont le parleur comme l'écouteur sentent le faux! Mais ce serait choquer toutes les convenances de cette confrérie que de ne pas se payer de fausse monnaie. Il faut gober je ne sais combien de sottises et ne pas se moquer des vérités fondamentales de leur religion, ou tout est perdu. (ii. 213)

As such the Grandet circle is little better than many of the inhabitants of Nancy whose reading is almost entirely confined to newspapers. The result is that these provincials are often at a loss for conversation, unless it be to repeat what the newspapers say (as Colonel Malher does) or to provide their own news in the form of gossip. Life in a town like Nancy being far from eventful, gossip is scarce, and so the only remedy is to find an excuse for its repetition, be it the arrival of a stranger or the omission of a detail:

quand le mari s'apprête à faire à cet étranger une histoire connue de sa femme et de ses enfants, on voit ceux-ci brûlant de prendre la parole et de la voler à leur père, pour narrer, eux-mêmes le conte; et, souvent, sous prétexte d'ajouter une nouvelle circonstance oubliée, ils recommencent l'histoire. (i. 230)

Accordingly social, and even sexual, success comes from being able to keep another amused with an anecdote. Thus story-telling is crucial to d'Antin's survival as Mme d'Hocquincourt's lover (ii. 43), as it is to the unprepossessing marquis de Sanréal's popularity with his fellows. It is Sanréal who has the great good fortune to see Lucien's first fall from his horse and who is therefore able to command attention when he announces it in Mme d'Hocquincourt's drawing-room. But his narrative skills desert him:

comme il embrouillait beaucoup un si beau récit, en voulant y mettre de l'esprit, on prit le parti de lui faire des questions, et il eut le plaisir de recommencer son histoire; mais il cherchait toujours à faire le héros plus ridicule qu'il n'était. (i. 143)[2]

---

[2] Cf. Stendhal's advice to Mme Gaulthier: 'faites faire quelque petite gaucherie à votre héros, parce qu'enfin nous autres héros, nous faisons des gaucheries' (*Corr.*, ii. 724 (8 Nov. 1834)). Perhaps Sanréal's lack of narrative skill derives from the fact that usually he is himself 'le héros de tous ses contes' (i. 225).

When he lets the art of story-telling take second place to his discovery
of an imminent increase in the price of oats,[3] he is simply exhibiting
a common provincial trait: 'en province, le moindre intérêt d'argent
éclipse à l'instant tout autre intérêt; on oublie la discussion la plus
piquante, on n'a plus d'attention pour l'histoire scandaleuse la plus
attachante' (i. 145). Free of financial worry he is readier to indulge his
amiable Regency habit of being more or less completely drunk before
midday and to give rein to a narrative facility which convinces Lucien
of his integrity and the sincerity of his political affiliation (i. 225–6).

The further one moves to the Right along the political spectrum,
the greater the performance. Thus Du Poirier the doctor is welcomed
by high society not only because of his 'opinions furibondes de
légitimité' (i. 182) but also because of his eloquence. He is full of
stories ('il prétendait avoir des anecdotes secrètes sur tout': i. 183)
and, despite 'les gestes d'une vulgarité si plaisante', can lend these
stories 'un tour si vif, si amusant, si peu offensant [...] qu'il fallait
tout lui passer'. Indeed his skills are so much those of the live
performer that the things he says 'perdent tout à être écrites' (i. 186).
But he is not just a brilliant raconteur for, like the marquise de
Puylaurens (i. 223–4), he even has the power to create his own
anecdotes. He is an inventor of plots ('un fameux intrigant': i. 182).
and his 'besoin de parler, de persuader, de faire naître des événements'
(i. 190) is most spectacularly fulfilled by the episode of the 'faux
accouchement'. Not only does he succeed in tricking Lucien, he also
has the supreme satisfaction of giving the bachelors of Nancy a false
and uninformative version of his own trickery:

l'orgueil de Du Poirier et sa manie de parler en public triomphaient. Il faut
avouer qu'il parla admirablement; il se garda bien d'expliquer pourquoi et
comment Lucien était parti, et cependant sut attendrir ses auditeurs [...]
La porte fermée, Du Poirier éclata de rire. Il venait de parler pendant quarante
minutes, il avait eu beaucoup de succès, il se moquait parfaitement des gens
qui l'avaient écouté. C'était là, pour ce coquin singulier, les trois éléments
du plaisir le plus vif. (ii. 110)

The lack of substance in Du Poirier's account raises a question
which has already occurred to Lucien: 'il serait bien plaisant qu'au
fond ce docteur amusant ne crût pas plus à Henri V qu'à [God the
father]' (i. 197 and n. 196). Perhaps Du Poirier is all form and no

---

[3] An incident which prefigures de Vaize and the king's use of advance information
for speculation on the Bourse.

content, a man ready to take on any role, provided it is challenging? If so, he is plainly very similar to Lucien's father. M. Leuwen is of course the supreme stylist in the novel. He is a keen, if occasionally tactless (ii. 186) story-teller who can pander to the needs of his audience, be they the aristocratic sensibilities of the influential Mme de Thémines (ii. 178) or the rather basic narrative requirements of his faithful 'députés': 's'il racontait des anecdotes, c'étaient des cochers de fiacre qui, à minuit, emmenaient dans la campagne des imprudents qui, ne connaissant pas les rues de Paris, hasardent de se retirer à cette heure' (ii. 320). He too can be the source of an anecdote (ii. 347). As a parliamentary orator he does not declaim like de Vaize. Not for him the provincial orator's recourse to 'la force de ses poumons', nor the 'voix de Stentor' by which Sanréal seeks to persuade, nor the 'voix éclatante' of M. de Torpet in the Grandet salon, but a 'voix presque imperceptible' which has the entire Assembly straining with attention.[4] Nor does he affect the periphrasis and gravity of elocution which may pass for eloquence; his speeches are simply 'du bavardage de société piquant et rapide' (ii. 327). Not the leaden chatter of a Mme Grandet with her imitations of Mme de Staël, but the sharp wit of an original epigrammatist, the wit of a 'Talleyrand de la Bourse' (ii, 139) who has his own version of 'n'ayez pas de zèle' (ii. 303, 306). Not the literary pretension of a M. Grandet who repeats what the newspapers say but the improvised genius of a man whose speeches Le Moniteur prints verbatim:

le style noble me tuerait, disait-il un jour à son fils. D'abord, je ne pourrais plus improviser, je serais obligé de travailler, et je ne travaillerais pas dans le genre littéraire pour un empire... (ii. 327)

M. Leuwen's style is oral, improvised, and unliterary,[5] and as such is akin not only to Du Poirier's but also to that of the Napoleonic veteran who charms Lucien with ungrammatical yet brilliantly detailed descriptions of the exploits of the Grande Armée: 'le vieux lieutenant était quelquefois sublime en racontant avec simplicité ce temps héroïque; nul n'était hypocrite alors!' (i. 162).

---

[4] i. 229, ii. 123, 213, 323, 328, 331, 370, 379. Thoughout the novel the vulgarity of 'le parler haut' (i. 96) is contrasted with the elegance of the soft-spoken (i. 223, ii. 119–23).
[5] As if to underline his lack of gravitas his speeches are based on a few notes jotted down on a playing card: ii. 324.

It is similarly comparable with the style of his female companions
at the Opéra, in particular that of Mlle Raimonde, who offers Lucien
much-needed respite from 'l'emphase lente et monotone du salon
Grandet' in the lively account of a duel and a conjugal row: 'sa petite
voix douce et bien timbrée parcourait les détails en sautillant
rapidement' (ii. 213). But whereas the soldier is retired and the opera-
girl an entertainer, M. Leuwen and Du Poirier are involved in running
the country. Their style must have political consequences. But does
it? Du Poirier seems to be a mere performer, upstaged by the much
greater performance that is M. Leuwen's rise to power. The latter's
election, his creation of the Légion du Midi, his manipulation of de
Vaize, his revenge on him for his offhand treatment of his son, these
are carried out with consummate skill by an 'homme de plaisir' whose
worst enemy is boredom. M. Leuwen's greatest asset is that he does
not care, that he does not take things seriously ('quand il n'avait
personne de qui se moquer, il se moquait de soi-même': ii. 191). But
in the end this becomes his greatest weakness:

je commence à songer sérieusement à tout ceci. Le succès est venu me
chercher; mais être *éloquent*, comme [disent] les journalistes amis, cela me
paraît plaisant: je parle à la Chambre comme dans un salon. Mais [si] ce
ministère, qui ne bat plus que d'une aile, vient à tomber, je ne saurai plus
que dire, car enfin je n'ai d'opinion sur rien, et certainement, à mon âge,
je n'irai pas étudier pour m'en former une. (ii. 357)

The supreme stylist has no substance. He has the ear of the king,
thanks to him the government may fall, but there is nothing he wants.
The 'chef de famille' described in the epigraph to the novel ('lequel
avait beaucoup d'esprit et de plus savait vouloir') now finds himself
in the paradoxical situation of being at once all-powerful and yet
powerless to devise an objective: 'il ne me vient pas une idée' (ii. 363).

At this point in the novel M. Leuwen first mentions that he is in
financial difficulty. Since the death of his partner Van Peters his
political activities have prevented him from visiting Holland, and
as a result his bank has suffered losses in two recent bankruptcies.
His own coming bankruptcy is now prefigured, and it seems here
to be not only financial but political and even moral. As he puts it
himself: 'mon éloquence et ma réputation sont comme une omelette
soufflée; un ouvrier grossier trouve que c'est viande creuse' (ii. 357).
Like Du Poirier he is all form and no content. When he decides to
aim at getting M. Grandet appointed Minister of the Interior, his

new objective is as grotesque as the *quid pro quo* he demands from Mme Grandet. These ambitions are forgeries, mere counterfeit politicking, and the fact that one of the most likely consequences is de Vaize's appointment as Minister for the Arts seems only too fitting a commentary on the vacuity of M. Leuwen's urbanity. At the end of the novel the reader may even come to see some justified criticism[6] in Grandet's remarks: 'il n'est pas difficile d'être aimable quand l'on se permet de tout dire', 'Leuwen sacrifiera toujours un ami à un bon mot' (ii. 391). There is a moral limit to the demands of style. M. Leuwen dies a bankrupt, unloved by the son for whom he thought he was doing so much. The *omelette soufflée* has collapsed.

So far we have seen that the political spectrum corresponds to a stylistic one. At one end is content, truth, virtue, earnestness, bad form, considered speech, newspaper reports; in the middle is conversation based on studious rehearsal of the written; at the other end is form, good form, falsity, corruption, gaiety, improvisation, oral anecdote. Where along this spectrum should one situate the novel's other two stylists, the narrator and Lucien?

The narrator professes to be a 'partisan modéré de la Charte de 1830' (i. 87), yet stylistically he seems to be well to the Right. According to the first preface he is uninterested in politics, and between people of different parties amiability is his only criterion of preference. Instead he has let himself be guided by the 'douces illusions de son art' and produced 'un roman frivole', 'ce roman futile' (i. 88). Almost as if he feared that these adjectives might not adequately forestall our expectation of something solemnly literary, he then refers to 'ce conte' (i. 93) which he is writing for pleasure (i. 94). It will be a contribution to 'la Bibliothèque bleue', that is, a chivalric romance full of exploit and adventure. From the outset the narrator emphasizes the resemblance to a tale by choosing an epigraph which begins like a fairy story and by opening the narrative with an expulsion reminiscent of the beginning of *Candide*.[7] He seeks to give the impression of oral narration, either by the ambiguous use of 'entendu' (i. 93) or by merging 'récit' and 'histoire': 'pendant qu'il [Lucien] est engagé dans la maussade besogne de rendre poliment dédain pour dédain au capitaine Henriet, nous demandons la permission de suivre un instant le lieutenant général comte N...' (i. 114). As a story-teller he knows what is good form.

---

[6] *Pace* Crouzet, *Quatre études*, 11.
[7] For other possible parallels with *Candide* see Crouzet, *Quatre études*, 94, n. 104.

Like M. Leuwen he will avoid periphrasis. He is modest about his own skills and generous in his praise of the Napoleonic veteran's. He is kind enough to omit what we can read in newspapers anyway and to spare us the tedium of long conversations, the repetitions of Gauthier's daily propaganda or the boring detail of an election: 'c'est un genre de vérité que nous laissons aux romans in–12 pour femmes de chambre' (ii. 124). He tries to be unobtrusive and while, in comparison with *Le Rouge*, there are more examples of omniscience and fewer instances of limited point of view, his presence as a commentator is much less pronounced than that of his counterpart in *Le Rouge*. Aiming as he is at a 'manque d'emphase' and a 'manque de but moral' (i. 93), he keeps abstract generalizations to a minimum, and when comment is called for, he cleverly attributes it to someone else. Thus the advice he would like to give Lucien is the hypothetical statement of 'un homme sage' (i. 158), and his abstract summary of Lucien's position at the beginning of Part II is disguised as the work of 'un ennuyeux moraliste qui avait divisé sa drogue par portraits détachés, comme Vauvenargues' (ii. 101).[8]

This is part of his technique of 'dialogisme'[9] whereby the novel offers a dialogue, even a dialectic, of styles by virtue of the different modes of discourse which are quoted within it. One of the most interesting examples of this dialogue of styles occurs as the narrator describes Mme de Chasteller's uncertainty about Lucien's sincerity after their visit to *Le Chasseur vert*:

le cœur de Mme de Chasteller n'était pas dans un état beaucoup plus enviable [than that of Lucien's]. Ils payaient tous les deux, et chèrement, le bonheur rencontré l'avant-veille au *Chasseur vert*. Et si les romanciers avaient encore, comme autrefois, l'heureux privilège de faire de la morale dans les grandes occasions, on s'écrierait ici: Juste punition de l'imprudence d'aimer un être que l'on connaît réellement aussi peu! Quoi! rendre en quelque sorte maître de son bonheur un être que l'on n'a vu que cinq fois! Et si le conteur pouvait traduire ces pensées en style pompeux et finir même par quelque allusion religieuse, les sots se diraient entre eux: Voilà un livre moral, et l'auteur

---

[8] Cf. the way in which the narrator also appears to transfer responsibility for the plot to his characters, especially M. Leuwen. See Brooks, *The Novel of Worldliness*, 256–7, and Crouzet, *Quatre études*, 20.

[9] Bakhtinian notions of heteroglossia and/or polyphony are particularly helpful to a study of the use of language in *Lucien Leuwen*. See Jean-Luc Seylaz, 'Un aspect de la narration stendhalienne: la qualification intensive dans le début de *Lucien Leuwen*', *Etudes de Lettres*, IV. iii. 3 (July–Sept. 1980), 31–49. See also Crouzet, *Quatres études*, ch. iii, espec. p. 94.

doit être un homme bien respectable. Les sots ne se diraient pas, parce qu'ils ne l'ont encore lu que dans peu de livres recommandés par l'Académie: avec l'élégance actuelle de nos façons polies, qu'est-ce qu'une femme peut connaître d'un jeune homme *correct*, après cinquante visites, si ce n'est son degré d'esprit et le plus ou moins de progrès qu'il a pu faire dans l'art de dire élégamment des choses insignifiantes? Mais de son cœur, de sa façon particulière d'aller à la chasse du bonheur? Rien, ou: il n'est pas correct. (i. 337)

Leaving aside for the moment the splendid Stendhalian irony that it is precisely a religious allusion which will give a moral point to *Lucien Leuwen* (ii. 399), we can see that this passage illustrates or refers to a wide variety of styles: matter-of-factness, exclamation, religious pomposity, gullible certainty, empty elegance, intelligent interrogation. The 'content' of this passage is that the truth behind elegant appearance will best be revealed by 'incorrectness'. Only when elegance is subverted will the real nature of things be evident; sincerity requires bad form. The 'form' of the passage tells the same story: its truth is couched in a style that is simple and questioning, that is, a style which is, within the novel's terms of reference, unliterary. In Stendhal's terms this is the style of the Code civil.

It may have seemed unduly pedantic to distinguish until now between the narrator and Stendhal and, in the case of the prefaces, even unfounded.[10] Clearly the foregoing account of the narrator's narrative techniques has been about Stendhal's art as a novelist. But it has seemed helpful to maintain the distinction, not only on the a priori ground that the narrators of *Le Rouge* and *La Chartreuse* are separable from their creator, but more especially in order to underline the way in which the narrative style of the novel is tied in with its story, its form with its content. For just at the point in the novel when M. Leuwen's 'éloquence' turns out to be an 'omelette soufflée' (as insubstantial as the courting lover's 'art de dire élegamment des choses insignifiantes'), the narrator begins to distance himself from M. Leuwen's style and to look more towards that of Lucien:

si nous écrivions des *Mémoires de Walpole*, ou tout autre livre de ce genre également au-dessus de notre génie, nous continuerions à donner l'histoire anecdotique de sept demi-coquins, dont deux ou trois adroits et un ou deux

---

[10] Especially as there has been occasion to quote the second preface as evidence of Stendhal's intentions. But this preface is after all called 'Deuxième Préface Réelle'!

beaux parleurs, remplacés par le même nombre de fripons. Un pauvre honnête homme qui, au ministère de l'Intérieur, se fût occupé avec *bonne foi* de choses utiles êut passé pour un sot; toute la Chambre l'eût bafoué. Il fallait faire sa fortune non pas en volant brutalement; toutefois, avant tout, pour être estimé, il fallait mettre du foin dans ses bottes. Comme ces mœurs sont à la veille d'être remplacées par les vertus désintéressées de la république qui sauront mourir, comme Robespierre, avec treize livres dix sous dans la poche, nous avons voulu en *garder note.*

Mais ce n'est pas même l'histoire des goûts au moyen desquels cet homme de plaisir écartait l'ennui que nous avons promis au lecteur. Ce n'est que l'histoire de son fils, être fort simple qui, malgré lui, fut jeté dans des embarras par cette chute de ministres, autant du moins que son caractère sérieux le lui permit. (ii. 361)

Here the narrator turns away from the Right's end of the spectrum and, his eyes directed with subdued irony towards the virtues of the Left, reaffirms his commitment to the story of Lucien, a story of seriousness. At the very point when Lucien recognizes his lack of love for his father, the narrator too seems to disown Leuwen *père.* As the novel approaches its provisional end, it is Lucien, not Leuwen, who matters more, the promise of substance more than the disappointment of style.[11]

[11] For further discussion of the relationships between Lucien, his father and the narrator, see D. A. Miller, *Narrative and its Discontents* (Princeton, 1981), 222–59.

3

Role and identity

'Que suis-je donc?'

(i. 158)

WHAT are we to make of 'ce fils silencieux d'un père si bavard' (ii. 391)? Who is this person who wants to be a Trappist monk?[1] One of the places along the shores of Lake Geneva which Lucien may have visited on his way to Italy is Saint-Gingolph, where the 'Avant-Propos' to Armance was ostensibly written.[2] Such a visit would have been most appropriate since Lucien clearly has much in common with Octave de Malivert.[3] In one sense luckier than Octave, in that no one prevents him from joining the army upon leaving the Ecole Polytechnique, Lucien is motivated by the same desire for self-esteem, and listening to Dévelroy's 'sermon' has the same effect on him as overhearing Armance's imputation of mercenariness does on Octave. Where Octave's first recorded words are: 'pourquoi me montrerais-je autre que je ne suis', Lucien's are exactly comparable: 'pour te plaire, disait Lucien [to Dévelroy], il faudrait jouer un rôle, n'est-ce pas? et celui d'un *homme triste*! et qu'est-ce que la société me donnera en échange de mon ennui?' (i. 98). Another Alceste (ii. 125) and just as prone to throwing people out of windows (i. 167), Lucien has a heightened sense of honour and personal integrity which can induce moods of deep depression about the venality of his fellow man, and such depression may vent itself in outbursts no less comic than Octave's supposedly pathological 'accès de fureur':

'à quoi donc sommes-nous bons? A faire du zèle en style de député vendu.' En faisant cette réflexion profonde, Lucien s'étendait, horriblement

---

[1] Given Lucien's repeated thoughts of monastic refuge (ii. 100, 129), it may be of interest to note that the Prémol which figures in one of the novel's projected titles is the name of a ruined Carthusian convent near Grenoble (i. 80, n. 7). The title was rejected because the Bois de Prémol were to appear in the abandoned third part of the novel, but the idea behind it proved fruitful when Stendhal came to write about Fabrice del Dongo.

[2] It was actually written in Paris.

[3] As several critics have noted. See especially Crouzet's introduction, i. 36; Bardèche, *Stendhal romancier*, 142, 264; Wood, *Stendhal*, 133; and Mouillaud, *Le Roman possible*, 162.

découragé, sur un canapé de province, dont un des bras se rompit sous le poids; il se leva furieux et acheva de briser ce vieux meuble. (i. 147)

Likewise he dreams of an errant life in the New World and the liberation of an assumed identity. He too forswears amorous entanglement only to fall unwittingly in love, and with a woman whose sense of duty to her own virtue is no less great than that of Armance and may lead no less readily to notions of conventual retreat.

So clear are the parallels between the two novels that one may come to see more than coincidence in the onomastic parallel between the prototypes of the two heroes, Latouche's Olivier and Mme Gaulthier's Olivier Leuwen. Was it perhaps the latter's Christian name which gave Stendhal the idea of returning to the character of Octave and of recreating him under a new name and within the context of a different story, a story which would set aside the question of sexual impotence and emphasize the theme of a quest for identity which had become obscured in *Armance*? Perhaps even to use the new version of Octave as a focus for the exploration of questions raised by the end of *Le Rouge et le Noir*? Because one of the most interesting things about *Lucien Leuwen* is the way it takes up the story of Julien Sorel, and even begins to tell it in reverse. At the beginning of the novel Lucien is determined to be himself and to live for the moment: 'il songeait dans chaque moment à faire ce qui lui plaisait le plus au moment même, et ne pensait point assez *aux autres*' (i. 97). The 'assez' here reflects the value-judgement of society: Lucien's disregard of others is a laudable part of his 'absence totale d'affectation', his 'franchise' and 'vivacité'. This, of course, is the state which Julien attains to in prison once he is released from the grip of his 'noire ambition' and the need to plan for the future. As such it assumes in *Le Rouge* the status of an ideal attitude to life, indeed of a kind of maturity. It is the 'beyliste' secret to 'la chasse au bonheur'. But such mental reservations as it may inspire—how imitable are the circumstances of Julien's accession to happiness? how would he put the lesson he has learnt into practice if he were released into society again? if he has learnt to be true to himself, how should he set about defining the person he is being true to?—may be made more acute at the beginning of *Lucien Leuwen* where Lucien's 'beylisme' is presented as mere childish heedlessness. Whereas Julien's 'disponibilité' may be hard-won, Lucien's is perhaps simply that of someone who has 'pris la peine de naître comme le fils d'un prince'

(i. 104–5). Ernest Dévelroy's quotation of Beaumarchais comes, of course, from the mouth of a solemn, indeed earnest, aspirant to the Académie des Sciences morales, and the reader may hesitate to side with such a spokesman for the 'parti prosaïque', but his warning to Lucien about the shaky foundations of his 'indépendance' is telling, as indeed is his prediction: 'tu sentiras la nécessité d'être quelque chose' (i. 99). But what? Merely an 'amateur fou de courses de chevaux', as Dévelroy suggests, or someone more substantial, something more than 'un brillant peut-être'? Again one is reminded of Gide, this time of Michel in L'Immoraliste: 'savoir se libérer n'est rien; l'ardu, c'est savoir être libre.'

Where Julien's development leads from hypocrisy and role-playing to sincerity and authenticity, Lucien's moves in the opposite direction. The affront to his pride occasioned by Dévelroy's disdain and his consequent desire to prove that he can fend for himself lead him to leave happiness behind and to set out on a road which he knows to be false. He knows he will have to suppress his easy laughter and subordinate his behaviour to the expectations of society but, as he later explains to Gauthier, the republican newspaper-editor, a higher duty to self has become paramount: 'pour me mettre en état de gagner quatre-vingt-dix-neuf francs par mois et ma propre estime, j'ai quitté une ville où je passais mon temps fort agréablement' (i. 166).[4] The result of this paradoxical situation is confusion, much of it comic, as Lucien struggles to find himself in a world where appearance and reality are seldom one, a world of theatre in which he must perform while yet not knowing what he would do or feel if he were not playing a role. Aware of his own insincerity, and aware of the inauthenticity of the milieux in which he is obliged to live (the garrison, the Legitimist salons, the Ministry of the Interior), he is left with but one option: to perfect his style of playing.[5]

This pattern is established at the outset when he joins the army. At first thrilled at the sight of his uniform and dazzled by heroic prospects of charging down a Prussian battery, he quickly appreciates that he will be serving not Napoleon but his tawdry successors, 'cette halte dans la boue'[6] (i. 102). Far from being wounded on a foreign

---

[4] Cf. CP, 177: 'à quoi bon aller si loin chercher le bonheur, il est là sous mes yeux'.
[5] Cf. Stendhal's comment about the hero of Armance: 'seul moyen pour Octave (comme pour toute personne timide) de devenir véritablement aimable: parler en se moquant du fond et ne songeant qu'au piquant et à l'élégance de la manière' (OI, ii. 85).
[6] The phrase was that of General Lamarque whose funeral is thought to be alluded to on the first page of the novel (i. 342, n. 7).

field he will more likely be killed by a chamber-pot thrown from a
fifth-floor window by some toothless crone (i. 103). Still, he says, as
he tries on his new uniform in front of the mirror: 'ils disent tous qu'il
faut être quelque chose. Eh bien, je serai *lancier*; quand je saurai
le métier, nous verrons' (i. 103). The paradox has already been made
explicit: 'par amour pour l'uniforme, il essaya de songer aux avantages
du métier: avoir de l'avancement, des croix, de l'argent...' (i. 102).
Genuine excitement looks to spurious gain for its justification.
Throughout Part I Lucien's imagination is offered tantalizing glimpses
of a heroic military past—in his commanding officer Filloteau's account
of Napoleon's Egyptian campaign, in the company of the 'other ranks',
in the comments of Bouchard the 'maître de poste', and in the anecdotes
of the Napoleonic veteran 'officier de la Légion d'honneur'—but these
serve only to emphasize the irony present in the description of military
life as 'la plus brillante carrière du monde et la plus gaie' (i. 151).
A noble career has become a mere job, a form of police work wherein
the only thing to fear is what the newspapers will say, and the honour
of Marengo has been replaced by the ignominy of 'la rue
Transnonain' where French workers become the victims of army
sabres. The nearest Lucien ever comes to military glory is in playing
toy soldiers with the 'maréchal des logis', and the only thing that
seems to require courage is facing up to the vulgarity of his fellow
soldiers: 'et pourtant je passerai par là, se dit-il, avec courage; je ne
me moquerai point de ces façons d'agir et je les imiterai' (i. 107).

Part of Dévelroy's lesson to Lucien had been that Filloteau, for
all his vileness, was at least a man of substance, whereas he, Lucien,
was a mere performer: 'toi, tu n'es qu'un enfant qui ne compte dans
rien, qui a trouvé de belles phrases dans un livre et qui les répète
avec grâce, comme un bon acteur pénétré de son rôle; mais, pour
de l'action, néant' (i. 105). Now the paradox is that, for Lucien,
going into action simply means learning a new part. First he will
have to be impassive or, better still: 'donner à ses traits une expression
contraire à celle qu'on s'attendait à y lire' (i. 112).[7] For a cavalry
officer horsemanship is all-important, so it must be displayed, as must
his generosity, his loyalty to the king and his readiness to duel. But
soon the role begins to pall, and even if there are moments of
sufficiently penitential boredom for him to contest Dévelroy's original

---

[7] Cf. *OI*, ii. 215 (12 Dec. 1834): 'Epigraphe *of the boock*: En toute espèce de
chose, faites et dites le contraire de ce à quoi on s'attend, et par ainsi le XIXe siècle
vous trouvera de bien bon ton.'

slur and to match his quotation of Beaumarchais with one that is more flattering ('*ma vie et un combat*': i. 167), Lucien is nevertheless now ready to answer in the negative when the amiable rogue Du Poirier puts the obvious question: 'un tel rôle est-il fait pour un homme comme vous?' (i. 185). And so he swaps parts: 'il ne me reste d'autre mascarade que celle d'ami des privilèges et de la religion qui les soutient. C'est le rôle indiqué par la fortune de mon père' (i. 196). He begins his new role with enthusiasm, like a hero of vaudeville: 'je suis ici comme M. Jabalot à Versailles: *je fais mes farces*' (i. 201). But soon, at the dinner-party given by Mme de Commercy, the tedious conversation and the need to cultivate the least prepossessing members of this set cause him severe misgivings. He has no need of advancement, so why bother? 'A quoi bon n'ouvrir la bouche que pour mentir, et au fond d'une province? et dans un dîner encore où il n'y a qu'une jolie femme! C'est trop héroïque pour votre serviteur' (i. 209). But he perseveres, particularly as his father has refused to help him with letters of introduction, and success soon comes:

'je serais bien dupe de dire un mot de ce que je pense à ces comédiens de campagne; tout, chez eux, même le rire, est une affectation; jusque dans les moments les plus gais, ils songent à 93'. Cette observation fut décisive pour le succès de notre héros. Quelques mots trop sincères avaient déjà nui à l'engouement dont il commençait à être l'objet. Dès qu'il mentit à tout venant, comme chantait la cigale, l'engouement reprit de plus belle [...] (i. 227)

And this success is crowned at Mme de Marcilly's ball, itself a manifestation of 'cet ignoble bal masqué qu'on appelle le monde' (i. 268).

Again the reader meets with paradox, as the precedence of style over substance is shown in the reason for Lucien's success at the ball:

on aime les uniformes dans l'est de la France, pays profondément militaire; et c'est en grande partie à cause de son uniforme porté avec grâce, et presque unique dans cette société, que Lucien pouvait passer pour le personnage le plus brillant du bal. (i. 257)

Here, at a Legitimist ball to honour Henry V, the uniform worn by one of Louis-Philippe's officers is able to command centre stage. Even if Lucien's initial fears about the green uniform of the 27th Lancers being less cheerful than the daffodil yellow of the 9th have proved unfounded, he was right that 'l'essentiel, pour un uniforme, est d'être joli au bal' (i. 101). Costume is all, and it is a bit late to start worrying whether Mme de Chasteller is attracted by his personality or whether he is being patronized for the low rank which his uniform proclaims. From the beginning he has known the importance of dress. His equestrian display in front of Mme de Chasteller's window to erase the indignity of his earlier fall into the mud is preceded by two hours spent on 'la toilette militaire la plus soignée' (i. 138), and this preparation, requiring two mirrors and offering an enthralling spectacle to hotel staff and landlady alike, is followed by the equally careful grooming of his horse, the newly acquired and Byronically named Lara. But Lucien also knows when to sacrifice cleanliness, and the gentle lowering of his white-trousered knees on to the dirty floor of the Chapelle des Pénitents is no less effective, nor any less theatrical. Part II of the novel brings further changes of role and costume. The 'faux accouchement' has turned him first into 'un jeune premier de tragédie' (ii. 94), then a comic cuckold: 'il se regardait comme un mari trompé et s'appliquait la masse de ridicule et d'antipathie dont le théâtre et le monde vulgaire affublent cet état' (ii. 103). The moment comes to don 'un uniforme de maître de requêtes', that is, an extremely uncheerful 'habit noir boutonné jusqu'au menton', and for his father to teach him how to dress the part:

mais comme te voilà fait, dit-il en s'interrompant. Tu as l'air bien jeune! Va prendre un habit moins frais, un gilet noir, arrange mal tes cheveux,... tousse quelquefois,... tâche de te donner vingt-huit ou trente ans. (ii. 126)

Now, after 'une grande heure de toilette', he is ready to make his début in this his most serious role, the one in which his costume will be dirtied not by falling off a horse but by the mud-slinging opprobrium of the people of Blois.

The world of *Lucien Leuwen* is a world of sham where appearances count for everything, where simulated emotion such as Lucien's for Mme Grandet meets with reciprocation while a sincere outburst of filial affection (i. 106-7) causes only shock and irritation. Lucien's bewildered reaction on the latter occasion—'je ne suis sûr de rien sur mon compte'—becomes a leitmotif in the novel. 'Que suis-je donc?', 'sous le rapport de la valeur réelle de l'homme, quelle est ma place? Suis-je au milieu de la liste, ou tout à fait le dernier?' (i. 158-9), these are the questions he asks himself subsequently when he becomes aware of a disparity between his personal tastes and his political beliefs. On the one hand he sides morally with the Left: 'excepté mes pauvres républicains attaqués de folie, je ne vois rien d'estimable dans le monde; il entre du charlatanisme dans tous les mérites de ma connaissance' (i. 158), and this opinion is doubtless the one which caused his expulsion from the Ecole Polytechnique. But that was two years ago, and since then he has become a happy pleasure-seeker. No Hampden, no 'fanatique de liberté américaine' but simply 'un jeune homme de vingt ans, pensant comme tout le monde' (i. 101), perhaps he is indeed simply covered in a 'vernis de républicanisme' (i. 155) while remaining inwardly aghast at the materialism of the New World and dependant upon the 'plaisirs donnés par une ancienne civilisation' (i. 157). His father may call him a Saint-Simonian[8] and express surprise that he is not one of the dirty, bearded variety (i. 106), but that is only because Lucien has scruples about taking his money (or later about being the 'coquin' his father thinks he ought to be),[9] just as Colonel Malher thinks he is republican merely because he senses insubordination in Lucien's ironic expression (i. 146). He may admire Gauthier's honesty and integrity but he cannot overcome 'sa grande objection contre la république: la nécessité de faire la cour aux gens médiocres' (i. 165). For all Gauthier's republican virtue Lucien prefers the amusing charlatanry of Du Poirier, and when he challenges to a duel, the accusation of being boring seems to weigh more than the charge of republicanism. Pleasure matters more than principle. Indeed such is the equation between radicalism, seriousness, truthfulness and tedium, on the one hand, and conversatism, flippancy, mendacity and entertainment on the other, that Lucien's motive for the duel can only be given as a paradox: 'républicain, je viens de me battre pour prouver que je ne le suis pas' (i. 196). And this paradox emerges again when Lucien dresses his servants up in expensive livery to show his father that he is not a Saint-Simonian, but soon afterwards takes exception to Legitimist desires to turn the political clock back to 1786 because he believes that 'c'était précisément à compter de 1786 que la France avait commencé à sortir un peu de la barbarie où elle est encore à demi plongée' (i. 215). A republican at heart, he regrets republican lack of style, and hence his confusion: 'il n'y a qu'un sot ou un enfant qui consente à conserver des désirs contradictoires' (i. 157).

---

[8] See Crouzet's comments on why Lucien is not a Saint-Simonian, i. 348, n. 44.
[9] For an account of politics as 'coquinerie' see Michel Crouzet, 'Lucien Leuwen et le "sens politique"', in Berthier et al., Le Plus Méconnu des romans de Stendhal, 99–139.

Similar confusion overwhelms Lucien during the experience of love. His early ridiculing of his cousin Edgard 'qui fait dépendre son bonheur, et bien plus, son estime pour lui-même, des opinions d'une jeune femme' (i. 159) gives way to sophistry as the attractions of Mme de Chasteller begin to take effect: 'j'étais bien bon de penser à l'amour et de me faire des reproches! Ce passe-temps ne m'empêchera pas d'être un homme estimable et de servir la patrie, si l'occasion s'en présente' (i. 242). Shame at being no better than his cousin soon follows, and then the most comic pomposity:

mais moi! à mon âge! quel est le jeune homme qui ose seulement parler d'un attachement sérieux pour une femme? [...] Je me crois des devoirs envers la patrie. Jusqu'ici je me suis principalement estimé parce que je n'étais pas un égoïste uniquement occupé à bien jouir du gros lot qu'il a reçu du hasard; je me suis estimé parce que je sentais avant tout l'existence de ces devoirs envers la patrie et le besoin de l'estime des grandes âmes. Je suis dans l'âge d'agir; d'un moment à l'autre la voix de la patrie peut se faire entendre; je puis être appelé; je devrais occuper tout mon esprit à découvrir les véritables intérêts de la France, que des fripons cherchent à embrouiller. Une seule tête, une seule âme, ne suffisent pas pour y voir clair, au milieu de devoirs si compliqués. Et c'est le moment que je choisis pour me faire l'esclave d'une petite ultra de province! (i. 248)

He who had thought of love as a rare phenomenon, a kind of dangerous cliff over which he was sure not to fall, now trembles at the approach of his beloved, and immediate thoughts of flight provoke the increasingly familiar shocked realization that he does not know himself:

il ne pouvait donc se répondre de rien sur son propre compte! Quelle leçon de modestie! Quel besoin d'agir pour être enfin sûr de soi-même, non plus par une vaine probabilité, mais d'après des faits! (i. 250)

This comedy of 'la surprise de l'amour' is followed by the equally Marivaudian sequence at the ball in which Mme de Chasteller undergoes the same 'surprise' and each lover seeks to gauge the sincerity of the other's feelings while not revealing his or her own love. Here there is much sophisticated interplay of truth and falsehood, and the reader's privileged awareness of the dramatic ironies may reinforce his sense of the lover's bewilderment. The tone is set as Lucien tries to interpret the expression in Mme de Chasteller's eyes, this gaze that has already proved the subject of several uncertain explanations (i. 125, 131, 134, 138). The narrator reveals that the eyes merely betray a curiosity to meet this much talked-about young man 'qui avait des passions extrêmes, qui, tous les jours, avait un duel' (i. 263), who falls off his horse in front of her house on purpose, and who showed bravery, albeit of a rather cold-blooded kind, when they were out boating. We of course can perceive the exaggeration in the first of these descriptions, and we know that the other incidents are better explained in terms of Lucien's nervousness. But we are only just ahead of Mme de Chasteller, who at once discovers by dancing with Lucien that 'il était timide à la gaucherie'—except that she does not put his timidity down to love but to his supposed memories of his ignominious fall. When this real timidity persists, she sees it as feigned; when it ceases, she sees his genuine brilliance as artifice, and classes Lucien among 'ces hommes adroits, aimables, et profondément dissimulés, que l'on voit dans les romans' (i. 269). Yet just as she decides that she should 'rompre toute relation avec cet homme dangereux, habile comédien', it is already too late: 'elle l'aimait déjà'. Now it is her turn to experience 'une surprise profonde' (i. 273), and during several minutes of blanching and blushing[10] she comes to the conclusion that she may trust 'l'évidence de l'extrême sincérité dans les propos de ce jeune homme', while during those same moments Lucien has come to doubt hers, wondering instead whether her involuntary frankness has not been merely 'une faveur banale', whether perhaps she simply fancies soldiers. As a result of his suspicion his 'propos' are now very carefully calculated: 'un mot peut me perdre à jamais'. As the ball draws to a close the ironies of masquerade are now enriched by Mme de Chasteller's sudden realization that the other guests may have been watching: 'j'en ai agi, pendant je ne sais combien de temps, comme si personne ne m'eût regardée, moi ni M. Leuwen. Ce public ne me passe rien' (i. 279). Her anguished thoughts return repeatedly to 'ce public cruel', 'un public mesquin', 'la cruauté de ce public', and lose themselves in a whirl of fervent paranoia: 'elle se figurait les regards que chacune des femmes dont elle se figurait le mépris devait lui avoir adressés en dansant le cotillon' (i. 291). She has forgotten the golden rule of which she later tells Lucien: 'une femme qui vit seule [...] doit être attentive aux moindres apparences' (ii. 57), and it seems therefore all the more ironic that Lucien should conclude from her behaviour

---

[10] Given the large number of references in the novel to sudden pallor or suffusion *Le Rouge et le Blanc* would have been an appropriate title for a reason other than the political one mentioned by Stendhal (i. 339).

at the ball that 'elle joue le sentiment' (i. 292), that she is but 'une coquette de théâtre' (i. 301).

Lucien's reaction to this turning-point in his relationship with Mme de Chasteller (i. 304–6) is characteristic: 'il ne comprenait rien à tout ce qui lui arrivait', and he throws himself into his old role with renewed vigour: ' "on ne peut trop charger un rôle avec ces gens-ci"; et il se mit à parler comme un véritable comédien. Toujours il récitait un rôle, et le plus bouffon qui lui venait à l'esprit.' Possessed of all the outward trappings of success, he is inwardly beset by gloom, so that his 'noire mélancolie' is now taken to be 'une imitation savante de Lord Byron' and even Mme de Chasteller begins once more to doubt him (i. 315). Their respective melancholy and doubts are dispelled by the sincerity of their conversation in the idyllic woods of Burelviller, but Lucien's confusion is all the greater when the presence of Mme de Chasteller's chaperone causes him to fall out of love just as surely as he had fallen into it. In a sequence reminiscent of Constant's *Adolphe* and pointing forward to Proust's account of 'les intermittences du cœur' in *A la recherche*, Lucien is assailed by renewed awareness of his inconsistency and the provisional, contradictory nature of his desires. As in his anguish about politics the parallels of child and madman come to his mind: 'Grand Dieu! Puis-je me répondre de rien sur moi-même? Qui me l'eût dit hier? Mais je suis donc un fou, un enfant! [...] Demain, je puis être un assassin, un voleur, tout au monde. Je ne suis sûr de rien sur mon compte' (i. 329). Who indeed can count on whom?

ces pauvres femmes, se disait-il, qui sacrifient toute leur destinée à nos fantaisies, qui comptent sur notre amour! Et comment n'y compteraient-elles pas? Ne sommes-nous pas sincères quand nous le leur jurons? Hier, au *Chasseur vert*, je pouvais être imprudent, mais j'étais le plus sincère des hommes. Grand Dieu! Qu'est-ce que la vie? Il faut être indulgent désormais. (i. 331)

These 'pensées philosophiques et sombres', accompanied by reference to Chactas and even to 'un René, duc de Lorraine', may be redolent of the *mal du siècle* and the rhetorical extravagance of Octave in *Armance*, but they are authentic none the less, and Stendhal's portrayal of the intermittence of love contributes substantially to the originality of this account of Lucien's relationship with Mme de Chasteller and helps to make it perhaps the most subtle analysis of love in any of his novels. Unlike Constant's Adolphe,

Lucien decides at once to confess his new lack of feeling and to make a sincere avowal of his recent insincerity:

je vous parle, madame, d'une façon un peu emphatique, mais en vérité je ne sais comment expliquer en d'autres mots ce qui m'arrive depuis la vue de votre demoiselle de compagnie. Le signe fatal en est que, pour vous parler un peu le langage de l'amour, il faut que je fasse effort sur moi-même. (ii. 6)

Mme de Chasteller's confusion is once again equal to Lucien's. His use of language seems insincere, yet his tone and gesture ring true: 'serait-il déjà un comédien aussi parfait?' If she is to believe him, how then should she appear in her reply: 'si elle ajoutait foi à cette étrange confidence, si elle la croyait sincère, d'abord elle ne devait pas paraître fâchée, encore moins attristée, et comment faire pour paraître ni l'un ni l'autre?' (ii. 7). Thus a belief in his sincerity entails an insincere response from her. Just as Mme de Chasteller's real distress at the ball leaves Lucien thinking she is an actress, so Lucien's extraordinary honesty leaves Mme de Chasteller with grave doubts about his integrity. In this world of masquerade only the mask is believed, and the real face behind it seems like a lie. 'Vous êtes un homme étrange!' she exclaims,[11] while he remains as baffled as ever: 'en vérité, je ne sais pas ce que je suis, et je donnerais beaucoup à qui pourrait me le dire' (ii. 9). This counterpoint of sincerity and pretence is maintained to the end of Part I, as the lovers continue to wonder about each other's feelings and about each other's choice of words or tone of voice. Moments of trust and 'sincérité parfaite' alternate with moments of anguish and doubt (ii. 60, 67). Not for them, it seems, the perfect understanding of M. and Mme Leuwen (ii. 375). Instead, a determination on Lucien's part to 'ne [...] croire que ce que j'aurai vu' (ii. 52) which leads to the final grotesque irony whereby Lucien believes he has seen Mme de Chasteller's new-born baby and trusts the evidence of his own eyes, when he has had so much evidence to the contrary from the depths of hers, 'ces yeux si pénétrants, mais si chastes' (i. 248).

An event such as the 'faux accouchement' is unlikely to strengthen one's faith in one's ability to judge others, and the Lucien who returns to the family fold at the beginning of Part II is even more confused than the playboy who left it. Where Dévelroy had preached, M. Leuwen now quotes La Fontaine: 'sera-t-il dieu, table ou cuvette?' (ii. 96) and offers him the job of principal private secretary to the Minister

---

[11] Cf. ii. 424 where 'étrange' is again a synonym for 'sincère'.

of the Interior: 'et il faut qu'avant demain matin, se disait-il [Lucien] avec terreur, je prenne une décision, que *j'aie foi en moi-même*... Est-il un être au monde dont j'estime aussi peu le jugement?' (ii. 100). Only the story of *Edgar, ou le Parisien de vingt ans*, this 'jeune homme qui ne connaît pas les hommes [...], qui] n'est sûr de rien ni sur les autres ni, à plus forte raison, sur soi- même' shames him into action: *'je serai un coquin'* (ii. 102) he exclaims, where once he had cried: 'eh bien, je serai *lancier'*. No particular reasons for the decision occur to him. He just might as well have a go, might as well see what happens. What has happened to the good intention to 'agir [...] non plus par une vaine probabilité, mais d'après des faits!' (i. 250)?

Lucien's crises of identity are far less frequent in Part II, and much more space is devoted to the machinations in which he is involved than to their impact on his attitude to life. Doubtless this may be a consequence of Stendhal the 'chroniqueur' taking over from Stendhal the 'psychologue' and of the original plan to return to Lucien's relationship with Mme de Chasteller in Part III. The effect nevertheless is to suggest that he may be growing out of 'cette maladie de *trop raisonner* qui coupe bras et jambes à la jeunesse de notre temps et lui donne le caractère d'une vieille femme' (i. 103). Such crises as do occur become gradually less violent. Certainly the incident at Blois causes him considerable pain and self-questioning: 'que faire? Quel état prendre?' (ii. 232), which the brutal honesty of Coffe does nothing to alleviate. But the next stage of his mission soon puts it out of his mind, and by the time he reports home on his electioneering, the questions have become calmer, more like requests for information than cries for help:

ai-je bien agi ou mal agi? dit Lucien. En vérité, je l'ignore. Sur le champ de bataille, dans la vivacité de l'action je croyais avoir mille fois raison, mais ici les doutes se présentent en foule [...] Mais mon orgueil est alarmé; quelle opinion dois-je avoir de moi-même? Ai-je quelque valeur, voilà ce que je vous demande, dit-il à son père. (ii. 316–17)

Soon he is coming to his own conclusions about himself: 'je suis trop simple, trop sincère, je ne sais pas assez dissimuler l'ennui, et encore moins l'amour que je sens, pour arriver jamais à des succès marquants auprès des femmes de la société' (ii. 403). He now trusts his own impulses, now knows that he could be financially independent, and has learnt to accept the rules of the game: 'faisons comme le monde, laissons la moralité de nos actions officielles' (ii. 407–9).

But only the morality of his actions as an official, not of his actions as a person. For Lucien has found a new certainty, a discovery which occurs during a consideration of content and form. Speculating about what it would be like to frequent the Parisian equivalents of Nancy's Legitimist hostesses, Mmes de Serpierre and de Marcilly, instead of the *juste milieu* salon of Mme Grandet, Lucien decides that the 'élégance parfaite' of the former is a sign of callousness: 'dans les livres elle me plaît, mais dans le monde elle me glace.' On the other hand the men whom he meets in the Grandet salon merit respect because they have 'au moins fait quelque chose [...] enfin ils ont agi'. Lucien concludes:

ce monde que je vois chez *ma maîtresse*, dit-il en riant, est comme une histoire écrite en mauvais langage, mais intéressante pour le fond des choses. Le monde de Mme de Marcilly, c'est des théories absurdes, ou même hypocrites, basées sur des faits controuvés et recouvertes d'un langage poli, mais l'âpreté du regard dément à chaque instant l'élégance de la forme. (ii. 399)

'Chez la Mme de Marcilly de Paris' no one pays attention to what you say but to how you say it, yet, when uttered by 'l'homme *accompli*' possessed of a modicum of good sense: 'ces discours élégants sont comme un oranger qui croîtrait au milieu de la forêt de Compiègne:[12] ils sont jolis, mais ne semblent pas de notre siècle.' As the narrator turned away from the vacuity of mere anecdote, so Lucien turns away from the heartless elegance of aristocratic society. But whereas the narrator was turning back towards the interesting enigma of Lucien, Lucien himself now seems set to accept his role as Mme Grandet's lover and to identify with the graceless 'canaille' that entertains 'cette âme de femme de chambre hôte d'un si beau corps' (ii. 201). There is complacency in his rejection of the style of the Faubourg Saint-Germain: 'le hasard n'a pas voulu me faire naître dans ce monde-là. Et pourquoi me changer? Que demandé-je au monde?' (ii. 399).

On the point of becoming part of the Grandets' 'histoire écrite en mauvais langage', Lucien is brought up short by a memory of Mme de Chasteller, just as once, some eighteen hundred years previously, 'cet homme faible qui devant le pouvoir venait de désavouer son ami arrêté pour opinions publiques fut averti par le chant du coq'. Lucien had been trying to dismiss his relationship with Mme de Chasteller

---

[12] Clémentine Curial, Stendhal's source of information about Legitimist circles, lived in the Château de Monchy near Compiègne.

as merely 'cette aventure de jeunesse et d'ambition', but now this latter-day Saint Peter realizes its sacred value and rushes out to buy a portrait which offers a close likeness of her, a portrait on porcelain to serve as icon, a 'sainte image' before which to weep in silent worship. The result? 'Lucien était un autre homme. Mme Grandet s'aperçut de ce changement dans ses idées' (ii. 400). Lucien now takes stock—of his father,[13] of his career prospects, of his political beliefs, of his future. Now for the first time he is sure of something:

'enfin, je ferai ce que Bathilde voudra...' Il raisonna longtemps sur cette idée, enfin elle l'étonna: il fut heureux de la trouver si profondément enracinée dans son esprit. 'Je suis donc bien sûr de lui pardonner! Ce n'est pas une illusion.' Il avait entièrement pardonné la faute de Mme de Chasteller. (ii. 408)

These realizations come to Lucien as he sits at the Opéra (where else?) watching Mlle Elssler in a ballet 'pendant que la musique donnait des ailes à son imagination'. This is a moment of enchantment comparable with those he once knew at the 'Chasseur vert', a moment of happiness: 'ce mélange de raisonnements et d'amour fit de cette fin de soirée, passée dans un coin de l'orchestre, un des soirs les plus heureux de sa vie' (ii. 409). The curtain falls, but Lucien now knows how to direct his own steps. Rejecting a return to the 'monde ennuyeux' of his parents, just as he has already rejected his father's box, he now exchanges the anonymity of the orchestra stalls for that of rented rooms. Here he is free, his own man at last, 'tout à fait à l'abri de la sollicitude paternelle, maternelle, sempiternelle!' (ii. 410). The hotel has asked for a passport. He will give them a false one: 'il faut un faux nom pour assurer encore plus ma liberté.' Having found himself, Lucien now sheds his patronym (as Stendhal would in his coming autobiography).[14] What will his new name be? Like Lucien's future, that must remain uncertain, 'un brillant *peut-être*' to go with 'le *peut-être* du bonheur' that may or may not await him 'chez Mme de Chasteller' in the rue de la Pompe in Nancy (ii. 407). By assuming a false identity he will be play-acting even more, of course, but he has now accepted the inherent theatricality of living in society and knows that behind whichever mask he may choose to wear will be the tender smile of sincere love.

[13] For an excellent account of the relationship between Lucien and his father see Berthier, *Stendhal et la Sainte Famille*, 72–82. See also Brombert, *Fiction*, 114–27.
[14] See Brombert, *Fiction*, 121–2, and Didier, *Stendhal autobiographe* (Paris, 1983), 276–83.

In reaching this conclusion he reverses his father's application of the image (in *Werther*) of the red thread which runs through all ropes belonging to the Royal Navy. 'Voilà', says M. Leuwen, 'l'image d'une corporation ou d'un homme qui a un mensonge *de fond* à soutenir. Jamais de vérité *pure et simple*' (ii. 105). From being the worthless Edgar he has become more like Jérôme Ménuel, the soldier, actor, forger and deserter, for whom living is a continuous performance and who finds freedom in the assumption of another's name.[15] Just as we never learn Jérôme Ménuel's real name, so the real identity of Lucien must remain provisional. But, as he reaches Capel at the end of the novel and assumes a new role, we know that his cadetship is at an end. He has learnt the ropes, and his love for Mme de Chasteller will provide the red thread that demonstrates continuity amidst the convolutions of experience. That is Lucien's 'vérité *de fond*'.

But what of the novelist's role? What is his red thread, his 'vérité *de fond*'? My argument has been that Stendhal faced a dilemma during the writing of *Lucien Leuwen*, and that this dilemma is reflected in the events and characters of the novel.[16] Indeed it pervades the work through a series of lexical oppositions: 'gai' or 'grave', 'plaisant' or 'sérieux', 'aimable' or 'triste', 'amusant' or 'ennuyeux', 'frivole' or 'plat', 'coquin' or 'honnête', 'se moquer' or 'prendre au sérieux', 'heureux' or 'malheureux', 'sublime' or 'bas'. The crux of Stendhal's dilemma is the relationship between the novel and reality. In the creation of his work of imagination he looks to the contemporary world at once for stimulus and for guarantees of plausibility, but his overriding aim is to portray 'la chasse au bonheur', the variety of often comically misguided ways in which humanity strives for fulfilment. In the process the gravity of the human condition under the July Monarchy is obscured by the gaiety of a comic novel in which governments are toppled for fun. Should he worry? Marginal comments of the kind 'le roman doit raconter',

---

[15] For a different approach to the story of Jérôme Ménuel, one which sees it as *La Chartreuse* in embryo, see Anne Léoni, 'Ménuel pseudonyme', *L'Arc*, 88 (1983), 64–71. See also Brombert, *Fiction*, 116.

[16] Both Peter Brooks and Michel Crouzet have noted that the form and content of the novel are closely connected, but both see in this an affirmation of the exemplary status of M. Leuwen's 'worldly' style, of his disinterested 'esprit' that transcends parochial 'vérités' through 'la liberté du jeu'. See Brooks, *The Novel of Worldliness*, 230–66, and Crouzet, *Quatre études*, chs i (especially 24–5) and iii. Only in passing does Crouzet acknowledge the 'liberté vide et un peu satanique de M. Leuwen' (23).

'le roman est un livre qui amuse en racontant' (ii. 591), 'rien qui fasse penser, mais au contraire quelque chose qui dispose à l'émotion' (ii. 579), 'jamais de satire' (i. 345) begin to look like reminders, and even reassurances. Is Stendhal perhaps worried that story-telling may be a frivolous irrelevance at a time when the army was massacring workers in the rue Transnonain? Worried that the one sure point of contact between the novel and reality, namely the reader's response, may be lost? That this novel may cease to be a violinist's bow and become a mirror, even a mirror 'qu'on promène le long d'une banqueroute'? By avoiding satire he can perhaps avoid bankrupting the reader's sympathy (ii. 91), by being original in his comedy he can perhaps avoid bankrupting the French comic tradition through excessive imitation (ii. 203), but can he avoid the bankruptcy of the 'histoire anecdotique' (ii. 361)? Confidently he denies a 'but moral' and purports to write for 'la Bibliothèque bleue' (i. 93–4), but is 'le romanesque' any more authentic than M. Leuwen's 'omelette soufflée'? May it not be just as insubstantial, mere (implausible) story for vicarious pleasure and quite without seriousness of purpose? It is all very well to exclude all 'réflexion philosophique sur le fond des choses' (ii. 525), thereby rendering the novel 'inintelligible pour les femmes de chambre' (ii. 477, n. 260), but how does one avoid the 'viande creuse' of the simple adventure story?

There is no question that the writing of *Lucien Leuwen* caused Stendhal grave doubts about the value and function of the novel as a genre, and it is of great interest in this respect to read Beatrice Didier's account of his 'refus du romanesque' in *Vie de Henry Brulard*.[17] When memory fails him in the recovery of his past he is frequently tempted to bring imagination to its aid, but that would be too easy, too tidy: 'mon souvenir n'est qu'un roman fabriqué à cette occasion.'[18] Truth and sincerity are better served by leaving gaps and preserving the fragmentation of his reminiscence. His life is like a fresco with blanks.[19] Curiously, so is *Lucien Leuwen*. Was its author already, consciously or unconsciously, experimenting with the open text as a more authentic means of expression than the neat directions and proportions of a 'roman d'éducation'? In *La Chartreuse de Parme* Stendhal found a solution to the problem of story and meaning. Here in *Lucien Leuwen* the problem itself constitutes both the story and the meaning. Throughout the novel Lucien's principal

---

[17] *Stendhal autobiographe*, 283–93.   [18] *OI*, ii. 951.   [19] Ibid. 644.

aim is to combine gaiety and gravity in an authentic way, and it is Mme de Chasteller who provides the model for such a combination, for she possesses both 'un caractère sérieux et tendre' (i. 279) and 'un caractère heureux et même gai' (i. 258-9). In choosing her as the one certainty in his shifting experiences Lucien has chosen wisely. For the novelist she is a symbol of the union of story and seriousness at which he is aiming. She is unique among the characters of the novel in that 'rêver était son plaisir suprême' (i. 259), and 'la rêverie' is 'le vrai plaisir du roman'.

This foregrounding of the problem of sincerity and style is the 'vérité *de fond*', the red thread which proclaims continuity in the endless round of episode and scene. *Lucien Leuwen* is unique among Stendhal's novels in that it provides an allegory not of reading but of writing, and this 'mise-en-abyme' is not the least of the many reasons why it could so easily have been called *Les Faux-Monnayeurs*.

V

REASON AND ROMANCE IN
LA CHARTREUSE DE PARME

The Reader Enchanted

'L'homme pensif, qui se berce l'imagination par les détails enchanteurs
de quelque roman dont il sent qu'il serait le héros si le ciel était juste,
va-t-il se retirer de cet océan de bonheur, pour jouir de la supériorité
qu'il peut avoir sur un Géronte disant de son fils: "Mais que diable
allait-il faire dans cette galère!"'

(*HPI*, ii. 78)

1

The Miraculous Novel

Le dessin laissé par Gros sur la table du café des *Servi* parut un miracle descendu du ciel; il fut gravé dans la nuit, et le lendemain on en vendit vingt mille exemplaires.

$$(7)^1$$

AS Lucien makes his way to Capel at the end of *Lucien Leuwen*, the narrator describes how 'il vit, avec plus de plaisir qu'il n'appartient de le faire à un ignorant, Milan, Sarono, la Chartreuse de Pavie, etc. Bologne, Florence, le jetèrent dans un état d'attendrissement et de sensibilité aux moindres petites choses qui lui eût causé bien des remords trois ans auparavant.' Milan, the charterhouse of Pavia, Bologna . . . Just as *Lucien Leuwen* seems to begin where *Le Rouge et le Noir* ended, so it seems to end where *La Chartreuse de Parme* begins: with the arrival of the French in Northern Italy. Now, as the narrator of *La Chartreuse* remarks: 'il y a lieu à un nouveau paysage comme à un nouveau roman' (2), and the reader too may have the sense of being in a new and foreign land. With *Le Rouge et le Noir* and *Lucien Leuwen* one at least remains within the bounds of a familiar kind of Europen nineteenth-century novel, the kind that offers a portrait of society, both provincial and metropolitan, and traces the emotional and intellectual development of one or more individuals with, perhaps, particular emphasis on their experience of love and sexual passion. But such bearings may not help to orientate the reader of *La Chartreuse de Parme*. The depiction of society seems less important than in Stendhal's earlier novels because of its anachronistic colouring, the events and values of Renaissance Italy having been transported without apology into the early nineteenth century.² Certainly the experience of love is still an

---

¹ Throughout Part V simple page-reference of this kind is to the Classiques Garnier edition by A. Adam.
² A point first made by Zola. See Talbot (ed.), *Critique stendhalienne*, 256. Cf. Bardèche, *Stendhal romancier*, 377, and Hemmings, *Stendhal*, 177 ('it is this moral anachronism, more than anything else, that gives the novel its specific savour').

important feature but, broadly speaking, it is presented without the complexity and concern for psychological precision to be found in the previous novels.[3] Similarly there is little analysis of the central hero Fabrice: he seems merely to act, indeed often only to re-act, and the elements of development, or education, may appear to be minimal. Also one may wonder if he is in fact to be regarded as the central character, for the narrator claims rather to be telling the 'histoire de la duchesse Sanseverina' (1). To some, like Sainte-Beuve, the narrative may appear labyrinthine and implausible,[4] to others little more than a series of adventure stories with a hasty, tragic ending.[5] For all that Gide placed the novel second to *Les Liaisons dangereuses* in his list of the greatest French novels,[6] the disconcerted reader may wonder whether *La Chartreuse de Parme* has any claim to serious consideration at all.[7]

The rapidity of the novel's composition (from 4 November to 26 December 1838) may, on the other hand, cause the reader to marvel: 'cette promptitude dans la perfection est un des miracles du métier littéraire',[8] writes Prévost, later echoed by Hemmings: 'for once it seems proper to apply the over-used word "miraculous" to this extraordinary eruption of a dense, intricate, dazzlingly poetic masterpiece.'[9] *La Chartreuse de Parme*, then, is a miracle? It is of course in the nature of a miracle to be at once accomplished with ease and yet difficult to explain, and this very contrast underlies much of the critical response to the novel. As Michael Wood writes: 'quel autre grand roman laisse tant de travail au critique tout en ayant l'air de se passer complètement de lui?'[10] Consequently, and in a

---

[3] Cf. Zola: 'Stendhal n'est même plus ici le grand psychologue; il devient un conteur, il frappe l'imagination', in Talbot (ed.), *Critique stendhalienne*, 261.

[4] Ibid. 167.

[5] Cf. Zola: '*La Chartreuse de Parme* est pour le moins autant un roman d'aventures qu'une œuvre d'analyse' (ibid. 261). See Bardèche, *Stendhal romancier*, 394, and Jones, *Ironie* 129.

[6] 'Les Dix Romans français que ...', in *Œuvres complètes*, ed. L. Martin-Chauffier, Nouvelle Revue Française (15 vols, n. p., n. d.), vii. 449–58.

[7] Cf. Elme Caro: 'dans la *Chartreuse de Parme*, je me demande où est l'intérêt. C'est une accumulation de scènes, sans aucun plan, sans l'ombre d'unité' (Talbot, *Critique*, 191).

[8] *Création*, 432. The term 'miracle' recurs on p. 454.

[9] *Stendhal*, 176. Cf. Balzac: 'je crois à quelque *lampe merveilleuse littéraire*' (Talbot, *Critique*, 27) and Bardèche: 'nous croyons assez à cette explication par le miracle' (*Stendhal romancier*, 418. See also p. 401: 'on ne sait par quel miracle'). Cf. also Strickland, *Stendhal*, 226.

[10] '*La Chartreuse de Parme* et le sphinx', *Stendhal Club*, 20 (1977/8), 161–9. Cf. the same critic's *Stendhal*, 157: 'one can't say less. And at first sight, it looks as if one can't say much more.'

curious inversion of normal procedures of evaluation, *La Chartreuse* is sometimes deemed a masterpiece before reasons are adduced by way of justification, with the result that critical analysis of the work may appear more like an act of faith. Reading is believing.[11] Thus Hemmings, for example, comments that 'the general consensus of critical opinion has for a long time now assigned *La Chartreuse* a high place among the masterpieces of European fiction in the nineteenth century. And the general consensus of critical opinion, at any rate when passing a positive judgement, is not often at fault. Where, then', he goes on to ask, 'does one look for that structural unity which is invariably a feature of the true work of art?' But, having accepted the consensus of critical opinion, he can only align himself with it by rejecting its methods:

the traditional vocabulary of criticism is of little help as a guide to the qualities that confer on *La Chartreuse de Parme* the excellence which the discerning mind divines in it. For once, it is better to discard the old framework of concepts—theme, characterization, plot—and look elsewhere for the unity underlying this intricate diversity.

In the place of analysis the critic is obliged to express a poetic impression:

one would have to say that the whole novel gives the impression of being balanced at the intersection of two inclined planes: the one rising with the rising sun from the warm mists of the morning of life, the other dipping with the lengthening shadows of evening towards the chilly darkness of cloister and tomb.[12]

Critical analysis is elided between eulogy (the 'dazzlingly poetic masterpiece') on the one hand and poetic analogy on the other. Equally one may sense a circular argument at work: *La Chartreuse* is excellent because the 'discerning mind' so deems it, while 'discernment' implies the ability to see excellence in *La Chartreuse*.

---

[11] Conveniently Stendhal has left clear evidence of how he would have reacted to such critical procedure: 'on ne peut s'empêcher de rire quand on lit le commencement de la description que le judicieux Richardson donne de cette statue [Michelangelo's Moses]: *"Comme cette pièce est très fameuse, il ne faut pas douter qu'elle ne soit aussi très excellente"* ' *(HPI*, ii. 354).

[12] *Stendhal*, 200–1. Ironically this last passage is prefaced by 'if one were to be more precise'.

Hemming's response to the 'miracle' of *La Chartreuse* is characteristic of the novel's reception.[13] Victor Brombert, for example, also tries his hand at the poetic impression, though in an appropriately 'oblique' way:

an impressionistic critic might stress the autumnal light of *La Chartreuse*. Distant details are repeatedly brought out in their sharpest outline. Yet this light, allowing for clarity and vast panoramas, does not provide a gay illumination. It has the softness of mellow sadness and resignation. It is a light that somehow suggests the eternity of the fleeting moment.[14]

And again one finds the same tendency to circularity:

the ambiguous tone of *La Chartreuse*, which transmutes playfulness into meaning and deals with the most serious events in an almost flippant manner, can easily unsettle the reader. This tone is hard to describe. Unconstrained and irreverent, it seeks out the sophisticated reader, willing and able to follow the author in his mental games and ironic capers.[15]

Playfulness and flippancy are meaningful and serious because a sophisticated reader so regards them: sophistication implies the ability to see playfulness and flippancy as meaningful and serious. And one finds the same kind of tautology in Prévost:

pour que le charme soit goûté, il faut que le lecteur n'ait aucun effort à faire. Le laisser-aller doit être égal à celui de l'auteur. Or la *Chartreuse* est l'un des ouvrages les plus limpides au monde—mais pour ceux qui ont le goût de l'esprit, une certaine culture, et qui ne sont pas trop prisonniers de leurs propres habitudes et de leurs propres mœurs. Pour tous les autres il y a difficulté, le laisser-aller de l'auteur fait impertinence.[16]

[13] See Bardèche, *Stendhal romancier*, 365: '[...] pour comprendre la composition et la conduite du récit dans la *Chartreuse*. On dirait une vigne vierge qui a poussée dans tous les sens. On a l'impression de pénétrer un beau jour d'été dans un jardin abandonné. Il y a des jeunes pousses, des fleurs imprévues, des baies sauvages. On se laisse aller avec délice à ce foisonnement heureux. Ne gâtons pas au lecteur cette exploration *merveilleuse*. Il faut le laisser dans ce jardin sauvage. Ce mouvement de fécondité et de grâce heureuse, c'est la poésie même de Stendhal, c'est la forme que prend chez lui la joie de créer, d'imaginer le bonheur et les âmes qu'il aime' (my italics). Bardèche momentarily takes issue with commentators for whom 'l'état de grâce [...] paraît expliquer tout': 'ne peut-on parfois', he ventures, 'expliquer l'état de grâce?' (366). But finally he concedes: 'cette grâce de la *Chartreuse*, il faut bien avouer aussi qu'elle échappe à tout "démontage" et même, en définitive, à toute explication' (396).

[14] *Fiction*, 149–50. Cf. Strickland, *Stendhal*, 233: 'one is left with the impression that the story of [Fabrice's] life takes place in an almost uninhabited Italian landscape on a glorious, though slightly melancholy afternoon.'

[15] *Fiction*, 151.   [16] *Création*, 438.

Membership of the charmed circle is both the condition and consequence of an ability to understand *La Chartreuse*. The charmed circle is a vicious one.

But how can this circle be broken (into)? It will perhaps already be evident to the 'discerning mind' how deeply the critical reception of *La Chartreuse* is imbued with the terminology and preoccupations of the novel itself. Miracles, interpretation and misinterpretation, even blindness and insight, these are some of the central concerns of the narrative. And perhaps there is a lesson for us here, because in the novel a belief in miracles is synonymous with ignorance and gullibility. The inhabitants of Milan regard Gros's cartoon as miraculous because the genre itself is unknown to them, while Fabrice sees his safe passage across the frontier after the murder of Giletti also as miraculous, but only because he is unaware that the police officer who inspects his passport is trying to protect Giletti. May one not suspect that the miraculous ease of *La Chartreuse*, its playfulness and 'limpidité', are beguiling? May it not be that the apparent simplicity of the narrative conceals difficulties which are open to rational, incredulous discussion? To believe so is of course gratifying to the critic who is anxious to justify his role, and nothing is more conventional in critical discussion than to begin with what appears to be true and to follow this with a different, purportedly more accurate account of the matter. But to discuss *La Chartreuse* in this way is in fact to re-enact the principal strategy of the novel, which, from first to last, presents itself to the reader both as 'merely a story' and as a text that is in danger of being misread. Thus in the 'Avertissement' the narrative is introduced with all the highly conventional trappings of pseudo-oral narration more often found in early nineteenth-century short stories than in the novel: the visit to friends, the chance reference in a conversation, the long after-dinner story (in the manner, say, of Balzac's *L'Auberge rouge*), even the discovered manuscript to provide supplementary evidence, all these suggest a 'true' story just waiting to be retold. Yet at the same time retelling it may prove difficult: the reader may be bored by Italians, the 'author' may be thought to condone immorality. The impression of an 'easy', traditional kind of story conveyed by the 'Avertissement' is then reinforced by the epic style of the opening sentence of chapter i: 'le 15 mai 1796, le général Bonaparte fit son entrée dans Milan à la tête de cette jeune armée qui venait de passer le pont de Lodi, et d'apprendre au monde qu'après tant de siècles

César et Alexandre avaient un successeur.' At the end of the novel and almost by way of a framework device (again in a manner more reminiscent of the short story), this impression is recalled by the fairy-tale style of the final sentence: 'les prisons de Parme étaient vides, le comte immensément riche, Ernest V adoré de ses sujets qui comparaient son gouvernement à celui des grands-ducs de Toscane.' But the sense of closure, of uncomplicated and tidy completion, is at once undermined by the notorious valedictory dedication 'TO THE HAPPY FEW' which reminds one of the narrator's anxieties in the 'Avertissement'. Things may appear simple, but have we understood? Have we found the Italians interesting after all? Have we looked beyond the 'aventures [...] blâmables' (2) in search of moral values that we can accept? Have we in fact been truly 'avertis'?

In this way La Chartreuse invites its reader to enjoy narrative in an innocent, childlike way as if it were an excellent zabaglione (1) and yet also to interpret, to understand, to discriminate with a maturity born of reading (only if the reader is young will he be scandalized: 162). At the same time the novel presents itself as a cryptogram: apparently simple, it yet purports to conceal a secret message which only the Happy Few will decipher.[17] Like Fabrice's letters to Fabio Conti and don Cesare (421) or his sermons to the congregations of Parma (529) it proclaims a surface meaning for public consumption and a deeper one for private contemplation. The reader anxious to achieve membership of the Happy Few is called upon to become an accomplice[18] in the novelist's conspiracy, to participate in a game of hermeneutic hide-and-seek. Reading is an adventure, and one might almost say that it is the danger of misreading which makes the novel exciting. Hence perhaps the inclusion of the lines from Ronsard as an epigraph to chapter ii. God's truth is displayed for all to see in the disposition of the stars, yet 'les hommes chargés de terre et de trépas, / Méprisent tel écrit et ne le lisent pas' (19). This puts us on our mettle: are we so shot through with error, so 'fallen' that we cannot see the truth of La Chartreuse? Or are we of the Happy Few? Are we to win grace and have revealed to us the reality which we in our ignorance call miraculous?

But how should we respond to this danger? Some, doubtless, will exaggerate it and seek out the most implausible of hidden messages,

---

[17] See William J. Berg, 'Cryptographie et communication dans La Chartreuse de Parme', and Landry, L'Imaginaire, 333–4.

[18] See Prévost, Création, 438, and Brombert, Fiction, 151.

while others may find that they are prompted to unusual insight: 'la présence du danger donne du génie à l'homme raisonnable, elle le met, pour ainsi dire, au-dessus de lui-même; à l'homme d'imagination elle inspire des romans, hardis il est vrai, mais souvent absurdes' (206). This quotation comes from the account of Fabrice's encounter with the border official who knows Giletti, and it may seem unduly fanciful to use it as an illustration of the ways in which we may respond to the novel. But just as we have found with *Armance* and *Le Rouge et le Noir*, there are close parallels in *La Chartreuse* between the experience of the central characters and the way in which the novel offers itself to be read. Here, as elsewhere in the narrative, reason and imagination are contrasted as alternative responses, not only to danger but to experience of all kinds. In this instance reason is equated with 'génie' (meaning intelligent ways of avoiding the danger in question) while imagination is equated with absurdity and nonsensical fantasy ('des romans')—in this case Fabrice's plan to jump into the Po and swim back to the other side, his subsequent speculation that if he kills the official he will be condemned to death or twenty years as a galley slave, and his dread of spending twenty years in the Spielberg with chains weighing 120 lbs on each foot and a mere eight ounces of bread a day to eat. Not only could reason have dispelled these particular fears ('la logique de Fabrice oubliait que puisqu'il avait brûlé son passeport, rien n'indiquait à l'employé de police qu'il fût le rebelle Fabrice del Dongo'), but knowledge of the truth would have shown them to be paltry ('notre héros était suffisamment effrayé, comme on le voit; il l'eût été bien davantage s'il eût connu les pensées qui agitaient le commis de police': 206). Imagination, then, is both erroneous and inadequate.

But if this passage is compared with another in which reason and imagination are again contrasted as possible responses to danger, then it becomes clear that the superiority of reason is not total. As Fabrice gazes down from Blanès' room at the top of the church tower in Grianta, he suddenly notices the arrival of ten gendarmes in the main street. At once he imagines the Spielberg and his legs shackled by chains weighing 110 lbs (this is an earlier incident: the weight of the fearsome chains increases as the novel unfolds). Reason tells him that the chances of his being seen by the gendarmes are slim: he is eighty feet up, in a darkened room, and any observer would also have to contend with the glare of the sun and the dazzle of the newly whitewashed houses of the village. And yet:

malgré des raisonnements si clairs, l'âme italienne de Fabrice eût été désormais hors d'état de goûter aucun plaisir, s'il n'eût interposé entre lui et les gendarmes un lambeau de vieille toile qu'il cloua contre la fenêtre et auquel il fit deux trous pour les yeux. (178)

Now it seems as if Fabrice's imaginings have added to the pleasure he experiences in watching the procession in honour of Saint Giovita. The danger of discovery is imaginary, but it has led to a need to hide and a fear of being found out, both of which are part of the cloak-and-dagger secrecy with which Fabrice's life, and much of the novel, is pervaded. Imagination provides the thrills: reason is unexciting.

From these two episodes it emerges that imagination creates 'des romans' which give pleasure, while reason brings clarity and understanding. The former is the lot of the Italian ('Fabrice était un de ces malheureux tourmentés par leur imagination; c'est assez le défaut des gens d'esprit en Italie': 205), the latter of the French ('un soldat français d'un courage égal ou même inférieur se serait présenté pour passer sur le pont tout de suite, et sans songer d'avance à aucune difficulté; mais aussi il y aurait porté tout son sang-froid': 205). It comes therefore as no surprise that the French narrator should describe Fabrice's reflections on astrology in the following way:

le raisonnement de Fabrice ne put jamais pénétrer plus loin; il tournait de cent façons autour de la difficulté sans parvenir à la surmonter. Il était trop jeune encore; dans ses moments de loisir, son âme s'occupait avec ravissement à goûter les sensations produites par des *circonstances romanesques* que son imagination était toujours prête à lui fournir. Il était bien loin d'employer son temps à regarder avec patience les *particularités réelles* des choses pour ensuite deviner leurs causes. Le réel lui semblait encore plat et fangeux; je conçois qu'on n'aime pas à le regarder, mais alors il ne faut pas en raisonner. Il ne faut pas surtout faire des objections avec les diverses pièces de son ignorance. (168: my italics)

According to Victor Brombert's analysis of this passage[19] Stendhal here intervenes in his novel as the 'porte-parole d'une éthique pragmatique et anti-romanesque', not only to protect himself, by appearing 'rationnel et adulte', against the reader's possible derision of his approval for the youthful Fabrice, but also, and more especially, to illustrate and dramatize the divide between the reasonable and the 'romanesque', to provide concrete evidence of

[19] *La Voie oblique*, 92–100.

'un monde trivialement réaliste' in conflict with the 'énergie souvent naïve de ses jeunes héros'. By implication any suggestion that this intervention might contain some truth would lead, in Brombert's eyes, to immediate disqualification from the Happy Few. Yet even Brombert admits that the tone of this particular intervention is 'un peu plus brutal que d'habitude' and that one may be 'quelque peu déconcerté par ce brusque mouvement d'humeur'. And in fact there is every reason to think that one may indeed take this passage at face value.[20] For is it not a reprise of the comments in *Le Rouge et le Noir* that Julien 'entreprenait de juger la vie avec son imagination' and that 'cette erreur est d'un homme supérieur' (*RN*, 343)? The narrator of *La Chartreuse* sympathizes with Fabrice ('je conçois qu'on n'aime pas à le regarder') and understands the 'ravissement' consequent upon perceiving the world imaginatively. What he criticizes is Fabrice's attempt to *judge* the world imaginatively. Thus, in the paragraph which follows, he honours Fabrice's credulity but derides his reasoning:

c'est ainsi que, sans manquer d'esprit, Fabrice ne put parvenir à voir que sa demi-croyance dans les présages était pour lui une religion, une impression profonde reçue à son entrée dans la vie. Penser à cette croyance c'était sentir, c'était un bonheur. Et il s'obstinait à chercher comment ce pouvait être une science *prouvée*, réelle, dans le genre de la géométrie par exemple. Il recherchait avec ardeur, dans sa mémoire, toutes les circonstances où des présages observés par lui n'avait pas été suivis de l'événement heureux ou malheureux qu'ils semblaient annoncer. Mais tout en croyant suivre un raisonnement et marcher à la vérité, son attention s'arrêtait avec bonheur sur le souvenir des cas où le présage avait été largement suivi par l'accident heureux ou malheureux qu'il lui semblait prédire, et son âme était frappée de respect et attendrie; et il eût éprouvée une répugnance invincible pour l'être qui eût nié les présages, et surtout s'il eût employé l'ironie.

There will be occasion later to discuss in detail Fabrice's attitudes to presages and to compare his imaginative response to the world with his (vain) attempts at a rational understanding of experience. What matters here is to consider the narrator's presentation of reason and imagination as alternatives, and to note the recurrence of the equivalences mentioned earlier. Imagination furnishes 'circonstances romanesques' to delight the soul: to imagine is to believe, to believe is to feel, to feel is to be happy. Reason, on the other hand, requires

---

[20] As does Durand, *Le Décor mythique*, 54.

a patient examination of the causes underlying the 'particularités réelles des choses' and a readiness to tolerate that reality can be 'plat et fangeux': to reason is to 'marcher à la vérité'. As has already been noted, this contrast may be seen in national terms. Imagination is the lot of the Italian: it brings him joys that are more intense and longer-lived than those experienced by the French (86) but also misconceived notions and unfounded fears (86, 205), and the inability to forgive or forget (107, 398); while reason is the lot of the Frenchman, bringing him a quieter life (63) but also the impoverishing experiences of vanity and self-interest (118, 219).

In *Armance* and *Le Rouge et le Noir* the reader is presented with a choice of readings: in *Armance* the tragic or the comic, in *Le Rouge* the prospective or the retrospective. To choose the former in each case is to be led into the errors of the central protagonist, to choose the latter is to understand the truth but to forgo the delights of imaginative illusion. A similar choice is open to the reader of *La Chartreuse*. We can read with innocent credulity as if we were Italian aristocrats faced with the prophecy of Saint Giovita: 'c'est que réellement et sans comédie ils croyaient à la prophétie. Tous ces gens-là n'avaient pas lu quatre volumes en leur vie' (15). Or we can read with the ironic distance of the narrator who is prepared to 'regarder avec patience les particularités réelles des choses pour ensuite deviner leurs causes' (168). In other words the reader of *La Chartreuse* must choose to read as an Italian or as a Frenchman. The Italian will delight in the miracle: the Frenchman will question it.

2

'Circonstances romanesques'

'To make of this sketch a romanzetto.'

(*OI*, ii. 324)

THE sense of miraculous ease which *La Chartreuse* may inspire in its reader derives in the first instance from the emphasis on story-telling, and of all the novels this is the one which most clearly illustrates Stendhal's determination to 'raconter narrativement selon le système de l'Arioste'.[1] It has already been noted how the 'Avertissement' locates the origins of the novel in post-prandial conversation. The story of Gina and Fabrice is first and foremost an entertainment, and the pleasures of narration are associated from the outset with 'la joie folle, la gaieté, la volupté, l'oubli de tous les sentiments tristes, ou seulement raisonnables' (11) which constitute the French 'liberation' of Milan. Just as the 'miracles de bravoure et de génie' effected by Napoleon's army awaken the people of Milan (5) from one hundred years of boredom (10), so on a winter's evening in Padua 'ce qui nous fit veiller surtout, ce fut l'histoire de la duchesse Sanseverina', and the narrator's subsequent transformation of this story into a 'nouvelle' is intended as an antidote to the boredom of the long evenings 'dans le pays où je vais' (1). And how else does lieutenant Robert, as a representative of this liberating power, overcome his early awkwardness with Gina and the marquise del Dongo but by the miracle of story-telling: 'enfin une idée descendue du ciel vint m'illuminer: je me mis à raconter à ces dames ma misère' (9)?

The narrative in *La Chartreuse* is essentially a narrative of events, and the novel seems to be packed full of incidents, each one crowding in on the last and threatening to overwhelm the story-teller: 'les événements nous pressent' (465), 'entraînés par les événements, nous n'avons pas eu le temps d[e ...]' (520). Such is the pressure on space that anything not absolutely germane to the main story is passed over rapidly (for example, Gina's two marriages), while events or

---

[1] *OI*, ii. 354. Cf. Stendhal's comment in the first draft of his projected reply to Balzac: 'quant à la perfection de la narration, c'est l'Arioste' (*Corr.*, iii. 396 [16 Oct. 1840]).

conversations which could cause delay are ruthlessly abbreviated (the consequences of Fabrice's lack of a passport, Gina's bribery of the citadel guards, the discussions between Aubry and the cantinière, or between Mosca and Rassi). Happiness, in particular, seems decidedly unnewsworthy: 'nous glissons sur dix années de progrès et de bonheur, de 1800 à 1810' (15), 'ici, nous demandons la permission de passer sans en dire un seul mot, sur un espace de trois années' (531)—the 'trois années de bonheur divin' enjoyed by Fabrice and Clélia. Because of this abbreviation the importance of events which *are* narrated seems to be increased by the very prestige of inclusion. This rapidity of narration produces a trace of breathless excitement which combines with the subject matter to suggest a *roman d'aventures* of the most swashbuckling kind. For both narrator and character it seems as if there is not a moment to lose, and for the reader too, no doubt, as he vicariously experiences the thrills attendant upon the cloak-and-dagger activities of the protagonists. Killing or getting killed, escaping or avoiding capture, sending and receiving secret messages, plotting and avenging, these are the principal events of *La Chartreuse*. One might be reading Dumas *père*. Or Ariosto. For the verve and compelling impetus of the narrative are complemented by stylistic reminiscences of epic and romance. The tone of the opening sentence of the novel is maintained in the hyperbolic description of setting and character. The del Dongo castle at Grianta occupies 'une position peut-être unique au monde' (11), while Lake Como and its environs offers 'aspects sublimes et gracieux, que le site le plus renommé du monde, la baie de Naples, égale, mais ne surpasse point' (27). Of Gina we read: 'personne dans la prospérité ne la surpassa par la gaieté et l'esprit aimable, comme personne ne la surpassa par le courage et la sérénité d'âme dans la fortune contraire' (9); of Clélia that she has a 'figure dans laquelle éclataient les grâces naïves et l'empreinte céleste de l'âme la plus noble' (284). Just as Clélia will marry, in Crescenzi, 'l'homme le plus riche de la cour' (343), so Gina marries, in the duc de Sanseverina, the owner of 'le plus beau palais de Parme et une fortune sans bornes' (117), and her success in usurping the marquise Balbi in the affections of Ranuce-Ernest is all the more notable for the fact that the marquise ('le plus parfait modèle du *joli italien*') is possessed of 'les plus beaux yeux du monde' and 'les plus belles dents au monde' (123). Such hyperbole extends both to the incidental—Anetta Marini's portrait of Fabrice is 'magnifique' and 'entouré du plus beau cadre que l'on eût doré à Parme depuis vingt ans' (519)—and to the ugly. Giletti, for example, is almost a caricature of the villain: 'ce Giletti était bien l'être le plus laid et le moins fait pour l'amour: démesurément grand, il était horriblement maigre, fort marqué de la petite vérole et un peu louche' (160–1).[2]

Hyperbole also characterizes the way in which the protagonists view themselves and each other. Fabrice reflects ruefully on his lot which is 'unique au monde' (533), while Gina sees Fabrice as 'l'un des plus jolis hommes de l'Italie' (141) and Mosca as 'l'homme le plus habile et le plus grand politique que l'Italie ait produit depuis des siècles' (305). Consequently the main characters in La Chartreuse seem to have all the advantages. Beauty, wealth, intelligence, courage and good fortune are theirs in the fullest measure, such that they appear to inhabit a fairy-tale world, a world of make-believe, and this is the impression conveyed by the final sentence. At the end of La Chartreuse we may well feel that we have been reading of the great and the good and their struggles against the mean and petty villainy of Rassi and his ilk.

The narrative ease of La Chartreuse derives, then, from its emphasis on action (rather than psychology), its pace and its occasional imitation of the facility to be found in epic and fairy-tale. The semblance of a simple, uncomplicated tale is further enhanced by the way in which the story seems to pre-exist the act of telling. In Le Rouge, it may be remembered, the opposite seems true. That novel's 'allure d'une chose présente' is due in part to the fact that the narrator seems never to know what is going to happen next and appears at times almost to be overtaken by events. Despite the use of conventional narration in the past, the immediacy of the chronicle (in the sense of a contemporary account) is paramount. Of course it is true that in La Chartreuse there is still much emphasis on the act of story-telling, and this contributes to the aura of easy comprehensibility[3] which we are discussing. It is also true that the narrator tries to involve his reader by such phrases as 'comme on voit', 'on voit que', 'on peut juger', 'on peut penser', as if he can perceive the reader's opinion of a particular incident or see his

---

[2] Durand (Le Décor mythique, 88–9) sees this monstrousness as a traditional element in myth and epic. Durand's book provides the fullest treatment of epic and mythic elements in La Chartreuse.

[3] See Alison Finch, Stendhal: 'La Chartreuse de Parme' (London, 1984), 11. The first chapter of this study, entitled 'Tone and Presentation', covers many of these points.

impatience and desire to get on with the story (216, 314, 465). Moreover on one occasion he addresses the reader directly (14), and since this follows soon after lieutenant Robert's similar direct addresses to the narrator (8, 9), we may well feel ourselves momentarily to be the 'destinataires' of an oral narration.

But for all the immediacy of these acts of story-telling the fact remains that the story of *La Chartreuse* is constantly presented as anterior to the novel (or 'nouvelle') itself.[4] Indeed it is already a twice-told tale: once in the 'annales' of the canon, and once by the canon's nephew at a dinner-party. The effect of this is to suggest that the story already has a shape and a pattern of its own before the narrator comes to it; that many people, including some of the protagonists, have already had a chance to assimilate all these events and to come to some balanced view about them, so that the narrator's task appears merely to be that of a faithful archivist or historian who is recording and handing down to us an account to which he has added no pattern or interpretation of his own. Part of the narrator's function seems to be to bridge the gap between our reading present and the past of the story, and to this end he anticipates within his narrative in a way which would be quite foreign to the narrator of *Le Rouge*. Thus 'Gina del Dongo [...] qui fut depuis cette charmante comtesse Pietranera' (9); 'ce fut huit jours après qu'eut lieu le mariage de la sœur du marquis Crescenzi, où la duchesse commit une énorme impudence dont nous rendrons compte en son lieu' (386); 'par excès de précautions, elle faillit faire manquer cette fuite, ainsi qu'on va le voir' (400); and in chapter xvii:

la nouvelle de la démission du comte eut l'effet de guérir de sa goutte le général Fabio Conti, comme nous le dirons en son lieu, lorsque nous parlerons de la façon dont la pauvre Fabrice passait son temps à la citadelle, pendant que toute la ville s'enquérait de l'heure de son supplice. (317)

Sometimes these prolepses involve the characters themselves, as when the narrator reports the evidence which they themselves have provided: 'elle [La Fausta] a dit qu'elle avait peur de lui [Fabrice]' (239). This happens extensively in chapter xxii when Fabrice is shown to have served as a source of information about his own escape: 'Fabrice a dit que', 'il raconte que', etc. These anticipations underline the pastness of the events narrated: everything seems to have been thoroughly gone into before the narrator begins his

---

[4] *Pace* Brombert, *Fiction*, 151–2.

narrative (in one instance a particular point has since been established in a court of law: 406) and each incident has its appointed place in the scheme of things.

The illusion that the narrator's material is immutable is all the greater for his initial reluctance to divulge certain parts of it. He feels that Fabrice's credulity may alienate the reader's sympathy: 'mais enfin il était ainsi, pourquoi le flatter lui plutôt qu'un autre?' (164), and he continues his narrative 'puisqu'il faut tout dire'. Similarly, politics in a work of literature (the famous 'coup de pistolet au milieu d'un concert') are 'quelque chose de grossier et auquel pourtant il n'est pas possible de refuser son attention'. They involve 'de fort vilaines choses' which the narrator would like to suppress: 'mais nous sommes forcés d'en venir à des événements qui sont de notre domaine, puisqu'ils ont pour théâtre le cœur des personnages' (435). Now of course such interventions help, in a very traditional way, to create and sustain the illusion of a true story, and they are designed also to defuse the reader's possible moral objections. Already in the 'Avertissement' we have been indirectly warned that 'cette histoire n'est rien moins que morale', and prophylactically shamed out of any unduly puritan reaction by the nephew's remark to the narrator that 'maintenant que vous vous piquez de pureté évangélique en France, elle [cette histoire] peut vous procurer le renom d'assassin'. (Only a prig will indict the narrator of *La Chartreuse*, just as only 'le commun des hommes' will see Julien as an 'assassin vulgaire' in *Le Rouge*). Throughout the narrative the narrator seems to say: life is like this, so don't blame me. Thus he asks rhetorically in respect of Gina's arranged marriage with the duc de Sanseverina:

pourquoi l'historien qui suit fidèlement les moindres détails du récit qu'on lui fait serait-il coupable? Est-ce sa faute si les personnages, séduits par des passions qu'il ne partage point malheureusement pour lui, tombent dans des actions profondément immorales? (118)

This too, of course, is a fairly traditional narrative strategy (cf. the reference to the mirror and the muddy road in *Le Rouge*). What is important once more, though, is the suggestion that the narrator has no control over the story he is telling. This is how things were ('mais enfin il était ainsi'), and his role is that of an impartial observer. Like the narrator of *Le Rouge* he can act as a kind of travel-guide, explaining to us the topography of Milan, Parma and the Italian lakes, particular meteorological conditions, and certain customs like the *mortaretti* or the exchange of visits between boxes at La Scala. But he is much less given to generalizations and *sententiae* than his counterpart in *Le Rouge*. The odd comment on courtiers and court life, the occasional remark about, say, intelligence in royal families or the nature of blood relationships (433), these constitute his rare attempts at being a *moraliste*. His main task is the faithful transmission of historical fact, and it is no accident that the novel begins with much emphasis on dates.

But what of the numerous comments about the various characteristics of the French and the Italians? Surely these are evidence of the narrator's ample role as a commentator? Here a problem arises which may cause one to begin to question the narrative simplicity of *La Chartreuse*. The 'Avertissement' introduces us to a man who was billeted in the house of a Paduan canon 'bien des années avant 1830, dans le temps où nos armées parcouraient l'Europe', a Frenchman then, enlisted in or attached to Napoleon's army, most probably a young officer like his friend lieutenant Robert (cf. 8–10). One might assume therefore that all the comparisons of the French and the Italians which stud the novel reflect the judgement of this erstwhile French soldier who loves Italy and returns there in later years. Yet this soldier is given the annals of the deceased canon, and in the one (translated) extract from these given verbatim in the novel we read:

ce ministre [Mosca], malgré son air léger et ses façons brillantes, n'avait pas une âme *à la française*; il ne savait pas *oublier* les chagrins. Quand son chevet avait une épine, il était obligé de la briser et de l'user à force d'y piquer ses membres palpitants. (107)

Not only does this suggest that the Italian canon is equally as well placed to compare the two nationalities as the Frenchman, but the opinion itself recurs throughout the novel (63, 86, 205, 398) in contexts where one might have presumed it to be that of the Frenchman. Do all these comments then come from the annals? In which case how much of this 'nouvelle' is borrowed from the canon and how much the original work of the soldier? The latter has heard directly of lieutenant Robert's experience (8–10), but surely it is the canon who reports on what Fabrice (409–11) and La Fausta (239) have said, just as it is the canon who possesses the letters of the protagonists. At the same time one must not forget that the French soldier hears the story from the canon's nephew, who may be basing it in part on what his wife, who knew Gina well, has told him. The sources of *La Chartreuse* are multiple, and the reader's choice between an Italian and a French reading of the novel is thus rendered all the more intriguing, for he cannot determine the nationality (or indeed the profession) of the narrator. As befits the story of a boy born of a French father and an Italian mother, and the story of a would-be Napoleonic hussar (16, 97), who becomes Archbishop of Parma, the narrative of *La Chartreuse de Parme* is both a collaboration between the army and the Church and a kind of Franco-Italian co-production.

Discovering that the identity of the story-teller is problematic,[5] we may then go on to question the miraculous ease of the story-telling, particularly since the novel itself describes how the same events can lead to different stories. Thus in the case of Fabrice's escape from prison we have the conflicting accounts (409–11, 425–6) given by Fabrice himself, the police (who invent a story of bribed guards to devalue Fabrice's courage and protect their own reputation), the liberal opposition (who put it about that the police have shot eight of these guards), a mediocre sonneteer (whose sonnet 'célébrait cette fuite comme une des belles actions du siècle, et comparait Fabrice à un ange arrivant sur la terre les ailes étendues') and Ferrante Palla (whose 'sonnet sublime' contains 'le monologue de Fabrice se laissant glisser le long de la corde, et jugeant les divers incidents de sa vie'). The 'real' Fabrice becomes submerged beneath the various political or artistic transformations of his exploits. Soon, thanks to his eloquence and self-abnegation, he becomes a sort of ecclesiastical pin-up. A portrait depicting him as a bishop sells out rapidly among the Parmesan populace (493), while the rich heiress Anetta Marini commissions a painting of Fabrice in non-ecclesiastical dress as an adornment for her bedroom wall and a focus for her star-struck crush (519). Fabrice's other female admirers turn him into a Napoleonic legend: 'elles inventèrent qu'il avait été un des plus braves capitaines de l'armée de Napoléon. Bientôt ce fait absurde fut hors de doute' (513). Such is the transformational power of gossip and story-telling that he has soon become 'l'un des plus braves colonels de l'armée de Napoléon' (524).

---

[5] As it is also in the *Chroniques italiennes*. See Jean-Jacques Hamm, 'Un laboratoire stendhalien: les *Chroniques italiennes*', *Revue d'Histoire Littéraire de la France*, 84 (1984), 245–54.

In the light of these travesties[6] how can we believe that the narrator's own version of Fabrice's life is reliable? How can we trust the epic simplicity of the narrative when the latter so clearly demonstrates that the chivalric world of Tasso and Ariosto is long gone? 'Le cheval des quatre fils Aymon' has become a figure of speech (42), and the walls and moats of the medieval castle at Grianta dry, empty relics of a vanished world (11), symbols rather than real instruments of power (32). Fabrice may begin his escape from prison 'comme un héros des temps de chevalerie' (410) by thinking of Clélia, and Ranuce-Ernest may attribute to Gina 'les beaux yeux d'Armide' (311), but the lesson of Waterloo is unambiguous: '[Fabrice] défaisait un à un tous ces beaux rêves d'amitié chevaleresque et sublime, comme celle des héros de la *Jérusalem délivrée*' (55).

Is there then something suspect about the narrator's simple adventure-story presentation of his material? For example, though he is almost as sparing in his use of the historic present as his counterpart in *Le Rouge*, and though he employs it for moments which are especially 'romanesques' (Fabrice as latter-day Horatio at the bridge, his escape from the lackeys of La Fausta's lover), one may think that its use in describing the immediate aftermath of Giletti's murder detracts from the possible seriousness of this incident by engaging our attention in the breathless excitement of Fabrice's flight from the scene. The peculiar repetition involved in the transition from chapters xxi to xxii and involving the first stages of Fabrice's great escape may not be a mistake[7] but evidence of the narrator's wish to highlight the valour and prowess of his quasi-epic hero.[8] When seen as conscious choices of the narrator (cf. the narrator's revealing jest before describing reactions to Gina's lavish party at Sacco: 'mais

---

[6] For other instances see Ann Jefferson's excellent account of representation and misrepresentation in the novel, which is based on the persuasive thesis that *La Chartreuse* lays claims to truthfulness by including reference to politics but then, by demonstrating how political power depends on the use and abuse of story-telling, calls into question this very truthfulness. See 'Représentation de la politique, politique de la représentation: *La Chartreuse de Parme*', *Stendhal Club*, 27 (1984/5), 200–13.

[7] Even if it is a 'mistake', why should one attribute it to Stendhal rather than the narrator? Why can the fiction of a narrator composing a 'nouvelle' not also apply, beyond the introductory 'Avertissement', to all aspects of the narration? There is a comparison to be made here with *La Religieuse* and the conventional, erroneous attribution to Diderot rather than Suzanne of the implausible 'innocence' of the narrative in respect of lesbianism. Suzanne's artfulness is revealed precisely by her decision to tell her story as if in ignorance of the lessons of her eavesdropping.

[8] Perhaps even a wish to imitate devices of repetition in medieval and Renaissance narrative?

ici il me faudrait chercher le style épique': 426), the stylistic features hitherto discussed may be seen as attempts to make the reader, like Fabrice, 'goûter les sensations produites par les circonstances romanesques' and ignore 'les particularités réelles des choses pour ensuite deviner leurs causes'. We are being made to read like Italians, Italians who are ready to acquiesce in the defusing of all moral and political issues for the sake of a cracking good story, the Italians of the novel itself.

Thus the narrator may be anxious that political issues will strike an ugly, discordant note, but they are so enveloped in the imagery of games[9] and play-acting,[10] and the political antagonists themselves so simplistically disposed in two opposing camps (Mosca versus Rassi and Raversi), that the reality of these issues is far from being immediately apparent.[11] Likewise, in the 'Avertissement', the narrator is moved to pompous pronouncements about the morality of his characters: 'je le déclare hautement, je déverse le blâme le plus moral sur beaucoup de leurs actions'. But he ends the introduction more ambiguously with reference to Gina and 'ses aventures, lesquelles sont blâmables'—blameworthy, but not actually to be blamed? Throughout the narrative he shows a scale of values and moral flexibility worthy of the protagonists. Thus the proposed marriage with the duc de Sanseverina is seen by Gina as 'fort immoral' (116) and is then classified by the narrator among the 'actions profondément immorales' (118) which it is his sad duty to relate. Yet when it comes to the murder of Giletti and the assassination of Ranuce-Ernest, there is no question of profound immorality. The murder is deemed of no consequence by the people of Parma ('une pareille vétille, un coup d'épée maladroit donné à un comédien': 407), by the Church as represented by Archbishop Landriani ('cette bagatelle': 227)

[9] For a detailed account of the theme, and presence, of play in the novel, see C. W. Thompson, Le Jeu de l'ordre et de la liberté dans 'La Chartreuse de Parme'.

[10] Given the many critics, like Durand (Le Décor mythique, 130) and Hemmings (Stendhal, 190–1), who see Part I of the novel as playful and Part II as serious, it is interesting that references to play-acting all occur in Part II: see pp. 259, 267, 268, 275, 450, 453, 462, 476, 527.

[11] A thesis propounded by J. D. Hubert in 'Notes sur la dévaluation du réel dans La Chartreuse de Parme', Stendhal Club, 2 (1959/60), 47–53, and subsequently maintained by Roland Barthes in 'On échoue toujours à parler de ce qu'on aime', Tel Quel, 85 (Autumn 1980), 32–8. In this unfinished paper, found in his typewriter after his death, Barthes describes the Italy of La Chartreuse as 'un Mythe' (p. 38). This view informs Michel Crouzet's Stendhal et l'italianité. Essai de mythologie romantique (Paris, 1982), and François Landry's account of the novel in L'Imaginaire de Stendhal.

and by Gina ('dans tous les cas, la mort d'un être ridicule tel que
Giletti ne lui semblait pas de nature à être reprochée sérieusement
à un del Dongo': 226; 'c'est un petit assassinat comme on en compte
cent par an dans ses heureux états': 301). As for the narrator, when
he recounts the immediate aftermath of the murder, he makes no
moral comment whatsoever and seems more apprehensive about the
need to tell us of Fabrice's fear in crossing the frontier and his 'autre
faiblesse' in being touched by the devotion of peasants and servants.
Moreover in his description of Fabrice's confession in the church of
San Petrone he seems tacitly to accept Fabrice's lack of remorse
(Fabrice confesses to having killed in self-defence) but is critical of
his failure to confess to simony. But surely the reader of *La Chartreuse*
will have moral doubts about Fabrice's killing of Giletti, since the
latter's death is caused by Fabrice's rage at thinking he has been
disfigured (200). Is it not, as Ranuce-Ernest says, 'un meurtre [...]
épouvantable' (223)? In the case of the assassination of Ranuce-
Ernest himself, the narrator is no less free from 'pureté évangélique',
and when he writes of it as 'une action non seulement horrible aux
yeux de la morale, mais qui fut encore bien funeste à la tranquillité
du reste de sa vie' (414), he is less concerned with conventional
morality than with Gina's peace of mind. For one moment of
'bonheur immoral' (398), one spectacular act of vengeance (because
Ranuce-Ernest has tricked her—in order to punish Fabrice for
murdering Giletti!) Gina has risked her future happiness, and for
the narrator this matters more than the life of a despotic Prince.

For the narrator, then, simony and arranged marriages are morally
more reprehensible than murder and assassination, doubtless because
he considers pecuniary practicalities to be unworthy while vengeance
and aristocratic superiority may be noble causes of manslaughter.
Whatever the reader's own reaction to this ethic, it is more than
evident that the narrator of *La Chartreuse* is far from being the
impartial historian he purports to be. The 'easy' narrative conceals,
indeed is part of, a system of values which sets imagination and the
'romanesque' above reason and the 'prosaic' as the surer guides in
our 'chasse au bonheur'. This is an eminently 'beyliste' position, of
course, but is it indicated by the events of the novel? What of 'les
particularités réelles des choses'? What if we read *La Chartreuse* as
a Frenchman?

3

'Particularités réelles'

'Il faut que l'imagination apprenne les droits de fer de la réalité.'

(OI, ii. 52)

SUCH is the emphasis on event in *La Chartreuse* and such the comparative absence of abstract commentary, the 'réflexion philosophique sur le fond des choses' which Stendhal saw as inimical to Ariosto's narrative purity, that a 'French' reading of the novel proves far from easy. *La Chartreuse* is a 'good read', we may concede, but has it depth? What can it tell us of human nature, of the right or wrong ways to conduct 'la chasse au bonheur'? What more specific lessons are to be drawn about politics, religion, the experience of love, Italy, etc.? What, if any, is the reality that underlies the bland, easy labels 'notre héros', 'l'aimable comtesse', 'la bonne marquise'? The questions are quickly posed, but how should reason proceed if it is to find answers beyond mere intuition or imaginative conjecture? Clearly, by reading between the lines or, rather, between the events. As C. W. Thompson puts it most succinctly:

pour bien suivre le jugement de Stendhal sur l'action et sur les personnages, il ne s'agit donc pas tellement de repérer dans cette façade pittoresque des ouvertures pratiquées afin de permettre l'inspection de la charpente morale. Il faut plutôt, en suivant de page en page le jeu mobile des mots, savoir tirer rien que de la juxtaposition et de la succession des événements—et du ton dont ils sont racontés—la portée morale essentielle.[1]

One of the fascinating aspects of *La Chartreuse* is the wide divergence of critical opinion about the nature of this 'portée morale essentielle'. Miracles, it seems, preclude easy consensus. A similar divergence, of course, exists in respect of Julien's shooting of Mme de Rênal yet the controversy which surrounds that central event is nevertheless contained within the bounds of some fairly firm, shared conclusions about the meaning of *Le Rouge* as a whole. There is a gap to be filled but at least it is clear where the edges are. With *La Chartreuse*, however, one may sense a yawning abyss of mystery,

---

[1] *Le Jeu de l'ordre*, 95.

a mystery that is epitomized in the very title of the novel. That this should denote Fabrice's ultimate destination places him at the centre of the narrative, yet what is the nature of the journey that leads him to that destination? Is it a quest, an education, a voyage of discovery, or a road to failure and withdrawal? Is monastic devotion to be seen as a feckless palliative or a moral advance on the immorality of court life? Is the charterhouse a bolt-hole or a summit? The novel comes to an end with its hero rapt in the silence of contemplation. But of what? Of his past, doubtless, of the past that is the novel, and it is the reader's task to fill that silence with his own speculation.

Despite the narrator's claim to be telling the 'histoire de la duchesse Sanseverina', *La Chartreuse de Parme* is above all the story of Fabrice del Dongo. 'N'est-ce pas la vie de Fabrice qu'on écrit', Stendhal wrote in the second of his projected letters to Balzac,[2] and not only does the novel end with its hero's death but it begins, like *Tristram Shandy*, with the circumstances of his conception. Fabrice is the leading man: youthful, handsome, intelligent, well-connected, beloved of the most charming woman at court and lover of an ethereal beauty beneath whose pious exterior beats a passionate and adoring heart. But Fabrice is also the man who resigns from an archbishopric to die in a monastery at the age of twenty-seven, having witnessed, perhaps even caused, the death of his mistress and his son. How has such a change in his fortune come about? Does one call this tragic failure or merely growing up?

For Bardèche, Fabrice is blessed with a 'disposition au bonheur': everything comes easily to him, he has no fears and takes nothing seriously, he lives life at one remove from reality. But in the last chapters of the novel 'ce paradis se ferme sur la souffrance': gaiety gives way to the discreet evocation of suffering which is for Fabrice 'la découverte de la maturité'. Bardèche admits that this tells us little: 'mais comment peindre un héros de Stendhal? Comment peindre cette grâce de jeune dieu, qui est grâce parce qu'elle est insaisissable? On aime Fabrice, on ne le décrit pas.'[3] Again, the inexplicable miracle. Victor Brombert and Alison Finch are just as inconclusive. For Brombert, in Existentialist frame of mind, the 'essence' of Fabrice is as elusive for Fabrice himself as it is for us: he is an 'oversensitive hero who is forced by the world's coarseness to withdraw within

---

[2] *Corr.*, iii. 399.   [3] *Stendhal romancier*, 405–9.

himself', an 'exceptional being' impelled 'to set out in quest of that undefinable "something" that fills the inner emptiness of the exiled individual', and this 'pursuit of an elusive identity' illustrates 'the eternal becoming and the disturbing "availability" of the individual'.[4] Once again the critic's inability to analyse and define is seen as a function of the text itself. Equally tentative, Alison Finch is nevertheless one of the few to be critical of Fabrice's much vaunted naïveté by noting in him a 'hampering of the ability to question' which results from the 'deficiencies and distortions of Jesuit education'. Yet ultimately she places value on this naïveté by seeing it transformed into a renunciation of urbanity—into a 'marginality which [...] offers some critique of Gina's and Mosca's worldliness, and goes beyond mere lack of sophistication'. At the same time Fabrice is also marginal to the novel whereas the 'marginal' Ferrante Palla becomes 'central' to an understanding of the work because of his 'artistic genius' and 'the boldness of his social views' and because he is 'the only character in anything like Stendhal's own situation during the writing of *La Chartreuse*'.[5]

The difficulty in extracting moral import from the biography of Fabrice has thus been circumvented by appeals to the indescribable, the indefinable, and the marginal. Other critics have met the difficulty head on and been prepared to see triumph and success in the midst of the 'scuffle of deaths'[6] with which the novel ends. Thus Grahame Jones argues that 'la tragédie de la fin du roman est atténuée, adoucie, par cette atmosphère poétique qui pénètre tout le reste du livre' and proclaims 'le triomphe du héros, le triomphe de celui qui refuse de s'incliner, de renoncer à son individualité, et qui accepte courageusement les conséquences de sa décision';[7] while François Landry concludes: 'malgré ces morts—ou en elles?—*La Chartreuse* s'achève sur la relative image de la réussite intérieure. La Sanseverina, Clélia et Fabrice ont à peu près trouvé ce qu'ils cherchaient dans l'ordre des sentiments; Mosca a imprimé le sceau de ses idées libérales au gouvernement de Parme.' What Fabrice and Clélia have found is 'la plus haute valeur que leur existence pût atteindre [...] une valeur morale, qui les a poussés à cultiver la spiritualité et l'intériorité

---

[4] *Fiction*, 159, 175. Cf. Bardèche's account of 'la morale du refus' (*Stendhal romancier*, 383–90).
[5] '*La Chartreuse de Parme*', 60–1, 65, 70. See also Coe, 'Portrait d'une réaction', 56.
[6] Wood, *Stendhal*, 185.   [7] *Ironie*, 144.

de l'amour plutôt que sa représentation extérieure'.[8] This view of spirituality as the principal value proclaimed by the novel finds strongest expression in the study of the novel by C. W. Thompson, who writes of 'cette transformation surprenante qui lui [Fabrice] permettra de passer des fantaisies d'un gentilhomme léger aux méditations élevées d'un chartreux' and of 'la découverte progressive d'un ordre de solitude et de contemplation, qu'il nous faudra appeler mystique'.[9] For Thompson, Fabrice's sense of literal and metaphorical superiority, his aesthetic detachment in the face of reality, his easy-going passivity and readiness to play the game, in short his aristocratic 'désinvolture', are the basis from which he 'accède à une morale supérieure par sa passion pour Clélia'. This 'morale supérieure' in turn inspires 'un désir irrésistible de tout quitter, même Clélia' in order to 'réaliser son être essentiel', so that the 'caprice de tendresse' (531, 532) which leads to Sandrino's death is seen as a voluntary cutting loose from terrestrial ties, while the final silence of the charterhouse is invested with the achievement of lucidity: 'on peut même croire que dans cette rêverie Fabrice atteint enfin cette connaisance plus approfondie de lui-même'. Where once, in the prison cell, there had been 'la contemplation fabricienne des harmonies universelles', now in the monastic cell there comes that rarest of Stendhalian triumphs: 'une véritable connaissance spirituelle'.[10]

While it may thus be seen that there is considerable divergence amongst critics about the moral import of La Chartreuse, a certain consensus does emerge in the marked reluctance to see anything negative in Fabrice. Alison Finch, for example, subordinates her criticism of him to the subsequent assertion of his valuable marginality. There is almost irresistible encouragement to accept Fabrice for what he is: 'parlez donc avec plus de respect, dit la comtesse souriant au milieu de ses larmes' (and after Fabrice has objected with 'une sorte de hauteur héroïque' that his mother and sisters will betray his plan to join Napoleon) 'du sexe qui fera votre fortune; car vous déplairez toujours aux hommes, vous avez trop de feu pour les âmes prosaïques' (33). But what might a prosaic,

[8] L'Imaginaire, 338–9.

[9] Le Jeu de l'ordre, 167–8. See also Michèle Hirsch, 'Fabrice, ou la poétique du nuage', Littérature, 23 (1976), 21–30: '[La Chartreuse de Parme] est le roman d'une éducation, l'analyse de la conversion au mysticisme des forces dont Fabrice a été doté à sa naissance' (22).

[10] pp. 203, 195, 201, 202, 181 and 175 respectively.

'masculine' reading of the life of Fabrice lead to by way of judgement about the moral import of the novel? Perhaps that *La Chartreuse* is about a naïve young man who learns little from experience and who, having been constantly surprised and bewildered by the discrepancies between appearance and reality, is finally destroyed by their unexpected coincidence.

To establish such a view one has first to rehearse some of the more obvious points about Fabrice's naïvety. From first almost till last he inhabits an apparently enchanted world, but while enchantment may justifiably characterize the natural beauty of his environment (27, 418), any distinctions between the horrors of war, the fatuity of amorous dalliance and the authenticity of passion are lost in his invariably 'enchanted' response to events such as Waterloo (46, 73), the pursuit of La Fausta (248) and his voluntary return to the Tour Farnese (469). Life is uniformly smooth thanks to 'cette disposition naïve à se trouver heureux de tout ce qui remplissait sa vie' (231), and even after his experiences at Waterloo, and later as a fugitive and then prisoner, he is still an 'âme naïve et simple' who 'rêvait comme à l'ordinaire' (432–3). From the start of the novel the story of his upbringing focuses on his ignorance, with the years 1800 to 1810 spent at home 'n'apprenant rien, pas même à lire', though later we are told that he did learn to read—by deciphering the captions on engravings depicting Napoleon's victories; and his subsequent schooling at a Jesuit college in Milan leaves him 'ignorant à plaisir, et sachant à peine écrire' (16). So unsullied at this point is the blank page[11] of Fabrice's mind and character that there is all the more room for the religious lessons of the Jesuits to make their mark upon it, as his mother learns to her surprise and chagrin: 'Fabrice avait pris au sérieux toutes les choses religieuses qu'on lui avait enseignées chez les jésuites' (18). But, as the narrator later suggests, the fruit of these lessons may well be ignorance of another kind: 'tel est le triomphe de l'éducation jésuitique: donner l'habitude de ne pas faire attention à des choses plus claires que le jour' (219), and one of the most obvious things to which the Jesuits' pupil may be oblivious is himself: 'cette religion *ôte le courage de penser aux choses inaccoutumées*, et défend surtout l'*examen personnel*, comme le plus énorme des péchés; c'est un pas vers le protestantisme' (218: Stendhal's italics). Fabrice's formal schooling has left him a credulous and unthinking ignoramus, while his reading, be it of the family

[11] See Bardèche, *Stendhal romancier*, 374.

history (15) or of Tasso and Ariosto (53), has imbued him with fond notions of chivalry and military heroism.

But what of the lessons of experience? Waterloo, his reflections on astrology or aristocratic privilege, his experience of love, his life in prison, none of these aspects of Fabrice's life seems to bring real knowledge. As Gérald Rannaud puts it: 'le roman de Stendhal raconte bien la perte des illusions, mais on n'y gagne pas le savoir. Rastignac y est impossible.'[12] What we get are repeated statements from the narrator that Fabrice has understood but no evidence of subsequent, or consequent, maturity. Thus at Waterloo his notorious bewilderment—'il n'y comprenait rien du tout', 'ceci est-il une véritable bataille?', 'c'est donc l'Empereur qui a passé là?' (49–52), 'ai-je réellement assisté à une bataille?' (70), 'ce qu'il avait vu, était-ce une bataille, et en second lieu, cette bataille était-elle Waterloo?' (83)—is followed by assertions of comprehension: 'car il commençait à réfléchir quelque peu et n'était plus si étonné des choses', 'les écailles tombèrent des yeux de Fabrice; il comprit pour la première fois qu'il avait tort dans tout ce qui lui arrivait depuis deux mois' (65–7), 'et Fabrice devint comme un autre homme, tant il fit de réflexions profondes sur les choses qui venaient de lui arriver' (83). The reality he had thought to encounter turns out to be chivalric (55) or Napoleonic (56) illusion. But he is still at a loss for an interpretation of what he has experienced, and it is significant that this should prompt in him the desire to read:

pour la première fois de sa vie il trouva du plaisir à lire; il espérait toujours trouver dans les journaux, ou dans les récits de la bataille, quelque description qui lui permettrait de reconnaître les lieux qu'il avait parcourus à la suite du maréchal Ney, et plus tard avec l'autre général. (83)

He needs someone else's account of what he himself has witnessed in order to understand and believe in that experience. During the battle there are two echoes of Diderot's *Jacques le fataliste*—Fabrice being led by his horse (46) and his remark about the 'cantinière': 'il est écrit que je ne la reverrai plus, se dit-il avec un soupir, brave et bonne femme!' (71–2)—and these suggest that Fabrice sees himself fatalistically as a character in a story that has already been written (which, as we saw, also happens to be the effect the narrator himself

---

[12] 'La Chartreuse de Parme roman de l'ambiguïté', in Liano Petroni (ed.), *Atti del IX Congresso Internazionale Stendhaliano dedicato a Stendhal e Bologna con alcuni itinerari dell'Emilia-Romagna* (2 vols, Bologna, 1977), i. 426–46 (443).

would create). It is as if during the battle of Waterloo Fabrice comes to realize that he has anticipated the wrong story and so turns to the written word of newspapers for the correct one. The last thing he thinks of is to interpret appearances for himself: he cannot write his own story.

This pattern repeats itself in the next stage of his formal education as well as in his attitude to aristocratic privilege. Thus Fabrice decides to re-educate himself: 'je ne sais rien, pas même le latin, pas même l'orthographe'. Now, instead of passively accepting religious doctrine: 'j'étudierai volontiers la théologie [...] c'est une science compliquée' (132). Once again experience supposedly produces great change. After his few years at Theological College in Naples Gina doesn't recognize this diamond 'qui n'avait rien perdu à être poli' (141), Fabrice is now prepared to see through people—'je tombe des nues' (148), he exclaims having met Landriani—and Mosca is much impressed: 'arrive-t-on à quelque détail où l'esprit soit nécessaire, son regard se réveille et vous étonne, et l'on reste confondu' (154). Yet the ensuing narrative shows that a knowledge of Latin, orthography and theology brings Fabrice no nearer to an independent assessment of experience, and Mosca's erroneous[13] judgement may be attributed to his jealous anxiety about Fabrice's effect on Gina. Equally his remark that 'tout est simple à ses [Fabrice's] yeux parce que tout est vu de haut' (154) may, as this discussion seeks to show, be an indication of Fabrice's weakness, not his strength.

As regards Fabrice's status as an aristocrat, there is at first an innocent assumption of the supposed rights and privileges of that class. Fabrice had only to 'se donner la peine de naître' (14) and 'en sa qualité de noble, se croyait fait pour être plus heureux qu'un autre et trouvait les bourgeois ridicules' (100). He has momentary scruples about his easy access to princely patronage but, albeit with

---

[13] For C. W. Thompson also 'Fabrice a de l'esprit et sait voir juste' (*Le Jeu de l'ordre*, 174), but his evidence is inconclusive. Fabrice's understanding of Landriani (*CP*, 148, 229) and his awareness of Marietta's circumstances (*CP*, 177) may both, as Thompson later acknowledges (p. 184), be seen as evidence of a certain snobbish smugness, just as his unease about aristocratic privilege is either temporary and inconsequential (*CP*, 167) or politic and patronizing (*CP*, 213–14). Certainly he realizes that love for Clélia, and not inherent 'grandeur d'âme', is the reason for his indifference to the rigours of prison life (*CP*, 338), but this lucidity does not extend to an understanding of Clélia's suffering. Which leaves Thompson's other evidence—two occasions when he admits he was scared (*CP*, 181, 212) and one when he shakes hands with a corpse (*CP*, 43–4). But honesty and courage are not the same as perspicacity.

a troubled conscience, argues that 'puisque ma naissance me donne le droit de profiter de ces abus, il serait d'une insigne duperie à moi de n'en pas prendre ma part' (167), and soon afterwards we see him reacting to news of his nomination as future archbishop of Parma 'en véritable grand seigneur qui naturellement a toujours cru qu'il avait droit à ces avancements extraordinaires, à ces coups de fortune qui mettraient un bourgeois hors des gonds' (197). But the murder of Giletti, itself invested with the same unreality as Waterloo ('il para plusieurs coups avec son couteau de chasse et porta plusieurs bottes sans trop savoir ce qu'il faisait; il lui semblait vaguement être à un assaut public': 200), ostensibly teaches Fabrice the limits of aristocratic privilege. While he 'de son côté, croyait qu'un homme de son rang était au-dessus des lois', he finds Ludovic's reaction to his repeated protestations of innocence revealing: 'cet homme me croit un assassin et ne m'en aime pas moins, se dit Fabrice, tombant de son haut'. And this revelation is subsequently stressed by the narrator: 'les écailles tombaient des yeux de Fabrice', 'Fabrice tout étonné [...] entrevoyait pour la première fois le véritable état des choses' (224–6). But once again the ensuing narrative provides no evidence that Fabrice acts upon this lesson or even remembers it, while there is repeated reference to his aristocratic indifference to the rest of mankind. Thus his delight in the airy solitude of his prison 'au-dessus des petitesses et des méchancetés qui nous occupent là-bas' (331) may be seen as a consequence of 'l'extrême réserve qui, chez Fabrice, provenait d'une indifférence allant jusqu'au dégoût pour toutes les affectations ou les petites passions qui remplissent la vie des hommes' (510–11). Reality is beneath him.

In the case of Fabrice's response to the abbé Blanès' practice of astrology, again there is a semblance of change which proves illusory. At first we see him imbued with 'romanesque' illusions, then baffled when he tries rationally to assess astrology, either as a con-trick or as a 'science *prouvée*, réelle, dans le genre de la géometrie par exemple' (166–8), and then supposedly cured or enlightened when he comes to see these astrological predictions as ridiculous or as a ploy to make him resist future temptations to violence in response to trickery (182, 185). Just as Waterloo and his subsequent exile make him want to educate himself properly, so it seems the murder of Giletti may have inspired in him a desire to learn astronomy, the real science of the stars (231). Yet for all this supposed intellectual advance he still believes in presages: 'les prédictions de Blanès, dont il se moquait fort en tant que prophéties, prenaient à ses yeux toute l'importance de présages véritables' (190). His own life is still a story that has already been written. Now, admittedly, he is able to look back and think how things might have been different, how the story could be rewritten (169, 234), but his tendency is still—in Brombert's terms but in contradiction of his thesis—to presume an essence that precedes any act he might consciously and voluntarily choose. The great happiness he feels in Blanès' observatory as childhood memories flood back apparently causes, but also, one suspects, in part derives from, Fabrice's view of his own life as a 'fait accompli': 'le bonheur le porta à une hauteur de pensées assez étrangère à son caractère; il considérait les événements de la vie, lui, si jeune, comme si déjà il fût arrivé à sa dernière limite' (176)—just as the pleasure which he finds 'à contempler ce qui arrivera dans dix ans' and which makes him forget to 'regarder ce qui se passe actuellement à mes côtés' (181) is the pleasure of someone wondering how the events of a story will turn out, not someone about to forge his own destiny. For a hero endowed with the great Stendhalian gift of being able to live spontaneously in the present, Fabrice is surprisingly interested in his past and future, and the present moment seems to be something he would rather not look at too closely. It might bring him down to earth.

As if to underline this point the demands of the present do now impinge in the form of Fabrice's anxiety about his relationship with Gina. Just before his visit to Blanès the perfect moment of happiness experienced on the shores of Lake Como leads to his brave resolution to tell Gina he cannot love her (166), but when he is subsequently brought face to face with an opportunity to do so, the demands of the present are shirked, albeit with lucidity:

je ne suis point changé, se disait-il; toutes mes belles résolutions prises au bord de notre lac quand je voyais la vie d'un œil si philosophique se sont envolées. Mon âme était hors de son assiette ordinaire, tout cela était un rêve et disparaît devant l'austère réalité. Ce serait le moment d'agir, se dit Fabrice en rentrant au palais Sanseverina sur les onze heures du soir. Mais ce fut en vain qu'il chercha dans son cœur le courage de parler avec cette sincérité sublime qui lui semblait si facile la nuit qu'il passa aux rives du lac de Côme. Je vais fâcher la personne que j'aime le mieux au monde [...] (193)

The metaphor of 'hauteur' which characterizes the simplicity, or simple-mindedness, of Fabrice's relation to reality leads on from the bell-tower at Grianta to the Tour Farnese and to Fabrice's experience of imprisonment and love, and here once more we meet with the pattern of erroneous anticipation, surprise and bewilderment, and a subsequent illusion of change and growing maturity. In the case of imprisonment itself Fabrice's imagination has long thrilled to the fear of being incarcerated by the Austrians in their redoubtable gaol upon a Moravian hill, the Spielberg. But this historically real prison becomes, as its name suggests, a plaything, a subject of fancy, a kind of bogeyman with which to frighten the children (187), and Fabrice finds himself instead in the Tour Farnese, in a cell with a magnificent view. His accommodation comprises a wooden cage more spacious than the meagre three feet allotted to the improbably named Grillo and his dog Fox, and conditions are improved by the presence of some antique gilt furniture, some Asti Spumante and the comedy of Fox chasing rats: 'au lieu d'apercevoir à chaque pas des désagréments et des motifs d'aigreur, notre héros se laissait charmer par les douceurs de la prison' (329). At Waterloo Fabrice had expected the noble and heroic only to meet with chaos and human fallibility, whereas now he had expected cruel torture and the direst confinement. He is not very good at predicting. The familiar bewilderment—'mais ceci est-il une prison?', 'est-il possible que ce soit là la prison?', 'suis-je un héros sans m'en douter?' (329–32)—is of course increased by the unexpected discovery of his capacity to love, and the realities of prison life became invisible to his starry eyes: 'il ne songea pas une seule fois, distinctement du moins, au grand changement qui venait de s'opérer dans son sort', 'Fabrice oubliait complètement d'être malheureux' (283), 'sans songer autrement à son malheur' (328). Yet still he believes he has matured. Love itself has made him 'un autre homme' (335), Clélia's glance as he arrives in prison has 'effacé toute ma vie passée' (338), and the nine months leading up to his escape are ostensibly the gestation period of a more serious and upright man: 'combien je suis différent, se dit-il, du Fabrice léger et libertin qui entra ici il y a neuf mois!' (410). But what has Fabrice learnt? At one point he remarks complacently to Clélia: 'n'est-il pas plaisant de voir que le bonheur m'attendait en prison?' to which she promptly replies: 'il y a bien des choses à dire sur cet article' (357). And so indeed there are, for this 'happy' imprisonment entails a great deal of unhappiness on the part of other people. It is ironic that so much of Fabrice's relationship with Clélia in and out of prison should hinge on the possibility of seeing her and being seen by her, for Fabrice's eagerness to see Clélia is accompanied by a blindness to the realities of the situation while her maidenly reluctance to look at him and her subsequent vow never to set eyes on him again are combined with lucid awareness.

We have already seen how Fabrice's easy dream of being honest with Gina evaporates before the 'austère réalité' of actually having to do so, how he then simply shuts his eyes to the problem and says nothing, and it is of interest to compare this with the reactions of Gina and Clélia to his two periods of imprisonment. When Gina first hears of Fabrice's capture, she consoles herself with impossible dreams of carrying him away on a magic carpet to Paris, there to live happily ever after, and these happy fantasies take her most of the night, for 'la pauvre femme avait horreur de revenir à la contemplation de l'affreuse réalité'. But at dawn she pulls herself together and resolves to do something: 'dans quelques heures, se dit-elle, je serai sur le champ de bataille; il sera question d'agir.' Again her imagination leads her into the realms of the implausible, as she envisages Ranuce-Ernest deciding to poison her rather than execute her publicly for fear that her emotive presence on a tumbril might stir the people to unrest. 'Mais quoi!' she exclaims, 'toujours le roman! Hélas! l'on doit pardonner ces folies à une pauvre femme dont le sort réel est si triste! Le vrai de tout ceci, c'est que le prince ne m'enverra point à la mort' (297–8). Whereupon she takes the painful decision to pretend publicly to break with Mosca. Throughout this moment of crisis, imagination and reason seem locked in combat for Gina's mind, but in the end the extravagant images of magic carpet and gallows must give way before the prosaic claims of 'l'affreuse réalité and 'le sort réel'. Reason prevails, and Gina acts—masterminding Fabrice's escape and the assassination of Ranuce-Ernest, and then securing Fabrice's escape from his second period of imprisonment in exchange for half an hour in bed with the young Prince. 'Circonstances romanesques' are replaced by the least glamorous of 'particularités réelles', and we see the accuracy of the narrator's view of her: 'quelquefois son imagination ardente lui cachait les choses, mais jamais avec elle il n'y avait de ces illusions volontaires que donne la lâcheté. C'était surtout une femme de bonne foi avec elle-même' (113).

And the same is true of Clélia. Her first two glimpses of Fabrice are purest romance: 'elle regardait avec étonnement ce jeune héros dont les yeux semblaient respirer encore tout le feu de l'action' (91), 'quelle noblesse! quelle sérénité! Comme il avait l'air d'un héros entouré de ses vils ennemis!' (283); and her imagination is quick to frighten her with thoughts of his imminent execution and to inspire her with implausible designs: 'moi j'irais poignarder le prince, comme l'héroïque Charlotte Corday' (338). The unsuccessful defence of her virtue, the failure of loyalty to her father, the sense of compassion for Gina, which turns to painful jealousy, the temptation to take refuge in a convent in paradoxical conflict with the fear of being banished to one (which fear leads her to the 'hideux et déshonorant mensonge de feindre d'accepter les soins et les attentions publiques du marquis Crescenzi': 346–7), the anguish at thinking herself partly responsible for the apparent poisoning of her father, the resultant decision to marry Crescenzi and the vow never to see Fabrice again, these are the ingredients of her 'sort réel'. While Fabrice is airily remarking on the twist of fate which has brought him happiness in prison, Clélia is 'profondément malheureuse' (341), and when Fabrice returns voluntarily to the prison which he was so reluctant to leave, we can appreciate the nature of Clélia's reaction: 'elle crut à une vision que le ciel permettait pour la punir; puis l'atroce réalité apparut à sa raison' (468).

'L'atroce réalité', 'l'affreuse réalité', 'l'austère réalité', these phrases echo through the novel as reminders of what lies behind the easy appearances of card-games and play-acting. All around Fabrice, indeed beneath him, this suffering is felt and these sacrifices are made, yet he never once seems to think of what either Gina or Clélia may be feeling. Gina's lamplit messages bring an unwelcome invitation to escape, while Clélia's gallant arrival in his prison-cell to prevent him eating his poisoned dinner is simply too good an 'opportunity' to be missed. 'Aucune résistance ne fut opposée' (472): to Fabrice it never is. In the end so great is the disparity between the latter's persistently Olympian view of life and the harsh realities of existence experienced by others that one may come to question whether the experience of love changes Fabrice at all.

Certainly it has brought him happiness, and doubtless the reader may share the tremulous excitement of Fabrice's first days in prison, and thrill to each successive stage in his pursuit of Clélia—the glances exchanged, the alphabets, the letters given and received, and the furtive meeting in the chapel. There is a strong element of innocent play in this relationship (cf. Clélia's reference to 'nos jeux d'enfant, avec des alphabets': 365), while at the same time their profane love is more than once merged with the sacred—the pastoral ring destined for Fabrice and entrusted to Clélia by Landriani, the meeting in the chapel, Fabrice's coded description of his feelings for Clélia in the margins of a folio edition of the works of Saint Jerome ('les grands événements n'étaient autre chose que des extases d'*amour divin* (ce mot divin en remplaçait un autre qu'on n'osait écrire)': 422).[14] And these ludic and religious elements persist in the account of Fabrice's pursuit of Clélia after he has finally been released from prison—the game of whist, the whispered couplet from a 'Petrarchan'[15] sonnet, the floral alphabet (510), the sermons which speak of compassion both human and divine (516, 529). Theirs is a classic love story, a courtly romance properly tinged with ritual and religious observance,[16] and culminating in the most famous line of the book: 'entre ici, ami de mon cœur' (530).

But what are the consequences of this romance? For Clélia, as we have seen, much suffering and sacrifice, and in the end an acceptance of the overwhelming power of her passion for Fabrice which is rewarded by three years of 'bonheur divin' (531). But for Fabrice? Has the experience of love and imprisonment brought him any discoveries about himself or the world? Is he more mature? Certainly he has suffered, particularly between leaving prison and receiving Clélia's gift of a fan (whereupon, as usual: 'tout changea aux yeux de Fabrice: en un instant il fut un autre homme': 503). But there is no evidence that he is any closer to forgoing his 'romanesque' view of life or to examining events 'pour ensuite deviner leurs causes', and this becomes clear when we examine the circumstances surrounding the death of Sandrino. During the three years of 'bonheur divin' Fabrice has reached a point in his life where he seems set fair to live happily ever after, the equivalent stage to Julien's when he says: 'voilà mon roman est fini, et à moi seul tout le mérite.' Every evening is shared with Clélia, he has become archbishop, and a good one at that, thanks to his piety, exemplary behaviour and eloquence; he has inherited the family fortune and can distribute his archiepiscopal

---

[14] And Fabrice's breviary provides the letters for their alphabet of love. On the mixture of sacred and profane love see J. D. Hubert, 'Notes sur la dévaluation du réel', Stirling Haig, 'La descente du paradis', *Stendhal Club*, 21 (1978/9), 139–45 (143), and Madeleine A. Simons, 'Stendhal et les métamorphoses du sacré. Le palimpseste à rebours', *Stendhal Club*, 28 (1985/6), 1–16.

[15] It is by Metastasio. See *CP*, 699, n. 11.

[16] *Pace* Thompson who sees love and religion as being in conflict. See *Le Jeu de l'ordre*, 196 ff. Cf. also Durand for whom the second part of *La Chartreuse* is 'une *descente*, un progressif retour, retour par delà les aimées, à la profondeur religieuse de l'amour' (*Le Décor mythique*, 158).

salary amongst his vicars and curates. In short: 'il eût été difficile
de rêver une vie plus honorée, plus honorable et plus utile que celle
que Fabrice s'était faite' (532). But now, fast on the heels of this
false denouement, comes the equivalent of Julien's shooting of Mme
de Rênal: Fabrice's 'mauvais caprice de tendresse' in wishing to have
his son Sandrino live with him and love him as his father. While
Fabrice's motives are of course much more straightforward than
Julien's, his whim nevertheless destroys the fragile happiness he had
achieved and leads at once to the death of all the main characters
in the novel, save Mosca. The passing glimpse of a happy ending
is thus quickly followed by the reality of a tragic outcome.

The question remains: is Sandrino's death just bad luck, or is
Fabrice to blame? While Clélia understands and sympathizes with
Fabrice's desire to bring up his own son ('elle sentait que Fabrice
avait une sorte de raison': 533), she responds to it with much anxiety.
Rationally and sensibly she considers the various options open to
her, and she is forced to accept as apparently 'le plus raisonnable'
(534) the stratagem whereby Sandrino will appear to fall ill and die.
At the same time the superstitious side of Clélia (526) warns her not
to tempt fate: Fabrice's plan 'avait quelque chose de sinistre augure',
'Clélia prétendait qu'il ne fallait pas tenter Dieu' (534). When
Sandrino actually falls ill, Clélia 'fut sur le point de perdre la raison'
and interprets the consequent breaking of her vow as 'un péché
horrible et qui présageait la mort de Sandrino' (535). The cruel irony
of *La Chartreuse* is that, when Fabrice least expects it, augury and
presage prove tragically accurate, and this may well be one of the
reasons why Stendhal twice claimed to have written *La Chartreuse*
with the death of Sandrino as a focal point.[17]

For the reference to augury and presage allows us to measure the
continuing immaturity of Fabrice. Instead of seeing reality in terms
of an explicable chain of cause and effect, Fabrice has from the start
entertained 'une confiance illimitée dans les signes qui peuvent prédire
l'avenir' (21). Thus priests and crows are bad omens, whereas the
flight of an eagle in the direction of Switzerland is a sure sign that
Fabrice should go in search of Napoleon. The important thing about
omens is that they seem to provide Fabrice with external approval
of his conduct. They prevent him from having to take responsibility
for his actions and they sustain him in the illusion previously

---

[17] *JL*, iii. 210, and *Corr.*, iii. 396.

mentioned that his life is already planned, that his story has already
been written. Faced with the big decision whether to go and join
up under Napoleon, he in a sense lets Providence decide for him.
If the young chestnut planted by his mother on the occasion of his
birth is already in leaf, he will go. It is, and he does. The tree decides.
But Fabrice only heeds it when it suits him. Later he returns to find
that the tree has been damaged, but he dismisses the broken branch
as 'un accident sans conséquence' (182) and even decides its removal
will help the tree flourish. In other words he rationalizes what many
critics, themselves suddenly become credulously superstitious, choose
to see as a presage of Sandrino's death.[18]

The same superstitious approach can be seen in Fabrice's reaction
upon assuming the identity of a soldier who died in prison: 'gare
la prison!... Le présage est clair, j'aurai beaucoup à souffrir de la
prison' (38); and he becomes obsessed with this omen (65, 70),
especially when the abbé Blanès makes a similar prediction (172).
In the end of course Fabrice does not appear to suffer in prison, but
his very surprise at this causes him to make further predictions:

serait-ce l'étonnement de tout ce nouvel établissement qui me distrait de la
peine que je devrais éprouver? Peut-être que cette bonne humeur
indépendante de ma volonté et peu raisonnable cessera tout à coup, peut-
être en un instant je tomberai dans le noir malheur que je devrais éprouver.
(332)

One way of looking at these statements is to see in them confirmation
of Blanès' warning about predictions:

toute annonce de l'avenir est une infraction à la règle, et a ce danger qu'elle
peut changer l'événement, auquel cas toute la science tombe par terre comme
un véritable jeu d'enfant [...] (173)

Perhaps then it is Fabrice's very conviction that he will suffer in prison
which leads him to underestimate the discomfort and deprivations
to which he is subject and to believe even that he is happy. Moreover,
since happiness is here the end-product of a prediction, perhaps there
is no harm in Fabrice's faith in the possibility of foreseeing the future.
But the phrases 'la peine que je devrais éprouver', 'le noir malheur
que je devrais éprouver' remind one at once of the Octave who lives

---

[18] Prévost, Création, 451, Durand, Le Décor mythique, 53–4. Gilman disagrees
(The Tower as Emblem, 46). Felman sees it as a symbol of castration prefiguring
the end of the novel ('Folie', 236–7, n. 181).

his life according to a 'règle antérieure à toute expérience' and the Julien
who preconceives his life according to his ambitions. Fabrice believes
his life to *have been* preconceived and is in danger here of losing his
natural spontaneity by feeling obliged to behave and feel according to
prediction. More especially, his fanciful and inconsistent belief in omens
prevents him from judging experience with an open, rational mind.

By the end of the novel Fabrice is no nearer being able to judge
in this way. The Sandrino episode shows Fabrice ignoring the possible
presages mentioned by Clélia, not because of any new-found maturity
or readiness to think in terms of cause and effect, but rather in the
name of a destiny over which he has no control:

puisque une fatalité unique au monde veut que je sois privé de ce bonheur
dont jouissent tant d'âmes tendres, et que je ne passe pas ma vie avec tout
ce que j'adore, je veux du moins avoir auprès de moi un être qui te rappelle
à mon cœur, qui te remplace en quelque sorte. (533)

When Clélia voices her superstitious and religious fears to him:
'Fabrice reparlait de sa destinée singulière'. How can one talk of
maturity or spirituality here? The simplest rational process might
have allowed him to foresee the possible result of his selfishness:
'l'enfant, retenu au lit plus qu'il ne fallait pour sa santé, devint
réellement malade', an announcement that is followed by the heavily
ironic question: 'comment dire au médicin la cause de ce mal?' Yet
even now Fabrice will not desist from attempting to fulfil his spurious
destiny. He insists on removing Sandrino to another house, having
enlisted Mosca's help in the removal of Clélia's husband, but 'cet
enlèvement, fort adroitement exécuté, eut un résultat bien funeste:
Sandrino [...] mourut au bout de quelques mois'. Fabrice has
compounded his original error, and with fatal consequences—for
Sandrino, for Clélia, for himself, and even for Gina, who is unable
to outlive him for long. And this surely is the role of the charterhouse.
It is a refuge. 'J'irai me réfugier dans quelque chartreuse' (489), he
surmises, if Clélia should refuse to see him, and she does just this
when she writes to him asking 'permission' to marry Crescenzi (492).
A week before the marriage he takes a vow of silence (494), and
after it reflects: 'il faudrait mieux pour moi [...] me faire chartreux;
je souffrirais moins dans les rochers de Velleja' (495). In each instance
his monastic aspirations result from the suffering caused by his
relationship with Clélia, and at the end of the novel his final retreat
follows upon her death:

Fabrice était trop amoureux et trop croyant pour avoir recours au suicide; il espérait retrouver Clélia dans un meilleur monde, mais il avait trop d'esprit pour ne pas sentir qu'il avait beaucoup à réparer. (536)

The silence of the charterhouse shrouds regret, remorse and even bewilderment. From a summit of achievement and 'bonheur divin' one single act, apparently inspired by fine paternal feelings, yet carried out with heedless indifference to the attendant dangers and to Clélia's feelings, has cast him down: things have taken a quite unexpected turn for the worse. How could he have foreseen it? What could he have done? Where did he go wrong? Are not these the questions Fabrice is asking himself as he sits upon his lonely bench in the charterhouse of Parma?

Certainly they are some of the questions a 'French' reader may ask as he comes to the end of the 'particularités réelles' of the narrative and faces the blank and silent space that follows TO THE HAPPY FEW, the more so as the rapidity of the conclusion increases the sense of inexplicable and disproportionate disaster.[19] Of course there is Stendhal's statement that he had much more to say but was obliged to abbreviate by a publisher anxious for a text that would fit nicely into two octavo volumes.[20] Yet the evidence of the endings in the *Chroniques italiennes* suggests also that Stendhal was conscious of the aesthetic benefit of abrupt conclusion.[21] The violin-reader is caught unawares, and the taut strings of his attention may well resonate that much longer after the final note has been played.

One resonance he may hear is that the death of Sandrino marks the symbolic conclusion of the theme of childhood in the novel: the adventure is at an end, and we are left with the realities of death and a lesson in survival. For part of the 'innocence' and apparent simplicity of the novel derives from the comparison of some of the characters to children at moments of delight and carefree happiness

[19] Cf. the end of Laclos's *Les Liaisons dangereuses* where the very excess and disproportion of the 'punishments' meted out, far from being evidence of poor craftsmanship or mere lip-service to contemporary moral requirements, suggests a providence, fate, or realm of bad luck, which is quite different from the fine proportions of (vain) human attempts to control destiny.

[20] *OI*, ii. 394.

[21] *Pace* Prévost, *Création*, 323; but see 100 and 411, and cf. 281. See also Wood, *Stendhal*, 86–7, and Attuel, *Le Style*, 500 ff. Cf. also *OI*, ii. 110. Jean Sgard takes the view that even the abrupt ending of *Vie de Henry Brulard* is intentional. See 'L'explicit de la *Vie de Henry Brulard*', *Revue d'Histoire Littéraire de la France*, 84 (1984), 199–205.

(30, 223, 365, 440), and indeed some of the adult behaviour in the novel is itself childish, such as Ranuce-Ernest having Mosca look for 'reds' under his bed (105) or kicking Rassi in the pants (271, 384). What better way to illustrate that 'l'atroce réalité' co-exists with the easy dream-like world of the naïve than to portray the sudden death of a child?[22] And what better way to link the episode with the paradigmatic account of Waterloo, which itself has the status of a story for children (56, note a)? At Waterloo the young Fabrice arrives full of superstitious and grand notions which are belied by appearances and leaves unable to understand or describe, or even to name, the reality that informs these appearances. To the abduction of Sandrino the adult Fabrice brings an inflated notion of his own destiny and a confident belief that he knows the difference between appearance and reality and can ignore superstition, only to discover that if you arrange for someone to appear ill, he will be ill, and if your intention is to pretend that he has died, he will die.

It is fitting that the 'Avertissement' of *La Chartreuse* should be dated on Stendhal's birthday (his fifty-sixth) because the novel is very much concerned with the passing of the years, with the fading of youth and the onset of middle age. It begins with the youthfulness of the French invaders whose oldest general is only twenty-seven (Fabrice's age at the end of the novel) and who rejuvenates Milan, just as the young Gina's return to Grianta rejuvenates her sister-in-law (27), and as Gina later rejuvenates Mosca (109). But the subsequent passing of time is punctuated by references to the ageing of the characters, and particularly of Gina herself—'elle se croyait une femme âgée' (113), 'je suis une femme de trente-sept ans, je me trouve à la porte de la vieillesse' (304), 'la jeune femme est morte en moi' (307):

> [Clélia] a vingt ans; et moi, changée par les soucis, malade, j'ai le double de son âge!... Il faut mourir, il faut finir! Une femme de quarante ans n'est plus quelque chose que pour les hommes qui l'ont aimée dans sa jeunesse! (434)

Thus the process of ageing is closely linked with the bitterness of experience. After the betrayal by Ranuce-Ernest and the capture of Fabrice Gina changes overnight: '[Mosca] fut atterré à la vue de la duchesse... Elle a quarante ans! se dit-il, et hier si brillante! si jeune!' (303), and Fabrice's indifference after his release from prison continues the process:

---

[22] Cf. Pierre Creignou, 'Illusion et réalité du bonheur dans *La Chartreuse de Parme*', *Stendhal Club*, 16 (1973/4), 310–34 (especially 313).

la duchesse n'était plus cette beauté éblouissante de l'année précédente; la prison de Fabrice, et, bien plus encore, le séjour sur le lac Majeur avec Fabrice, devenu morose et silencieux, avaient donné dix ans de plus à la belle Gina. Ses traits s'étaient marqués, ils avaient plus d'esprit et moins de jeunesse. (453)

Nor is it only Gina who ages: 'depuis sa faute, la physionomie de Clélia avait pris un caractère de noblesse et de sérieux vraiment remarquable; on eût dit qu'elle avait trente ans' (488). And so much has Fabrice aged that Clélia does not recognize him: 'celui-ci est un homme de quarante ans' (501). The changes in Clélia and Fabrice add extra poignancy to the lines of their favourite sonnet: 'Non, vous ne me verrez jamais changer,/Beaux yeux qui m'avez appris à aimer' (503); and indeed one might even argue that it is ageing which precipitates the denouement, for Fabrice's motive in wanting Sandrino to live with him is that he should come to love the real Fabrice behind the off-putting exterior: 'il doit me trouver une figure sérieuse, ce qui, pour les enfants, veut dire triste' (533).

Seriousness, the child must learn, is not the same as sadness. And so must we; for here perhaps is the principal lesson of the novel (and an aid to understanding how its author also wrote Lucien Leuwen). The passage of time of course brings sadness and a sense of loss, and the ageing and premature death of the main protagonists makes the end of the narrative a bleak and tragic experience. It is true that this sad decline is characterized by an increase in seriousness, be it in Fabrice's 'figure sérieuse', the 'caractère [...] de sérieux' in Clélia's, the 'plus d'esprit' in Gina's, and it is also the case that much of the first part of the novel orchestrates a stark contrast between the happiness of youthful insouciance and the kind of seriousness epitomized by the Austrian chief of police, Baron Binder. Receiving representations on behalf of Fabrice after his return from Waterloo and being asked 'comment l'on pouvait prendre au sérieux l'incartade d'un enfant de seize ans', this 'homme sage et triste' replies: 'mon métier est de tout prendre au sérieux' (92). Seriousness for him means wisdom and sadness. But with the introduction of Mosca we encounter wisdom and seriousness with a smiling face, the Mosca who would already have been Prime Minister 's'il eût voulu prendre une mine plus grave' (104). His lack of self-importance, his air of simple gaiety, his erstwhile youthful idealism in the cause of Napoleon (103) make of him a kind of grown-up Fabrice, and he therefore understands only too well how dangerous to his own chances of success with Gina is the irresistible charm of Fabrice's 'joie naïve et tendre' which seems to proclaim that 'il n'y a que l'amour et le bonheur qu'il donne qui soient choses sérieuses en ce monde' (154). But while he might share Fabrice's priorities, he realizes too that there are other 'choses sérieuses'. Where Fabrice trusts to presage, Mosca has foresight. He understands how to maintain his power over Ranuce-Ernest (106) and Landriani (148), knows what will happen if he lets his jealousy be known (153), and is doubtless accurate in his account of what would have happened had he not intervened and put down Ferrante Palla's uprising (444–5). For all his prudence (152) and his cool, detached view of politics as a game of chess (104) or backgammon (444), he is far from being unfeeling, and it seems that his easy laughter conceals a profound awareness of the fragility of human destiny, an awareness born perhaps of the memory of his own moments of sudden passion and violence (109, 154, 441).

For a 'French' reading of the text Mosca's ultimate survival suggests the benefits of seriousness and implies that Fabrice's Olympian view of things condemns him to tragic failure. The attractions of the imaginative response are everywhere to be seen, but the 'oubli de tous les sentiments tristes, ou seulement raisonnables' (11) with which the novel begins cannot withstand so many reminders of 'l'atroce réalité'. The spontaneous and charming Gina who acts on a whim but never changes her mind (151, 267) is caught up in an act of vengeance which is 'bien funeste à la tranquillité du reste de sa vie' (414), and the delights of marriage and social success are hollow: 'la comtesse en un mot réunissait toutes les apparences du bonheur, mais elle ne survécut que fort peu de temps à Fabrice, qu'elle adorait' (537). And Clélia loses her son and, in the end, her own life because love is stronger than reason: 'elle aimait trop Fabrice pour se refuser constamment au sacrifice terrible qu'il lui demandait' (534). But Mosca lives on because he understands the seriousness of the game he is playing. Indeed he can even predict its outcome:

c'est que nous sommes environnés d'événements tragiques, répliqua le comte aussi avec émotion; nous ne sommes pas ici en France, où tout finit par des chansons ou par un emprisonnement d'un an ou deux, et j'ai réellement tort de vous parler de toutes ces choses en riant. (188)

4

Choices

THE reader of *La Chartreuse* has a choice of readings: either his imagination may respond with delight to the thrill of the adventure story and identify with the passionate zest for living exhibited by some of the protagonists, or his reason will analyse with ironic detachment the events and values of a far from impartial narrative. The 'circonstances romanesques' conduce to entertainment, the 'particularités réelles' to instruction. But how instructive has a prosaic, 'French' reading of the novel been? And would an 'Italian' reading have its lesson to impart?

In the case of Fabrice we may have noted the fatal consequences attendant upon an inability to engage with reality and the debonair refusal to examine either oneself or the world about one, but that is not all there is to Fabrice. We can equally well admire his honesty and courage, applaud his sensitivity to natural beauty and the poetry of memory (170, 176), envy his lack of doubt and hesitation and see it as evidence of an integrated authentic being. He sets himself the highest standards (181) and refuses to be like other young men (100, 140)—except, that is, during an idle moment in Bologna when he suffers 'une misérable *pique* de vanité' and decides to pursue La Fausta. The narrator denounces this as 'l'une des plus mauvaises actions de Fabrice' (235), which may appear ironic in view of some of Fabrice's other actions but can be taken to be perfectly serious, given that Fabrice is here at his least authentic. He is merely playing a role: 'n'est-ce pas ainsi qu'en agissent messieurs les amants? se disait-il' (247), as he serenades La Fausta like some latter-day Don Giovanni. But this episode is merely a comic deviation from Fabrice's normal behaviour, which displays the charm of a life lived with enthusiasm and imagination, free from the inhibitions of prudence and cool reason. In other words the charm of an 'âme italienne' who may never understand the world but whose joys are all the more intense and lasting (86) for the unqualified commitment to passion.

Mosca, on the other hand, may, by the very fact of his survival, finally forfeit the reader's sympathy. He may have exemplified the possibility of seriousness without sadness, and his smiling reason may well have combined with a middle-aged capacity to fall passionately

in love in a way no Frenchman could ever understand (113, 308),
but the end of the novel excludes him from the élite who die for love.
For Stendhal the government of the grand-dukes of Tuscany created
an atmosphere of torpid security from which passion and gaiety were
absent,[1] and it is over this that Mosca comes finally to preside. He
has defined old age as 'n'être plus capable de ces enfantillages
délicieux' (108), and one senses indeed that by the end old age has
overtaken him and that the last spark of idealism or imagination has
been quenched by the cold waters of realism and reason in a way
which he himself predicted:

un être à demi stupide, mais attentif, mais prudent tous les jours, goûte très
souvent le plaisir de triompher des hommes à imagination. C'est par une
folie d'imagination que Napoléon s'est rendu au prudent *John Bull*, au lieu
de chercher à gagner l'Amérique. John Bull, dans son comptoir, a bien ri
de la lettre où il cite Thémistocle. De tous temps les vils Sancho Pança
l'emporteront à la longue sur les sublimes don Quichotte. (189)

Not that Mosca is either vile or half stupid, but such a process as
he describes can happen not only between people but within them:
the Sancho Panza in Mosca has outlived the Quixote. When we
remember that Fabrice towards the end of his life comes increasingly
to venerate Mosca 'à mesure que les affaires lui [Fabrice] apprenaient
à connaître la méchanceté des hommes' (513), we may even feel that
retreat and death have saved Fabrice from a worse fate—a loss of
faith in himself and mankind. Or is that what the silence of the
charterhouse conceals?

And what of Gina? Again imagination may thrill but reason
question. 'Cette vivante et ravissante créature', exclaims Balzac, 'vous
la trouverez grande, spirituelle, passionnée, toujours vraie.'[2] 'one of
the most glamorous and vital women of modern fiction', writes
Robert M. Adams, created by 'boldly ignoring anything which
sounded like meat-and-potatoes reality or middle-class morality'.[3]
Many readers have responded with delight to the portrait of the
duchesse Sanseverina, to her energy and passion, her love of danger
and thirst for excitement, her theatricality and taste for the grand
gesture, her spontaneity and capacity to improvise, above all her
sublime indifference to the petty and prosaic. In certain respects

---

[1] *VIT*, 494, and *VR*, i, 59, n. 1. See Thompson, *Le Jeu de l'ordre*, 164. Cf. also
HPI, i. 54.
[2] Talbot, *Critique*, 33.   [3] *Notes on a Novelist*, 84.

she seems to combine the virtues of Fabrice and Mosca. She shares the former's sensitivity to beauty and nature, his sense of fun and disposition to happiness, while she has Mosca's talent for intrigue, his capacity to act promptly and efficiently as the occasion demands. As we have already seen, she can dream of magic carpets but she knows that the battlefield awaits. In her, it seems, imagination and reason are in perfect harmony. But like Fabrice and Mosca she is also open to criticism.[4] The sense of theatre is not far removed from vanity, that need for public acclaim which made Mathilde's heroism so inauthentic (and so tiring). Her tendency to break the rules may suggest a free spirit, but she insists on having power over others, that they should obey her rules. Pride demands that she never change her mind, so she loses the freedom to go back on her intention to assassinate Ranuce-Ernest, which itself was born of injured pride. She becomes too involved in the games she is playing and overplays her hand (her overstepping of the mark with Ranuce-Ernest: 308; the excess of poison administered to Fabio Conti: 400). It may be that hell hath no fury like a woman scorned, but the prevention of Fabrice's marriage to Clélia (434, 495) and the assassination of a ruler are hellish to the point when one may speak, not of noble vengeance, but of vindictiveness in its purest form. Yet she may not forfeit all sympathy since these are the actions of a loser. Ranuce-Ernest has tricked her over Fabrice, the latter's escape may be due more to Clélia's efforts than her own (420), the grand gesture of flooding Parma has been ineffectual and gone unnoticed (427) and, above all, Fabrice loves another. As Thompson rightly remarks; 'la vie est autrement tragique que ne le voudrait Gina dans son énergie si généreuse.'[5]

If we turn from character to event, the same choice has to be made between reasoned and imaginative response. As has already been noted, political affairs in the novel are so enveloped in the imagery of games and play-acting that it is difficult to infer any serious political considerations, and many critics have been content to see the depiction of Parmesan court life in terms of high comedy[6] or a game of chance.[7] The easy division into ultras and liberals, the lack of principle suggested by the equally easy changing of sides as Mosca

[4] The following remarks are derived from Thompson, *Le Jeu de l'ordre*, 103–39.
[5] p. 125.   [6] e.g. Bardèche, *Stendhal romancier*, 378–82.
[7] e.g. Hemmings, *Stendhal*, 190. Cf. J. D. Hubert, 'Notes sur la dévaluation du réel'.

and Rassi exchange places (as Rênal and Valenod do at the end of *Le Rouge*), the manœuvres and intrigues, the role of the mistress, the absurdity of Ranuce-Ernest's imitations of Louis XIV, all these suggest that politics are simple and can be seen 'de haut'. But for others there are serious, general issues at stake, not least the nature of tyranny and the workings of reactionary politics,[8] and of course there is the occasional echo (130, 146, 465) of the anti-American, anti-democratic notions of *Lucien Leuwen*. At the same time the supposed anachronistic flavour of the novel does not preclude specific relevance to nineteenth-century Italian politics, and the place of the Napoleonic invasion in the pre-history of the Risorgimento emerges clearly enough.[9]

As far as the moral issues raised by the novel are concerned, one may be inclined to presume the characters (and even the Happy Few) devoid of conscience[10] and to give oneself up to what Bardèche calls 'la poésie de l'indifférence morale': 'on entre tout doucement dans une demeure où la morale est au vestiaire, on l'a quittée en entrant.'[11] Or perhaps we have left conventional morality in the cloakroom the better to don the different moral values which the novel proposes—Bardèche's own 'morale du refus', or Brombert's 'authentic complex of values founded on truth and merit [...] a code of honor that freely binds human beings capable of mutual esteem'.[12] Whichever the case, Adams is right to talk of Stendhal deliberately raking 'our sympathy-judgments across the teeth of our moral judgments',[13] and the effect must be to sharpen the reader's self-awareness in both respects. Imaginatively we may be carried along by the narrative, willing victims of the narrator's defusing of moral issues and eager that our heroes and heroines should succeed. A bribe here, a murder there, what does it matter as long as they are happy? Or we may keep our distance and either, like Sainte-Beuve[14] and Henry James,[15] roundly condemn these characters as

---

[8] Coe, 'Portrait d'une réaction'. Cf. Wood's account of 'lucid conservatism', *Stendhal*, 167–8.

[9] See Finch, '*La Chartreuse de Parme*', 40–51. Finch is right to stress the literal, as well as the symbolic, role of prisons in this portrait of repression (49–50). On the symbolic function of prisons see Victor Brombert, *La Prison romantique. Essai sur l'imaginaire* (Paris, 1975).

[10] Hemmings, *Stendhal*, 186 (echoing Henry James's comments in the *Nation*, 17 Sept. 1874. See 'Henry Beyle', in *Literary Reviews and Essays*, ed. Mordell (New York, 1957), 151–7.)

[11] *Stendhal romancier*, 370–1. Cf. Jones's view of Fabrice's amorality, *Ironie*, 140.

[12] *Fiction*, 165.

[13] *Notes on a Novelist*, 103. Cf. Finch, '*La Chartreuse de Parme*', 61.

[14] Talbot, *Critique*, 166.   [15] See above, n. 10.

moral monsters or, more moderately, analyse the nature of their crimes, setting one against the other, wondering which may be the perhaps excusable crimes of passion and which are the truly base and evil acts, and constructing a series of moral judgements accordingly. The novel offers all these possibilities.

And so also with the experience of love and the matter of omens. Thanks to the allusions to incest (125–6, 156–7) the relationship between Gina and Fabrice seems to belong in the category of forbidden romance until we remember that Gina is not even Fabrice's aunt, let alone his stepmother, and that anyway Fabrice is not in love with Gina. Equally, as we have seen, the relationship between Fabrice and Clélia has all the hallmarks of a classic love story, but perhaps reason might lead one to question the reality of this 'grande passion'. These lovers who fell in love at first sight are in the end denied that sight of each other, so that at every stage of its development, this relationship remains incomplete. When Fabrice and Clélia manage to see each other (despite the wooden screen outside Fabrice's window and the barrier of Clélia's reserve), they can't talk to each other; when they can communicate with each other, they can't be with each other and when they can be with each other, they can't see each other. Their love-affair is as much of an obstacle race as that between Octave and Armance, and one may legitimately wonder if the obstacles, as well as being part of the fun, do not also offer both partners a kind of security in permitting them to keep reality at a distance.

When we come to superstition, omens, and predictions, imagination may respond as to the marvellous in epic or romance.[16] The numbers seven and thirteen, the eagle, the chestnut-tree, all appear invested with talismanic significance and, together with the horoscopes of Blanès, enhance the magical atmosphere of the novel, its aura of naïve and primitive simplicity. But reason may take note at the beginning of the novel of the way in which the prophecy of Saint Giovita has been misinterpreted, and later take Blanès' account of a mistaken prediction in respect of himself as a *caveat* following Blanès' own predictions about Fabrice. And a salutary *caveat* too, for Blanès' predictions (172) will prove far from accurate[17] and are reminiscent, in their mixture of truth and falsehood, of Mme de Rênal's letter about Julien. Thus indeed Fabrice ought to prepare

---

[16] See Durand, *Le Décor mythique*, 43–56.
[17] *Pace* e.g. Wood, *Stendhal*, 175, and Strickland, *Stendhal*, 230.

himself for 'une autre prison' (beyond that which held him before Waterloo: 36-8) but, thanks to Clélia, it will not be 'bien autrement dure, bien plus terrible'. It is not at all clear that Fabrice eventually leaves this prison thanks to someone else's crime, unless the bribery of the guards, Clélia's betrayal of her father or—for the second departure from prison—Gina's prostitution be so regarded. But Blanès' tone ('grâce au ciel') suggests something more serious. Is then the assassination of Ranuce-Ernest in question? But surely this is not what secures Fabrice's release. Blanès then rightly predicts that 'il sera question de tuer un innocent' (i.e. the 'valet de chambre' (183) and Giletti) but he is wrong to add 'qui, sans le savoir, usurpe tes droits'[18] and wrong to predict a temptation to violence 'qui semblera justifiée par les lois de l'honneur', since self-defence and a belief that he has been disfigured are the two causes (183 and 200). In one case Fabrice does not resist the temptation, so the rest of Blanès' prediction might be deemed invalid. Yet it continues with the same blend of truth and falsehood. The statement that 'ta vie sera très heureuse aux yeux des hommes..., et raisonnablement heureuse aux yeux du sage' is difficult to assess:[19] in the eyes of the people of Parma, and indeed of some critics, the young archbishop may seem happy, but 'raisonnablement heureuse' seems an inadequate description from the point of view of the Happy Few for a life that contains such extremes of joy and suffering. The prediction that 'tu mourras comme moi, mon fils, assis sur un siège de bois, loin de tout luxe' seems accurate, but 'détrompé du luxe' is a cliché that is irrelevant to Fabrice's final disposal of his worldly goods, and 'n'ayant à te faire aucun reproche grave' will be flatly contradicted ('il avait trop d'esprit pour ne pas sentir qu'il avait beaucoup à réparer': 536). In his concluding remarks Blanès adjusts the focus of his predictions with the result that the assassination of Ranuce-Ernest seems more accurately foretold: 'après la prison, mais je ne

---

[18] Unless this is a reference to Crescenzi. See I. H. Smith, 'Brief Note on the Predictions of the Abbé Blanès', *AUMLA*, 45 (1976), 96-7. This theory is countered by Geneviève Mouillaud-Fraisse, 'Le titre comme chimère', *L'Arc*, 88 (1983), 77-86 (85). Mouillaud-Fraisse also entertains the possibility that the innocent in question is Sandrino. For further discussion of this theory see François Landry, 'Le crime dans *La Chartreuse de Parme*', in Berthier (ed.), *Stendhal: l'écrivain, la société, le pouvoir* 329-44.

[19] *Pace*, Landry, *L'Imaginaire*, 339.

sais si c'est au moment même de la sortie, il y aura ce que j'appelle un crime, mais par bonheur je crois être sûr qu'il ne sera pas commis par toi.' But Blanès is still wrong about the 'paix de l'âme' which he expects Fabrice to enjoy at the end of his life.

Blanès' predictions add to the 'circonstances romanesques' of the novel by whetting the reader's curiosity, but the detached reader will in retrospect see their inaccuracies and may even, as has already been suggested, adduce one of Blanès' own remarks by way of explanation: 'toute annonce de l'avenir est une infraction à la règle'. Perhaps it is childish to think one can foresee the future? And of course we have already seen the immaturity and inconsistency in Fabrice's response to omens like the eagle and the chestnut-tree. But once again it is the Sandrino episode which gives one pause for thought, for here precisely an omen—ignored by Fabrice, as he ignored the damaged tree—proves accurate. What if Fabrice's earlier 'confiance illimitée dans les signes qui peuvent prédire l'avenir' (21) was not misplaced? What if the novel were to contain—*unannounced*—such pointers towards subsequent events? And would this not explain why in *La Chartreuse* history seems so frequently to repeat itself?

Because it unquestionably does. There is a whole series of incidents and details which repeat themselves in such a way that moment *a* appears, on first reading, to recall another moment *b* while on a second reading, *b* appears to presage moment *a*.[20] Thus, for example, Fabrice's first experience of prison and his night with the gaoler's wife prefigure the Tour Farnese and his love for Clélia, just as his first view of Clélia surrounded by prisoners prefigures his arrival in the citadel. The role of a church in his pursuit of La Fausta (238) and Clélia (529), the setting of his meetings with Marietta (230) and Clélia (530), his reluctance to leave places, be it Zonders (81), Grianta (177), or the Tour Farnese (378), these are all repetitions which are perhaps susceptible of rational explanation such as the suitability of a church for clandestine meetings, the uniformity of Parmesan architecture or Fabrice's gift for being happy where he finds himself. So too the repetitions in Gina's life. The honour of princely visits to her salon by Ranuce-Ernest, both IV and V (136–9, 505),

---

[20] Some of these are dealt with by Finch, '*La Chartreuse de Parme*', 18–20, as illustration of her argument that the structure of *La Chartreuse* 'shows two opposite tendencies: towards harmony and towards uncertainty' (17); and many of them by Thompson, *Le Jeu de l'ordre*, 75–85, in support of his thesis that Stendhal was seeking to reconcile an aesthetic need for order with the freedom and spontaneity of his improvisation.

her threats to leave the court (259–66, 507), her successes in securing release from prison by direct appeal to the ruler (23–4, 126, 265–6), the sacrifices of her finer feelings (95, 508) may all be seen as the ends and means of an astute politician who sees no reason to change her winning stratagems. Again it is plausible that borrowing dead men's clothes is a familiar routine on the battlefield (9, 38) and even that both the pro-Austrian marquis del Dongo and Ranuce-Ernest should live in almost paranoid fear (11–12, 105). But all these repetitions may nevertheless create a sense of 'déjà vu' in the reader such that he may posit some hidden order beneath the apparent jumble of adventures, and certainly the strong pattern of recurrence which embraces the castle and bell-tower at Grianta, the citadel of Parma,[21] and both the Palais Contarini and the Palais Crescenzi seems to encourage the conclusion that a providential view of human affairs has not been invalidated by Blanès' fumbled horoscopes. The del Dongo castle, a fifteenth-century fortress towering 150 feet above Lake Como and provided with all manner of moat, drawbridge and escutcheons and with walls some 80 feet high and 6 feet wide, prepares for the citadel of Parma of similar date, position and proportions (125–6, 325–7). At the same time the amateur astronomy sessions upon 'la plate-forme d'une des tours gothiques du château' (29) prepare for Blanès' observatory at the top of the bell-tower and the 'plate-forme' of the citadel upon which the Tour Farnese is built. Most importantly Fabrice's visit to Blanès at the bell-tower is the hub of the novel's circular pattern. There in the 'cage de planches qui formait son observatoire' (170) and which can seem like a prison (175, 176), Fabrice can look down on the sparrows looking for breadcrumbs on the dining-room balcony of the castle and the terra-cotta vases filled with orange-trees, one of which vases has been removed to serve as an ingenious lighted frame for Blanès' map of the heavens, and—after concealing himself behind a rag in which he has cut two holes for his eyes and with the aid of Blanès' telescope—he can witness the procession in the square beneath. And from here he escapes as fortunately (180) as later from the Tour Farnese where, incarcerated in a 'cabane en planches' he has been able to see through the screened window to receive the lamplit messages of Gina and to look down on the 'jolies cages'(328) of Clélia's aviary and imagine the orange-trees which she has caused to be placed at

---

[21] Cf. Gilman, *The Tower as Emblem*, especially, 29–31, 42–3, and 46.

the foot of the tower (333–4). At the Palais Contarini (485) it is Clélia's turn to watch a procession, only to see Fabrice looking at her from a window opposite through panes of the same oiled paper that obscured his prison-windows (333). Finally the lovers are reunited through a barred window in the orangerie of the Palais Crescenzi (530).

Towers, cages, prisons, windows, screens, bars; birds, trees; lamps, stars, the heavens;[22] height, imprisonment, flight, concealment, vision, divination; the images and themes of the novel are woven together in an unyielding skein, leading one through the labyrinth of adventure from childhood home to spiritual home ('l'abbé Blanès était son véritable père': 170) to the beloved's home, to Sandrino's home, to the final home—the monastic cell of the charterhouse of Parma, a refuge freely entered, the antechamber of death. So compelling is this pattern and progression that the reader's imagination cannot but be caught by the mystery of the multiple echoes and interconnexions of the text. While reason may deny all notions of providence and the supernatural and may question the power of prophecy or the validity of omens, the violin of the reader's soul must surely resonate to the tantalizing unity and poetic coherence which a retrospective view of the novel displays. Indeed such resonance, or reverie, may be prompted even as we proceed through the novel, for each stage in the development of theme and image may seem already familiar, each motif already a leitmotif even if we don't know where it leads . . . as if in fact Fabrice's story has already been written.

La Chartreuse, it may be said, images, or imagines the world more cogently than our reason can dismantle it. Yet the recurrent opportunities to 'regarder les particularités réelles des choses' are essential in that they complement the surface charm of the narrative with the depth of moral consequence, the lightness of touch with the weight of mature reflection, and the immediacy of vicarious involvement with the distance of irony and mental reservation. Curiously—though not so if one thinks back to Stendhal's previous novels—this blend is reflected in the very landscape of the novel: 'il y a lieu à un nouveau paysage comme à un nouveau roman' (2).[23]

---

[22] The list is incomplete. See Thompson, *Le Jeu de l'ordre*, 42–3, 73–4, 169–71, for ropes, boats, horses, air . . .

[23] Some of the following details have also been noted by Michel Crouzet in his much fuller account of the matter but he draws different conclusions. See 'Sur la topographie de la *Chartreuse de Parme*, et sur le rapport des lieux et des lieux communs', in Crouzet (ed.), *Espaces romanesques* (Paris, 1982), 99–139.

Thus in chapter ii we learn of Gina's 'retirement' to the castle at Grianta and how she begins to revisit, with Fabrice, 'tous ces lieux enchanteurs voisins de Grianta':

la villa Melzi de l'autre côté du lac, vis-à-vis le château, et qui lui sert de point de vue; au-dessus le bois sacré des *Sfondrata*, et le hardi promontoire qui sépare les deux branches du lac, celle de Côme, si voluptueuse, et celle qui court vers Lecco, pleine de sévérité [...] (27)

Here reflected in the topography of Lake Como is the blend of the novel itself. Surrounding it are the hills which recall[24] the world of Tasso and Ariosto: 'tout est noble et tendre, tout parle d'amour, rien ne rappelle les laideurs de la civilisation'. But then if one lifts one's eyes:

par-delà ces collines, dont le faîte offre des ermitages qu'on voudrait tous habiter, l'œil étonné aperçoit les pics des Alpes, toujours couverts de neige, et leur austerité sévère lui rappelle des malheurs de la vie ce qu'il en faut pour accroître la volupté présente.

Again the mixture of the 'voluptueux' and the 'sévère', but now with a rider, which is important to an understanding of the novel, that the presence of 'malheurs' enhances happiness.[25] This is the 'langage de ces lieux ravissants' (28), a language which the reader of the novel must master, and a language which is heard again by Fabrice as he gazes from the citadel:

ces sommets, toujours couverts de neige, même au mois d'août où l'on était alors, donnent comme une sorte de fraîcheur par souvenir au milieu de ces campagnes brûlantes [...] (325–6)

The contrast is the same, even if the terms are reversed, and what better way to describe the final impression left by the novel than as 'une sorte de fraîcheur par souvenir'? No wonder too that it begins with this quotation from Ariosto: '*gia mi fur dolci inviti a empir le carte/I luoghi ameni*'. 'At one time these charming places were sweet invitations for me to fill the pages': one explanation of the 'miracle' of *La Chartreuse* lies among the summits of the Alps—where France and Italy meet.

[24] Not only to Gina's mind but also to the narrator's, it seems, since the division between her interior monologue and the resumption of the narrator's discourse is impossible to locate. (But cf. Creignou who argues that Gina and the narrator have a different conception of happiness: see 'Illusion et réalité', 314.)

[25] Cf. Creignou, 'Illusion et réalité', 317–18.

VI

TAKING A BOW

'La difficulté n'est plus de trouver et de dire la vérité, mais de trouver qui la lise.'

(*OI*, ii. 833)

1

Lamiel

'Ces regards étaient archets: *Mulier plectrum viri.*'

(OI, ii. 371)

STENDHAL collapsed in the rue Neuve-des-Capucines on the evening of 22 March 1842, after dinner with Guizot at the Ministry of Foreign Affairs, and he died in his lodgings at 2 a.m. on the following morning. Among the various unfinished works which he left behind was his last novel *Lamiel*. The latter's incompletion, however, may be attributed less to a fatal stroke than to a recurrence of its author's fatal tendency to let improvisation conflict with design. As F. W. J. Hemmings has shown,[1] there are essentially two *Lamiel*. The idea for the first came to Stendhal exactly one week after the publication of *La Chartreuse de Parme* (on 6 April 1839) and, like death, it came on the streets of Paris:

je comptais me délasser de la *Chart*[*reuse*] avec *le Curieux de province*, comédie.[2] Mais j'ai vu ce soir, 13 avril, Amiel de la station près la Bastille à la rue Saint-Denis qu'elle a prise puis suivie. Beaucoup d'esprit à Amiel et à un autre personnage. Un personnage vaniteux pour accrocher la sympathie des Français. (226–7)[3]

The chance glimpse of a young girl, perhaps even a prostitute, had set the process of novelistic 'cristallisation' once more in train,[4] and after some preliminary work in May, Stendhal wrote a first version back in Civitavecchia, between October and December.[5] In this version Lamiel is an orphan girl in Normandy who is adopted by a M. and Mme. Hautemare and subsequently employed as a reader by the ageing duchesse de Siossens (later Miossens or Myossens)

---

[1] See 'Les Deux *Lamiel*'.

[2] Even towards the end of his life Stendhal still had thoughts of writing a play. Given the title and Lamiel's own curiosity, perhaps the novel takes over situations which he had envisaged for the stage.

[3] Simple page-references of this kind are to Anne-Marie Meininger's edition for Gallimard (Folio) (Paris, 1983).

[4] For full documentation see Meininger's edition, 225–314.

[5] From 1/2–10 October, and 19 November–3 December. The reason for the interruption was a protracted and increasingly unwelcome visit from Mérimée.

whose eyesight is beginning to fail her. Through the duchess she meets the hunchback docteur Sansfin and then the duchess's son Fédor with whom she elopes to Rouen. Bored by his devotion she sends him back to his mother and becomes the mistress of the comte d'Aubigné (later de Nerwinde) and then of the marquis de la Vernaye, who confirms his links with Julien Sorel by offering her dinner 'dans les bois de Verrières' (221). In a plan dated 25 September 1839 Stendhal writes of his intention to finish this version of the novel with Lamiel falling in love with Valbayre, a fictional equivalent of the famous murderer and outlaw Lacenaire (1800-36). Having married Fédor upon the death of the duchesse de Miossens, the new duchess was to abscond with her marriage settlement and join Valbayre and his gang. When Valbayre is finally arrested, tried and executed, Lamiel 'incendie le Palais de Justice pour venger Valbayre; on trouve des ossements à demi-calcinés dans les débris de l'incendie,—ce sont ceux de Lamiel' (242).

When Stendhal resumed writing on 3 January 1840, his conception of the novel had clearly changed, and a second *Lamiel* emerges during his revision of the first version.[6] In this second *Lamiel* the importance of Lamiel herself is diminished,[7] and the main emphasis shifts on to the nascent relationship between Sansfin and a much younger duchesse de Miossens. In the latest notes and drafts for the novel Lamiel has become merely the person who first introduces Sansfin to the duchess. Where previously the secondary characters and the social and historical background had been mentioned simply in passing, now there is a desire to portray the workings of a whole society, to portray its politics and, above all, its moral decline. Having set out to write a *Le Rouge et le Noir* for feminists, Stendhal ended up working on a cross between *Lucien Leuwen* and *Beauty and the Beast*.

Thereafter his problem was that the second *Lamiel* fitted ill with the first. As Hemmings has noted, the first version is a kind of 'conte philosophique' in which a young girl of independent mind and quick intelligence discovers the world and learns to see through its

---

[6] This revision was carried out 3-15 January and on 5, 6 and 10 February 1840. Stendhal returned to it in March 1841 and March 1842.

[7] In her introduction Meininger puts forward the debatable idea that, in basing the character of Lamiel on Mélanie Guilbert, Stendhal came retrospectively to realize that Mélanie was lesbian and then lost interest. Hence, in Meininger's view, his marginal jotting: 'je ne puis travailler à rien de sérieux for this little gouine' (271). See Meininger, ed. cit. 23-30.

hypocrisy and duplicity. This Lamiel is related anagrammatically not
only to Mélanie Guilbert but also to Rousseau's Emile, so that this
first version may be seen as a kind of anti-*Emile*. But the second
version brings the hunchback doctor Sansfin into the centre of the
stage, and this sinister, if still slightly comic character comes to
dominate the action. He becomes a Svengali figure, moulding the
innocent Lamiel to his cynical view of the world, while she now is
a dependent Trilby, ready to carry out her mentor's orders. Stendhal
seems to have understood this disparity between his two conceptions
of the heroine when, during revision of the first version, he reached
the famous scene where Lamiel takes Berville off to the woods and
pays him to show her what people mean by 'l'amour'. Such a
forthright pursuit of the truth is entirely characteristic of the first
Lamiel, whereas the second Lamiel might more plausibly have been
told by Sansfin. This impasse defeated Stendhal, and when he
returned to the novel a year later in March 1841, he had a third
or even fourth version in mind: 'mon talent, s'il y a talent, est
celui d'*improvisateur*. J'oublie tout ce qui est écrit. Je pourrais
faire quatre romans sur le même sujet, et j'oublierais tout également'
(279). The talent for improvisation which had stood him in such
good stead during the dictation of *La Chartreuse de Parme* was now
proving as detrimental to *Lamiel* as it had to *Lucien Leuwen*. Indeed
the novel was no longer to be called *Lamiel*. More appropriate, he
thought, would be a title along the lines of *Les Français du King
Philippe*.

The interest of *Lamiel* consists less in any coherence it may have,
therefore, than in the novelistic ambitions informing the various false
starts which constitute it. When the novelist-violinist took up his final
bow, what music did he hope to play? The same as before, or
something quite new? Obviously several aspects of *Lamiel* recall
Stendhal's previous novels. The opening description of Carville from
the point of view of a hypothetical Parisian visitor and the various
comments on provincial mentality put one immediately in mind of
Le Rouge et le Noir. Similarly Lamiel's social ascent from orphanage
to bourgeois household to ducal château, and the parallel progression
from Carville to Rouen/Le Havre and Paris, lend weight to the view
that Lamiel is a female Julien Sorel—a foundling who becomes a
duchess only to throw it all away by eloping with a criminal and
committing arson and suicide within society's sanctuary of justice.
Where Julien was the avatar of proletarian revolt, Lamiel is the

'prototype de la guérilla urbaine'.[8] In a world of cant, crime is the only authentic act.

At the same time the reader of *Lamiel* may be reminded of *La Chartreuse de Parme*, partly by the heroine's flamboyant disregard of social and moral conventions, partly by the 'tour d'Albret' and the magical refuge it offers from the world, and partly by the narrator. 'Un *mauvais livre*', 'aventures [...] peu édifiantes', 'notre histoire fort immorale' (52–3), these titillating references to the nature of the tale he is about to recount recall the 'Avertissement' to *La Chartreuse* and the 'aventures, lesquelles sont blâmables'. More especially the presence of a fictional narrator at the beginning of *Lamiel* shows how far Stendhal's handling of narratorial voice has evolved since his first novel. The narrator of *Armance* is essentially anonymous, a worldly-wise figure who nostalgically apes the extravagant language of his[9] protagonists while yet introducing many moments of irony and prosaic deflation. The narrator of *Le Rouge* is a more complex figure, a Parisian socialite who is in two minds about the value and function of imagination. The narrator of *Lucien Leuwen* marks a return to the anonymity of *Armance* and again gives the impression of someone who would rather delegate the narration of the story to the language and dialogue of his characters. The narrator of *La Chartreuse* is both French soldier and Italian canon, a double identity which gives pseudo-biographical and symbolic expression to the ambivalence which exists within the apparently unambiguous narrator of *Le Rouge*. Coming after all these, not to mention the distinctive narratorial presences in the *Chroniques italiennes* and the *Mémoires d'un touriste*, is the narrator of *Lamiel*. The son of a local notary who worked for the duchesse de Miossens, he inherits an estate in Havana where he spends five years before returning to Paris and then Carville. Here he learns about Lamiel's 'aventures': 'j'ai pris la fantaisie de les écrire afin de devenir homme de lettres' (53). Where once the narrator sought to hold a mirror up to society (*Armance*, *Le Rouge*, *Lucien Leuwen*) or to help us while away a dull evening (*La Chartreuse*), now he is a professional man returned from abroad, rather out of touch but desirous of a literary reputation—a figure whose

---

[8] See Gita May, 'Le féminisme de Stendhal et *Lamiel*', *Stendhal Club*, 20 (1977/8), 191–204 (201).

[9] Or her, given that in the preface Stendhal claims merely to have corrected the style of the 'femme d'esprit' who wrote the book.

circumstances may resemble, *mutatis mutandis*, those of Henri Beyle the consul on leave,[10] but a fictional character none the less.

Clearly, however, the most interesting feature of Stendhal's final novel is Lamiel herself and the depiction of the relationship between imagination and crime. Like Octave she is an angry misanthrope (107, 147); like Julien she has 'trop de vivacité et d'énergie pour marcher lentement et les yeux baissés' (78); like both Julien and Fabrice she has 'un cœur et un esprit romanesques qui se figuraient les chances de bonheur qu'elle allait trouver dans la vie' (145); like Lucien she is prone to laughter (211); and like Julien she is avid for knowledge: 'l'unique passion de Lamiel était alors la curiosité; jamais il ne fut d'être plus questionneur' (184), 'elle étudiait, elle doutait, elle ne savait à quel parti s'arrêter sur toutes choses; la curiosité était toujours son unique et dévorante passion' (212). Where she differs from Stendhal's male heroes is in her attraction to the forbidden, and the novel shows how an innocent imagination is gradually warped—or liberated?—by the lure of the illegal and the unseemly until it is capable of a violent, pyrotechnical attack upon a symbol of social order—or repression?—namely, the Palais de Justice. May it even be that Stendhal chose a woman as his protagonist because, quite simply, more things have traditionally been denied to women: education, sexual freedom, financial independence, even the possibility of travelling alone? In *Lamiel* society appears as a conspiracy to conceal knowledge, to keep people from the truth, and the heroine's quest for answers is representative of a human desire for emancipation from ignorance. Geometry (176), mathematics (209), the meaning of words (164), the point of a comedy and the purport of literature (175), the nature of sexual intercourse (153), these are the things to which all should be privy, yet Lamiel has to prostitute herself (or rather Jean Berville) in order to learn them. Denial of knowledge corrupts the pursuit of knowledge.

In the absence of knowledge the imagination provides speculative answers, and here *Lamiel* goes beyond even *Le Rouge et le Noir* in depicting the dangers of reading. Lamiel reads 'tous les livres du maître d'école', but because no one will expound their wisdom, she is left 'n'y comprenant pas grand'chose; mais elle jouissait des *imaginations* qu'ils lui donnaient' (68). Her own imagination is prey to the delights of the twelfth-century romance, the *Histoire des*

---

[10] Cf. *OI*, ii. 423: 'je n'ai point de réputation en 1842.'

quatre fils Aymon, and of Virgil's account of Dido's love in the *Aeneid* (67–8). When she then reads biographies of the notorious eighteenth-century criminals Cartouche and Mandrin, who is she to distinguish between chivalry and crime, or between the legendary ancestor of the Romans and a murderer of tax officials? The *Bildungsroman* of the future gangster's moll is already under way. This supremacy of the imagination over moral reflection persists when she acts as a reader for the duchesse de Miossens. For the latter, the *Dictionnaire des Etiquettes* is 'l'ouvrage le plus profond du siècle', while she also insists on explaining to Lamiel the meaning of certain articles in the right-wing newspaper *La Quotidienne* so that Lamiel should 'comprendre même les anecdotes malignes sur les femmes des banquiers, et autres dames libérales' (80). Nefarious conjugal practices are on a par with the rules of decorum. Similarly Lamiel is required to read aloud *Les Veillées du château* by Mme de Genlis, 'et ensuite les romans les plus moraux de cette célèbre comédienne' (80), while Sansfin in turn reads to her selected passages from the *Gazette des Tribunaux* (85). Needless to say the court case appeals more than the moral tale: 'les crimes l'intéressaient' (85). The confusion which this eclectic reading produces in Lamiel's view of the world is at once comic and indicative of her future destiny. As she reads from Mme de Genlis:

Lamiel n'était attentive qu'aux obstacles que les héros rencontraient dans leurs amours. Allaient-ils rêver aux charmes de leurs belles au fond des forêts éclairées par le pâle rayon de la lune, elle pensait aux dangers qu'ils couraient d'être surpris par des voleurs armés de poignards, dont elle lisait les exploits détaillés, tous les jours, dans *la Quotidienne*. Et encore, à vrai dire, c'était moins le danger qui l'occupait que le désagrément du moment de la surprise, quand, tout à coup, de derrière une haie, deux hommes mal vêtus et grossiers s'élançaient sur le héros. (117–18)

Given the projected circumstances of Lamiel's death one might almost see ironic confirmation here of the duchess's opinion that 'c'étaient les romans qui avaient perdu la France' (79)!

Thanks to the stupidity of her adoptive parents, crime is a concept devoid of moral significance for her. When M. Hautemare considers love a crime and when his wife uses the same word to describe the adding of meat stock to Friday's soup (118), how is Lamiel to come to any moral understanding of the world? This stupidity is what Sansfin compares to the ivy threatening the fine oak of her native wit (94), and in Stendhal's rewriting of his first version of the novel, Lamiel's ultimate criminality is potentially seen to derive not only from her reading and the effects of this on her imagination but also from the influence of Sansfin's disabused philosophy of life. Reason, like romance, leads to the inevitable conclusion that crime is the only mature way to undertake 'la chasse au bonheur'.

For Sansfin, as for Lucien Leuwen, 'le monde n'était qu'une mauvaise comédie, jouée sans grâce, par d'infâmes menteurs' (105). In this comedy performance and costume again are all. And disguise. The ugliness of the hunchback Sansfin is a convenient, if involuntary, camouflage for his erotic ambitions, just as Lamiel's fake consumption (simulated by spitting the blood of a bird freshly beheaded by Sansfin) secures for him renewed and respectable access to his pupil in evil. Where the sixteen-year-old girl of *Le Rouge* gilds the lily of her rosy complexion by wearing rouge to a ball, Lamiel smears pulverized holly-leaf on her face to discourage the advances of male travelling-companions. The deformed and the diseased provide cover for the operation of diabolical complicity. Yet this is simply emblematic of what happens in society as a whole:

le monde [says Sansfin] n'est point divisé, comme le croit le nigaud, en riches et en pauvres, en hommes vertueux et en scélérats, mais tout simplement en dupes et en fripons. Voilà la clef qui explique le XIXe siècle depuis la chute de Napoléon; car, ajoutait Sansfin, *la bravoure personnelle, la fermeté de caractère* n'offrent point prise à l'hypocrisie. (119)

Sansfin's education of Lamiel along these lines begins with a demonstration that the duchesse de Miossens's 'bonté' is actually condescension or *Schadenfreude* (120), and doubtless the extra chapters which Stendhal intended to devote to Sansfin would have contained much social comedy of this kind. What he had called 'cet ignoble bal masqué' in *Lucien Leuwen* is here being subjected to a rigorous unmasking. In the first *Lamiel* this operates through the device of a feminine Candide bringing instinctive empiricism and probing literal-mindedness to bear upon the fictions and taboos of society. In the second version Stendhal clearly finds such an unmasking easier to accomplish by having an instructor complement the lessons of experience.

In one sense, therefore, Sansfin could be said to take over the role of the novelist, leaving Lamiel both literally and metaphorically as the reader. Where once she had learnt about society through her

imagination (via novel, newspaper and book of etiquette), now
Sansfin teaches her to read society for herself: 'peut-être que tout
ce que je vous dis est un mensonge. Ne m'en croyez donc point
aveuglément, mais observez si, par hasard, ce que je vous dis ne serait
point une vérité' (120). Moreover, like Stendhal with his reader, he
wants her to use her reason as well as her imagination: 'il voulait
surtout qu'elle se donnât la peine de réfléchir.' Accordingly, in her
efforts to acquire what Sansfin terms 'le bon sens', she reads between
the lines of social hypocrisy in search of a truth, a personal truth,
the truth of courage and integrity. Previously her reading had
rendered her 'sensible à la fermeté d'âme déployée par certains
scélérats' (85), that quality which Sansfin tells her has disappeared
with Napoleon. Now she sees how she may proceed with her own
'chasse au bonheur': 'je ne puis voir la guerre, mais quant à la fermeté
de caractère, je puis non seulement la voir chez les autres, mais je
puis espérer de la mettre en pratique moi-même' (120). If society's
truth may be summed up in the word 'friponnerie' (cf. Stendhal's
recurrent description of Louis-Philippe as 'le plus fripon des Kings'),
then frank villainy offers the surest alternative to bad faith.
Appropriately, when Lamiel's education is complete and she turns
her lovers into dupes, she becomes a kind of novelist:

Lamiel vit la nécessité de raconter son histoire à Mme Le Grand, mais pour
cela il fallait la composer; elle se méfiait de son étourderie; elle était hors
d'état de mentir, parce qu'elle oubliait ses mensonges. Elle écrivit son histoire,
et, pour pouvoir la laisser dans sa commode, elle donna à cette histoire la
forme d'une lettre justificative adressée à un oncle, M. de Bonna. (184)[11]

The duchesse de Miossens's reader has become a writer, the violin
a bow playing upon the heart-strings of others.
    And what of the reader of *Lamiel*? If we acknowledge the truth
about society which Lamiel discovers and Sansfin proclaims, do we
then also accept the corollary that crime is the most authentic act? Or
does our reason shun such logic? If we complain of the power which
the written word has exerted over Lamiel in making her admire the
fortitude of outlaws, do we then also condemn our own complicity
in innumerable works of literature which present as sympathetic and
even admirable men and women who have transgressed religious,

---

[11] Note the reminiscence of Diderot's *La Religieuse*. Note also that Lamiel's
forgetting of her fictions provides a 'mise-en-abyme' of Stendhal's difficulties in writing
Lamiel.

moral or social laws in the name of a personal truth? Or does our imagination disclaim such similarity? The story of Lamiel presents a 'situation limite', and a completed version of the novel might well have left its reader with the uncomfortable feeling of being an oak-tree covered in the ivy of 'bêtise'. Imagine that Stendhal had completed those chapters on Sansfin; imagine that we had laughed our way through a ruthless exposé of hypocrisy and cant; imagine that we were then presented with the heartwarming spectacle of true love between Valbayre and Lamiel and a glorious *Liebestod* amid the flames of the Palais de Justice.[12] Would we then be ready to accept the terrorists as tragic hero and heroine (for that would be the logical consequence of our earlier laughter)? Or would the desire not to accept such an ennobling interpretation make us realize that we had laughed in bad faith, that we had treated comedy as a mere entertainment without relevance to our actual lives. Valbayre, like his model Lacenaire, has read both Corneille and Molière, but neither has stayed his hand from murder. Stendhal has offered in *Lamiel*, as in all his novels, a unique blend of tragedy and comedy; but will *Lamiel*, or his other novels, keep us from the crime of complacency? We have been shown 'la vérité, l'âpre vérité', but will we do anything about it? Is the bow mightier than the terrorist bomb? But perhaps such questions are too earnest, as well as too fanciful. Stendhal claims simply to have been writing a comedy: 'le grand objet actuel est le RIR[E]' (274). Regrettably he could not finish it, and so perhaps the reader of *Lamiel* must forgo speculation and admit defeat. As its author noted on 7 March 1841: 'pour juger des chapitres de Sansfin il faut les voir faits, on ne peut pas juger les choses Komi[ques] sur la théorie, sur le plan, sur l'imagination' (278). In the absence of such evidence, the violin must finally fall silent.

---

[12] And of hell? Lamiel is *'la fille du diable'* (49), as well as something of a female Don Juan.

2

Reverie

'Ton affaire est de faire des co[médie]s sans fin.'

(*OI*, ii. 423)

'Donc, *to make novels.*'

(*LL*, ii. 467)

LE docteur Sansfin: the name of the character which came to occupy Stendhal's mind during his last days is filled with connotation. Is he a representative of clinical reason, an endlessly cynical opponent of life-enhancing imagination? Or is he a representative of intelligence without ulterior motive, of Stendhalian 'lo-gique', an observer who notes the facts which imagination would honey-coat (*'facta, facta, nihil praeter facta*, sera un jour l'épigraphe de tout ce qu'on écrira sur l'homme')?[1] Is he the counterpart of an ugly and infirm Henri Beyle who would like to have abdicated wisdom in youthful pursuit of the mysterious Earline,[2] or the counterpart of a Stendhal who may always have been able to offer an anatomy of society but who also preferred to leave the larger questions unanswered? Of the Stendhal who always found it easier to begin his novels than to end them?

One of the principal, and perhaps most engaging, features of Stendhal's novels is the absence of grandiose pronouncements on the human condition. 'La bêtise consiste à vouloir conclure' wrote Flaubert,[3] and so might Stendhal have before him. Unlike the German historians whom he castigates in *Rome, Naples et Florence (1826)*, Stendhal gives the turbot without the sauce, that is, the facts without the philosophy.[4] In doing so he aims to please: 'que sommes-nous? Où allons-nous? Qui le sait? Dans le doute, il n'y a de réel

---

[1] *HPI*, ii. 88.   [2] See *OI*, ii. 362 and n. 5.

[3] To Louis Bouilhet (4 Sept. 1850).

[4] *VIT*, 498: 'A Paris, on sert à part le turbot et la sauce piquante. Je voudrais que les historiens allemands se pénétrassent de ce bel usage; ils donneraient séparément au public les faits qu'ils ont mis au jour, et leurs réflexions *philosophiques*. On pourrait alors profiter de l'histoire, et renvoyer à un temps meilleur la lecture des idées sur l'*absolu*. Dans l'état de mélange complet où se trouvent ces deux bonnes choses, il est difficile de profiter de la meilleure.'

que le plaisir tendre et sublime que donnent la musique de Mozart
et les tableaux du Corrège'.[5] The pleasure which he envisages does
not, however, exclude intellectual speculation: 'tel est le plaisir d'aller
voir les œuvres des grands artistes: ils jettent sur-le-champ dans les
grandes questions sur la nature de l'homme.'[6] Rather it subsumes
it and combines it with emotion. This blend is well conveyed by
Stendhal's analysis of his own response to music:

je viens d'éprouver ce soir que la musique, quand elle est parfaite, met le
cœur exactement dans la même situation où il est quand il jouit de la présence
de ce qu'il aime et qu'il voit que ce qu'il aime l'adore. C'est-à-dire qu'elle
donne le bonheur apparement le plus vif qui existe sur cette terre. Si cela
était vrai pour tous les hommes, rien au monde ne disposerait plus à l'amour.
Mais j'ai observé il y a longtemps que la musique parfaite comme la
pantomime parfaite me fait songer à ce qui fait actuellement l'objet de mes
méditations, et me fait venir des idées excellentes.[7]

This response is what Stendhal calls 'la rêverie', in which, as in the
'rêveries' of Rousseau's 'promeneur solitaire', the distinction between
reason and feeling seems to be superseded by an experience of
perfection. Thus, for Stendhal, the subtle *chiaroscuro* of Correggio
'donne à l'âme plongée dans une douce rêverie cette sensation de
bonheur qui l'élève et la transporte hors d'elle-même, et que l'on a
appelée le sublime.'[8]

In Stendhal's view 'la rêverie' is, as I have already had occasion
to quote, 'le vrai plaisir du roman'. This comment is followed by
another which suggests the futility of all literary criticism:

cette rêverie est innotable. La noter, c'est la tuer pour le présent, car l'on
tombe dans l'analyse philosophique du plaisir; c'est la tuer encore plus
sûrement pour l'avenir, car rien ne paralyse l'imagination comme l'appel
à la mémoire.[9]

But what Stendhal is referring to here is the re-reading of novels in
which are recorded his impressions of previous readings. Comparison
of his present response with a previous one may add to his
'connaissance de l'homme', but it prevents an authentic reading:
'adieu pour longtemps le laisser-aller des sensations tendres'.[10]
Where a novel is empty of such marginal records, however, then a
re-reading may be as authentic as a first reading:

[5] *VIT*, 885.   [6] *HPI*, ii. 240.
[7] *OI*, ii. 42 (25 Feb. 1820). Clearly his unrequited love for Matilde Dembowski
underlies this response.
[8] *VHMM*, 108.   [9] *DLA*, 36.   [10] Ibid. 37.

je remarque que je puis relire un bon roman tous les trois ans avec le même plaisir. Il me donne des sentiments conformes au genre de goût tendre qui me domine dans le moment, ou me procure de la variété dans mes idées, si je ne sens rien.[11]

An authentic reading, then, is one which affords a pleasure born of tender sentiment and intellectual stimulation, a pleasure which is, once more, comparable with that provided by music:

je puis aussi écouter avec plaisir la même musique, mais il ne faut pas que la mémoire cherche à se mettre de la partie. C'est l'imagination uniquement qui doit être affectée; si un opéra fait plus de plaisir à la vingtième représentation, c'est que l'on comprend mieux la musique, ou qu'il rappelle la sensation du premier jour.[12]

It has been my argument in this book that Stendhal's novels lend themselves to be read and re-read in this way. On the one hand, our imagination may involve us in the lives of Stendhal's characters to such an extent that we see tragic pathos, heroism and romance. On the other hand, our reason may distance us so that we see comedy, misguidedness and superficiality. We may sympathize and identify or smile and disown. It seems to me that we oscillate between these in the course of our reading, or that we read in one way and then find ourselves re-reading in another.[13] Michel Crouzet has written in this context of Stendhal's 'esthétique du sourire':

il faut s'en tenir à noter qu'il y a chez Stendhal une esthétique du sourire, opposé au rire de distance et de supériorité et à l'émotion de participation; à mi-distance de l'un et de l'autre, le *sourire* est le plaisir de culture, l'émotion de l'amateur, qui savoure avec le succès de l'œuvre le bien joué de l'artiste.[14]

But this 'émotion de l'amateur' and 'plaisir de culture' are reminiscent of the dialogue from *Racine et Shakespeare* which I referred to in my preface and, in particular, of the academician's admiration for Racine's fine verse. Crouzet seems to deny the 'émotion de participation', whereas the provoking of such an emotion (in the dialogue, the Romantic's 'illusion parfaite') is an important feature of Stendhal's aesthetic. These moments of illusion may be fleeting, but they do exist. There is a 'femme de chambre' in all of us. Stendhal, I think, is not aiming to provoke a response which falls half-way

---

[11] Ibid. 36. [12] Ibid.
[13] Particularly in the case of *La Chartreuse de Parme*. Cf. Wood, 'Le sphinx', 163, and Finch, '*La Chartreuse de Parme*', 9. [14] *Quatre études*, 7.

between irony and vicarious thrill, but rather one which combines a full experience of both of these—the response of the theatre-goer in *Racine et Shakespeare* who knows that he is watching a play and yet momentarily, and repeatedly, forgets this.[15]

This is also, of course, the response of Culler's 'divided reader', the reader who has, for example, a 'simultaneous interest in characters as people and in characters as devices of the novelist's art' (see my preface). For Culler, critics tend to turn such a reader into the hero of a kind of *Bildungsroman*. Like Culler himself in his book on Flaubert (as he acknowledges) they tell 'stories of reading' which follow 'an innocent reader, confident in traditional assumptions about structure and meaning, who encounters the deviousness of texts, falls into traps, is frustrated and dismayed, but emerges wiser for the loss of illusions. It is as though', continues Culler, 'what permits one to describe reading as misadventure is the happy ending that transforms a series of reactions into an understanding of the text and of the self that had engaged with the text.'[16] My own readings of *Armance, Le Rouge et le Noir* and *La Chartreuse de Parme* have followed a similar course (while *Lucien Leuwen*, as was seen, provokes a 'story of writing' rather than a 'story of reading'). But in each case I have tried to show that there is no 'happy ending' for the reader as Culler describes it. A 'steam-age' reading of *Armance* may alert us to the absurdities of Octave, but we may yet prefer the pathos of a 'poetic' reading; a retrospective reading of *Le Rouge* may show us that Julien missed his chance at Vergy, but we may yet give precedence to the values previously suggested by a proleptic reading; and in *La Chartreuse* a French reading may reveal the inauthenticity of romance, but we may yet choose to be Italians. This accounts for the presence of 'and' rather than 'or' in the titles of Parts II, III, and V above, as no doubt also for the presence of 'et' in *Le Rouge et le Noir*. As Culler writes in his exposition of Paul de Man:

---

[15] Crouzet comes closer to this position in the last two sentences of *La Poétique de Stendhal* (itself the conclusion to his monumental doctoral thesis): 'car il y a deux émotions: l'une plus proche de la réalité et du moi, l'autre plus détachée. Et il faut soit les séparer, comme font le comique, la satire, ou la musique, soit les réunir, ce qui serait la fonction du roman.' But in my view 'le comique' and 'la musique' belong with 'le roman'. Cf. *JL*, iii. 24, where Stendhal envisages 'quelque chose d'aérien, de fantastique dans le comique, quelque chose qui donne des sensations analogues à celles que produit la musique'.

[16] *On Deconstruction*, 79.

in undoing the oppositions on which it relies and between which it urges the reader to choose, the text places the reader in an impossible situation that cannot end in triumph but only in an outcome already deemed inappropriate: an unwarranted choice or a failure to choose [. . .] The reader may be placed in impossible situations where there is no happy issue but only the possibility of playing out roles dramatized in the text.[17]

The 'ending', therefore, lies in each individual reader. Jean-Jacques Hamm has written felicitously that 'l'achèvement stendhalien passe par le public', but for him this is because the reader can achieve 'une connaissance absolue des valeurs qu'il cache'.[18] Hamm, therefore, is restating in more modern parlance that the Happy Few will get the message, that they will know what sauce to serve with the turbot. In my view the great virtue of Stendhal as a novelist is to take account of the fact that each individual reader will bring his own unique blend of emotional and intellectual experience to his reading. It is for the reader alone to face up to the paradox, central to Stendhal's work and no doubt to all works of fiction, which is expressed in *Le Rouge*: 'il entreprenait de juger la vie avec son imagination. Cette erreur est d'un homme supérieur.' What the novelist is doing is to 'faire rêver' and, when it comes to sauces, Stendhal thinks the proper thing to do, as with French dressing, is to leave it to us to mix our own.

The Happy Few are those who will know to do so, but many of course have not known. One of the most famous of these is Henry James who completely fails to respond to Stendhal's invitation to surmise: 'among writers called immoral there is no doubt that he best deserves the charge'; '*Le Rouge et le Noir*, *L'Amour* [*sic*], and certain passages in his other writings have an air of unredeemed corruption—a quality which in the novel amounts to a positive blight and dreariness.' James is bewildered by Stendhal's perception of authentic passion within immorality and crime and quite out of sympathy with Stendhal's refusal to draw the line: 'it seems to him that one may perfectly well live a scandalous life and sit up half the night reading Dante in a glow of pure rapture.'[19] A slightly less celebrated but perhaps more representative example of the failure to co-operate intellectually in reading Stendhal is afforded by Frank O'Connor in *The Mirror in the Roadway*. No wonder Stendhal worried that he might be thought to be writing for ladies' maids when someone of O'Connor's own skills can entitle his chapter 'The Flight

---

[17] Ibid. 81.   [18] 'L'achèvement', 28–9.   [19] 'Henri Beyle', 156–7.

from Reality' and argue that 'Stendhal's gifts as a novelist are more limited than his worshippers realize' because he is 'without the intellectual detachment of the really great novelist'. How impoverishing, too, to see *Le Rouge* as being, 'as no romantic novel was, an exploration of reality by means of the romantic temperament'.[20]

I mention O'Connor because he is typical of those who find Stendhal inconsequential and 'romantic' and then go on to question his status as a novelist. O'Connor, for example, considers that 'what [Stendhal] wished to do is only very doubtfully the business of the novelist, since he looked on the novel merely as an extension of his journals and autobiographies, a new means of exploring his own ill-balanced character.'[21] A similar view has long been held by Henri-François Imbert who has expressed it thus in a recent article: 'Stendhal ne fut jamais un romancier d'instinct. Son domaine, c'était la biographie, le récit de voyage mêlé de considérations politiques et artistiques, le récit bref, ou, plus précisément, ce qu'il appelait le récit qui prouve.'[22] But it seems to me that Stendhal is indeed a 'born' novelist, in the sense that so much of his writing, be it autobiographical, fictional, epistolary, journalistic, or 'touristic', is above all *narrative*. Imbert is right to stress 'le récit qui prouve', the telling story,[23] but wrong, I think, to suggest that Stendhal was better suited by the shorter form. Stories such as *Le Coffre et le revenant* (1829) and *Le Philtre* (1830) do not stand out from the many similar stories being published in the press at the time, and the best of the *Chroniques italiennes* is the longest (*L'Abbesse de Castro*). As I have argued in Part I, Stendhal sought to narrate stories which would intrigue the mind in 'moments de philosophie rêveuse'.[24] The more numerous the facts and the wider the ramifications, the greater the consequent 'rêverie', as any comparative reading of a 'chronique italienne' and *La Chartreuse* will show. He certainly did not find novels easy to write but he saw well how they worked, and he may even have been mindful of Rousseau's important observation in the preface to *La Nouvelle Héloïse* that the longer a novel is, the more likely it is to seduce: 'c'est une longue romance, dont les couplets pris à part n'ont rien qui touche, mais dont la suite

---

[20] *The Mirror in the Roadway*, 48, 53.   [21] Ibid. 43.
[22] 'Fonction de *Lucien Leuwen* dans l'œuvre romanesque de Stendhal', *Stendhal Club*, 26 (1983/4), 165–78 (165).
[23] Cf. Coe, 'The Anecdote and the Novel'.   [24] *MT*, i. 75.

produit à la fin son effet'.[25] At the very least this may help explain why someone who found it so hard to construct a novel actually wrote such long ones.

Another notable absentee from the Happy Few is Flaubert, who found *Le Rouge et le Noir* 'mal écrit et incompréhensible, comme caractères et intentions' and could not understand Balzac's enthusiasm for it (nor, presumably, Balzac's even greater enthusiasm for *La Chartreuse*). In the letter where he shares these opinions with Louise Colet[26] (because he has dutifully just borrowed *La Chartreuse* from the library), he goes on to extol another novel: 'ce qu'il y a de prodigieux dans *Don Quichotte*, c'est l'absence d'art et cette perpétuelle fusion de l'illusion et de la réalité qui en fait un livre si comique et si poétique.' Yet what better description could there be of Stendhal's own novels? Similarly, when Flaubert subsequently describes his aesthetic ideal to Louise Colet, one may sense a certain affinity of purpose between the two novelists:

ce qui me semble, à moi, le plus haut dans l'Art (et le plus difficile), ce n'est ni de faire rire, ni de faire pleurer, ni de vous mettre en rut ou en fureur, mais d'agir à la façon de la nature, c'est-à-dire de *faire rêver*. Aussi les très belles œuvres ont ce caractère. Elles sont sereines d'aspect et incompréhensibles.[27]

Certainly Stendhal does want to make us laugh and cry, but his overriding ambition is to stimulate 'la rêverie'. Equally his novels have a certain serenity in that they seem artless and somehow incontrovertible (cf. the 'miracle' of *La Chartreuse*), and they may even seem 'incompréhensibles', not, as Flaubert thought of *Le Rouge*, because they are obscure but, on the contrary, because they can seem so straightforwardly narrative and thus lacking in points of purchase for critical analysis to gain a hold on them. This is what Gide (most decidedly one of the Happy Few) had in mind when he later wrote of his own desire to purge the novel of 'tous les éléments qui n'appartiennent pas spécifiquement au roman' and of how 'ce *pur* roman, nul ne l'a donné [...] pas même l'admirable Stendhal, qui, de tous les romanciers, est peut-être celui qui en approche le plus.'[28] But it is the phrase 'agir à la façon de la nature' which most suggests

[25] *Julie ou la Nouvelle Héloïse*, ed. R. Pomeau (Classiques Garnier, Paris, 1960), 744.
[26] 22 Nov. 1852.   [27] 26 Aug. 1853.
[28] *Journal des Faux-Monnayeurs*, in *Œuvres complètes*, ed. L. Martin-Chauffier, xiii. 40, 41.

Stendhal, because it recalls his theory of mimesis which I outlined
at the end of Part I. The novelist-musician cannot reproduce nature
but he can attempt to provoke in the reader-listener the same response
as the natural phenomenon itself would have provoked.

For Stendhal, famously, 'un ouvrage d'art n'est qu'un beau
mensonge',[29] and beauty is in the character, as well as the eye, of
the beholder. In the case of sculpture, he argues,[30] it is possible to
envisage a 'beau idéal' which is universal because 'la différence des
formes du corps humain dans les divers pays est beaucoup moins
grande que celle des tempéraments donnés par les climats.' But when
it comes to the arts of literature and music which 'mettent en jeu
les diverses affections', response will vary enormously: 'ce qui
paraîtra charmant à Naples sera trouvé fou et indécent à
Copenhague.' For the Stendhal of 1814 the writer had but to choose;
'le poète doit donc prendre son parti, et chercher à plaire aux uns
ou aux autres.' The composer, on the other hand, had a much more
serious problem:

quel doit donc être l'embarras du musicien, celui des artistes qui peint de
plus près les affections du cœur humain, et qui encore ne peut les peindre
qu'en faisant agir l'imagination et la sensibilité de chacun de ses auditeurs,
qu'en mettant, pour ainsi dire, chacun d'eux de moitié dans son travail.

It seems to me that Stendhal began to question the starkness of the
writer's choice and to see virtue in the musician's plight. What if he
could appeal to both the Neapolitan *and* the Dane? What if he tried
to purge language of its generalizing elements and used words as
musical notes?

je conterais trente anecdotes, et je supprimerais toutes les idées générales
sur les mœurs: tout ce qui est *vague*, en ce genre, est faux. Le lecteur qui
ne connaît que les mœurs de son pays, entend par les mots *décence, vertu,
duplicité*, des choses matériellement différentes de celles que vous avez voulu
désigner.[31]

In this way perhaps he can forestall unthinking, stock reactions
on the part of his reader, perhaps even wean him from too
immediately and conventionally literary a response: 'j'écrivais en
langue française, mais non pas certes en *littérature française*. Dieu
me préserve d'avoir rien de commun avec les littérateurs estimés

[29] *VIT*, 1136.   [30] *VHMM*, 209–11.
[31] *VIT*, 37 (9 Feb. 1817). Cf. *VIT*. 518, and *MT*, i. 361.

d'aujourd'hui.'[32] Perhaps too he can finally reverse the decline which, like Pacchiarotti in the realm of bel canto, he observed in the art of story-telling:

le sublime Pacchiarotti voyait avec larmes la décadence d'un art qui avait fait le charme et la gloire de sa vie. De quel mépris ne devait pas être inondée l'âme de ce véritable artiste, lui qui jamais ne s'était permis un son ou un mouvement sans le calculer sur les besoins *actuels* de l'âme du spectateur, le but unique de tous ses efforts, lorsqu'il voyait un chanteur n'avoir pour toute ambition que le mérite mécanique de devenir le rival heureux d'un violon dans une variation à trente-deux biscromes par mesure! L'art le plus touchant autrefois se change tranquillement sous nos yeux en un simple métier.[33]

Bring back the narrative 'bel canto' of Ariosto, says Stendhal, and may the reader's soul, 'la caisse du violon *qui rend les sons*', respond, neither mechanically nor as it 'theoretically' thinks it ought, but with a fullness of heart and mind. Stendhal takes a bow to provoke 'rêverie', that plenitude of human response which Mallarmé also compared with the music of a violin:

je crois que pour être bien l'homme, la nature en pensant, il faut penser de tout son corps, ce qui donne une pensée pleine et à l'unisson comme ces cordes de violon vibrant immédiatement avec sa boîte de bois creux. Les pensées partant du seul cerveau [...] me font maintenant l'effet d'airs joués sur la partie aiguë de la chanterelle dont le son ne réconforte pas dans la boîte,—qui passent et s'en vont sans se *créer*, sans laisser de traces d'elles.[34]

This is the violin which Stendhal hoped to play, this the music of the Happy Few. Where Flaubert wrote alone, for art ('il faut donc faire de l'art pour soi, *pour soi seul*, comme on joue du violon'),[35] Stendhal the supposed egotist wrote for others. For him the reader was no mere 'violon d'Ingres' but his central preoccupation. How appropriate, then, that some of his last published words were devoted to Raphael, and in particular to Raphael's *Parnassus* in the Vatican.[36] There Raphael depicts Apollo among the Muses, Apollo

[32] *DLA*, 160.   [33] *VR*, ii. 125–6.
[34] *Correspondance*, ed. H. Mondor and J.-P. Richard (vol. i), H. Mondor and L. J. Austin (vols ii–xi) (Gallimard, 1959–85), i. 249.
[35] To Louise Colet, 30 May 1852.
[36] See A. Constantin, *Idées italiennes sur quelques tableaux célèbres, deuxième édition revue et annotée par Stendhal* (Paris, 1931), 280–2, especially 281, n. 4: 'L'Apollon est de la main de Raphaël et peint avec beaucoup de soin.' Cf. *OI*, ii. 377, and n. 5.

the god of music and poetry: he is playing the violin.[37] And for
those engaged in the pursuit of the Stendhalian sign how appropriate
too that Apollo the violinist should adorn the 'Stanza de la Segnetura',
the Room of the Signature.

[37] Cf. *VIT*, 828: 'Apollon joue du violon; on prétend que le pape voulut que
Raphaël représentât un fameux joueur de violon alors vivant.'

Bibliography

The following bibliography includes all editions and critical works which have been referred to in the preceding pages, as well as some which have not been mentioned but which have nevertheless been of interest. It may be completed and kept up to date by reference to the comprehensive bibliography published annually in the October issue of *Stendhal Club*, to whose editor, Victor Del Litto, and editorial assistants all students of Stendhal owe a considerable debt of gratitude.

I. THE WORKS OF STENDHAL

A. *Collected Editions*

Correspondance, Bibliothèque de la Pléiade, ed. Henri Martineau and V. Del Litto (3 vols, Paris, 1968).

Chroniques italiennes, ed. Béatrice Didier (Paris, 1977).

Chroniques pour l'Angleterre, ed. K. G. Watters and R. Dénier (vols i– ; Grenoble, 1980–).

Courrier anglais, ed. Henri Martineau (5 vols, Paris, 1935–6).

Œuvres (Romans—Voyages—Autobiographie), ed. V. Del Litto and E. Abravanel (18 vols, Lausanne, 1960–2).

Œuvres complètes, Cercle du Bibliophile, ed. V. Del Litto and E. Abravanel (50 vols, Geneva, n. d. [1967]–1974).

Œuvres intimes, Bibliothèque de la Pléiade, ed. V. Del Litto (2 vols, Paris, 1981–2).

Romans abandonnés, ed. Michel Crouzet (Paris, 1968).

Romans et nouvelles, Bibliothèque de la Pléiade, ed. Henri Martineau (2 vols, Paris, 1948–52).

B. *Individual Editions*

Armance, ed. Georges Blin (Paris, 1946).

Armance, Classiques Garnier, ed. Henri Martineau (Paris, 1962).

Armance, ed. H.-F. Imbert (Paris, 1967).

La Chartreuse de Parme, Classiques Garnier, ed. A. Adam (Paris, 1973).

De l'amour, Classiques Garnier, ed. Henri Martineau (Paris, 1959).

Histoire de la peinture en Italie (2 vols, Paris, 1980: reprint of Henri Martineau's edn for Le Divan in 1929).

Lamiel, ed. Anne-Marie Meininger (Paris, 1983).

Lucien Leuwen, ed. Michel Crouzet (2 vols, Paris, 1982).

Lucien Leuwen, Collection de l'Imprimerie Nationale, ed. Anne-Marie Meininger (2 vols, Paris, 1982).

Mémoires d'un touriste, ed. V. Del Litto (3 vols, Paris, 1981).

Racine et Shakespeare, ed. Roger Fayolle (Paris, 1970).

Le Rouge et le Noir, Classiques Garnier, ed. Henri Martineau (Paris, 1960).

Le Rouge et le Noir, ed. Michel Crouzet (Paris, 1964).

Le Rouge et le Noir, Classiques Garnier, ed. P.-G. Castex (Paris, 1973).

Vie de Rossini (2 vols, Paris, n. d. [1977]: reprint of Henri Martineau's edn for Le Divan in 1929).

Voyages en Italie, Bibliothèque de la Pléiade, ed. V. Del Litto (Paris, 1973).

Also: Constantin, A., *Idées italiennes sur quelques tableaux célèbres, deuxième édition revue et annotée par Stendhal* (Paris, 1931).

II. STUDIES OF STENDHAL

A. Studies of Individual Novels

1. Armance

Barbéris, Pierre, '*Armance*, Armance: quelle impuissance?', in Berthier (ed.), *Stendhal. Colloque de Cerisy-la-Salle* (q.v.), 67–86.

Bayard, Pierre, *Symptôme de Stendhal. Armance et l'aveu* (Paris, 1979).

Bellemin-Noël, Jean, *L'Auteur encombrant: Stendhal/'Armance'* (Lille, 1985).

Birnberg, Jacques, 'Notes sur la citation moliéresque dans *Armance* et dans *Le Rouge et le Noir*', *Australian Journal of French Studies*, 22 (1985), 68–77.

Brotherson, L., 'Impotence in *Armance*: a Medium for Social Criticism', *Australian Journal of French Studies*, 16 (1979), 55–67.

Chessex, Robert, 'Ambiguïté fâcheuse', *Stendhal Club*, 22 (1979/80), 374–5.

Crouzet, Michel, 'Le réel dans *Armance*. Passions et société ou le cas d'Octave: étude et essai d'interprétation', in *Le Réel et le texte* (Paris, 1974), 31–110.

Del Litto, V., 'Stendhal lecteur d'*Armance*, (Exemplaire interfolié Bucci)', *Stendhal Club*, 18 (1975/6), 193–205, 277–82.

Gaillard, Françoise, 'De la répétition d'une figure: *Armance* ou le récit de l'impuissance', *Littérature*, 18 (May 1975), 111–26.

Gans, E., 'Le secret d'Octave: secret de Stendhal, secret du roman', *Revue des Sciences Humaines*, 40 (1975), 85–9.

Gleize, Jean-Marie, '*Armance* oblique', in *Le Réel et le texte* (Paris, 1974), 111–21.

—— 'Bordures de buis', *L'Arc*, 88 (1983), 43–8.

Jones, Grahame C., 'L'emploi du point de vue dans *Armance*', *Stendhal Club*, 18 (1975/6), 109–36.

Mölk, U., 'Stendhal's *Armance* und die Motivgeschichte des impotenten Helden', *Romantische Zeitschrift für Literaturgeschichte*, 1 (1977), 413–32.

Mouillaud, Geneviève, 'Stendhal et le mode irréel. A propos de l'impuissance dans *Armance*', *Modern Language Notes*, 83 (1968), 524–42.

O'Keefe, C., 'A Function of Narrative Uncertainty in Stendhal's *Armance*', *French Review*, 50 (1976/7), 579–85.

Place, David, 'The Problems of Stendhal's *Armance*', *French Studies*, 33 (1979), 27–38.

Rosa, George M., 'Un présage de la mort d'Octave dans *Armance*', *Stendhal Club*, 23 (1980/1), 15–21.

——— 'Byronism and "Babilanisme" in *Armance*', *Modern Language Review*, 77 (1982), 797–814.

Shillony, Helena, 'Le dénouement d'*Armance* ou la mort du héros', *Stendhal Club*, 21 (1978/9), 193–200.

Stivale, Charles J., 'Ordre et duration: la structuration temporelle d'*Armance*', *Stendhal Club*, 24 (1981/2), 141–56.

Sykes, J. M., '*Armance*, roman romantique?', *Stendhal Club*, 16 (1973/4), 127–35.

Talbot, Emile, 'The Impossible Ethic: A Reading of Stendhal's *Armance*', *French Forum*, 3 (1978), 147–58.

Thompson, C. W., 'Les clefs d'*Armance* et l'ambivalence du génie romantique du Nord', *Stendhal Club*, 25 (1982/3), 520–47.

2. Le Rouge et le Noir

Bassette, Louis, 'Sur une épigraphe de *Rouge et Noir*. Stendhal et Saint-Réal', *Stendhal Club*, 9 (1966/7), 241–53.

Bibas, Henriette, 'Le double dénouement et la morale du *Rouge*', *Revue d'Histoire Littéraire de la France*, 49 (1949), 21–36.

Bokobza, Serge, '*Le Rouge et le Noir*: jeu de hasard ou réalité politique?' *Stendhal Club*, 21 (1978/9), 163–6.

——— '*Rouge et Noir*: le blason de Julien?', *Stendhal Club*, 22 (1979/80), 37–41.

——— *Contribution à la titrologie romanesque: variations sur le titre 'Le Rouge et le Noir'* (Geneva, 1986).

Borgerhoff, E. B. O., 'The Anagram in *Le Rouge et le Noir*', *Modern Language Notes*, 68 (1953), 383–6.

Castex, P.-G., '*Le Rouge et le Noir*' de Stendhal (Paris, 1967).

Cellier, Léon, 'Rires, sourires et larmes dans *Le Rouge et le Noir*', in *De Jean Lemaire de Belges à Jean Giraudoux. Mélanges d'histoire et de critique littéraire offerts à Pierre Jourda* (Paris, 1970), 277–97.

Combe, T. G. S., 'A Snake and Ladders in Stendhal's *Le Rouge et le Noir*', *Cambridge Review*, 104 (3 June 1983), 151–5.

Crouzet, Michel, 'Julien Sorel et le sublime: étude de la poétique d'un personnage', *Revue d'Histoire Littéraire de la France*, 86 (1986), 86–108.

Didier, Béatrice, 'Lieux et signes dans *Le Rouge et le Noir*', *Studi Francesi*, 20 (1976), 40–4.

Fonvieille, René, *Le Véritable Julien Sorel* (Paris, 1971).

Godfrey, Gary M., 'Julien Sorel—Soldier in Blue', *Modern Language Quarterly*, 37 (1976), 339–48.

Gormley, Lane, ' "Mon roman est fini": fabricateurs de romans et fiction intratextuelle dans *Le Rouge et le Noir*', *Stendhal Club*, 21 (1978/9), 129–38.

Grant, Richard B., 'The Death of Julien Sorel', *L'Esprit Créateur*, 2 (1962), 26–30.

Hamm, Jean-Jacques, 'Le dénouement de *Rouge et Noir*. Un parvenu qui ne parvient à rien', *Stendhal Club*, 17 (1974/5), 250–66.

—— 'Hypothèses sur quelques noms propres de *Rouge et Noir*', *Stendhal Club*, 18 (1975/6), 228–34.

—— '*Le Rouge et le Noir* d'un lecteur d'épigraphes', *Stendhal Club*, 20 (1977/8), 19–36.

Hemmings, F. W. J., 'Julien Sorel and Julian the Apostate', *French Studies*, 16 (1962), 229–44.

Hoog, Armand, 'Le "rôle" de Julien', *Stendhal Club*, 20 (1977/8), 131–42.

Imbert, H.-F., 'Conjectures sur l'origine scottienne du titre de *Rouge et Noir*', *Revue de Littérature Comparée*, 45 (1971), 305–22.

Ishikawa, Hiroshi, 'Réflexions sur le réalisme subjectif dans *Le Rouge et le Noir*', *Stendhal Club*, 19 (1976/7), 144–52.

Jefferson, Ann, 'Stendhal and the Uses of Reading', *French Studies*, 37 (1983), 168–83.

Jones, Grahame C., 'Réel, Saint-Réal: une épigraphe du *Rouge* et le réalisme stendhalien', *Stendhal Club*, 25 (1982/3), 235–43.

Le Breton, André, '*Le Rouge et le Noir*' de Stendhal (Paris, 1950).

Liprandi, Claude, 'Sur un épisode de *Rouge et Noir*. Un roi à Bray-le-Haut', *Revue des Sciences Humaines*, 15 (1950), 141–60.

—— *Au cœur du 'Rouge'*. *L'Affaire Lafargue et 'Le Rouge et le Noir'* (Lausanne, 1961).

—— 'De "l'origine du nom Sorel" à l'origine de *Rouge et Noir*', in V. Del Litto (ed.), *Communications présentées au Congrès Stendhalien de Civitavecchia (IIIe Journée du Stendhal Club)* (Florence and Paris, 1966), 233–55.

—— '*Le Rouge et le Noir*: Quiroga Rouge et Morillo Noir', *Stendhal Club*, 18 (1975/6), 219–27.

Longstaffe, Moya, 'L'éthique du duel et la couronne du martyre dans *Le Rouge et le Noir*', *Stendhal Club*, 18 (1975/6), 283–306.

Martino, Pierre, '*Le Rouge et le Noir*–la signification du titre', *Le Divan*, 93 (1923), 575–7.

Maugham, W. Somerset, *Ten Novels and Their Authors*, 2nd edn (London, 1963), 68–98.

Mauldon, Margaret, 'Generic survival: *Le Rouge et le Noir* and the Epistolary Tradition', *French Studies*, 38 (1984), 414–22.

Mitchell, John, *Stendhal: 'Le Rouge et le Noir'* (London, 1973).

Mossman, Carol A., *The Narrative Matrix. Stendhal's 'Le Rouge et le Noir'* (Lexington, Ky., 1984).

Mossop, D. J., 'Julien Sorel, the vulgar assassin', *French Studies*, 23 (1969), 138–44.

Mouillaud, Geneviève, *'Le Rouge et le Noir' de Stendhal. Le roman possible* (Paris, 1973).

Neri, F., 'Note stendhalienne, *Rosso e Nero*', *Ambrogiano*, 2 May 1925.

Pollard, Patrick, 'Colour Symbolism in *Le Rouge et le Noir*', *Modern Language Review*, 76 (1981), 323–31.

Purdy, Anthony, 'Un cheval nommé Sorel et une taupe régicide. Réflexions onomastiques sur *Le Rouge et le Noir*', *Stendhal Club*, 22 (1979/80), 144–52.

Reizov, Boris, 'Pourquoi Stendhal a-t-il intitulé son roman *Le Rouge et le Noir?*', *Studi Francesi*, 11 (1967), 296–301.

Schehr, Lawrence R., 'A Chronicle of Production: the Creation of an Enunciative Framework in *Le Rouge et le Noir*', *Australian Journal of French Studies*, 22 (1985), 43–60.

Schneck, Jerome M., 'Legal insanity, moral insanity, and Stendhal's *le Rouge et le Noir*', *Medical History*, 10 (1966), 281–4.

Stivale, Charles J., 'Le vraisemblable temporel dans *Le Rouge et le Noir*', *Stendhal Club*, 21 (1978/9), 299–315.

Trouiller, Dominique, 'Le monologue intérieur dans *Le Rouge et le Noir*', *Stendhal Club*, 11 (1968/9), 245–77.

West, John, 'Eléments du récit prophétique dans *Le Rouge et le Noir*: cloches et horloges', *Australian Journal of French Studies*, 20 (1983), 130–8.

3. Lucien Leuwen

Crouzet, Michel, *'Lucien Leuwen* et le "sens politique" ', in Philippe Berthier et al., *Le Plus Méconnu des romans de Stendhal* (Paris, 1983), 99–139.

—— *Stendhal. Quatre études sur Lucien Leuwen* (Paris, 1985).

Durand, Gilbert, *'Lucien Leuwen* ou l'héroïsme à l'envers', *Stendhal Club*, 1 (1958/9), 201–25.

Imbert, H.-F., 'Fonction de *Lucien Leuwen* dans l'œuvre romanesque de Stendhal', *Stendhal Club*, 26 (1983/4), 165–78.

Jones, Grahame C., 'L'intrusion de l'auteur en particulier dans *Lucien Leuwen*', *Stendhal Club*, 25 (1982/3), 50–66.

Léoni, Anne, 'Ménuel pseudonyme' in *L'Arc*, 88 (1983), 64–71.

Rousset, Jean, 'Variations sur les distances: aimer de loin', in Philippe Berthier *et al.*, *Le Plus Méconnu des romans de Stendhal* (Paris, 1983), 75–87.

Seylaz, Jean-Luc, 'Un aspect de la narration stendhalienne: la qualification intensive dans le début de *Lucien Leuwen*', *Etudes de Lettres*, IV. iii. 3 (July–Sept. 1980), 31–49.

Weiand, Christof, 'En marge de *Lucien Leuwen*. *L'orange de Malte* titre ou énigme', *Stendhal Club*, 24 (1981/2), 450–8.

4. *La Chartreuse de Parme*

Barthes, Roland, 'On échoue toujours à parler de ce qu'on aime', *Tel Quel*, 85 (Autumn 1980), 32–8.

Bellemin-Noël, Jean, 'Le motif des orangers dans la *Chartreuse de Parme*', *Littérature*, 5 (1972), 26–33.

Berg, William J., 'Cryptographie et communication dans *La Chartreuse de Parme*', *Stendhal Club*, 20 (1977/8), 170–82.

Brooks, Peter, 'L'invention de l'écriture (et du langage) dans *La Chartreuse de Parme*', *Stendhal Club*, 20 (1977/8), 183–90.

Cellier, Léon, 'Rires, sourires et larmes dans *La Chartreuse de Parme*', in *Omaggio a Stendhal, II*, Atti del 6° Congresso Internazionale Stendhaliano (Parma, 1967), 18–33.

Coe, Richard N., '*La Chartreuse de Parme*. Portrait d'une réaction', in *Omaggio a Stendhal, II* (q.v. above), 43–61.

Creignou, Pierre, 'Illusion et réalité du bonheur dans *La Chartreuse de Parme*', *Stendhal Club*, 16 (1973/4), 310–34.

Crouzet, Michel, 'Sur la topographie de la *Chartreuse de Parme*, et sur la rapport des lieux et des lieux communs', in Michel Crouzet (ed.), *Espaces romanesques* (Paris, 1982), 99–139.

Didier, Béatrice, '*La Chartreuse de Parme*, ou l'ombre du père', *Europe*, 519–21 (July–Sept. 1972), 149–57.

Durand, Gilbert, *Le Décor mythique de la 'Chartreuse de Parme'. Contribution à l'esthétique du romanesque* (Paris, 1961).

Finch, Alison, *Stendhal: 'La Chartreuse de Parme'* (London, 1984).

Gilman, Stephen, *The Tower as Emblem. Chapters VIII, IX, XIX and XX of the Chartreuse de Parme* (Frankfurt am Main, 1967).

Haig, Stirling, 'The Identities of Fabrice Del Dongo', *French Studies*, 27 (1973), 170–6.

Hirsch, Michèle, 'Fabrice, ou la poétique du nuage', *Littérature*, 23 (1976), 21–30.

Hubert, J. D., 'Notes sur la dévaluation du réel dans *La Chartreuse de Parme*', *Stendhal Club*, 2 (1959/60), 47–53.

Jefferson, Ann, 'Représentation de la politique, politique de la représentation: *La Chartreuse de Parme*', *Stendhal Club*, 27 (1984/5), 200–13.

Kogan, Vivian, 'Signs and Signals in *La Chartreuse de Parme*', *Nineteenth-Century French Studies*, 2 (1973/4), 29–38.

Landry, François, 'Le crime dans *La Chartreuse de Parme*', in Berthier (ed.), *Stendhal: l'écrivain* (q.v.), 329–44.

Nehrlich, Michaël, '*La Chartreuse* est-elle *Le Prince Moderne*? Sur l'unité retrouvée du texte stendhalien', in Berthier (ed.), *Stendhal: l'écrivain* (q.v.), 311–27.

Rannaud, Gérald, '*La Chartreuse de Parme* roman de l'ambiguïté', in Liano Petroni (ed.), *Atti del IX Congresso Internazionale Stendhaliano dedicato a Stendhal e Bologna con alcuni itinerari dell'Emilia-Romagna* (2 vols, Bologna, 1977), i. 426–46.

Russell, Lois Ann, 'Les jeux de l'écriture dans *La Chartreuse de Parme*', *Stendhal Club*, 25 (1982/3), 67–77.

Smith, I. H., 'Brief Note on the Predictions of the Abbé Blanès', *AUMLA*, 45 (1976), 96–7.

Thompson, C. W., *Le Jeu de l'ordre et de la liberté dans 'La Chartreuse de Parme'* (Aran, Switzerland, 1982).

Wood, Michael, '*La Chartreuse de Parme* et le sphinx', *Stendhal Club*, 20 (1977/8), 161–9.

B. *Studies of Stendhal as a Novelist*

Adams, Robert M., *Stendhal: Notes on a Novelist* (London, 1959).

Arrous, Michel, 'L'odieuse réalité. Le procès stendhalien du miroir', *Europe*, 652–3 (Aug.–Sept. 1983), 55–61.

Bardèche, Maurice, *Stendhal romancier* (Paris, 1947).

Bertelà, Maddalena, 'Les couleurs dans quelques titres stendhaliens', *Australian Journal of French Studies*, 22 (1985), 35–42.

Blin, Georges, *Stendhal et les problèmes du roman* (Paris, 1954).

Boll Johansen, Hans, *Stendhal et le roman. Essai sur la structure du roman stendhalien* (Aran and Copenhagen, 1979).

Booker, John T., 'Retrospective Movement in the Stendhalian Narration', *Romanic Review*, 72 (1981), 26–38.

—— '*Style direct libre*: the case of Stendhal', *Stanford French Review*, 9 (1985), 137–51.

Brombert, Victor, *Stendhal et la voie oblique. L'auteur devant son monde romanesque* (New Haven and Paris, 1954).

—— *Stendhal. Fiction and the Themes of Freedom* (Chicago and London, 1968).

Coe, Richard N., 'The Anecdote and the Novel: a Brief Enquiry into the Origins of Stendhal's Narrative Technique', *Australian Journal of French Studies*, 22 (1985), 3–25.

Geninasca, Jacques, 'L'invention du détail vrai', *Stendhal Club*, 24 (1981/2), 388–402.

Hemmings, F. W. J., *Stendhal. A Study of his Novels* (Oxford, 1964).

—— 'Les deux *Lamiel*. Nouveaux aperçus sur les procédés de composition de Stendhal romancier', *Stendhal Club*, 15 (1972/3), 287–316.

Jefferson, Ann, '*De l'Amour* et le roman polyphonique', *Poétique*, 14 (1983), 149–62.

Jones, Grahame C., *L'Ironie dans les romans de Stendhal* (Lausanne, 1966).

—— 'Le mouvement dramatique de la narration stendhalienne', *Stendhal Club*, 20 (1977/8), 46–56.

Lampedusa, Giuseppe Tomasi di, 'Notes sur Stendhal', *Stendhal Club*, 2 (1959/60), 155–68.

McWatters, K. G., *Stendhal lecteur des romanciers anglais* (Lausanne, 1968).

Trout, Paulette, *La Vocation romanesque de Stendhal* (Paris, 1970).

Weiand, Christof, '*Ernestine* prototype de la narration stendhalienne', *Stendhal Club*, 26 (1983/4), 263–79.

—— *Die Gerade und der Kreis: Zeit und Erzählung in den Romanen Stendhals* (Frankfurt am Main, 1984).

C. General Studies of Stendhal

Alain, *Stendhal* (Paris, 1935).

Albérès, F. M., *Le Naturel chez Stendhal* (Paris, 1956).

Alter, Robert, in collaboration with Carol Cosman, *Stendhal. A. Biography* (London, 1980).

André, Robert, 'Harmonie et mélodie chez Stendhal', *Stendhal Club*, 18 (1975/6), 15–33.

Aragon, Louis, *La Lumière de Stendhal* (Paris, 1954).

Attuel, Josiane, *Le Style de Stendhal. Efficacité et romanesque* (Bologna and Paris, 1980).

Berthier, Philippe, *Stendhal et ses peintres italiens* (Geneva, 1977).

—— *Stendhal et la Sainte Famille* (Geneva, 1983).

—— (ed.), *Stendhal: Colloque de Cerisy-la-Salle (30 juin–10 juillet 1982)* (Paris, 1984).

—— (ed.), *Stendhal: l'écrivain, la société, le pouvoir. Colloque du Bicentenaire (Grenoble, 24–27 janvier 1983)* (Grenoble, 1984).

Bishop, Michael, 'Laughter and the Smile in Stendhal', *Modern Language Review*, 70 (1975), 50–70.

Blanchard de Farges, A., 'Un peu de Stendhal inédit. Petite récolte de notes marginales', *Le Correspondant*, 81 (1909), 1077–119.

Blin, Georges, *Stendhal et les problèmes de la personnalité* (Paris, 1958).

Blum, Léon, *Stendhal et le beylisme*, 3rd edn (Paris, 1947).

Bourgeois, René, 'Lacenaire, héros stendhalien', *Stendhal Club*, 16 (1973/4), 219–29.

Bourget, Paul, 'Stendhal (Henri Beyle)', in *Essais de psychologie contemporaine* (Paris, 1886), 251–323.

Butor, Michel, 'Fantaisie chromatique à propos de Stendhal', in *Répertoire V et dernier* (Paris, 1982).

Caramaschi, Enzo, 'Praxis et art dans l'*Histoire de la peinture en Italie*', *Studi Francesi*, 28 (1984), 228–49.

Claudon, Francis, 'Stendhal et Cimarosa', in *Stendhal e Milano*, Atti del 14° Congresso Internazionale Stendhaliano (2 vols, Florence, 1982), ii. 563–89.

—— 'Stendhal et Winckelmann', *Stendhal Club*, 25 (1982/3), 297–309.

Coe, Richard N., 'Introduction', in *Lives of Haydn, Mozart and Metastasio by Stendhal (1814)*, trans. and ed. Richard N. Coe (London, 1972), pp. ix–xxxii.

—— 'From Correggio to Class Warfare: notes on Stendhal's ideal of "la grâce"', in D. G. Charlton, J. Gaudon and A. R. Pugh (eds), *Balzac and the Nineteenth Century. Studies in French Literature presented to Herbert J. Hunt* (Leicester, 1972), 239–54.

Colomb, Romain, 'Notice sur la vie et les ouvrages de Henri Beyle (de Stendhal)', in *Romans et nouvelles* (Paris, 1854), pp. iii–civ.

Constans, Ellen, 'Stendhal et le public impossible', in Berthier (ed.), *Stendhal: l'écrivain* (q.v.), 33–55.

Crouzet, Michel, *Stendhal et le langage* (Paris, 1981).

—— *Stendhal et l'italianité. Essai de mythologie romantique* (Paris, 1982).

—— *La Vie de Henry Brulard ou l'enfance de la révolte* (Paris, 1982).

—— *La Poétique de Stendhal. Forme et société. Le Sublime. Essai sur la genèse du romantisme* (Paris, 1983).

Del Litto, V., *La Vie intellectuelle de Stendhal. Genèse et évolution de ses idées (1802–1821)* (Paris, 1959).

Denton, Michel, 'Le lecteur idéal de *Henry Brulard*', *Etudes de Lettres*, IV. vii. 3 (July–Sept. 1984), 39–46.

Didier, Béatrice, *Stendhal autobiographe* (Paris, 1983).

—— 'Le secret du journal', *L'Arc*, 88 (1983), 5–9.

—— 'L'adresse au lecteur dans les textes autobiographiques de Stendhal', in Berthier (ed.), *Colloque de Cerisy-la-Salle* (q.v.), 119–33.

Diefenbach, Dieter, 'Stendhal et la franc-maçonnerie', *Stendhal Club*, 27 (1984/5), 329–38.

—— 'Stendhal: un pseudonyme et ses variantes', *Stendhal Club*, 29 (1986/7), 43–8.

Faguet, Emile, 'Stendhal', *Revue des Deux Mondes*, 109 (1892), 594–633.

Felman, Shoshana, *La 'Folie' dans l'œuvre romanesque de Stendhal* (Paris, 1971).

Genette, Gérard, ' "Stendhal" ', in *Figures II* (Paris, 1969), 155–93.

Gleize, Jean-Marie, 'Stendhal: le travail du texte', *Romantisme*, 1 (1971), 156–63.

Green, F. C., *Stendhal* (Cambridge, 1939).

Haig, Stirling, 'La descente du paradis', *Stendhal Club*, 21 (1978/9), 139–45.

Hamm, Jean-Jacques, 'Stendhal et l'autre du plagiat', *Stendhal Club*, 23 (1980/1), 203–14.

—— 'L'achèvement et son envers: de l'œuvre au lecteur', in Berthier (ed.), *Colloque de Cerisy-la-Salle* (q.v.), 13–31.

—— 'Un laboratoire stendhalien: les *Chroniques italiennes*', *Revue d'Histoire Littéraire de la France*, 84 (1984), 245–54.

Hazard, Paul, *La Vie de Stendhal*, 18th edn (Paris, 1927).

Hemmings, F. W. J., 'Stendhal, Self-plagiarist', *L'Esprit Créateur*, 2 (1962), 19–25.

Imbert, H.-F., 'Stendhal et *Tom Jones*', *Revue de Littérature Comparée*, 30 (1956), 351–70.

—— *Les Métamorphoses de la liberté, ou Stendhal devant la Restauration et le Risorgimento* (Paris, 1967).

Jacobs, Helmut C., *Stendhal und die Musik. Forschungsbericht und Kritische Bibliographie 1900–1980* (Frankfurt am Main, 1983).

James, Henry, 'Henry Beyle', *The Nation* (17 Sept. 1874), reprinted in *Literary Reviews and Essays*, ed. Mordell (New York, 1957), 151–7.

Landry, François *L'Imaginaire chez Stendhal. Formation et expression* (Lausanne, 1982).

Martineau, Henri, *L'Œuvre de Stendhal. Histoire de ses livres et de sa pensée* (Paris, 1945).

—— *Le Cœur de Stendhal. Histoire de sa vie et de ses sentiments* (2 vols, Paris, 1952–3).

May, Gita, 'Le féminisme de Stendhal et *Lamiel*', *Stendhal Club*, 20 (1977/8), 191–204.

Mertès-Gleize, Joëlle, 'L'action de lire', *L'Arc*, 88 (1983), 57–63.

Moinet, Gisela M., 'La quête de la comédie chez Stendhal', in V. Del Litto and H. Harder (eds), *Stendhal et l'Allemagne* (Paris, 1983), 135–51.

Mossman, Carol, 'Les gravures de la *Vie de Henry Brulard*. Iconographie brulardienne: les figures d'une écriture', *Stendhal Club*, 28 (1985/6), 339–53.

Mouillaud-Fraisse, Geneviève, 'Le titre comme chimère', *L'Arc*, 88 (1983), 77–86.

—— 'La question du destinataire dans l'écriture de Stendhal', in Berthier (ed.), *Colloque de Cerisy-la-Salle* (q.v.), 151–61.

Pouillon, Jean, 'La Création chez Stendhal. A propos du livre de Jean Prévost', *Les Temps modernes*, 7 (1951–2), 173–82.

Poulet, Georges, 'Stendhal', in *Etudes sur le temps humain* (4 vols, Edinburgh and Paris, 1949–68), iv (*Mesure de l'instant*), 227–51.

Prévost, Jean, *La Création chez Stendhal. Essai sur le métier d'écrire et la psychologie de l'écrivain* (Paris, 1951).

Richard, Jean-Pierre, 'Connaissance et tendresse chez Stendhal', in *Littérature et sensation* (Paris, 1954), 15–116.

Ringger, Kurt, *L'Ame et la page. Trois essais sur Stendhal* (Aran, Switzerland, 1982).

Rousset, Jean, 'Les échanges à distance', *Etudes de Lettres*, IV. vii. 3 (July–Sept. 1984), 3–12.

Rude, Fernand, *Stendhal et la pensée sociale de son temps*, 2nd edn (Brionne, 1983).

Sabatier, Pierre, *Esquisse de la morale de Stendhal d'après sa vie et ses œuvres* (Paris, 1920).

St Aubyn, F. C., 'Stendhal and Salome', *Stanford French Review*, 4 (1980), 395–404.

Seylaz, Jean-Luc, 'L'effet Cimarosa dans les romans stendhaliens', *Stendhal Club*, 25 (1982/3), 40–9.

Sgard, Jean, 'L'explicit de la *Vie de Henry Brulard*', *Revue d'Histoire Littéraire de la France*, 84 (1984), 199–205.

Simons, Madeleine A., *Sémiotisme de Stendhal* (Geneva, 1980).

—— 'Stendhal et les métamorphoses du sacré. Le décor gothique: "scena tragica" et "scena comica" ', *Stendhal Club*, 26 (1983/4), 329–43.

—— 'Stendhal et les métamorphoses du sacré. Le palimpseste à rebours', *Stendhal Club*, 28 (1985/6), 1–16.

Starobinski, Jean, 'Stendhal pseudonyme' in *L'Œil vivant* (Paris, 1961), 189–240.

Strickland, Geoffrey, *Stendhal. The Education of a Novelist* (Cambridge, 1974).

Talbot, Emile (ed.), *La Critique stendhalienne de Balzac à Zola* (York, S. Carolina, 1979).

Thibaudet, Albert, *Stendhal* (Paris, 1931).

Thiede, Carsten, 'Stendhal à Stendal. Le pseudonyme sur les lieux', *Stendhal Club*, 16 (1973/74), 335–40.

Thompson, C. W., 'L'armée ou l'église: sur les ressorts latents du dilemme héroïque chez Stendhal', *Stendhal Club*, 21 (1978/9), 228–52.

Tillett, Margaret, *Stendhal. The Background to the Novels* (London, 1971).

Valéry, Paul, 'Stendhal', in *Œuvres*, Bibliothèque de la Pléiade (2 vols, Paris, 1957–60), i. 553–82.

Vigneron, Robert, 'Beylisme, romanticisme, réalisme', *Modern Philology*, 56 (1958/9), 98–117.

Weill Goudchaux, Guy, 'Steindal, Winckelmann et Stendhal', in V. Del Litto and H. Harder (eds), *Stendhal et l'Allemagne* (Paris, 1983), 177–89.

Wood, Michael, *Stendhal* (London, 1971).

III. MISCELLANEOUS

Abrams, M. H., *The Mirror and the Lamp. Romantic Theory and the Critical Tradition* (New York, 1953).

Alter, Robert, *Partial Magic. The Novel as a Self-Conscious Genre* (Berkeley, 1975).

Auerbach, Erich, *Mimesis. The Representation of Reality in Western Literature*, trans. Willard R. Trask, 2nd impr. (Princeton, 1968).

Balchin, Nigel, 'Introduction', in David Footman, *Pig and Pepper. A Comedy of Youth*, 2nd edn (London, 1954).

Barthes, Roland, *Le Bruissement de la langue* (Paris, 1984).

Bennington, Geoffrey, *Sententiousness and the Novel. Laying Down the Law in Eighteenth-Century French Fiction* (Cambridge, 1985).

Bersani, Leo, *Balzac to Beckett. Center and Circumference in French Fiction* (New York, 1970).

Bory, Jean-Louis, 'Le cinéma: périlleux salut du roman', *Revue des Lettres Modernes*, 5 (1958), 249–55.

Brombert, Victor, *La Prison romantique. Essai sur l'imaginaire* (Paris, 1975).

Brooks, Peter, *The Novel of Worldliness. Crébillon, Marivaux, Laclos, Stendhal* (Princeton, 1969).

—— *Reading for the Plot. Design and Intention in Narrative* (Oxford, 1984).

Carpani, Giuseppe, *Le Haydine, ovvero lettere sulla vita e le opere del celebre maestro Giuseppe Haydn* (Milan, 1812: 2nd edn, 1823).

Chatelain, Danièle, 'Récit itératif et concrétisation', *Romanic Review*, 72 (1981), 304–16.

Culler, Jonathan, *Flaubert. The Uses of Uncertainty* (London, 1974).

—— *On Deconstruction. Theory and Criticism after Structuralism* (London, 1983).

De Man, Paul, 'The Rhetoric of Temporality', in *Blindness and Insight. Essays in the Rhetoric of Contemporary Criticism*, 2nd edn (London, 1983), 187–228.

Didier, Béatrice, *La Musique des lumières: Diderot—'L'Encyclopédie'— Rousseau* (Paris, 1985).

Duchet, Claude, *'La Fille abandonnée* et *La Bête humaine'*: éléments de titrologie romanesque', *Littérature*, 12 (1973), 49–73.

Duras, duchesse de, *Olivier ou le secret*, ed. Denise Virieux (Paris, 1971).

Fellows, O. E., *French Opinion of Molière (1800–1850)* (Providence, 1937).

Gautier, Théophile, *Histoire du romantisme, suivie de Notices romantiques et d'une Etude sur la poésie française 1830–68* (Paris, 1874).

Genette, Gérard, 'Vraisemblance et motivation', in *Figures II* (Paris, 1969), 71–99.

—— 'Discours du récit: *essai de méthode*', in *Figures III* (Paris, 1972), 65–282.

—— *Nouveau Discours du récit* (Paris, 1983).

Gide, André, *Œuvres complètes*, ed. L. Martin-Chauffier, Nouvelle Revue Française (15 vols, n. p., n. d.).

Girard, René, *Mensonge romantique et vérité romanesque* (Paris, 1961).

Giraud, Raymond, *The Unheroic Hero in the Novels of Stendhal, Balzac and Flaubert* (New Brunswick, N. J., 1957).

Howe, Irving, *Politics and the Novel* (New York, 1970).

[Hugo, Adèle], *Victor Hugo raconté par un témoin de sa vie* (2 vols, Paris, 1863).

Iknayan, Marguerite, *The Idea of the Novel in France: The Critical Reaction 1815–1848* (Geneva and Paris, 1961).

—— *The Concave Mirror: from imitation to expression in French aesthetic theory 1800–1830* (Stanford, 1983).

Imbert, Jean, *La Peine de mort* (Paris, 1972).

Iser, Wolfgang, *The Act of Reading. A Theory of Aesthetic Response* (London and Henley, 1978).

Levin, Harry, *The Gates of Horn. A Study of Five French Realists* (New York, 1966).

Lubbock, Percy, *The Craft of Fiction*, 2nd edn (London, 1965).

Mallarmé, Stéphane, *Correspondance*, ed. H. Mondor and J.-P. Richard (vol. i), H. Mondor and L. J. Austin (vols ii–xi) (Paris, 1959–85).

Marc, Edmond, *Mes Journées de juillet 1830*, ed. G. de Grandmaison (Paris, 1930).

Miller, D. A., *Narrative and its Discontents. Problems of Closure in the Traditional Novel* (Princeton, 1981).

O'Connor, Frank, *The Mirror in the Roadway* (London, 1957).

Prendergast, Christopher, *The Order of Mimesis. Balzac, Stendhal, Nerval, Flaubert* (Cambridge, 1986).

Proust, Marcel, *A la recherche du temps perdu*, Bibliothèque de la Pléiade (3 vols, Paris, 1954).

Rousseau, Jean-Jacques, *Julie ou la Nouvelle Héloïse*, ed. R. Pomeau (Classiques Garnier, Paris, 1960).

Schöning, Udo, *Literatur als Spiegel. Zur Geschichte eines kunsttheoretischen Topos in Frankreich von 1800 bis 1860* (Heidelberg, 1984).

Sénart, P., 'Un martyre du romantisme: Custine', in Custine, *Aloys ou le religieux du Mont Saint-Bernard* (Paris, n. d. [1971]), pp. vii–xxii.

Suleiman, Susan R. and Crosman, Inge (eds), *The Reader in the Text. Essays on Audience and Interpretation* (Princeton, 1980).

Sullivan, E. D., 'The Actor's Alceste: Evolution of the Misanthrope', *Modern Language Quarterly*, 9 (1948), 74–89.

—— 'Molé's Interpretation of Molière's Misanthrope', *Modern Language Quarterly*, 9 (1948), 492–6.

Todorov, Tzvetan, 'All against humanity', *Times Literary Supplement*, 4 Oct. 1985, pp. 1093–4.

Tompkins, Jane P. (ed.), *Reader-response Criticism. From Formalism to Post-Structuralism* (Baltimore and London, 1980).

Turnell, Martin, *The Novel in France* (London, 1950).

Index